Routledge A Level Religious Studies

Routledge A Level Religious Studies: AS and Year One is an engaging and comprehensive textbook for the new 2016 OCR A Level Religious Studies syllabus. Structured closely around the OCR specification, this textbook covers philosophy, ethics and Christianity, in an engaging and student-friendly way.

Each chapter includes:

- An OCR specification checklist, to clearly illustrate which topics from the specification are covered in each chapter;
- Explanations of key terminology;
- Review questions, thought points and activities to test understanding;
- An overview of key scholars and theories;
- Chapter summaries.

With a section dedicated to preparing for assessment, *Routledge A Level Religious Studies: AS and Year One* provides students with all the skills they need to succeed. This book comes complete with diagrams and tables, lively illustrations, a comprehensive glossary and full bibliography. The companion website hosts a wealth of further resources to enhance the learning experience.

Jon Mayled is a chief examiner. He is author and editor of many popular books for the GCSE and GCE specifications.

Jill Oliphant was formerly Head of Religious Studies at Angley School in Kent, UK.

Sam Pillay is Subject Leader in Religious Studies at the Axe Valley Academy in Devon, UK.

D1440591

Routledge
A Level
Religious Studies

AS and Year One

JON MAYLED,

JILL OLIPHANT AND

SAM PILLAY

Routledge
Taylor & Francis Group

LONDON AND NEW YORK

First published 2018
by Routledge
2 Park Square, Milton Park, Abingdon, Oxon OX14 4RN

and by Routledge
711 Third Avenue, New York, NY 10017

Routledge is an imprint of the Taylor & Francis Group, an informa business

British Library Cataloguing-in-Publication Data
A catalogue record for this book is available from the British Library

Library of Congress Cataloging-in-Publication Data
Names: Mayled, Jon, author.
Title: Routledge A level religious studies : AS and year one /
    Jon Mayled, Jill Oliphant, and Sam Pillay.
Description: 1 [edition]. | New York : Routledge, 2017. |
    Includes bibliographical references and index.
Identifiers: LCCN 2017028283 | ISBN 9781138631397 (pbk.) |
    ISBN 9781315208725 (ebook)
Subjects: LCSH: Religion—Philosophy—Textbooks. |
    Religious ethics—Textbooks. | Theology textbooks. |
    Christianity—Philosophy—Textbooks.
Classification: LCC BL51 .M47625 2017 | DDC 200.76—dc23
LC record available at https://lccn.loc.gov/2017028283

ISBN: 978-1-138-63139-7 (pbk.)
ISBN: 978-1-315-20872-5 (ebk)

Typeset in Charter ITC
by Apex CoVantage, LLC

Visit the companion website: www.routledge.com/cw/mayled

Printed and bound by
CPI Group (UK) Ltd, Croydon, CR0 4YY

Contents

Acknowledgements

We are very grateful to the many people who have helped us prepare this book, particularly to Rebecca Shillabeer of Taylor & Francis for commissioning us to write this text. We much appreciate the support we have received from Taylor & Francis staff. We also wish to thank greatly the people who have read drafts of the book and made so many helpful suggestions, for all their assistance and support, not to mention their patience while waiting for parts of the text.

We are also very grateful to the friends and family members who have supported and encouraged this project. We would like to thank in particular the sixth-form students of The Axe Valley Community College.

The scripture quotations contained herein are from The New Revised Standard Version of the Bible, Anglicised Edition, copyright © 1989, 1995 by the Division of Christian Education of the National Council of the Churches of Christ in the United States of America, and are used by permission. All rights reserved.

Extracts from specification details are produced by the kind permission of Oxford, Cambridge and RSA Examinations (OCR).

Every effort has been made to trace copyright holders. Any omissions brought to our attention will be remedied in future editions.

How to use this book

This book has been written for OCR students but it will be of use to all AS and A level Religious Studies students, as well as students taking the Ethics section of A level Philosophy and Scottish National Examinations at Higher Level.

The book is designed for students to use in class and at home. Every chapter provides an overview of the major themes and issues of Philosophy of Religion, Religious Ethics and Developments in Christian Thought on the OCR specification for Religious Studies. The following six features are designed to help you make the most effective use of the book.

1 **What you will learn about in this chapter**
   This highlights the key issue or issues you should think about while studying each chapter.

2 **OCR checklist**
   The box in each chapter about the OCR specification tells you which topics from the AS/A Religious Studies course are covered.

3 **Essential terminology box**
   At the beginning of every chapter there is a box listing the key terminology for the chapter. You should be able to use this terminology accurately in examinations.

4 **Review questions**
   The review questions in every chapter are designed to test your understanding of topics discussed in the chapter. Make use of this section as a way to assess your learning about and from the issues in the chapter.

5 **Examination questions practice**
   At the end of every chapter there is a section about answering examination questions on the topic, with an exam-style question.

6 **Further reading**
   The reading suggested at the end of each chapter gives ways of exploring topics in greater depth.

Answering examination questions

To be successful in AS and Advanced Level Religious Studies you must learn examination techniques. Some advice to guide you is given ahead, but there is no substitute for practising writing examination questions. There are example questions at the end of the chapters in this book, and your teacher will give you plenty of other questions with which to practise. Some important aspects to answering examination questions are explained ahead.

Your work will be assessed on how well you meet the following two Assessment Objectives (AO).

AO1

Demonstrate knowledge and understanding of religion and belief, including:

- religious, philosophical and/or ethical thought and teaching
- influence of beliefs, teachings and practices on individuals, communities and societies
- cause and significance of similarities and differences in belief, teaching and practice
- approaches to the study of religion and belief.

AO2

Analyse and evaluate aspects of, and approaches to, religion and belief, including their significance, influence and study.

All questions are in one part. This combines both AO1 and AO2.
For AS the AOs are weighted at 50% for AO1 and 50% for AO2.
For A level the AOs are weighted at 40% for AO1 and 60% for AO2.

All questions are marked according to the OCR Levels of Response. See: www.ocr.org.uk/qualifications/as-a-level-gce-religious-studies-h173-h573-from-2016/ Assessment Materials

SUBJECT KNOWLEDGE

At AS and A level the majority of marks are given for your demonstration of a good understanding of the topic the question is examining. It is important not only that you learn the work you have studied but also that you are able to select the knowledge that is relevant to an answer. For example if the question says to assess how a follower of natural law might approach the issue of abortion, your answer should be focused on the natural law approach to abortion, not writing everything you know about natural law or abortion.

When preparing for examination questions, it is a good idea to think about not only what a question is asking but also what material you have studied that is relevant to the question.

TIMING

It is very important that you learn how to complete questions in the time available. In an examination the time available is very limited. It is a good idea to practise timing yourself writing answers to examination-style questions. You will get a low mark if a question is incomplete, as this limits the maximum level your answer can reach.

Practise writing answers

It is very important that you practise answering questions for Religious Studies examinations by handwriting answers. In an examination you have very little time to write answers and you have to write, not type. This takes practice; try to avoid typing answers when you practise doing examination questions at home.

Selecting the correct information

Think about how you would answer the two questions ahead. Make a list of the topics and information you need to include in any answer and be specific.

1   Assess the view that utilitarianism provides the best approach to euthanasia.
2   To what extent is the cosmological argument successful in proving the existence of God?

Always try to spend equal amounts of time on each whole question you answer, as each question is worth the same number of marks.

UNDERSTANDING THE QUESTIONS

It is very important that you think carefully about what a question is asking you. The table ahead focuses on some of the common instruction words used in OCR questions and what they mean.

Instruction word	Explanation
Discuss as in: 'People are not free to make moral decisions.' **Discuss**.	The word **Discuss** in a question is telling you that you should examine the strengths and weaknesses of arguments for and against the statement in the question. You need to consider whether arguments in favour of and against the statement are successful. To do this, you will need to demonstrate an accurate understanding of one or more philosopher's views and the strengths and weaknesses of these views.
'Kant's ethical theory is too inflexible.' **Discuss**.	If a question uses the word **Discuss**, as well as considering arguments for and against the statement in the question, you need to explain accurately and in detail the philosophers' views and ideas to which the statement is referring.
Assess as in: '**Assess** a utilitarian approach to euthanasia.'	By **Assess** the examiner means that you should first explain the issue you are being asked to assess and second you should present arguments for and against the issue you have been asked to assess. Part of your assessment should present reasons analysing the strengths and weaknesses of arguments supporting or disagreeing with the issue. You should finish your answer with a conclusion which presents the result of your assessment. In the case of the example question, you would need to explain clearly and precisely the anthropomorphism of utilitarianism and the application of the principle of utility. Second, you should present philosophers' and theologians' arguments for and against a utilitarian approach. You should analyse the strengths and weaknesses of the philosophers' and theologians' arguments concerning a utilitarian approach to the environment.
To what extent as in: '**To what extent** can conscience be considered to be the voice of God?'	The instruction **To what extent** commonly appears, such as 'To what extent can conscience be considered to be the voice of God?' The question asks why some philosophers and theologians might hold this view. Next, you need to assess the strengths and weaknesses of reasons for holding these views and compare the strengths of the different reasons for holding this view with

continued overleaf

each other. The extent will be limited or defined by the strongest view you have considered. In the example question you need to explain the strengths and weaknesses of reasons philosophers and theologians give when discussing the ways conscience comes from God. The extent of the role of God in forming conscience will be decided by comparing the different reasons and arguments you present and deciding which one is strongest.

Evaluate as in: '*Evaluate* Plato's view that the soul is separate from the body.'

The instruction *Evaluate* commonly appears in questions, such as '*Evaluate* Plato's view that the soul is separate from the body.' Here you need to present all the relevant evidence which you have and make a judgement from that as to the strength or weakness of the statement.

Critically compare as in: '*Critically compare* the *via negativa* and *via positive* as ways of expressing religious beliefs in words.'

When a question begins with *Critically compare* it is asking you to explain the concepts and to identify the similarities and differences between them. The strength or weakness of the concepts will be decided by your balancing of them and deciding if one is better than the other.

Timeline
Scientists, ethicists and thinkers

This timeline gives the names and dates of people whose great ideas are discussed within the book. This list is not a comprehensive list of every important or significant ethicist of Western civilisation.

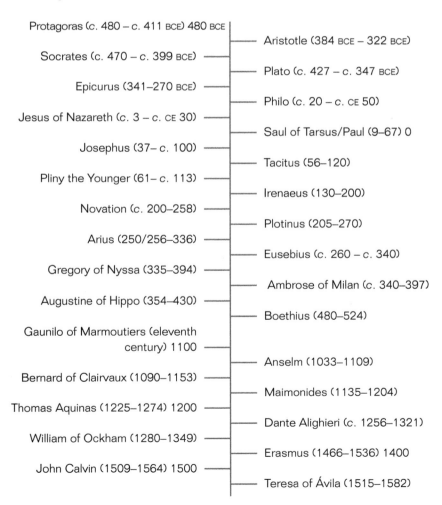

Protagoras (c. 480 – c. 411 BCE) 480 BCE

Aristotle (384 BCE – 322 BCE)

Socrates (c. 470 – c. 399 BCE)

Plato (c. 427 – c. 347 BCE)

Epicurus (341–270 BCE)

Philo (c. 20 – c. CE 50)

Jesus of Nazareth (c. 3 – c. CE 30)

Saul of Tarsus/Paul (9–67) 0

Josephus (37– c. 100)

Tacitus (56–120)

Pliny the Younger (61– c. 113)

Irenaeus (130–200)

Novation (c. 200–258)

Plotinus (205–270)

Arius (250/256–336)

Eusebius (c. 260 – c. 340)

Gregory of Nyssa (335–394)

Ambrose of Milan (c. 340–397)

Augustine of Hippo (354–430)

Boethius (480–524)

Gaunilo of Marmoutiers (eleventh century) 1100

Anselm (1033–1109)

Bernard of Clairvaux (1090–1153)

Maimonides (1135–1204)

Thomas Aquinas (1225–1274) 1200

Dante Alighieri (c. 1256–1321)

William of Ockham (1280–1349)

Erasmus (1466–1536) 1400

John Calvin (1509–1564) 1500

Teresa of Ávila (1515–1582)

Théodore de Bèze (1519–1605)

Pierre Gassendi (1592–1655)

René Descartes (1596–1650)

John Milton (1608–1674) 1600

John Locke (1632–1704)

Gottfried Wilhelm Leibniz (1646–1716)

David Hume (1711–1776) 1700

Adam Smith (1723–1790)

Immanuel Kant (1724–1804)

William Paley (1743–1805)

J.J. Griesbach (1745–1812)

Jeremy Bentham (1748–1832)

Thomas Malthus (1766–1834)

Friedrich Schleiermacher (1768–1834)

Charles Lyle (1797–1875)

John Stuart Mill (1806–1873) 1800

David Strauss (1808–1874)

Charles Robert Darwin (1809–1882)

Karl Marx (1818–1883)

William James (1842–1910)

Sigmund Freud (1856–1939)

A.N. Whitehead (1861–1947)

Rudolf Otto (1869–1937)

Bertrand Russell (1872–1970)

G.E. Moore (1873–1958)

Albert Schweitzer (1875–1965)

W.D. Ross (1877–1971)

Albert Einstein (1879–1955)

C.H. Dodd (1884–1973)

Rudolf Bultmann (1884–1976)

Paul Tillich (1886–1965)

Karl Barth (1886–1968)

Emil Brunner (1889–1966)

Reinhold Niebuhr (1892–1971)

Martin Niemöller (1892–1984)

Alister Hardy (1896–1985)

Charles Hartshorne (1897–2000)

Gilbert Ryle (1900–1976) 1900

Karl Popper (1902–1994)

Oscar Cullmann (1902–1999)

Bernard Lonergan (1904–1984)

Jean-Paul Sartre (1905–1980)

Joseph Fletcher (1905–1991)

Dietrich Bonhoeffer (1906–1945)

William Barclay (1907–1978)

Frederick Copleston (1907–1994)

Abraham Maslow (1908–1970)

Richard Brandt (1910–1997)

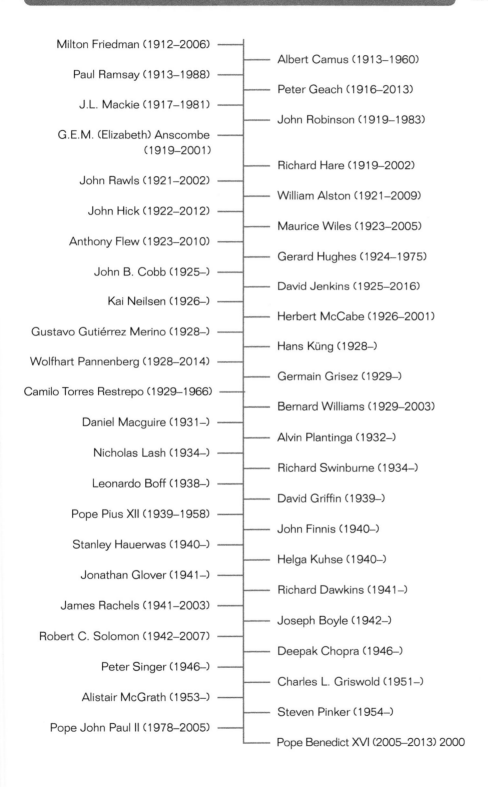

Milton Friedman (1912–2006)

Albert Camus (1913–1960)

Paul Ramsay (1913–1988)

Peter Geach (1916–2013)

J.L. Mackie (1917–1981)

John Robinson (1919–1983)

G.E.M. (Elizabeth) Anscombe (1919–2001)

Richard Hare (1919–2002)

John Rawls (1921–2002)

William Alston (1921–2009)

John Hick (1922–2012)

Maurice Wiles (1923–2005)

Anthony Flew (1923–2010)

Gerard Hughes (1924–1975)

John B. Cobb (1925–)

David Jenkins (1925–2016)

Kai Neilsen (1926–)

Herbert McCabe (1926–2001)

Gustavo Gutiérrez Merino (1928–)

Hans Küng (1928–)

Wolfhart Pannenberg (1928–2014)

Germain Grisez (1929–)

Camilo Torres Restrepo (1929–1966)

Bernard Williams (1929–2003)

Daniel Macguire (1931–)

Alvin Plantinga (1932–)

Nicholas Lash (1934–)

Richard Swinburne (1934–)

Leonardo Boff (1938–)

David Griffin (1939–)

Pope Pius XII (1939–1958)

John Finnis (1940–)

Stanley Hauerwas (1940–)

Helga Kuhse (1940–)

Jonathan Glover (1941–)

Richard Dawkins (1941–)

James Rachels (1941–2003)

Joseph Boyle (1942–)

Robert C. Solomon (1942–2007)

Deepak Chopra (1946–)

Peter Singer (1946–)

Charles L. Griswold (1951–)

Alistair McGrath (1953–)

Steven Pinker (1954–)

Pope John Paul II (1978–2005)

Pope Benedict XVI (2005–2013) 2000

PHILOSOPHY OF RELIGION

PART I

Ancient philosophical influences

1 Plato

THE ISSUES

1 Plato: one of the most important philosophers in the history of the Western world.
2 Is there a world of Forms beyond the physical world?

WHAT YOU WILL LEARN ABOUT IN THIS CHAPTER

In this chapter you will learn about some of the ideas of Plato, such as his reliance on reason rather than the senses, his theory of Forms, their nature and hierarchy, and the Analogy of the Cave. Some of the criticisms of his ideas will be discussed.

Thought point

Five-minute challenge

Draw sketches of some of the following animals:

- Lion
- Gorilla
- Donkey
- Frog
- Sheep

When all the drawings are finished, ask other people to identify which species the animal comes from. Let people try to work out what they are. Do not tell them.

Thought point

What do we mean by 'beauty'?

THE OCR CHECKLIST

The philosophical views of Plato, in relation to:

*   understanding of reality – Plato's reliance on reason as opposed to the senses
*   the Forms – the nature of the Forms; hierarchy of the Forms
*   the Analogy of the Cave – details of the analogy, its purpose and relation to the theory of the Forms.

Plato, *Republic* 474c – 480; 506b – 509c; 509d – 511e; 514a – 517c

PLATO'S UNDERSTANDING OF REALITY

Plato was a rationalist so the most important source of knowledge for him was a priori – not based on sense experience. To say that an idea is a priori is simply stating that experience is not necessary to say if it is true or not. So, for example, to know that 'all bachelors are unmarried men' is true and it is not necessary to examine all the bachelors to see if any are actually married, as to be a bachelor is to be unmarried. However, to discover if 'all bachelors are called George' it would be necessary to go and find out. Innate ideas (ones which are present from birth) are a sort of a priori knowledge. Plato was one of the first philosophers to hold the theory of innate ideas. In the *Meno* Plato writes about an uneducated slave boy who cannot be assumed to have knowledge of mathematics, yet, as Plato shows, the boy is able to arrive at mathematical truths. According to Plato all knowledge was simply memory, as he considered all knowledge was possessed from birth and we simply use our reason to uncover and remember it.

Plato considers that sense experience does not guarantee that what we experience is true, as any experience we get from our senses is constantly changing and can be unreliable. Plato distrusted information that came from our senses as imagination and reality can so easily be confused – so a

Plato and his times (427–347 BCE)

Plato is one of the most famous philosophers in the Western world and his ideas have had considerable influence. Plato lived in what we know as ancient Greece, which consisted of a series of self-governing city states or areas. These states were often at war with each other, but there was much more that united them than divided them, such as religion, language and ideas. Plato was an Athenian. Athens was a democracy governed by its citizens (excluding women, slaves and foreigners). Plato was taught by Socrates and devoted his life to continuing his philosophical tradition. Socrates wrote nothing down as far as we know and taught by questioning, but this and aspects of his personal life did not improve his reputation as far as the people of Athens were concerned. As a result, Socrates was put on trial, accused of mocking the gods and corrupting the young. He refused to back down and was convicted and sentenced to death by drinking hemlock. Most of Socrates' ideas and thoughts have

continued overleaf

been preserved by his follower Plato. Most of Plato's early books contain and develop the thinking of Socrates, but the later ones are mainly his own thinking.

Much of this work is written in the form of dialogues, often with Socrates as the speaker. Plato wrote about many subjects, from the existence of the soul and the nature of beauty to who should run a government. The idea of the Forms, which is so central to Plato's philosophy, does not appear in the earlier books and so would seem to come from Plato's own thinking. Plato also used the Academia or Academy to continue philosophical teaching.

School of Athens
Nick Fielding/Alamy

stick, for example, can seem bent when in water, but when it is picked up it is perfectly straight. Plato praised mathematics as one of the only forms of true knowledge, and disliked art because he thought that we distort our perception even further when we attempt to copy an imperfect image.

PLATO'S THEORY OF FORMS

The starter exercises drew your attention to the difference between ideas and ideas expressed in reality.

Thus, it is possible to recognise a dog from having an idea of what a dog is and for Plato this is all important – we begin with knowledge of what a dog is before we actually see a dog. Now we might think that we know what a dog is because we have experienced dogs and are familiar with them, and so we recognise any dog as being a dog, but, according to Plato, knowledge of what a dog is comes first. Additionally, Plato suggests that the world we live in is a world of *appearances* but the *real world* is a world of ideas that he calls *Forms*.

In *The Republic* Book V 478a-b Socrates tries to persuade Glaucon that anything that is beautiful can also appear less than beautiful. Can a beautiful woman be completely beautiful? She may be beautiful only according to some standards, and not according to others. Compared to a goddess, for example, she would probably appear plain. So, the beautiful woman is not completely beautiful. And her beauty will not last as nothing is sweet forever; fruit eventually withers and rots. The beautiful woman is changing and so the way we see her will change as well. Since knowledge, for Plato, is limited to eternal, unchanging, absolute truths, it cannot apply to the ever-changing details of the sensible world. It can apply only to what is stable and eternally unchanging.

Plato then assumes that there must be something which is unqualifiedly beautiful and which does not change. These are the Forms – the Form of beauty is always completely beautiful. There is only one Form of beauty for many beautiful things; they are like a kind of reflection of beauty.

The world we live in is a world of appearances, but it is not the most important or real world. In the material world things that exist, like animals and plants, will all die. What makes a flower a flower, however, or a dog a dog, is the way in which it corresponds to the Form of flower or dog.

By *Form* Plato meant the idea of what a thing is. There are many types of dogs but they all conform to or match to some degree the idea of what a dog is. Plato argues that the true Form of dog must exist somewhere; it exists in the world of Forms. A Form is unchanging because it is a concept – it is not like physical objects that imitate or copy the Form; they die. The Form is everlasting. The Forms thus exist in a different reality.

According to Plato the world we live in is a poor imitation of the real world. Our world is constantly changing and we rely on our senses to understand what is going on. Plato was therefore sure that the real world is outside the one we live in. This real world is unchanging and eternal. It is the world of ideas and not senses, where there are perfect Forms of the things we know on earth.

Plato was not really interested in the Forms of objects, like tables or, indeed, animals, like dogs. What mattered to Plato were concepts such as beauty, truth, justice and the Good. Plato saw that concepts like beauty may be applied to many different objects. A flower and a person can both in some way reveal what beauty is, but many other things can be beautiful, such as paintings and landscapes. Therefore Plato suggested that underlying all these images and examples of beauty is the real Form of beauty, to which these things correspond to a greater or lesser extent.

Form

By 'Form' Plato meant the idea of something – for example people have some idea of what a dog is and can recognise lots of different types of dogs. All the different breeds of dogs embody the Form of a dog: some set of characteristics that show what a dog is. The Form of anything is not a physical representation but the eternal idea of what a thing is.

Thought point

If you attempted the challenge about beauty and found it difficult, this may interest you. Scientific research has shown that part of our definition of beauty relates to symmetry. Subconsciously our minds assess the symmetry of anything we see. What scientists have shown is that people who are seen as beautiful, such as fashion models, have bodies that are more symmetrical than other people.

Forms, for Plato, are unchanging, timeless and eternal. Thus, for Plato the real world of Forms is more important than the world of appearances, which is constantly changing. In the world of appearances there are only shadows and images of the Forms. Objects in the world imitate a form – for example a beautiful person is only a shadow or image of the Form of beauty. Plato also talks of things in the world of appearance participating in the world of Forms – meaning that the Form of beauty, for example, is somehow present in a beautiful person. The Forms such as beauty capture the essence of a Form – they are pure, but what we see as particular examples of beauty are never completely pure. For example the painting of the Mona Lisa may be considered beautiful from a Western point of view, but not all cultures would consider it so, and thus the Mona Lisa is not unqualified pure beauty. So, the statement 'The Mona Lisa is beautiful' is both true and not true, and for Plato, this is opinion, not knowledge

Plato thinks that when we are born we have a dim recollection of what Forms are, because he says we have an immortal soul that observed the Forms before being incarnated in a body. However, in the body the memories of the soul are only dim. Plato claimed that the fact that people can have a basic understanding of something like truth, justice or beauty without being taught it shows that we have this instinctive knowledge, and so we can know something is beautiful even if we do not know about the Form of beauty. This leads Plato to claim that humans have an immortal soul.

He believes that reason itself leads us to genuine truths, and so it is the person who uses reason who will try to escape the world of appearances in order to see the Forms that lie behind – this is the philosopher. For Plato, it is the philosophers who should rule society as they have knowledge of the Forms.

Thought point

Justice and injustice

All the beliefs listed ahead are unjust according to many people, yet they are examples of practices that have occurred or are occurring in different parts of the world today.

1   Is this behaviour just or unjust?
2   Is there a single idea of justice that all these actions break? (Also, can you think of a culture where this behaviour is seen to be just?)

  a   Discriminating against people on the grounds of race;
  b   Keeping women at home and not educating them;
  c   Discriminating against homosexual people;
  d   Stoning to death rebellious sons who refuse to obey their parents;
  e   Sterilising people who are mildly mentally disabled.

Archetype
An initial model or idea from which later ideas and models of the same thing are all derived.

Hierarchy of the Forms

The idea of a hierarchy is present in the hierarchy of knowledge in the *Republic*, illustrated by Plato's Analogy of the Divided Line, in which knowledge (of the world of Forms) and opinion (about the physical world) are distinguished and ranked.

Plato also divides the Forms themselves, by claiming that there is a superior Form that the rest are dependent on; however, all the Forms are eternal and unchanging. This is the Form of the Good, which relates both to that which is the most perfect example of something and to good in a moral sense. Plato says that not only is the Form of the Good the highest Form but also it is the source of all the other Forms. In our world of appearances, we say certain things are good, but we cannot know everything about goodness.

By hierarchy Plato only seems to imply that the Form of the Good is superior to the others and from it all the others emanate. Additionally,

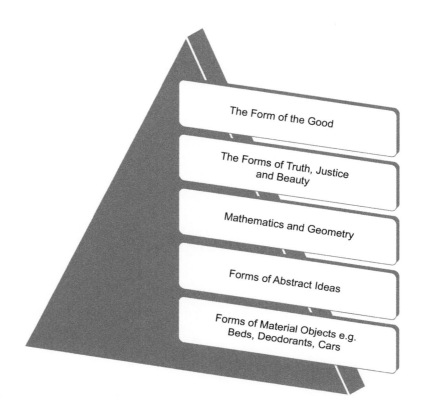

The Form of the Good

The Forms of Truth, Justice and Beauty

Mathematics and Geometry

Forms of Abstract Ideas

Forms of Material Objects e.g. Beds, Deodorants, Cars

Charles Griswold suggested that it is debatable whether Plato thought there were Forms of material objects, like beds and tables.

To explain what he means by this Plato uses three analogies: The Sun, the Divided Line and the Cave.

The Analogy of the Sun

In order to see an object, we need not only eyes but also light as provided by the sun. Plato considers that this applies also to the mind or soul and this is the knowledge and truth which come from the Form of the Good that enables knowledge of the other Forms.

In this analogy, Plato claims that just as the sun enables us to see clearly so the Form of the Good makes everything clear and knowable, so the Form of the Good is the source of all other Forms. It is the most important and it is vital.

Just as sight need slight and eyes to see clearly, without knowledge of the Form of the Good people cannot see clearly. The Form of the Good is symbolised by light, and just as nobody can see clearly without light, neither can a person see clearly without knowledge of the Form of the Good. Additionally, the Form of the Good has an ethical dimension – the Form of the Good allows the philosopher who understands it to recognise good people, good actions and so become good himself.

Thought point

What is the good?

- How would you explain to a child what the word 'good' means? Justify your answer.
- Would you say: good is a matter of what I approve of?
- Would you say: good is what pleases me?
- Would you say: good is what the government decides?
- Would you say: good is what my community decides?
- Would you say: good is what my religion says?
- Would you say: good is what God says?
- Something else?

The Analogy of the Divided Line

This analogy continues the Analogy of the Sun and helps us to understand the Analogy of the Cave.

The divided line is used to illustrate different levels of truth and show how someone can move up the line in order to arrive at the Form of the Good. He also uses it to justify why mathematics is an important part of the education of a philosopher.

The lower end of the line A-B represents opinions and beliefs. B-C represents scientific knowledge, which is knowledge of the physical world, C-D is mathematical knowledge and finally D-E is philosophical knowledge, knowledge of the Forms and most importantly the Form of the Good.

According to Plato philosophical knowledge is the most important, as shown by the length of D-E. B-C and C-D are equal, which suggests that there is an interdependent link between the physical world and mathematics. Finally, A-B represents the view of reality held by the prisoners in the Analogy of the Cave.

The Analogy of the Cave

The Analogy of the Cave is the third and the most important of the similes that Plato uses to explain his theory of the Forms. It encapsulates the similes of the sun and the divided line, while also representing Plato's concerns. It aims to:

- show Plato's ideas about appearance and reality and knowledge and belief, and the process of education as the philosopher moves towards knowledge of the Form of the Good;
- reinforce the role of the Form of the Good by extending the Analogy of the Sun;
- illustrate the role of the Form's in Plato's ethical theory and the political implications;
- show what Plato thinks what the role of the philosopher in society should be, his actual status and why it is not valued.

It is sometimes said to be allegorical as the different elements of the story are symbolic of the situation people find themselves in, and as a result philosophers debate as to its interpretation.

The story goes as follows:

Imagine people who have spent all their lives chained up in an underground cave. They are all facing the back wall of the cave and are chained up in such a way that they can only look ahead of them at the wall itself. There is a wall behind the prisoners, behind which there is a fire burning, giving the only light in the cave and casting shadows on the wall which the prisoners face. Behind the wall is a walkway where other people are walking up and down carrying different objects. What the prisoners chained to the chairs see is the shadows cast by the objects on the wall in front of them; all they hear is the occasional voices of the people carrying the objects. Thus, for the prisoners these shadows and voices are the only reality they know.

The prisoners believe that the shadows are reality and if they hear the people behind the wall speaking they assume that the voices come from the shadows. They even play games, trying to guess which object will appear next.

Plato then asks us to imagine that one of the prisoners is set free. At first, he will be confused and not understand what he sees but slowly the released prisoner becomes used to the firelight and is able to see the people and the objects they carry. He had formerly believed that the shadows were reality, but now he understands that they were merely an illusion.

Then if the released prisoner is dragged up a steep, long ramp at the back of the cave into the sunlight, he will not be able to see and will try to flee back into the cave. However, bit by bit he will be able to see the world around him. Finally, he will look up and realise the role of the sun, which enables sight and allows him to understand that it gives life to everything else. Once he realises this, he will not wish to return to the cave.

However, out of duty the prisoner goes back to the cave again to tell the other prisoners about reality. When he goes back underground from the light of the sun to the darkness, he once again cannot see clearly and at first sees nothing at all. When the other prisoners hear his story, and see that not only does he see little but also he no longer wishes to play their guessing games, they are convinced it is better not to go above ground, even wishing to put to death anyone who tries to free another prisoner. The prisoners would mock the returning escapee and might kill him.

Analogy

The act of comparing one thing with another that shares similar characteristics, to help a person learn about the first thing. For example if you say a person is 'as cunning as a fox', you are explaining something about how cunning and crafty the person is.

The Cave

A famous analogy written by Plato which he uses to explain some parts of his theory of Forms.

Thought point

Philosopher

Before reading the commentary on the cave discuss what your image of a philosopher is.

The Analogy of the Cave

The text of the Analogy of the Cave is in Plato's *Republic* at 514a–521b. The 'Further Reading' section suggests some books that are good guides to Plato's text.

Key features of the Analogy of the Cave

The cave corresponds to the visible realm, the world of appearances and illusions, while the world outside the cave corresponds to the intelligible realm, the world of reality and the Forms. The prisoners are at the level of illusion – all they see are shadows and reflections. It is not obvious whether seeing nothing but shadows is ever a feature of everyday life. We must assume that, as the cave dwellers are at the level of opinion, the shadows and reflected noises stand for opinions picked up from others, and possibly raw sensory experience. According to Plato people do not see the Forms clearly, only the illusory physical world. Also, being prisoners means that people need to be set free. In this sense the physical world imprisons a person by stopping him or her from seeing the Forms.

The journey of the prisoner who is mysteriously released from his bonds then illustrates the results of thorough philosophical education for one who is suited to it.

Plato's other analogies

Plato's Cave is one of a set of three analogies that he used to explain some of the features of his theory of the Forms. The other two analogies, the Analogies of the Line and the Sun, can be found in Plato's Republic at 506e–511e.

When the prisoner turns and becomes accustomed to the light he notices men making shadows with objects, which are images of the forms. However, these objects are only copies of the Forms. This is known as double deception, sometimes characterised by those who carry them who are believed to shape the views of the prisoners as they share the same views, having no more idea of the Forms than the prisoners. Plato criticised politicians and philosophers who are like the people carrying the objects – they lead others but they themselves have no knowledge of the truth: the Forms.

The passage of the prisoner from seeing the shadows are not real to the fact the objects are not real, to the fact that the men are carrying the objects is indicative of the passage from ignorance to even firmer belief.

The fire performs the same role in the cave as the sun does outside – the fire is a false Form of the Good that the prisoner's opinions are based upon and judged upon. Robin Waterfield (ed. Plato, *Republic*, 1994) suggests that the prisoners being attracted to the shadows from the firelight rather than the real world above represents the way in which culture, tradition and upbringing limit people's ability to see the world differently.

The prisoner is forcibly dragged up the steep slope – this represents the rigours of education. Presumably, those forcing him along are his teachers. Every stage in the simile is either difficult to traverse or painful on the eyes. The implication is that many will either turn back or stop before they reach the final stage; they are reluctant to see the truth.

Above ground the prisoner adjusts to the light and begins to see. This is an analogy to the philosopher gradually learning to distinguish Forms from the images and copies of them in the world. At first the Forms can be seen only in a dim manner, but as the philosopher's training reaches completion, he is able to see them in the full light of the sun, or Good, and finally look at the sun itself. It is by looking at the objects in relation to the sun that he is able to understand the seasons and so forth, which is to say how the forms relate to, and partake of, the Form of the Good, which is the source of all the other Forms.

The released prisoner wants to stay above ground to contemplate the Forms, but is duty-bound to return to the cave to educate the other prisoners. This represents Plato's idea that those who can see the Forms (i.e. what is true) should be the leaders of society, not the politicians who want to rule out of a desire for power and fame. For Plato, knowledge of the Forms is an essential quality of any ruler, so that a ruler governs wisely for society's good, not to further her or his self-interests.

When the released prisoner returns to the cave he is unable to see clearly, illustrating the difficulties of seeing the Forms within the world. The other prisoners mock him and Plato remarks that they would kill him if they could. It is possible that Plato could have had two things in mind here: first, the general view of philosophers in ancient Greek society was that they were rather odd; secondly, the statement that the other prisoners would kill the released prisoner if they could is, perhaps, a reference to the death of Socrates.

The death of Socrates

Socrates was one of the first Western philosophers. Although he wrote nothing himself, many of his ideas were recorded by Plato, his student. Socrates died after drinking hemlock, a poison. He had been condemned to death by a court in Athens for impiety and corrupting the youth of Athens by teaching them philosophy. The duty of a citizen was to end his or her own life if condemned to death; Socrates put obeying the law above himself and drank the poison.

Plato records the days leading up to Socrates' death in *Crito* and *Phaedo*. These books contain ideas from Plato as well as from Socrates.

Throughout his life Plato defended Socrates' memory and was distrustful of all politicians because of what had happened to Socrates.

The Analogy of the Cave raises issues about who is the most suitable person to rule society and about the state in which most people exist – one of ignorance of the Forms – and also the fact that people do not want to be released from this state.

The cave analogy – in summary

1 The prisoners are chained in an underground cave so they cannot turn their heads.	People who do not understand the knowledge of the Forms are trapped in the physical world, imprisoned by desires, temptations, superficiality and possessions.
2 There is a wall behind the prisoners and behind it is a fire.	Shadows are thrown onto the wall in front of the prisoners and voices can be heard.
3 People walk up and down between wall and fire with objects; some of them are talking.	Everything that is carried creates shadows on the wall in front of the prisoners. The objects are copies of things in the world above, so the shadows are copies of copies.
4 One prisoner is released and turns around to see the wall and the fire.	The released prisoner realises that the world of shadows is not actually the *real* world.

continued overleaf

The cave analogy – in summary

5 The prisoner is dragged up to the surface.	It is difficult to be forced to see the world in a different way.
6 At first the released prisoner is overwhelmed by the brightness of the light above ground.	The adjustment takes time.
7 The released prisoner first sees shadows, then reflections in the water, then the moon and stars and finally plants, trees and the sun by day.	Gradually an understanding of the true, real nature of the world is gained. The world above the cave represents the Forms; the sun is the highest Form and represents the Form of the Good. The sun gives light and symbolises the Form of the Good as the source of the other Forms of knowledge.
8 Remembering the prisoners still in the cave the released prisoner feels sorry for them and returns to the cave.	The released prisoner feels sorry for the prisoners who still don't see what the true reality is.
9 The people still imprisoned in the cave do not believe anything he says.	People in the cave are trapped in their own lives and may not want to be freed from it. The released prisoner has a better understanding of how things really are.
10 The people still imprisoned in the cave would, if they could, kill the released prisoner.	The released prisoner's ideas are threatening to the whole way of life and thinking of the prisoners.
11 The released prisoner would prefer not to descend once again to the cave.	Once someone has seen the reality of the Forms and how things are, it is not easy to go back to the state of ignorance of the prisoners.

The Analogy of the Cave questions who are the best people to rule society and also raises the fact that most people live in ignorance of the Forms and do not even want to acquire knowledge of the Forms. There is no one way to interpret the Analogy of the Cave. Plato used it as an illustration of the theory of Forms, but it does not explain everything about the theory of Forms. How do you interpret the Analogy of the Cave?

ANALYSIS OF THE THEORY OF FORMS

Why are the Forms important in Plato's thinking?

Plato never directly answers this, although many ideas can be deduced from Plato's *Republic*. In the *Republic* Plato attempts an answer to the challenge that people are good only because they have to be and if they can get away with not being good they will, and so nobody will be good simply because it is the right thing to do. According to Plato the Forms are the answer to this challenge: the Form of truth is real and so is an independent standard of truth – being truthful is good in itself. The Forms also mean that Plato can explain why concepts such as truth and beauty are unchanging in a world that is subject to constant change. The idea of the Forms allows Plato to explain why ideas known through reason are eternal and unchanging.

In the Analogy of the Cave the sun represents the Form of the Good and the sun is the source of all the other Forms. Just as the sun allows life to exist and people to see, so the Form of the Good enables the philosopher to know the other Forms and to know that objects in the physical world are images or copies of the Forms. The Form of the Good for Plato is the source of anything that is knowable and of the knowable world: 'The good therefore may be said to be the source not only of the intelligibility of the objects of knowledge, but also of their being and reality' (*Republic*, 509b). One interpretation of this is that the Form of the Good (symbolised by the sun) enables us to know what things are and also it is the source of what is knowable because without knowledge we do not know that there are objects of knowledge and we can know nothing about them. For example koi carp in a pond cannot understand the world above and outside the pond and do not have knowledge of the world; there are no objects of knowledge for koi carp, as they cannot understand or have knowledge of the world in the way humans do.

Additionally, if the Form of the Good is understood in a moral sense, morality is part of all areas of knowledge. Plato does not make a distinction between moral knowledge and other types of knowledge. So, for Plato, you could not have, for example, scientific knowledge of an automatic Kalashnikov assault rifle that is independent from moral values. Knowledge cannot be morally neutral. If you make an automatic Kalashnikov assault rifle this is not a morally neutral action in which you say it is up to people how they use it. So was Mikhail Kalashnikov right when he said, '*I wanted my invention to serve peace. I didn't want it to make war easier . . . If it was not guns, it would be knives or axes. Guns are not guilty. People are guilty*'? Plato attempts to answer the challenge posed by the story of Gyges' ring of invisibility.

For Plato, the Form of the Good cannot be separated from all other knowledge. This conflicts with modern views of morality that suggest that moral values are something imposed on the world by human beings, such as whether an action brings an individual pleasure. It is also different from the views expressed by Mikhail Kalashnikov.

However, trying to claim that the Forms are successful as a challenge to the idea that people are good only because they have to be depends on whether the theory of the Forms is successful. There are many arguments that have been put against this theory.

> **Gyges' ring**
>
> A famous story in the *Republic* concerning whether any person who had a magic ring of invisibility could resist using it and the effect such a ring might have on the user's moral identity. If you do not know the story look Gyges' ring up on the Internet and also think about similarities with Frodo Baggins' ring in *The Lord of the Rings*, by J.R.R. Tolkien.

Shadow worlds and real world

If you want to watch a film playing with the idea of a shadow world and the real world with a rather different twist from Plato, watch the film *The Matrix* (1993).

ANALYSIS OF THE THEORY OF FORMS

Forms could be just ideas preserved in people's minds

It could be argued that the ideas of justice or beauty are not Forms but simply ideas that people have in their minds that they pass on to others, such as their friends and children. If people die without passing on the idea, the idea dies out. Richard Dawkins suggested that ideas are passed on from person to person. He called the passing on of ideas like this *memes* (*The Selfish Gene*). He has compared bad ideas (he gives the example of religion) spreading from one person's mind to another's to a virus.

The Form of the Good

Plato's views of the 'Good' have also been criticised. Plato was a moral absolutist: he said that there is an absolute Good that is eternal and unchanging and which can be discovered through using reason (i.e. it is a priori). According to Plato, once we understand the Good people will not disagree about moral issues and there will be no differences between cultures about what is right or wrong.

Others hold a relativist approach to morality and argue that there is no such thing as an absolute good, but that ideas of right and wrong develop in the world in human relationships and situations (i.e. they are a posteriori). Society's values and morality change over time and also differ in different parts of the world, and so there is no Form of the Good.

Does everything have a Form?

Are there really Forms of everything, such as tables, chairs, televisions and so on? Plato is not concerned with the question of Forms of material objects; he is concerned with the Forms of concepts, such as good, truth and justice. He rarely discusses the Forms of material objects. According to Bertrand

Russell, his idea of the Forms when taken to its extreme falls into '*a bottom-less pit of nonsense*'. Plato himself seemed confused on this point; sometimes he says there is a Form for everything but at other times he seems uncertain. He does mention the Form of a bed in the *Republic*, but Charles Griswold has suggested this was a joke.

It is possible to think of Forms of good things, but it is more difficult to imagine the ideal Form of bad things, such as disease or handicap, or even death. It is confusing to see what the world of the Forms applies to as even if we could know the true ideas of beauty, truth and justice from the world of the Forms, how could they affect our everyday lives?

The link between Forms and the physical world

Plato never really explains the link between world of the Forms and the world of appearances in which we live (e.g. what is the link between the Form of truth and instances of truth in the world?). This is not clear.

Also, Plato presents a really depressing picture of the world of appearances in which we live, presenting it as a gloomy cave. Plato sees the world as evil and changing and ignores any beauty in the physical world. However, Popper thought that Plato's world of the Forms was simply a way of coping with the uncertainty of life in a world that is continually subject to change.

Aristotle also suggested that something does not have to be eternal to be pure. Something white does not become whiter if it is eternal – eternity and whiteness are different qualities. Thus, for something to be real does not depend on remaining unchanged, as Plato thought.

The world of Forms

There is, in fact, no evidence for the world of the Forms and knowledge comes through sense experience (a posteriori), not only a priori through reason.

Plato's dualist view about the nature of reality has been criticised by others who believe that abstract ideas, such as truth and beauty, are only names that have been invented to help people describe their experiences of the physical world. This approach claims that the ordinary, material world is the true reality and that ideas develop only because of our experience of physical things. From this point of view, the idea of 'dog' exists only because people have had experience of dogs and needed an idea or word to describe them. 'Dog' is not some eternal idea waiting to be discovered independently with the mind – we come up with the idea only because we have first experienced the physical object. Our knowledge is a posteriori – knowledge that comes after sense experience. Aristotle argued that the ideas or Forms are developed from our experience of physical things – they do not exist eternally or independently. They exist only in language, not in some independent world of Forms.

In Plato's defence . . .

Plato's argument can to some extent be supported by modern genetics. People and animals are members of a particular species because they share a common genetic code. The genetic code comes first, and the individual is able to grow and become a member of a certain species only as a result of the genetic code.

Also, rationalist philosophers, such as Descartes, support Plato's ideas to some extent, as he argued that we have concepts that exist in the mind first and are then used to help us construct reality. However, Descartes believed that these ideas existed in the mind and not somewhere else, such as the world of the Forms.

Kant was also a rationalist and thought there were two realities: the world of sense experiences, which he called the phenomenal world, which depends on the mind; and the world of things themselves, the reality or noumenal world. He thought that our ideas of the world come from how we ourselves perceive or interpret it, whereas the noumenal world can never really be known.

If Kant's ideas are right then he would support Plato's ideas of the world of the Forms, as according to Kant we can never really know the world around us as it really is as we interpret it through our sense experiences.

The physical world seems to have evidence to support its existence, but quantum physics shows that no one can be sure that their experience of the physical world is accurate, so maybe there does exist some noumenal world that exists beyond experience.

The third man argument

Plato's student Aristotle put forward a criticism of the theory of Forms known as the 'third man' argument. It is, however, quite an obscure argument and not always easy to follow.

The third man argument was first given by Plato himself in his dialogue *Parmenides*. The resemblance between any two material objects is explained by Plato in terms of their joint participation in a common form. A red book and a red flower, for example, resemble each other because they are copies of the form of redness. Because they are copies of this form, they also resemble the form. But this resemblance between the red object and the form of redness must also be explained in terms of another form. And this will lead to an infinite regress. Whenever someone proposes another form that two similar things copy, you can always ask them to explain the similarity between the form and the objects. This will always require another form. Therefore, to explain the similarity between a man and the form of man, one needs a third form of man, and this always requires another form. This argument is known as the third man argument, as Aristotle formulated it using the concept of a man and claimed that a copy of a Form could turn out to be an infinite series that never stopped; this would render the theory of Forms meaningless as a way of explaining the ultimate origin of concepts, such as the Good, truth and justice.

SUMMARY

1 Forms

Two worlds
Appearances (this world) and reality (the Forms)

Characteristics of the Forms
Transcendent and unchanging
Archetype for things that physically exist; immortal

Form of the Good
Highest Form
Source of the other Forms

Criticisms
Forms could just be ideas in the mind
Unclear link between Forms and the world of appearances
No proof that the world of Forms exists
The third man argument

2   **Cave analogy**

Key elements
Tied-up prisoners – people trapped in the world of appearances
The fire and shadows – imitations and copies of the Forms
The world above ground – the world of Forms
The sun – the Form of the Good

REVIEW QUESTIONS

Look back over the chapter and check that you can answer the following questions:

1   Explain in less than a side of A4 what is meant by Plato's theory of Forms.
2   Do you agree with Plato that Forms exist? Justify your answer with reasons.
3   Explain the link between Plato's Forms and the Analogy of the Cave.
4   Explain the Analogy of the Cave.
5   Is there any reason to believe that anything exists except what we can observe?

Terminology

Do you know your terminology?

Try to explain the following ideas without looking at your books and notes:

*   Form
*   Form of the Good
*   The Analogy of the Cave.

Examination questions practice

When writing answers to questions about Plato, make sure you avoid the mistake of only describing what Plato says.

SAMPLE EXAM-STYLE QUESTIONS

1 **Explain Plato's Analogy of the Cave.** (30 marks)

(a) Explain how the analogy was used by Plato to explain his theory of Forms. Key elements to include in your answer would be:
   (i) The sun – represents the Form of the Good, which is the source and origin of the other Forms. This links in with Plato's earlier Analogy of the Sun.
   (ii) The real world – the world of ideas; more important than the physical world for Plato.
   (iii) Shadows on the wall – the illusions of the physical world. Only shadows and images of the Forms are seen in the physical world.
   (iv) The prisoners – represent people trapped in the physical world and unable to see the reality of the world of Forms. The prisoner who is dragged out of the cave takes time to adjust to the sunlight. This represents the person who gradually adjusts to seeing the world differently when he or she recognises the reality that Forms exist.

2 **'Plato does not value experience enough.' Discuss.**

AO1 (15 marks)
You would need to explain Plato's theory of the Forms and the analogies he uses to explain them, particularly the Analogy of the Cave. But do not spend too much time simply telling the story of the cave. Pick out the points in the simile that apply to the question – experience of the real world and especially the Form of the Good.

AO2 (15 marks)
• You could argue that Plato's emphasis on the Forms limits knowledge to the few (the philosophers) who see the Forms clearly. You could explain that in daily life most people gain knowledge from experience of the physical world around them. You could argue that experience and study of the physical world, not knowledge of the Forms, have led to discoveries, such as electricity and cures for diseases.
• You could suggest that there is no way to prove whether the Forms exist. Some philosophers might say that the Forms cannot be verified and therefore are philosophically meaningless, whereas the physical world is visible and available for us to study through science.
• On the other hand, you could argue that Plato's suggestion of the existence of the Forms has developed from studying the physical world and realising that there is more to reality than just what can be seen and observed.
• Plato's theory of the Forms might also suggest that a moral life is possible only if you understand the Forms yourself or follow the instructions of those who understand them; however, people can be moral even if they do not believe in or see the Forms.
• You need to produce a balanced argument and use evidence to back up your claims.

Further possible questions

• **'Plato's Forms are no more than an invention.' Discuss.**
• **Critically assess Plato's idea of the Form of the Good.**
• **'The Forms teach us nothing about the physical world.' Discuss.**
• **'Plato is wrong to say that most people live in a shadow world.' Discuss.**

FURTHER READING

Annas, J. 1998. *An Introduction to Plato's Republic*. Oxford: OUP. There are many versions of Plato's *Republic* available. Two very readable editions that both contain helpful footnotes and commentaries are those translated by Desmond Leigh (2003) and Robin Waterfield (2001).

Ancient philosophical influences

2 Aristotle

Essential terminology

The body
The Four Causes
The Prime Mover

THE ISSUES

1 How do we explain the existence of things?
2 What did Aristotle mean by the Prime Mover?

Key scholars

Plato (c. 427 BCE – c. 347 BCE)
Aristotle (384 BCE – 322 BCE)

WHAT YOU WILL LEARN ABOUT IN THIS CHAPTER

In this chapter you will examine Aristotle's idea about reality, cause and purpose in the world and the Prime Mover.

'ALL MEN DESIRE TO KNOW'

This phrase begins Aristotle's book *Metaphysics* and it sums up Aristotle's desire to learn about and understand the world. Part of Aristotle's philosophy investigated the nature of things and how we explain why things exist.

THE OCR CHECKLIST

The philosophical views of Aristotle, in relation to:

* understanding of reality – Aristotle's use of teleology
* the Four Causes – material, formal, efficient and final causes
* the Prime Mover – the nature of Aristotle's Prime Mover and connections between this and the final cause

continued overleaf

Learners should have the opportunity to discuss issues related to the ideas of Plato and Aristotle, including:

* comparison and evaluation of Plato's Form of the Good and Aristotle's Prime Mover
* comparison and evaluation of Plato's reliance on reason (rationalism) and Aristotle's use of the senses (empiricism) in their attempts to make sense of reality

Aristotle, *Physics* II.3 and *Metaphysics* V.2

Aristotle's understanding of reality

Aristotle wanted to explain 'why' things exist as they do. However, he rejected Plato's idea that things which exist in some way participate in or imitate an ideal Form of that object. Instead, Aristotle focused on why a particular piece of matter existed: a car is made of matter, but all the bits of matter in it have a particular arrangement and structure as part of the car. They have a particular 'form'; but this form is not a copy of an ideal Platonic 'Form' of a car.

Aristotle suggested that there are four different types of causes or explanations of why any object exists; this is what we now call the 'Four Causes'.

ARISTOTLE'S FOUR CAUSES

Aristotle looked for answers to questions about the nature or substance of things. What does it mean for an object to exist? What gives an object its particular characteristics and so forth? When Aristotle talked about the form of something he meant its structure and characteristics which can be perceived by the senses. This is a completely different approach to that of Plato. Aristotle identified Four Causes that explain why a thing or object exists as it does.

The material cause

The material cause answers the question, what is it made of?

The material cause refers to the matter or substance that something is made from (e.g. a table which is made of wood). The material cause also explains the properties of something: wood can be carved, it can be sawn, it can be burned and so forth. Without the material nothing would exist.

However, knowing what something is made of does not give a complete answer. We know that a table is often made of wood, and perhaps glue, nails, screws and so forth, but knowing this does not help us understand exactly what a table is.

The formal cause

The formal cause answers the question, what are its characteristics?

The formal cause refers to what gives the matter its 'form' or 'structure'. A table is not just a piece of wood, but it is wood arranged in a particular way. So, the difference between a pile of pieces of wood and a table is that a table has properties and functions that come from the particular arrangement of the wood and shape of the table. It would not be a table if the wood was put together in a different way.

The efficient cause

The efficient cause answers the question, how does it happen?

The efficient cause refers to the cause of an object or thing existing – in other words, the answer to 'why' the thing exists. A table exists because a carpenter made it. The carpenter is the cause of the table existing rather than it just being a pile of wood.

The final cause

The final cause answers the question, what is it for?

The final cause is the most important part of Aristotle's thinking and is concerned with the function of any thing or object. If you take the example of a table, you could ask why it has been made the size and in the way it is, and of course an answer would be to say that it is laid out in this way so as to be used for eating, working and so forth. According to Aristotle everything is made for a purpose. This final cause is teleological – it is concerned with the function of a particular object or the reason an action is done (Aristotle, *Metaphysics*).

Aristotle is not saying that there is a purpose or sign of design in nature; he is saying that when you consider any object or thing it has some function, which is the ultimate reason why the thing is as it is.

The Four Causes

1 *The material cause* – what a thing is made of.
2 *The efficient cause* – the agent or cause of the thing coming to exist as it is. The existence of a painting or work of art is brought about by the artist who makes it. The artist is the efficient cause.
3 *The formal cause* – what makes the thing recognisable: its structure, shape and activity.
4 *The final cause* – the ultimate reason why the thing exists.

Metaphysics

Metaphysics means 'after physics'. This is nothing to do with what you more commonly mean by 'physics' – what this is actually referring to is Aristotle's book *Physics*; 'after physics' is just a reference to the fact that this book was classified by later philosophers as following on from his book *Physics*.

Aristotle's teleology

For Aristotle every single object and even the universe itself have a purpose, by which he means a reason for existing. Something is good if it achieves its final purpose, and this telos defines it as good. According to Aristotle if we could discover the telos of an organism, we could also discover what needs to be done to reach that purpose. He also believed that people have a purpose, and a good person is one who fulfils this purpose. Everything for Aristotle exists for a purpose.

Aristotle gave many examples to explain these ideas, such as that that of a marble statue. If someone asked what caused the statue he might get the following answers:

Material cause: it is made of marble.
Formal cause: it has the shape of a statue.
Efficient cause: a mason made it.
Final cause: its function is to be a beautiful statue that honours, remembers or recalls someone/something.

Thought point

Aristotle's four causes

How would you explain each item on the list in terms of Aristotle's Four Causes?

1 A house
2 A car
3 The sun
4 A flower
5 A human being

Teleological

The world 'teleological' originates from the Greek word 'telos'. 'Telos' refers to the final goal or purpose of something. So any argument that is 'teleological' is concerned with making points about either the 'goal' or the 'purpose' of something.

ARISTOTLE

Aristotle was a remarkable person. He tutored students on most traditional subjects that are taught at universities today. He was fascinated with understanding the physical world around him and the universe. His biology books were not superseded by anything better until 2,000 years later. Aristotle also wrote about other areas of study, including drama, rhetoric (public speaking), meteorology, sport and physics.

Plato and Aristotle

Aristotle was Plato's student and continued to study many of the areas of study that first interested Plato. However, Aristotle's approach was completely different from that of Plato. Plato was a rationalist, whereas Aristotle was an empiricist. Knowledge, for Aristotle, was not something remembered from the world of the Forms, but the physical world and experience were the basis of knowledge. Aristotle's idea of education was also different from that of Plato, who thought that education consisted of bringing out knowledge that was already in the mind. Aristotle emphasised the value of studying the physical world, and thought that there were a variety of ways that people acquired knowledge: through observation, through being taught and through practice of what was taught. Aristotle's approach is empirical and he is not as concerned as Plato with the world of Forms.

However, Aristotle's writings always recognised the value of what he had learned from Plato and his books often refer to the ideas of Plato. Anthony Kenny has stated that 'Aristotle always acknowledged a great debt to Plato, whom on his death he described as the best and happiest of mortals "whom it is not right for evil men even to praise"' (Kenny, *A Brief History of Western Philosophy*). The picture on p. 4 shows Plato pointing upwards towards heaven and the world of ideas and carrying his book *Timaeus*, while Aristotle carries his book *Ethics* and points towards the earth and the physical world. Why?

Evaluating Aristotle's theory of causality

Aristotle criticised Plato's belief in the world of the Forms as there is no empirical evidence for its existence, but one could also say that there is no evidence for considering that only the material world is the source of true knowledge.

Many scientists and philosophers would also disagree with Aristotle over his belief that everything has a telos, final cause or purpose. Some would say that things exist simply by chance, or as Bertrand Russell said, the universe simply is – it is 'brute fact' and it does not make sense to ask what caused it or to think that it has a purpose. Existentialist philosophers, such as Albert Camus and Jean-Paul Sartre, also thought it was pointless to think that the universe or anything in it had any purpose.

Some things do not seem to fit into Aristotle's theory of causality, such as emotions: love, hate, despair and so forth.

Both Hume and Kant considered that causation is simply the way we as humans see things in the world around us – causation is simply a mental construct.

Formal cause

Make sure you do not confuse Aristotle's formal cause and forms with those of Plato.

Aristotle the man (384–322 BCE)

Aristotle was born in Macedonia. At the age of 17 he moved to Athens, where he joined Plato's Academy. In 347 BCE he moved to Turkey due to the growing political tensions between Macedonia and Athens. He spent his time there investigating science and particularly biology. In 341 BCE he moved with his family back to Macedonia to become tutor to King Philip II of Macedonia's son, Alexander (who would later become Alexander the Great). After Alexander became king, Aristotle returned

continued overleaf

However, even today scientists do work in a similar way to Aristotle as theories about the universe are based on experience and observation of it.

Aristotle's theory also shows that there can be several explanations for something's existence, all of which increase our understanding of it. For example we are aware of the material cause of a human and all the chemical components involved, but we can also accept other explanations for human existence, such as life being a gift from God. Aristotle shows that both scientific and religious explanations can work together – the Big Bang could be seen as the efficient cause of the universe and at the same time God could be seen as the final cause. Aristotle's ideas have also been developed by Christian thinkers, such as Thomas Aquinas.

THE PRIME MOVER

According to Aristotle's observations of the world around him everything that exists is always in a state of movement or motion. In other words, everything is in a state of continual change; nothing stays the same, as things are always developing, growing larger or older or shrinking in size and so forth.

Aristotle observed four things:

1   The physical world was continually in a state of motion and change.
2   The planets appeared to be moving eternally.
3   Change or motion always has a cause.
4   Objects in the physical world were in a state of actuality and potentiality.

Aristotle, therefore, concluded that something must cause the movement or change without being moved and that is eternal. He observed that if something can change it moves from the actual state it is in and so has the potential to become another state: an actual tadpole is potentially a frog. He also concluded that for things to come into existence something else must have caused it to exist. Finally, it was his understanding of the eternal motion of the planets that made him realise that there must be an eternal cause of motion – a prime or first mover.

Aristotle was not talking about a sequence of events in time. His ideas about the Prime Mover are not simply that it started everything off in motion in the first place. It is more subtle than that. Change, in Aristotle's view, is eternal; there cannot have been a first change, because something would have to have happened just before that change which set it off, and this itself would have been a change, and so on. Aristotle goes on to say that certain things (i.e. the planets and the stars) that we see 'in the heavens' are always moving, in circles, without any apparent beginning or end, and this is clear to our observation.

to Athens and founded a school called the Lyceum. He remained in Athens, teaching until 323, when Alexander the Great died. After Alexander's death, it became difficult for Aristotle to stay in Athens as he was a Macedonian. Worried that he might die like Socrates, Aristotle and his family moved to Chalcis, where he died a year later.

Empirical

The word 'empirical' is used in philosophy to refer to a view or claim that is supported by observable evidence that you can study. 'Empiricists' (people who use an 'empirical' approach) believe that only truth claims based on empirical evidence are meaningful.

The Prime Mover

The unchanging cause of all that exists.

Thought point

Potentiality and actuality

How does Aristotle's distinction between potentiality and actuality apply to the following?

1   An acorn
2   An embryo
3   The prime minister
4   A computer
5   A pig

N.B. Aristotle never suggested that the Prime Mover started everything off like pushing a line of dominos so that they all fall down. For Aristotle, the Prime Mover is the originating cause of all motion eternally which sustains the pattern of change from actuality to potentiality in the physical world.

What are the characteristics of the Prime Mover?

According to Aristotle the Prime Mover exists by necessity – meaning that the Prime Mover could not fail to exist and nothing caused it to exist. The Prime Mover cannot change and so Aristotle said that it is pure actuality by nature, and that nature is good. If it were not good it would have the potentiality to be better and so could change. Something which has pure actuality does not need to change.

The Prime Mover causes the movement of other things, not as an *efficient* cause, but as a *final* cause or even the final cause. In other words, it does not start off the movement by giving it some kind of push, but it is the purpose, or the end, or the teleology, of the movement. Aristotle was keen to establish that the Prime Mover is itself unmoved, or unaffected; otherwise the whole concept would break down. It is the object of everything. It causes movement *as the object of desire and love*.

The Prime Mover is Aristotle's final cause, as it is the ultimate explanation of why things exist (think of Aristotle's Four Causes – if all objects in the universe have a purpose then the universe itself would also have a purpose – a final cause). Aristotle suggested that the final cause leads to movement like the action of being loved, as love is about not just actions but also attraction. The Prime Mover is the ultimate reason and final goal of movement. An alternative way to understand this could be to think of a magnet that will attract iron objects towards it. Aristotle says that all action is ultimately aimed at the Prime Mover and this is like attraction because the Prime Mover is the cause of all motion.

In his book *Metaphysics* Aristotle also links the Prime Mover with God and concludes that God is '*a living being, eternal, most good, so that life and duration continuous and eternal belong to God; for this is God*' (Aristotle, *Metaphysics*). If God caused motion by efficient physical means – pushing, or the equivalent, depending on the kind of 'moving' – he himself would be changed, so he must instead move by drawing things towards himself, while remaining unaffected. The final cause of movement, according to Aristotle, is a love of and desire for God. God is perfection, and everything wants to imitate perfection and is drawn towards it.

For Aristotle, God is the Prime Mover who is without parts and indivisible. In philosophy the term for being without parts is 'divine simplicity'. God is pure actuality, containing no potentiality. God is also described as being 'complete reality'.

So, what would this God as Prime Mover think about? It must be the best of all possible things to think about, because God is perfectly good. God could not think about anything which caused him to change in any way, nothing which could affect him, or make him react, or even change him from not-knowing to knowing. Aristotle concludes that God thinks about himself only. Nothing else is a fit subject. He even defines God as 'thought of thought', or 'thinking about thinking'. At the end of this line of argument, Aristotle comes to the conclusion that God knows only himself; so he does not know this physical world that we inhabit, he does not have a plan for us, and he is not affected by us. He does not even think about the universe and what happens in it as this would mean that God changes as his knowledge would change.

God thinks only about being God.

Finally, Aristotle suggests how God relates to the universe. He suggests two ways (Aristotle, *Metaphysics*):

1   As a leader
2   In the order of the universe.

Aristotle argued that the first is more important than the second as the universe depends on the Prime Mover for its existence, but he also suggests that all things in the universe are ordered to some 'final cause' and ultimately to the Prime Mover. This fits in with the importance he places on the last of his Four Causes.

To sum up:

- The final cause behind everything is the unmoved mover, which is a pure immaterial being or pure immaterial thought, self-subsistent and self-contained.
- The unmoved mover is intelligence or thought. Aristotle never talked about God in personal terms or in anthropomorphic terms as the Greek gods were described.
- God has no divine plan and does not know the world.
- The God of Aristotle is an eternal, transcendent and impersonal being.

The Prime Mover and Plato's Form of the Good

Aristotle, we know, was Plato's pupil and, therefore, was influenced by him. Like Plato, Aristotle believed that the universe was in a state of constant change or motion. Like Plato's Form of the Good, Aristotle describes the Prime Mover as being transcendent and not involved with this world. Both are impersonal beings. According to Plato, the Form of the Good is absolute and the source of all morality, of all good actions in the world; however, this does not seem to be the function of the Prime Mover.

In the writings of Plato, however, the roots of Aristotle's Prime Mover are to be found. In the *Laws*, Plato saw 'religion' as necessary to ensure order in the city. Basically, humans have to hold three key tenets: that gods exist (i.e. that the world is not a purely 'material' thing, product of chance or necessity); that they care for the world; and that they cannot be 'bought' or corrupted by people's gifts or prayers. However, he makes clear that he does not pretend to give the last answer on such difficult questions. Plato does not elaborate and seems to give only a partial insight into possible answers. But Aristotle seems to want the answers to be more complete and so gives a more literal meaning.

Plato held that there are degrees of reality, with the forms constituting the highest reality, sensible objects a middle level, and images of things the lowest level. Using the Analogy of the Sun, Plato held that the Forms, especially the Form of the Good, are the source of the reality of all things. Aristotle, on the other hand, did not distinguish between degrees of reality between sensible objects and the non-sensible Prime Mover. The role of the Prime Mover is that of a cause of motion, rather than the origin of reality itself.

Both Plato and Aristotle seek coherent, consistent, comprehensive explanations for all of nature.

Evaluating Aristotle's Prime Mover

Aristotle does not make clear the relationship between the Prime Mover and the universe, which the mover causes to move. According to Aristotle the

Necessary being

This is a phrase used in philosophy of religion to refer to something which always exists and cannot fail to exist. Usually it is a phrase that philosophers apply to God.

In medieval philosophy Anselm stated that God is a 'necessary being', by which he meant God is a being that must exist and it is impossible for God not to exist.

Prime Mover started the chain of cause and effect in the universe without himself being moved. This idea seems contradictory, for how can something that is unmoved itself initiate movement in other things? While Aristotle does link the Prime Mover with God, Aristotle's Prime Mover is transcendent and cannot interact in the universe in the way that believers often talk about God's activity in the world. Aristotle's idea of God is not a God who answers prayers or who can be experienced in any way.

It is also unclear as to the causal relationship between the Prime Mover thinking and the universe. Aristotle said that the Prime Mover was pure thought, but how can something which is pure thought move the physical universe? There is a disparity between an entity powerful enough to set the universe in motion and one unable to know it.

This immaterial view of God contradicts his materialist and empirical view of the universe as explained in his theory of the Four Causes. There are problems with the efficient cause because Aristotle's Prime Mover becomes the efficient cause of his universe, although Aristotle argues it causes movement not as an efficient cause but as a final cause.

Modern physics seems to suggest that the universe has a definite beginning. This would indicate that the universe and matter are not eternal. Therefore, Aristotle makes an assumption that matter is eternal and does not explain where it comes from.

However, the Prime Mover does share characteristics with the Christian view of God in that he is eternal and omnipotent. It makes sense to say that there must be a first cause for the universe, and his ideas again influenced Christian philosophers, such as Thomas Aquinas and his cosmological argument.

SUMMARY

1   Aristotle

Aristotle's Four Causes
The material cause – the matter or substance from which something is made
The formal cause – what gives the matter its 'Form' or 'structure'
The efficient cause – the cause of an object or thing existing
The final cause – the reason why something is the way it is

2   Plato and Aristotle

Aristotle's philosophy is different from Plato's
It emphasises the value of studying the physical world.
It rejects Plato's theory of Forms.
It rejects dualism.

3   The Prime Mover

Something that causes the motion and change of the universe without
being moved and that is eternal.
The Prime Mover exists by necessity.
The Prime Mover is the final cause.
The Prime Mover is linked with God.
The Prime Mover is related to the universe.
As a leader.
In the order of the universe.

Problems
The relationship between the Prime Mover and the universe is unclear.
Aristotle's Prime Mover is transcendent and cannot interact in the uni-
verse in the way that believers often talk about God's activity in
the world.
The causal relationship between the Prime Mover thinking and the uni-
verse is unclear.
Is there a final cause or purpose to the universe?

REVIEW QUESTIONS

1   What is the difference between Plato's and Aristotle's use of the word
'Form'?
2   What is the connection between the final cause and the Prime
Mover?

Terminology

Do you know your terminology?

Try to explain the following ideas without looking at your books and
notes:

- Aristotle's Four Causes;
- Necessary being;
- Prime Mover.

Examination questions practice

Make sure that you do not confuse the philosophy of Plato and Aristotle. Students often lose marks in this way, which is a great pity. In addition, in examination questions try to show that you understand Aristotle's ideas rather than just describing them.

SAMPLE EXAM-STYLE QUESTION

'Aristotle's theory of the Four Causes is convincing.' Discuss.

AO1 (15 marks)

Here you need to make sure that the theory is explained clearly – give examples to illustrate it.

AO2 (15 marks)

There are a range of ways to answer this question. Some relevant points to assess are as follows:

- Aristotle's theory can be defended because it is derived from reflection on his studies of the natural world. This could be seen as a strength of Aristotle's Four Causes compared with Plato's Forms, which are not observable in the physical world. You can also point to the fact that the Four Causes may be readily applied to things that exist within the world as a way of explaining them.

- You could argue that the idea of a Prime Mover and final cause who is eternal and transcendent is unpersuasive as there is a lack of evidence for the existence of a Prime Mover.
- You could also discuss Aristotle's views about the world having a purpose and the role of the final cause.

Further possible questions

- **Critically assess the strengths and weaknesses of Aristotle's views on causality.**
- **To what extent does the concept of the final cause teach us anything about the real world?**
- **'Aristotle's Prime Mover is a convincing explanation for the origins of the universe.' Discuss.**

FURTHER READING

A good starting point for further reading is the useful *Dialogue* article introducing Aristotle's thinking (2001, *Dialogue* 17).

Magee, B. 2016. *The Story of Philosophy*. Oxford: Dorling Kindersley.

Raeper, W. and Smith, L. 1991. *A Beginner's Guide to Ideas*. Oxford: Lion Books.

Ancient philosophical influences

3 Soul, mind and body

Essential terminology

Dualism
Life after death
Materialism
Monism
Soul

SOUL

The word 'soul' is used to refer to the spiritual or non-physical part of a human being, or to the mind. The soul is often seen as the centre or core of identity of a person.

Key scholars

Plato (c. 427 BCE – c. 347 BCE)
Aristotle (384 BCE – 322 BCE)
Descartes (1596–1650)

WHAT YOU WILL LEARN ABOUT IN THIS CHAPTER

The philosophical language of soul, mind and body in the thinking of Plato and Aristotle.

- Plato's view of the soul as the essential and immaterial art of a human, temporarily united with the body.
- Aristotle's view of the soul as the form of the body; the way the body behaves and lives; something which cannot be separated from the body.
  Metaphysics of consciousness, including
- substance dualism
  - ○ the idea that mind and body are distinct substances
  - ○ Descartes' proposal of material and spiritual substances as a solution to the mind/soul and body problem
- materialism
  - ○ the idea that mind and consciousness can be fully explained by physical or material interactions
  - ○ the rejection of soul as a spiritual substance.

You should discuss issues related to ideas about soul, mind and body, including:

- materialist critiques of dualism
- whether the concept of 'soul' is best understood metaphorically or as a reality
- the idea that any discussion about the mind-body distinction is a category error.

THE OCR CHECKLIST

Soul, mind and body

- The philosophical language of soul, mind and body in the thinking of Plato and Aristotle
    - ○ Plato's view of the soul as the essential and immaterial part of a human, temporarily united with the body
    - ○ Aristotle's view of the soul as the form of the body; the way the body behaves and lives; something which cannot be separated from the body
- metaphysics of consciousness, including:
    - ○ substance dualism
        - ▪ the idea that mind and body are distinct substances
        - ▪ Descartes' proposal of material and spiritual substances as a solution to the mind/soul and body problem
- materialism
    - ▪ the idea that mind and consciousness can be fully explained by physical or material interactions
    - ▪ the rejection of a soul as a spiritual substance.

Learners should have the opportunity to discuss issues related to ideas about soul, mind and body, including:

- materialist critiques of dualism, and dualist responses to materialism
- whether the concept of 'soul' is best understood metaphorically or as a reality
- the idea that any discussion about the mind-body distinction is a category error.

Thought point

Ask five people to explain what the following words mean to them:

- Soul
- Body

INTRODUCTION

What is meant by body and soul? Grammatically, I speak of 'my' body as if it were a possession, but is that really what I mean? When describing the body, we tend to use possessive terms – my arm, my head and so forth. If we take as granted that we live in a material world and what we see using our senses is valid, then we consider our bodies as occupying a space which we do not share with anyone. But is it true to say that 'I am a body' or 'I have a body'? We recognise each other by our bodies but we do not say 'I saw your body in town the other day,' but 'I saw you in town the other day.' If we identify the individual as the body they possess, then why talk of having a soul?

Additionally, there is the whole issue of personal identity: the problem of explaining what makes the identity of a single person *at a time* or *through time*, especially when there is a *change* in the person in time. Just what is it that makes you the person you are now, and what is it that makes you the same person now as you were in the past?

People change both mentally and physically, and yet these changes take place in the same person. For instance, your body is not the same size as it was when you were a child, but we say that you are the *same person* in spite of this physical change. And you are more developed mentally than you were when you were a child, but we also say that you are the same person in spite of this mental change. How can you be the same person in spite of these changes? One solution to this problem is that of John Locke, who said that it is *consciousness* on which the notion of self or personal identity is dependent. And he says that personal identity consists in consciousness and memory. This means that we are *not* to be identified essentially with our bodies.

And where does the mind fit in? When Vladimir Lenin died in 1924, Soviet scientists razor-sliced his brain to discover the secrets of his genius, but all they found was that it was just a brain. The slices of brain have, however, been preserved, so in one sense Lenin lives for ever.

So what, if anything, survives death? This brings us back to the question of what is meant by a 'person' – what are you? This is the philosophical debate about the mind-body problem and personal identity.

Two main approaches have been taken to this problem:

- The *dualist* approach argues that human beings consist of a body and soul. The soul is spiritual and the 'real me' which will survive after death. For a dualist the body is less important than the soul as it will not live on.
- The *monist* approach says that human minds cannot be separated from the body. Body and soul are united as one.

HOW DO YOU KNOW WHO YOU ARE?

Thought point

- Who are you?
- How do you know who you are?
- How do other people recognise you as you?
- Are you the same person today as yesterday?
- Will you be the same person tomorrow morning as today?
- Are you:

  - Your mind?
  - Your body?
  - Something else?

The mind-body problem

There are many books published about this topic. A helpful starting point is Quentin Smith and L. Nathan Oaklander's book *Time, Change and Freedom: Introduction to Metaphysics*. This book is set out in the form of a series of discussions between four philosophers. It is worth reading and discussing.

So is personal identity linked to our bodies? Or does the soul give us personal identity?

The mind-body question considers how our thoughts and decisions relate to our bodies. Philosophers such as Plato and Descartes are dualists and see the mind/soul and body as completely separate. We may experience pain in our bodies but the experience happens in our minds, so in many ways we do experience ourselves as separate from our bodies. Monists, on the other hand, argue that we exist in a physical world – the mind is simply the functioning of the brain and the brain is a physical organ in the body. This is a materialist view. This view also accords with the way we experience the world around us.

PLATO – A DUALIST VIEW

Plato believed that the human person has different parts: the physical body, the mind and the immortal soul. The body, like everything else physical, is in a constant state of change, but the soul is both immortal and unchanging.

In Plato's philosophy the soul is separate from the body. The soul is immortal and eternal, but the body is mortal. At death the soul is freed from the body. Plato (*Phaedo*) wrote that a person is a soul 'imprisoned' in a body. According to Plato the soul's aim is to get to the world of Forms.

According to Plato it is the soul that gives us real knowledge of Forms and when we learn anything we are remembering knowledge about the Forms that the soul has brought from the world of the Forms. The body distracts the soul from seeking knowledge of the world of Forms. He considered the body rather a nuisance, needing food, getting ill and full of desires that take away all power of thinking (Plato, *Phaedo*).

Thought point

Death and philosophy

In *Phaedo*, Plato suggests that philosophy is a preparation for death. Why do you think Plato says this?

Here the influence of the Pythagoreans is clear, with the stress on the spiritual soul or psyche and the material body with all its distracting needs. The philosopher would avoid these bodily distractions and centre on gaining knowledge of the Forms. Plato's analogy of the chariot shows the difference between the desires of the body and those of the soul. Plato explains this tripartite division of the soul by this allegory. The charioteer driving the horses represents the rational part of the soul who directs the entire chariot/soul, trying to stop the horses from going different ways, and to proceed towards the world of the Forms. The black horse represents the appetitive part of the soul, which is kept in check by the white noble horse, which represents the spirited part of the soul. Both horses pull in different directions, but the rational part of the soul tries to direct them to work in harmony.

Plato's description of the soul

In his earlier dialogues, Plato gave a fairly simple account of the duality between the body and the soul. In the *Republic* (608d–612a) he said that the soul is 'simple' and 'without parts', which means that the soul cannot be divided or split. Then as his thought developed, and he followed his own recommendation to challenge his previously held beliefs, Plato's ideas about the soul became more complex. The soul is divided into three different parts, roughly translated as reason, emotion and desire, and Plato became less certain about which parts of the soul are immortal. However, when Plato talked about the soul in the body he described it as 'complex'. By this, Plato meant that there are different aspects of the soul. For example a cut gemstone has different aspects or faces but it is still a single gem. When Plato talked about the complexity of the soul, it is still 'simple' and 'without parts'.

For Plato it was important that all parts of the soul were in harmony and worked together so that the person could obtain knowledge of the Forms. Thus a person should do the right thing just because it is a good thing to do and will help lead the person to knowledge of the Forms, not because it would bring any material benefits, such as wealth or popularity.

Soul and psyche

The word 'soul' originates from the Greek word *psyche*. It is translated as 'soul' not 'psyche' because in ancient Greek *psyche* means life or the principle that keeps a person alive. Plato means more than this when he talks about the 'soul'.

Thought point

Disharmony in the soul

Plato suggests that the soul consists of various aspects: spirit, reason and desire. How could the following crimes be explained in terms of disharmony between the aspects of the soul?

- Vandalism
- Perjury (lying in court)
- Fraud
- Drink-driving
- Rape
- Murder

Plato talking about desire, the third aspect of the soul

The third has so many manifestations that we could not give it a label which applied to it and it alone, so we named it after its most prevalent and powerful aspect: we called it the desirous part, because of the intensity of our desires for food, drink, sex and so on, and we also referred to it as the mercenary part, because desires of this kind invariably need money for their fulfilment (*Republic*, ed. Waterfield).

Virtue in the soul

In *Ethics* a classical argument against doing good, the myth of Gyges, is from the *Republic*. Part of Plato's answer to the challenge that people do good only because it brings them some benefit (e.g. not being sent to prison) is his discussion of the importance of harmony in the soul.

DOES THE SOUL EXIST?

Plato clearly believed that each person has a soul which lives on after the body dies; he also wanted to show that this belief is reasonable and can be justified through logical argument. His dialogue *Phaedo* is mainly concerned with these arguments; Cebes, the person who is in dialogue with Socrates, suggests that perhaps the soul just disappears, like smoke, into nothingness when the body dies, and he asks for some kind of persuasive argument to justify Socrates' belief in the immortality of the soul.

The argument from opposites

Plato's first argument relied on the idea that every quality comes into being from its own opposite. It depends on the existence of its opposite, or it would not exist at all. He argued that big things would not be bigger or small things smaller without their opposites; they depend on their opposites for their existence. In the same way, people who are awake are just people who were asleep but then woke up, while people who are asleep are just people who were once awake.

Plato argued that it follows that death must come from life, and life from death. That is people who are dead are just people who were once alive but then experienced the change we call dying, and people who are alive are just people who were among the dead but then experienced the change we call being born. Plato's thought suggests an endless chain of birth, death and rebirth. For death to be a thing rather than 'nothing', the soul must exist, so that one can talk of living and death as opposites.

The argument from knowledge

Plato thought that the most important kinds of human knowledge are really remembering things which we already knew. For example according to Plato, we have our knowledge of equality, even though we have never seen any two things that are perfectly equal, because there will always be some minute difference; and yet we know what true equality (or the Form of equality) must be.

Plato thought that the same was true of many other abstract concepts: even though we only ever experience imperfect examples, we have genuine knowledge of truth, goodness and beauty, just as we have true knowledge of equality and circularity. Plato distinguished this kind of knowledge from the sort of inferior, temporary, unreliable 'knowledge' that we might gain through the senses but which he considered to be merely opinion. Plato believed that this knowledge of the Forms must be innate, and must have been gained by our souls before we were born. When we come to understand something that is the object of true knowledge, such as the square root of 81, which will always be 9 and −9 and is true for all time and is not gained by the senses, we have a sense of recognition. For Plato, this was evidence that the soul pre-existed the body.

Problems with Plato's views on the soul

Peter Geach rejects Plato's views. He challenges the view that the disembodied soul can see the Forms, because seeing is a process that is linked to the body and experienced through one's senses. Geach also questions whether existence without a body is really human.

> If after a lifetime of thinking and choosing in this human way there is left only a disembodied mind whose thought is wholly non-sensuous and whose rational choices are unaccompanied by human feelings – can we still say there remains the same person?
>
> (Geach 1969)

While this does not necessarily mean that the existence of a soul without a body is impossible, it questions what exactly it would mean to say that a soul can exist without a body.

Other philosophers have rejected Plato's argument from opposites as a way to demonstrate the existence of the soul. Although many things in the universe are paired (and this is true in modern physics as well as in philosophy), there is no evidence to suggest that just because of this, death is a state opposite to but analogous to life.

Additionally, part of Plato's defence of the existence of the soul depends on the theory of the Forms. And Chapter 1 showed that there are many challenges to the theory of Forms. If Plato's theory of Forms is debatable, this also undermines his theory of the soul.

THE SOUL IN ARISTOTLE

Aristotle's understanding of the relationship between the body and the soul is found in Chapter 1 of Book 2 of his work *de Anima*. According to Aristotle, a living creature is a 'substance'. He saw the body as being the matter of a living thing, and the soul as its 'form', understood as its characteristics and covering every function of living things, including the ability to sense, move and reproduce.

The soul (*psyche*) is a much broader concept than the mind or the 'soul' in the way in which we usually use the word. The word *psyche* has numerous meanings in ancient Greek but it does not mean that the soul is what gives a person identity and which survives death. A living being is a composite whole – the body is the matter, and the soul is its form.

For Aristotle the soul cannot be separated from the body. Thus, for Aristotle, the soul and the body are not, as Plato would have it, two distinct entities, but are different parts of aspects of the same thing. The soul, in Aristotle's understanding, is the structure of the body, its function and its organisation. Aristotle gave three examples to illustrate this idea:

1   Aristotle used the example of an imprint in wax to show that just as the imprint cannot be separated from the wax, the soul and the body cannot be separated. '*We can dismiss as wholly unnecessary the question whether the body and soul are one: it is as meaningless to ask whether the wax and the shape given to it by the stamp are one.*'
2   Aristotle used the example of an axe, suggesting that if the axe was living, its body would be the handle and the axe head, while its Form would be what makes it an axe – for example the fact that it has the shape of the axe and is suited to chopping.
3   Aristotle suggested that if the eye were a body its soul would be the capacity to see. '*Suppose then that the eye were an animal – sight would have been its soul . . . when seeing is removed the eye is no longer an eye, except in name – it is no more a real eye than the eye of a statue or of a painted figure.*'

The particular nature of any soul will depend on the kind of living thing that it is, and these are arranged in a kind of hierarchy. Plants, for example, have only a vegetative sort of soul, with the powers of nutrition, growth and reproductive appetite for their kind. Animals are above plants on the scale of things, and their souls have appetites as well as the powers found in plants, so that animals can have desires and feelings, which in turn give them the ability to move. Even the human soul is simply the organisation of the body, but it has a special quality in addition to plant and animal qualities: the power of reason. Through the working of the soul, people develop their intellects and their ethical characters.

Aristotle also claimed that a dead animal is an animal in name only; it has its body, its matter, but it no longer has its soul. When it is dead, it has lost its capacity to do all the things that animals usually do. In general, then, Aristotle's concept of the soul does not allow for the possibility that it is

The soul

The principle of activity and life of the body. It also gives the body Form (structure and shape). It is an inseparable unity with the body.

The body

In Aristotle's thinking the body refers to the matter that a living creature is made of.

Faculty

In Aristotle's writings the word 'faculty' is used to refer to the capacities that are innate to something. For example the faculty of the eye is sight and that of the ear is hearing.

immortal. It is not separable from the body, if it is that which makes the body a person rather than just material. Therefore, without the body, it cannot exist, just as the characteristics and functions of a dog cannot exist on their own, without any material dog.

However, Aristotle did not stop at this point, with a clear view that the soul dies along with the body. He made an exception to the rule. All the faculties of the soul are inseparable from the body, he thought, with the exception of reason, and the extent to which they are dependent on the physical body. This is among the most obscure and most debated of all of his writings. It is not at all clear whether Aristotle thought that the reason was immortal; however, if the reason lives on after a person dies, it does not seem to be in a personal, individual kind of way; we could not say that *this person* is immortal, with a recognisable identity.

Aristotle did not believe in an afterlife or the immortality of the soul. He thought that the 'soul' was the part of the body that gave it life. It is what turns the physical form into a living organism of its particular type. For example a dog has a doggy soul, and a human has a human soul. There is no problem for Aristotle about how the soul and body work together; soul and body are inseparable. The soul develops the person's skills, character or temper, but it cannot survive death. Body and soul are a unity, and when the body dies, the soul ceases to exist. *This would appear to be materialistic* but Aristotle believed that the body and the soul were different. Human beings have a soul or self that is capable of an intellectual life. Only humans can reflect on feelings and sensations and grasp 'universals' (goodness as opposed to an individual good thing). In this way, we come to understand eternal truths.

THE LEGACY OF PLATO AND ARISTOTLE

In Greek thought it was common to separate the soul, which was wholly spiritual, from the material body. For Plato, the soul was eternal, not simply because it had no end but because it had no beginning. It was not capable of destruction, because as a simple substance it had no parts into which to disintegrate. For Plato, its true home was in the realm of the Forms – this body is temporary and corruptible, but the soul would live on.

This view was very different from that held by Christianity, which does not believe that the soul is immortal in the same way as Plato. To claim that nothing could destroy the soul would be to limit the power of God. Christians believe that any eternal life which the soul might have is a gift of God, and neither do they believe that souls transmigrate as Plato thought – there is only one earthly life.

Aristotle was a dualist like Plato – he believed there was a distinction between body and soul. However, for Aristotle, the soul was the animating principle of the body and it was not immortal. The difference between a live body and a corpse is the presence of the soul. When the soul dies, so does the body. The soul is, in Aristotle's sense, the 'form' of the body. It is not eternal; it dies. Aristotle speculated that perhaps reason, in some form, might continue eternally, but he had no notion of personal survival.

The early Christians were influenced by Platonism. This does not mean that Christian thinkers adopted every aspect of Greek thought, but Greek philosophy provided the principal tools for the development of doctrine. The language of scholarship was mainly Greek – the New Testament was written in Greek. The thought patterns, the vocabulary in which religious thought was expressed, was Greek, and the natural point of reference was to think of the human as body and soul: following Plato, it was the soul that was the 'real' person.

Plato's thought had perhaps more influence over Christian thinking than that of Aristotle, but in the Middle Ages his ideas came to affect Christian thinking through the work of Jewish and Muslim scholars in Spain. St Thomas Aquinas was more than a little influenced by Aristotle when it came to his view of the soul. Aquinas wrote that

> the soul is defined as the first principle of life in living things: for we call living things 'animate,' [i.e. having a soul], and those things which have no life, 'inanimate.' . . . it is the 'first principle of life . . . Now, though a body may be a principle of life, or to be a living thing, as the heart is a principle of life in an animal, yet nothing bodily can be the first principles of life. It is clear that to be a principle of life, or to be a living thing, does not belong to a body as a body; because, if that were the case, *every* body would be a living thing, or a principle of life. Of course, a body is able to be a living thing or even a principle of life, because it is a body. When it is a living body, it owes its life to some principle which is called its 'act'. Therefore, the soul, which is the first principle of life, is not a body, but the act of a body; just as heat . . . is not a body, but an act of a body.
>
> (*Summa Theologiae*)

Aquinas did not say that the soul *is* me. It is the principle of life, rather as Aristotle argued: life needs the body to be animated. He goes on to argue this more precisely: 'the human soul, which is called the "intellect", or the "mind", is something incorporeal and subsistent.' It is not material and to be understood as the mind, not something separate from it. The body is needed to be me.

SUBSTANCE DUALISM

In philosophy, a substance usually means something which does not depend on another thing in order to exist. Substance dualism says that there are two distinct things: material substances or bodies and mental substances or minds. This means that according to substance dualism minds do not depend on bodies in order to exist. Those who believe that the mind is the soul and that the soul can exist after death are substance dualists.

Materialism is the opposite of substance dualism as materialists believe that there is only one substance: matter. For a materialist everything that exists is a material thing or depends on a material thing for its existence.

DESCARTES AND SUBSTANCE DUALISM

René Descartes' ideas about the soul are found in both *Meditations* and *The Passions of the Soul*. The ideas of Plato had influenced Christianity, and in the seventeenth century, when Descartes lived, it was common to understand people as part angel and part beast. Descartes defended this dualistic view not by theology but by epistemology.

The Aristotelian/Thomist view, in which the soul was the principle of life, played no part in Descartes' view and he considered the body and soul to be wholly separate substances. He included in the 'mind' all the feelings and sensations that he could describe but which he could not locate physically. He accepted that everything that is non-physical becomes part of the mind. Descartes considers that he can doubt that he has a body as he sees his body as a result of his perceptual experiences and these could be hallucinations caused by some evil demon. All sense experience can be mistaken. Descartes considers that he could be mistaken in believing that he has a body but he cannot doubt that he has a mind – he thinks. So, he knows that he exists even though he is not so sure that he has a body, and from this Descartes considers that it is possible for him to exist without a body. He concluded '*I think therefore I am*,' and therefore the mind is distinct from the body, although the two interact. He would not cease to be himself if he did not have a body, but he would no longer be himself if he did not have a mind.

In the *Meditations on First Philosophy*, he argues,

> There is a very great difference between a mind and a body, because a body is by nature divisible, but the mind is not. Clearly, when I think about the mind, that is, of myself as far as I am a thing that thinks, I am not aware of any parts in me – that is, I understand myself to be one whole person. Although the whole mind seems united to the whole

Dualism
The view that a human person consists of two distinct elements: the mind/soul and the body. The mind/soul is immaterial, whereas the body is physical.

Materialism
The view that human beings are physical beings rather than consisting of a physical body and an immaterial soul.

body, if a foot, or an arm, or another limb were amputated from my body, nothing would be taken from my mind. Mental faculties, such as 'willing', 'sensing', 'understanding' cannot be called its 'parts', because it is always the same mind that wills, senses or understands. But any corporeal or physically extended thing I can think of, I can easily think of as divided into parts. . . . This reasoning alone would be enough to teach me that the mind is wholly different from the body.

(Meditation VI)

Descartes' dualism of mind and body depended on the following ideas:

* The mind is a 'non-corporeal' substance, which is distinct from material or bodily substance. The mind and body are different things.
* Every substance has a property or special character. So, for example, the property of the material body is to take up space, whereas the mind is a substance 'whose whole essence is to think' and so takes up no space.
* The mind is the place in which all feelings, sensations and thoughts are known only to the person experiencing them.
* The body performs all physical activities which everyone can see.
* The mind and body interact with each other as the mind can cause events to occur in the body and the body can cause events to occur in the mind.
* The mind and body are separate.

Descartes concluded that as our identity comes from our ability to think and reason, then it was quite possible that we could survive without our bodies and remain the same person; thus he concluded that the mind could survive the death of the body. For him, the mind is 'I', which thinks and makes us who we are.

We can drastically change our bodies and our physical appearance without changing our personalities, and even if a person underwent a radical physical transformation, we would still be able to recognise the person by reference to his or her character and memories. Descartes thought that when a person died, his or her soul could continue after death with God as the same individual, which existed in a physical form on earth. 'Our soul is of a nature entirely independent of the body, and consequently . . . it is not bound to die with it. And since we cannot see any other causes that destroy the soul, we are naturally led to conclude that it is immortal' (*Discourses on the Method*, 1637). In *The Passions of the Soul*, Descartes suggests that 'There is a little gland in the brain where the soul exercises its functions more particularly than in the other parts of the body.' In his *Treatise on Man*, he said that the pineal gland is the seat of the imagination and common sense – here it becomes (perhaps) the link between body and soul. The argument for this function is rather thin: he says that all the parts of our brain are double, and we have also two bodily organs for each sense – two nostrils, eyes and ears — but our mind perceives only a single thought or impression. Here Descartes is arguing, like Plato, that the mind does not have any parts and cannot be divided; having parts is an essential property of bodies as bodies exist in space and so can be divided.

The pineal organ is the bit of the brain that is singular, so Descartes thought that it must be the home of the single thought.

PROBLEMS WITH SUBSTANCE DUALISM

The obvious problem here is that simply to pick on the pineal gland leaves open the question of how that physical thing can encompass the non-material thought: the mind-brain identity problem has moved no nearer to a solution. Additionally, substance dualism seems to make a person with both body and mind two things which are connected to each other, but it is not clear how they relate to each other. Also, we experience ourselves as a single thing.

Descartes does not explain how the mind, which is so different from the body, can cause physical events in the body. If minds are independent of bodies how can it be possible to simply infer that other people have minds because they behave as I do and I have a mind?

MATERIALISM AND MONISM

Monism

The belief that human beings are a single unity of body and mind. The mind's existence is dependent on the body.

Materialists in general do not argue for any concept of the afterlife; however, a materialist could believe in bodily resurrection. Materialists are often called monists. A monist believes that there is only one substance – matter – and therefore dualism is incorrect, since it postulates the existence of matter and a non-physical substance (body and soul).

> *Thought point*
>
> **Materialism and bodily resurrection**
>
> If you are a materialist you cannot be a dualist or believe in rebirth, but you could believe in bodily resurrection.

continued opposite

Can you explain why?

For materialists, a person's identity is linked to the physical body. When the physical body's life ends that person ends. Emotions, feelings and thoughts are caused by our brains and are simply mental processes in the brain. According to materialism, all these characteristics of our experience are explainable by reference to the mental activity of the brain.

Identity theory says that all mental activities are centred in the brain. There is just one kind of substance and mental properties are in fact physical properties. This view can be supported by the fact that our moods, behaviour and even character can be changed by drugs, such as antidepressants or alcohol, meaning that mental activity is to be linked not to an immaterial soul or identity but to our brain. When our physical life ends, mental activity ceases.

GILBERT RYLE AND THE CONCEPT OF MIND

Gilbert Ryle was an important philosopher in the British analytical tradition. He published his famous book *The Concept of Mind* in 1949, arguing against dualism and saying that Descartes represented what he called 'the dogma of "the ghost in the machine"', a vision of the human which made the mind a separate substance somehow attached to the body, acting like the pilot of a ship. Ryle argued that philosophers often make a category error by assuming that mind and the body can be spoken of as though they are the same kind of thing:

> 'the dogma of the ghost in the machine'. I hope to prove that it is entirely false, and false not in detail but in principle. It is not merely an assemblage of mistakes. It is one big mistake and a mistake of a special kind. It is namely a category mistake. It represents the facts of mental life as if they belonged to one logical type or category . . ., when they actually belong to another.
>
> (*The Concept of Mind* 2000 [1949, 1984])

He illustrates his point by three examples:

1   Suppose a foreign visitor went to Oxford or Cambridge to look at its sights. He is shown the different colleges, the Fitzwilliam Museum, the library and so on. At the end of the tour, he then asks, 'But where is the university?' He is guilty of a category error – assuming that the university is something separate from and other than all those individual bits, which collectively *are* the university.

Gene

A gene is the term which scientists use for the smallest unit of DNA which can have an effect on the growth of the organism containing the DNA. DNA directs the development of every cell in a living organism. Different genes in isolation or combination have different effects as they can cause different tissues or cells to develop. Similarly, the reason that human beings are different from monkeys, earthworms or yeast is precisely because the DNA in every cell of each of these living organisms is different.

Biologists refer to the effect that a gene has on its environment (i.e. how the organism develops) as its phenotypic effect.

If you want to know more about genes and modern scientific discoveries about the nature of life read Richard Dawkins' book *The Selfish Gene* (1989).

2   A boy is watching a military parade in which he knows a division is marching by. Someone points out to him different squadrons, battalions, batteries and so on. At the end he asks when the division will arrive, unaware that all the units he has seen are collectively the division.

3   Consider the foreigner who goes to see a game of cricket, having previously read a book about it. He is shown the stumps and the ball, and the various fielding positions. Then he asks, 'But where is the team spirit?' – a category error.

In the same way, Descartes is guilty of a category error because he assumes that sentences about causes, sensations or events must be *either* mental *or* physical, which presupposes an unjustified assumption that they cannot be both.

Ryle's view is, in many ways, not too dissimilar from the views of Aquinas and Aristotle – for different reasons, they do not make the radical separation of soul and body found in Descartes, Plato and so much of the Western tradition. Ryle, therefore, was not a materialist – as Ryle said himself,

> Both Idealism and Materialism are answers to an improper question. The 'reduction' of the material world to mental processes and states, as well as the 'reduction' of mental states and processes to physical states and processes, presupposes the legitimacy of the disjunction 'Either there exist minds or there exist bodies (but not both)'. It would be like saying, 'either she bought a left-hand and right hand glove or she bought a pair of gloves (but not both)'.

Richard Dawkins
Jeff Morgan 07 / Alamy

RICHARD DAWKINS – THE HARD MATERIALIST?

Writing in *River Out of Eden* (1995), Dawkins puts forward a case for biological materialism: 'There is no spirit-driven life force, no throbbing, heaving, pullulating, protoplasmic, mystic jelly. Life is just bytes and bytes and bytes of digital information.' Dawkins argues that individuals cannot survive death. The only way in which people survive death is through the memories of them in other people's minds or through their genes, some of which are passed on to the next generation of offspring. This may be seen in Richard Dawkins' discussion of God's covenant with Abraham:

> He didn't promise Abraham eternal life as an individual (though Abraham was only 99 at the time, a spring chicken by Genesis standards). But he did promise something else. And I will make my covenant between me and thee, and will multiply thee exceedingly . . . and thou shalt be a

father of many nations . . . And I will make thee exceeding fruitful, and I will make nations of thee, and kings shall come out of thee.

Abraham was left in no doubt that the future lay with his seed, not his individuality. God knew his Darwinism.

(*Unweaving the Rainbow*)

However, although Dawkins' approach is far removed from that of Plato and Descartes, it is not so very different from that of Aristotle and Aquinas. For Dawkins, there is no pre-existent soul that is by nature divine. According to Dawkins scientific beliefs are supported by scientific evidence and are reliable, whereas religious beliefs, such as the concept of the soul, depend on myth and faith, for which there is no empirical evidence.

Dawkins claims that the belief in a soul is a result of human inability to accept that evil and suffering have no purpose. Humans themselves, he believes, are no more than the sum total of his or her DNA. The purpose of life is DNA survival. DNA is locked up in living bodies, and humans are no more than machines preprogrammed to replicate to ensure their DNA's survival into the next generation.

Dawkins does discuss the soul but he makes a distinction between two versions of the soul, which he calls Soul One and Soul Two.

Soul One refers to a particular theory of life. It's the theory that there is something non-material about life, some non-physical vital principle. It's the theory according to which a body has to be animated by some anima. Vitalized by a vital force. Energized by some mysterious energy. Spiritualized by some mysterious spirit. Made conscious by some mysterious thing or substance called consciousness. You'll notice that all those definitions of Soul One are circular and non-productive. It's no Julian Huxley once satirically likened vitalism to the theory that a railway engine works by 'force-locomotif.' I don't always agree with Julian Huxley, but here he hit the nail beautifully.

In the sense of Soul One, science has either killed the soul or is in the process of doing so.

(www.edge.org/conversation/richard_dawkins-steven_pinker-is-science-killing-the-soul)

Dawkins rejects this view of the soul.

Soul Two is very different.

But there is a second sense of soul, Soul Two, which takes off from another one of the Oxford dictionary's definitions:

Intellectual or spiritual power. High development of the mental faculties. Also, in somewhat weakened sense, deep feeling, sensitivity.

For Dawkins, Soul Two is real, part of what we are. He admits that

> there are, of course, many unsolved problems, and scientists are the first to admit this. There are aspects of human subjective consciousness that are deeply mysterious . . . We don't know. We don't understand it.
>
> There's a cheap debating trick which implies that if, say, science can't explain something, this must mean that some other discipline can. If scientists suspect that all aspects of the mind have a scientific explanation but they can't actually say what that explanation is yet, the of course it's open to you to doubt whether the explanation ever will be forthcoming. That's a perfectly reasonable doubt. But it's not legitimately open to you to substitute a word like soul, or spirit, as if that constituted an explanation. It is not an explanation, it's an evasion. It's just a name for that which we don't understand. The scientist may agree to use the word soul for that which we don't understand, but the scientist adds, 'But we're working on it, and one day we hope we shall explain it.' The dishonest trick is to use a word like soul or spirit as if it constituted an explanation.
>
> (www.edge.org/conversation/
> richard_dawkins-steven_pinker-is-science-killing-the-soul)

Dawkins therefore places his faith in DNA as the source of the answer he seeks. He does not for a moment deny imagination or poetry or any other aspects of conscious life. Genes do not have any sense of goal or direction. Instead, genes are what DNA is made of. DNA is a protein that makes copies of itself. Dawkins argues that genes are 'potentially immortal' as they are the 'basic unit of natural selection' (Dawkins, *The Selfish Gene*). Our genes have been passed on from previous generations of living organisms. The role of the body is as a '*survival machine*' for genes.

Thus, for Dawkins the soul is a mythological concept which people have invented to explain what they do not understood – the mystery of consciousness. Dawkins believes that, although we cannot explain consciousness at the present time, in the future science will be able to do so.

JOHN LOCKE – ANOTHER VIEW OF CONSCIOUSNESS

John Locke thought that personal identity consisted neither in sameness of body nor in sameness of soul but, rather, in what he called 'sameness of consciousness'. For Locke it is consciousness that creates personal identity. He thought that consciousness is enclosed in a spiritual substance. He understood there to be a difference between a human and that human's personal identity. What he meant was that an individual should remember enough of his or her past states of consciousness, and it is this awareness of self in different places and times that is the personal identity. This means that an individual can have different bodies and yet still have continuity.

Locke used the example of the soul of a prince transformed from the prince's body into the body of a cobbler whose soul has departed. The price still has princely thoughts and his personal identity as a prince, even though his body is different. Therefore, according to Locke, he is still the prince even though 'he would be the same cobbler to everyone besides himself.'

Locke holds that consciousness can be transferred from one soul to another, and that personal identity goes with consciousness. Locke considers that consciousness can be transferred from one substance to another and thus while the soul is changed, consciousness remains the same, so personal identity is preserved through the change. Since, for Locke, a person is to be identified with his consciousness and memories, in order for a person to survive the death of his body, his consciousness with its memories must continue on. If the human soul is not consciousness, then even if the entity called 'the soul' survives the individual does not survive.

JOHN HICK'S REPLICA THEORY – AN ALTERNATIVE MATERIALIST VIEW

John Hick rejects dualism and Plato's view of the soul and does not consider the soul as a separate part of a person. In some ways Hick's view is similar to that of Aristotle, and is often called 'soft materialism'. He accepts that we are our bodies, but thinks that our bodies do have a spiritual dimension. When considering about any sort of afterlife Hick uses his replica theory as a way of understanding of resurrection. Hick argues that resurrection is a divine action in which an exact replica of ourselves is created in a different place. The replica is in all respects the same as us, but the location of the replica is not on earth. However, the replica of the person is not the same as a copy. Hick uses the word 'replica' because each person can exist in only one place and time. Hick insisted that there is continuity because the replica has the '*consciousness, memory, emotion and volition*' of the person and there can only ever be one replica of an individual. However, if physical continuity of the body is important when explaining identity, then replica theory is problematic.

Hick does reject dualism but at the same time defends bodily resurrection. He considers that human beings are a 'psycho-somatic unity' – in other words human beings are a unity of physical body and the mind or soul. The two cannot be separated. He does not think that a soul is like Gilbert Ryle's ghost in a machine.

The concept of mind or soul is thus not that of a 'ghost' in the 'machine' but of the more flexible and sophisticated ways in which human beings behave and have it in them to behave (Hick, 'Resurrection of the Person').

SUMMARY

1 Plato

People consist of a body and a soul.
The soul is imprisoned in the body.
After death, the souls of wrongdoers would be re-imprisoned in a body.
Two related arguments to support his belief in an immortal soul:
Argument from opposites
Argument that education is about remembering
Challenges to Plato's view:

> Peter Geach questioned what it can mean for the disembodied soul to see the Forms and whether existence without a body is real human existence.
>
> There is no evidence to suggest that death is a state opposite to but analogous to life.

2 Aristotle

The soul cannot be separate from the body.
The body and the soul are aspects of the same thing.
The soul is the part of the body that gives it life.

3 Descartes

Substance dualism
The mind and body are different things.
The mind and body interact with each other as the mind can cause events to occur in the body and the body can cause events to occur in the mind.
The mind and body are separate.
The mind is 'I', which thinks and makes us who we are.

4 Monism and materialism

The belief that the mind is one with the body and inseparable from it. 'Monist' refers to anyone who believes that there is only one substance. Typically, monists are materialists.
For materialists the identity of a person is linked to the physical body. Identity theory claims that all mental activities are centred in the brain. Materialists can support life after death only if that life is physical, such as in religious teaching about resurrection.

5   **Gilbert Ryle**

The ghost in the machine
Category error

6   **Richard Dawkins**

The only sense in which human beings survive death is through the
memories of them in other people's minds or through their genes,
some of which are passed on to the next generation of offspring.
Soul One
Soul Two
Human beings' consciousness has evolved because of the survival
advantage it gives.

7   **John Hick**

Rejects dualism, while at the same time presenting a defence of belief in
bodily resurrection.
Human beings are a 'psycho-somatic unity' (Hick, 'Resurrection of the
Person').
Resurrection is a divine action in which an exact replica of ourselves is
created in a different place.
The replica exists in a 'different space' from us that is observable by God
and not by us.
The replica of the person is not the same as a copy.

REVIEW QUESTIONS

Look back over the chapter and check that you can answer the following
questions:

1   Which are more coherent: arguments in favour of dualism or monism?
2   What is the appeal of materialism?
3   Is replica theory more persuasive than belief in a soul?

Terminology

Do you know your terminology?

Try to explain the following ideas without looking at your books and
notes:

continued overleaf

- Replica theory
- Soul
- Consciousness
- Materialism
- Dualism

 Examination questions practice

SAMPLE EXAM-STYLE QUESTION

Assess Descartes' view that the mind can exist independently of the body.

AO1 (15 marks)
- You will need to explain Descartes' idea of substance dualism. You could include the idea that the mind is a 'non-corporeal' substance, which is distinct from material or bodily substance.
- You could explain how Descartes understood the difference between the mind and the body and how he saw them as separate. You could use the ideas of Plato to back up this view. You could explain how Descartes thought that as our identity comes from our ability to think and reason, then it was quite possible that we could survive without our bodies and remain the same person; thus he concluded that the mind could survive the death of the body.

AO2 (15 marks)
- In assessing Descartes' views you could use the ideas of Ryle that the soul becomes the ghost in the machine. The body becomes simply a machine, with the mind the mysterious, non-physical 'real me', like an operator somehow outside that body. You could also contrast the views of Descartes with those of Dawkins, who says that the belief in a soul comes from human inability to accept that evil and suffering have no purpose, and that we simply exist to pass on our DNA.
- You need to assess the different approaches as you explain them and use your evaluation to reach a conclusion.

Further possible questions

- **Critically compare Aristotle's concept of body and soul with that of Plato.**
- **'Plato's understanding of the distinction between body and soul is easy to criticise.' Discuss.**
- **'Aristotle's concept of body and soul is more coherent than that of Plato.' Discuss.**

FURTHER READING

Aristotle. 1986. *De Anima* (translation, introduction and notes, Lawson-Tancred, H.). London: Penguin.

Geach, P. 1969. *God and the Soul*. London: Routledge and Kegan Paul.

Plato. 2000. 'Life After Death: An Ancient Greek View', in *Philosophy of Religion: A Guide and Anthology*, Davies, B. (ed.), Oxford: OUP.

Ryle, G. (1949) 2002. *The Concept of Mind*. Chicago: University of Chicago Press.

Swinburne, R. 1997. *Evolution of the Soul*. Oxford: Clarendon Press

Williams, B. 1978. *Descartes: The Project of Pure Enquiry*. New Jersey: Humanities Press.

The existence of God

4 Arguments based on observation

THE ISSUES

1 Why does anything exist rather than nothing?
2 Does God cause everything to exist?
3 If we examine the world around us, is it obvious that someone designed it?
4 If someone did design the world, was that someone 'God'?

WHAT YOU WILL LEARN ABOUT IN THIS CHAPTER

The details of the teleological argument, including reference to:

- Aquinas' fifth way
- Paley

The details of the cosmological argument, including reference to Aquinas' first three ways Challenges to the arguments from observation:

- details of Hume's criticisms of these arguments for the existence of God from natural religion
- the challenge of evolution

You should be able to discuss:

- whether a posteriori or a priori is the most persuasive style of argument
- whether teleological arguments can be defended against the challenge of 'chance'
- whether cosmological arguments simply jump to the conclusion of a transcendent creator, without sufficient explanation
- whether there are logical fallacies in these arguments that cannot be overcome.

THE TELEOLOGICAL ARGUMENT

Look at the pictures opposite and try to answer the following questions:

1   Which picture(s) show(s) things that have been designed? List the features of these things that show they have been designed.
2   What purpose, if any, do the things in the picture have?
3   Is there any evidence that the things in the picture were made or designed by someone/something?

THE OCR CHECKLIST

Arguments based on observation

*   the teleological argument – details of this argument, including reference to:
    *   Aquinas' fifth way
    *   Paley
*   the cosmological argument – details of this argument, including reference to:
    *   Aquinas' first three ways
*   challenges to arguments from observation
    *   details of Hume's criticisms of these arguments for the existence of God from natural religion
    *   the challenge of evolution

Learners should have the opportunity to discuss issues related to arguments for the existence of God based on observation, including:

*   whether a posteriori or a priori is the more persuasive style of argument
*   whether teleological arguments can be defended against the challenge of 'chance'
*   whether cosmological arguments simply jump to the conclusion of a transcendent creator, without sufficient explanation
*   whether there are logical fallacies in these arguments that cannot be overcome.

continued opposite

More philosophical terms

A posteriori

'A posteriori' is the philosophical term for an argument in which a conclusion is reached based on evidence that has been observed. For example detectives investigating a crime collect evidence such as fingerprints, DNA samples and eyewitness statements and put together a case. Because the argument is based on the interpretation of evidence, the argument is only as convincing as the evidence.

A priori

'A priori' is the philosophical term for an argument which starts from a set of principles (called premises) and deduces conclusions from these principles. If the principles are correct, the conclusion is absolute and cannot be challenged. A priori arguments are common in philosophy, critical thinking and mathematics.

A famous example of an a priori argument is:

Premise 1: Socrates is a man.

Premise 2: Men are mortal.

TELOS AND TELEOLOGICAL ARGUMENTS

'*Telos*' is the Greek word for the ultimate object or aim of an action. It can also mean goal, target or purpose.

These arguments ask if there is a designer of things that appear to be designed and if that designer is in fact God.

The teleological arguments for the existence of God look at the universe and everything in it and attempt to show that it has all been designed for a purpose. Teleological arguments examine if there is a designer of things that appear to have been designed, and whether the designer is God. It looks at the features of the universe and asks whether they can account for their own existence.

Usually teleological arguments infer the existence of God from a particular aspect or character of the world – namely the presence of order, regularity and purpose. Order, regularity and purpose are seen as marks of design, and the arguments conclude that God must be the source of that design. The kind of thing that is usually appealed to as evidence of order in the universe is the solar system, with the planets revolving in their predictable orbits, or the human eye.

More popularly it is referred to as the 'argument from design', but this wording assumes the very thing that has to be proved. A better description would be the 'argument for design'.

Both the teleological argument and the cosmological argument are a posteriori arguments. The teleological argument begins from looking at that which seems to be designed or appears to be ordered in the world and attempts to show that there is a designer – in other words it starts from the results and tries to work backwards to the cause.

THE TYPES OF TELEOLOGICAL ARGUMENTS

Teleological arguments are often divided into types by philosophers:

1   *Arguments based on purpose* (e.g. William Paley's ideas)
2   *Arguments based on regularity* (e.g. Thomas Aquinas' ideas).

Paley's and Aquinas' ideas and the meaning of these two types of arguments are explained ahead.

TELEOLOGICAL ARGUMENTS BY THOMAS AQUINAS

Thomas Aquinas set out five ways (Aquinas, *Summa Theologiae*) in which he thought he could show that God exists. The fifth way is a form of design argument.

This argument was influenced by the ideas of Aristotle, that everything cooperates to produce and maintain cosmic order – an end, purpose or telos. Aquinas' teleological argument is influenced by Aristotle's theory of the Four Causes. Aquinas linked Aristotle's idea of a *final cause* to God.

Thus, as this end or purpose is achieved by non-intelligent beings, it requires an intelligent being to bring it about: God. So, for Aquinas, the final reason that things have a particular design, goal and purpose and follow natural laws is because God caused it to be so.

Here is a summary of Aquinas' fifth way:

1   When we look at the natural world it is clear that everything in it follows natural laws, even if the things are not conscious, thinking beings.
2   Things that follow natural laws have a goal or purpose.
3   If something cannot think for itself it will have this goal or purpose only if an intelligent thinking being gives it this purpose.
    For example an arrow can be directed to its goal and used for its purpose only by an archer.
4   *Aquinas concluded*: Everything in the natural world that is not an intelligent being heads towards its goal or purpose because it is directed by an intelligent being. That intelligent being we call 'God'.

Note what Aquinas wrote next:

Similarly, even though human beings think for themselves and cause things to be aimed at some goal or result, the reason why human beings exist has to be explained, as human beings are not immortal and die.

Argument by regularity

Aquinas' argument is one of *regularity of succession*. That is to say that he based his argument on the fact that nature follows specific laws that lead to specific results. For example if you drop a mug of coffee and it falls to the floor, the event that follows is that the mug smashes and the coffee is spilt. Natural laws, such as the law of gravity, are examples of regularities of succession: events follow scientific laws which are predictable, regular and never vary.

Aquinas gave the example of an archer shooting an arrow. Just as the arrow needs an archer to shoot it, so everything in the natural world that does not think for itself needs to be directed to follow natural laws by something intelligent – this is God.

The argument could be set out as follows:

1   An arrow hits a target even though it is not an intelligent being (*an effect*).

Conclusion: Socrates is mortal.

There are three ways in which an a priori argument can be criticised:

(a) A challenge to the validity (truthfulness/ accuracy) of the starting principles.
(b) A challenge to the coherence of the argument (whether its steps are logical).
(c) A challenge to the appropriateness of the assumptions the argument makes.

Telos

The Greek word for 'end' or 'result' of a process or course of action.

Assumption

A belief or statement which is accepted without being supported by evidence or argument.

Inference

The philosophical word for a conclusion that is reached through a process of reasoning in an argument.

Aristotle and Aquinas

Aquinas read and used Aristotle's philosophy. It is a good idea to review Aristotle while studying the teleological argument.

Natural laws

When discussing the teleological argument this phrase refers to the physical laws of science, such as gravity. It must not be confused with the ethical theory called natural (moral) law.

Effect

The result of an action.

Weaknesses of analogies

For more information about weaknesses of analogies, see this chapter's sections on David Hume.

Cause

Something which brings about a result. In philosophy this concept is often linked to the so-called Four Causes of Aristotle (see Chapter 2).

2 The archer (an intelligent being) shot the arrow (*a cause*).
3 Everything in nature follows natural laws even if they are not intelligent beings (*an effect*).
4 An intelligent being caused the natural world to behave in this way: someone God (*a cause*).

This analogy is not faultless as it could be argued that that an arrow being shot at a target is of a very different order and type from things following natural laws.

Thought point

Try to explain the Aristotle's Four Causes without looking at your notes, and then check your answers.

WEAKNESSES IN AQUINAS' ARGUMENT

Aquinas made certain assumptions but does not use any evidence to support them:

1 He assumed that everything has a purpose, but did not provide any examples to support this assumption, but he did explain this point in much greater detail in *On the Truth* (Aquinas, *De Veritate*), in which he discussed God's providence.
2 Can we simply assume that everything follows a general law set down by a designer? It may be that the world is just the way it is by chance and does not need any sort of intelligent designer behind it. Nor does it seem to be possible to find a purpose in everything that exists. The philosopher Anthony Flew suggested that evidence does not support the view that everything in nature has a purpose.
3 Richard Swinburne suggested that Aquinas' argument is not entirely correct as it states that '*everything in the natural world that does not think for itself heads towards its goal or purpose because it is directed by something which does think.*' According to Swinburne this is mistaken as it assumes what is at issue – whether God imposes regularity and laws on the universe (Swinburne, 'The Argument from Design'). Although the existence of order may be good evidence of a designer, it is just as compatible with the non-existence of one.

Natural selection

For more information see p. 71 ahead.

Thought point

A problem

If you found a rock, an apple and a smartphone on the ground, which one would you say was suited to a particular purpose or activity? Why would you make this choice?

If you had never seen any of these objects before, would there be any way of deciding whether the objects occurred 'just like that' or whether they were 'designed'?

Paley the man (1743–1805)

William Paley
The Granger Collection/Alamy

William Paley was the archdeacon of Carlisle. He was fascinated by discoveries being made about the natural world in his time, particularly the increase in knowledge of the complex organs and systems in the bodies of people and animals. He was famously impressed by the structure of the human eye: its sophistication, complexity, its fitness for seeing and so forth. This fascination with the natural world influenced his book *Natural Theology: or, Evidences of the Existence and Attributes of the Deity*, which was published in 1802.

WILLIAM PALEY'S TELEOLOGICAL ARGUMENT

William Paley's argument is the most well-known teleological argument and it is in two stages:

- It tries to establish that there is order and purpose in the universe.
- It then makes the step to the conclusion that there is something divine behind this order and purpose.

Paley used analogy to express his argument and based it on the argument that similar effects imply similar causes. Evidence of design is those features in which natural objects are similar to man-made machines. Three kinds of these features particularly impressed eighteenth-century thinkers: the world as a whole, especially the solar system as described by Newton's gravitational theory; the bodies of all sorts of plants and animals, especially certain organs like the eye; and the providential arrangement of things on the earth.

One of the man-made objects which impressed people at that time was the pocket watch, which had just been invented. Paley's most famous argument compares a rock and a watch.

In crossing a heath, suppose I pitched my foot against a stone, and were asked how the stone came to be there, I might possibly answer, that, for anything I knew to be the contrary, it had lain there forever; nor would it perhaps be very easy to show the absurdity of this answer. But suppose I found a watch upon the ground, and it should be inquired how the watch happened to be in that place, I should hardly think of the answer which I had before given, that, for anything

I knew, the watch might always have been there. Yet why should not this answer serve for the watch, as well as for the stone? Why is it not as admissible in the second case as in the first? *For this reason, and for no other, viz., that, when we came to inspect the watch, we perceive (what we would not discover in the stone) that its several parts are framed and put together for a purpose, e.g. that they are so formed and adjusted to produce motion, and that motion so regulated as to point out the hour of the day;* that, if the different parts had been differently shaped from what they are, if a different size from what they are, or placed after any other manner, or in any other order than that in which they are placed either no motion at all would have been carried on in the machine, or none which would have answered these that is now served by it.

(Paley, *Natural Theology* 1838)

William Paley's argument is comprised of the following two parts.

Part 1

1   Paley suggested that a rock would not inspire anyone to wonder how it came to be there; however, if someone found a watch he could examine it and look at the moving cogs, which show that:

(a) The watch was made for a *purpose*: telling the time.
(b) The parts *work together* or are *fit* for a purpose.
(c) The parts are *ordered* and put together in a certain way to make the watch work.
(d) If the parts were *arranged* in a different way the watch would not work – that is it does not fulfil its purpose.

This first part of the watch analogy is known as *design qua purpose*.

2   Conclusion: the watch had a maker who '*must have existed, at some time, and at some place or other, an artificer or artificers who formed it for the purpose which we find it actually to answer; who comprehended its construction and designed its use*' (Paley, *Natural Theology*).

Note: Paley also stated that it is not important if the watch sometimes stops working or is not perfect. The point is that the fact that the watch exists shows it was designed for a purpose. This point is important when you study David Hume's writings about the teleological argument.

Part 2

Paley continued his watch analogy:

1   Imagine that the watch had another purpose: that of producing other watches.
2   In this case, the person's admiration for the watchmaker would increase.

> *Conclusion*: Anyone finding such a watch would conclude that the design of the watch implies 'the presence of intelligence and mind' (Paley, *Natural Theology*).

Paley also used evidence from astronomy and Newton's laws of motion and gravity to show that there was design in the universe. The universal laws governing the rotation of the planets could not, he said, have come about by chance. This is *design qua regularity*.

What does the watch analogy show?

The watch presupposes a watchmaker, and in the same way the order in the universe presupposes a designer. Paley pointed out that the complexity of nature is far greater than any machine human beings can make. Thus the whole of nature requires a grand designer. That designer is God.

Thought point

Think about why Paley would liken the working of the natural world to that of a watch. Why is Paley's assumption considered to be weak by many philosophers?

Note the assumption that supports the analogy. Paley's watch is a machine – it is mechanistic. Paley's analogy assumes that the natural world is mechanistic in a similar manner to a watch.

One weakness of using analogy is that Paley's argument is only as strong as his analogy. For example Paley is impressed with the human eye, but would it really be appropriate to compare the working of an eye to that of a camera?

The difference between arguments from regularity and from purpose

Design arguments that are based on the idea of 'purpose', like Paley's, suggest that everything is designed to fulfil some function or purpose – for example the eye for seeing. Something must cause everything to have this purpose: God.

Design arguments that are based on 'regularity' claim that regularity and order can be observed in the universe, such as the scientific laws of nature. Something must cause this regularity: God.

Another famous example Paley gave to illustrate this is that of the complexity of the human eye.

Paley's analogy is all about a machine – a watch – and he presumed that the universe is also like a machine. This comparison shows that Paley's argument works only if the analogy works. The example of the human eye shows the weaknesses of the argument for the twenty-first century; whereas a modern automatic camera shows obvious signs of

continued overleaf

having been designed, the human eye, however, is not the result of an intelligent design, but evolved over millions of years from simple light-sensitive organisms. The analogy works only if you consider that the elements in the analogy are comparable; if you cannot argue that the causes of each effect are similar then the analogy will not work.

Paley is often shown as someone who was trying to prove God to unbelievers; however, in the conclusion to his book he implied that he was more concerned with making things clearer to those who believe in God already.

Many writers have criticised the comparison Paley makes of nature with machines, arguing that the natural world is not mechanistic in the sense of a man-made machine.

Thought point

Give a reason why the natural world is not like a machine.

How is Paley's argument different from that of Aquinas?

The main difference is that Paley focuses on the manner in which things like a watch fit together in a particular way for a purpose. Hence, this type of argument is sometimes called a *purpose argument*.

Paley considered the human eye, the complexity of its parts and the way in which the parts fit together for the purpose of seeing. He did not consider one thing following another according to some law, as Aquinas argued.

CRITICISMS OF PALEY'S ARGUMENT

William Paley himself showed that there were a number of possible weaknesses in his argument and attempted to respond to them.

He suggests that there is little point in talking about natural laws without considering that there must be some agent who is responsible for them.

Thought point

David Hume's books

When was David Hume's *Dialogues Concerning Natural Religion* first published? Why does the date matter?

The answer is important: William Paley published his book 24 years after David Hume's book was published. Curiously this was 27 years after Hume's death, as *Dialogues Concerning Natural Religion* was published posthumously. Do not make the mistake of claiming that David Hume criticised William Paley. It is much better to point out that Paley tried to respond to some of the criticisms of teleological arguments that were being made around that time. Some of Paley's responses are explained in the main text.

DAVID HUME'S CRITICISM OF TELEOLOGICAL ARGUMENTS

David Hume's book *Dialogues Concerning Natural Religion* was published posthumously in 1779 and pointed out a number of weaknesses in teleological arguments.

David Hume rejected the use of analogy to prove the teleological argument

According to Hume the strength of the argument depends upon the similarity between the things held to be analogous (i.e. the machine and the world). The greater the similarity, the stronger the argument; the weaker the similarity, the weaker is the argument. Hume criticised this analogy as he said that the world is *not* like a machine at all since it is composed of vegetables and animals. It is more organic than it is mechanical. This criticism can be applied to Paley's watch analogy, but not to Aquinas' teleological argument, which focuses on things following natural laws, although it could be applied to Aquinas' example of the archer and the arrow.

Hume gave an alternative analogy by suggesting that one could conclude that a house had a builder and an architect, but this cannot be applied to the universe in the same way as there is no similarity between a house and the universe. Additionally, if a house is faulty this suggests that the designer is not very good, and so if God designed the world he would be responsible for the faults and evil in it.

Paley rejected this criticism as he was concerned with signs of design within the universe rather than the quality of the design and the finished product. According to Paley it was not important if the watch sometimes stops working or is not perfect. The point is that the fact that the watch exists shows it was designed for a purpose, and by analogy so was the universe.

Hume considered that any analogy is weak as there is nothing within the universe to which the universe can be compared. Hume was not questioning belief in a God or deity, but instead whether the teleological argument can show that God or a deity exists.

William Paley rejected this argument, saying that because we do not know how something is made we will have an even greater admiration for the creator, whether this be a man-made object or a universe.

Hume the man (1711–1776)

David Hume

Alan King engraving/Alamy

David Hume was born in Edinburgh and went to university there. As a young man he became passionately interested in philosophy and started to develop the ideas for which he would become famous posthumously. During his life he worked as a clerk for a sugar merchant, and later carried out diplomatic work in Vienna and Turin. However, in later life, while working as a librarian in Edinburgh, he published his *History of England* (1754–62), which became a bestseller. It was this book of history rather than his philosophy which made him famous in his own lifetime. His *Dialogues Concerning Natural Religion* was published in 1779.

Natural selection

The phrase coined by Charles Darwin to explain his idea that *'If variations useful to any organic being ever do occur, assuredly individuals thus characterised will have the best chance of being pre-served in the struggle for life; and for the strong principle of inheritance, these will tend to produce offspring similarly characterised'* (in M. Palmer, *The Question of God*).

David Hume argued that there are other possible explanations than God for apparent design in the universe

Hume argued that rather than there being some great designer of the universe it could be argued that *'matter may contain the spring of order originally within itself, as well as mind does'* (Hume, *Dialogues Concerning Natural Religion and the Natural History of Religion*). According to Hume it is not philosophically sound to argue that intelligence is the necessary governing principle behind the world. Hume pointed out that there were lots of alternative governing principles (generation, vegetation, gravity); why should different principles not rule over their own natural domains: vegetation in plants, generation in animals, gravity in movement of planets? We cannot project from one limited area to another part or to the whole of nature.

He also argued that any effects observed in that natural world could have any number of causes and that 'the world plainly resembles more an animal or vegetable than it does a watch or a knitting loom'. He even argued that the world could be compared to a carrot. This analogy shows that the evidence of design in the world could be caused by generation. The natural world may possess some inner self-regulation and growth. Had Hume lived long enough he may well have quoted Darwinism as a possible example. This sees beneficial adaptations explained in non-personal terms by means of natural selection.

Hume went on to question whether there is evidence that the world has a single designer. He used the analogy of a ship, which could be the result of several years of trial and error and could have been the result of many designers, not just one great mind. He concluded that there is no evidence to suggest the *'unity of the deity'* (Hume, *Dialogues Concerning Natural Religion and the Natural History of Religion*). He even suggested that the universe with all its faults could be the first attempt of an inferior deity. Additionally, Hume listed some of the more unpleasant features of the natural world, such as earthquakes, war, disease, and questioned how this could have been designed by a just and good God. He argued that it is not possible to attribute to the cause anything more than is needed to produce the effect. He concluded that a better hypothesis was that of an immoral God or even two forces, one good and one bad.

Richard Swinburne disagreed with Hume's objections because he claimed that they were making the explanation unnecessarily complex – in other words breaking the philosophical principle of *Ockham's razor*. Hume claimed that this principle did not apply to the universe because it is a matter of debate whether one or more gods caused the universe. According to Swinburne it is better to postulate as few entities as possible as; Ockham's razor says, 'Do not multiply entities beyond necessity':

When postulating entities postulate as few as possible. Also, suppose one murderer, unless the evidence forces you to suppose a second. If there were more than one deity responsible for the order of the Universe, we should expect to see the characteristics of different deities in different parts of the Universe, just as we see different kinds of workmanship in different houses of a city . . . it is enough to draw this absurd conclusion to see how ridiculous the Humean objection is.

(Swinburne, 'The Argument from Design')

David Hume argued that random activity can lead to orderliness rather than disorder

Hume also considered the idea that matter could have been arranged randomly, by pure chance. He considers that there is always a tendency to move from disorder to order, so an ordered world could arise out of disordered chaos in the past. That means that the universe is the way it is and has life in it because of random changes which brought about order rather than disorder, not because anyone directed these changes in a particular way. This is often called the Epicurean hypothesis as this idea of the random arrangement of matter comes from the ancient Greek philosopher Epicurus.

Paley disagreed and said that it was an unsatisfactory idea that something which is clearly ordered, such as the watch, came about by pure chance. 'Nor . . . would any man in his senses think the watch, with its various machinery, accounted for, by being told that it was one out of possible combinations of material forms' (Paley, *Natural Theology*).

Thought point

Look at the weather outside today. Can you explain all the different possible causes that make the weather as it is? Is it a matter of chance if it is sunny, cloudy or rainy?

WHERE DO HUME'S IDEAS LEAVE THE TELEOLOGICAL ARGUMENT?

David Hume criticised the teleological argument, but did not suggest any other explanation for the apparent order in the universe. As Richard Dawkins put it,

Ockham's razor

Ockham's razor is a philosophical principle named after William Ockham, a fourteenth-century English philosopher and friar. The principle states, '*Do not multiply entities beyond necessity.*' It is used in philosophy to suggest that when explaining anything you should do so in the most straightforward way possible, because usually the simplest explanation of any event or occurrence is the correct one. Often, Ockham's razor is expressed as '*the simplest explanation is usually the last one.*'

Paley's criticism does not really address the issue which Hume raises. Hume claims that random changes will tend to produce orderly situations rather than disorder, as disorder brings the process of change to an end, while order may continue the process of change. Hume's idea would later be viewed more positively due to the work of Charles Darwin (see p. 70 ahead).

That great Scottish philosopher disposed of the argument from design a century before Darwin. But what Hume did was criticise the logic of using apparent design in nature as positive evidence for the existence of a God. He did not offer any alternative explanation for apparent design, but left the question open.

(Dawkins, *The Blind Watchmaker*)

MILL'S CRITICISMS OF TELEOLOGICAL ARGUMENTS

In his work *Nature, the Utility of Religion, and Theism*, first published in 1874, Mill claimed the amount of evil and cruelty was a major objection to any idea that the universe was designed. Richard Dawkins gave the following illustration of this cruelty in the natural world:

A female digger wasp not only lays her egg in a caterpillar (or grass hopper or bee) so that her lava can feed on it but, according to Fabre and others, she carefully guides her sting into each ganglion of the prey's central nervous system, so as to paralyse it but not kill it.

(Dawkins, *River Out of Eden: A Darwinian View of Life*)

Mill thought that the universe is not a pleasant place. He saw instances of events which, if carried out by a human, would be punished with the full force of the law. He also considered that the amount of suffering in the world far outweighed the goodness.

DARWIN'S THEORY OF EVOLUTION AS A CRITICISM OF TELEOLOGICAL ARGUMENTS

> ### Thought point
>
> Who was Charles Darwin? Why is he famous?

Thomas Malthus' idea

Malthus argued that the earth regulated population growth as a result of famine and disease. However, since his time modern medicine and farming methods have challenged these ideas. Using Malthus' ideas Darwin realised that

---

Darwin the man (1809–1882)

Charles Darwin came from an educated and wealthy background. Having commenced university life studying medicine, and later divinity, he became interested in botany – the study of plants. As a result, at the age of 22, he became the ship's naturalist on the now famous voyage of *HMS*

continued opposite

other species would also die if their population grew more quickly than the available food supply, and so he developed the idea that *'life struggles to exist.'*

Darwin extended this idea to work out that if two species were after the same food and one species evolved in a way that makes it better at getting food than the other, this species will survive while the other one will die out. He also worked out that any offspring would inherit characteristics from both parents, and any advantageous characteristics would be passed on to the next generation and so on.

Natural selection

Darwin called this 'natural selection': advantageous characteristics would be passed down through the generations to aid survival. Darwin himself wrote that

> If variations useful to any organic being ever do occur, assuredly individuals thus characterised will have the best chance of being preserved in the struggle for life; and for the strong principle of inheritance, these will tend to produce offspring similarly characterised. This principle of preservation, or the survival of the fittest, I have called Natural Selection.

> (Darwin, *On the Origin of Species*)

Natural selection as a challenge to the teleological argument

Natural selection challenges the teleological argument because it can explain how Paley's examples of regularity and order in the world, like an eye, can exist without needing a designer. Darwin showed why advantageous characteristics would be passed on to the next generation, whereas non-advantageous ones would not.

This idea supports Hume's suggestion that there may be other explanations of apparent design in the universe than a designer.

Evolution through natural selection has been proved by many further scientific studies and so portrays a world where species survive more by chance than by design.

THE COSMOLOGICAL ARGUMENT

The cosmological argument attempts to show that from the existence of the universe it is possible to discover the cause of its existence.

Beagle. During the five-year mission of the ship he studied a huge range of plants and animals, and he began to think about the 'species problem'. By the phrase 'the species problem', Darwin meant the question concerning the origins, development and relationship of different species. By 1842 he had developed an outline of what would eventually become his famous theory of evolution by 'natural selection'. His most famous work, *On the Origin of Species*, was published in 1859 and became a bestseller. He went on to write other works developing and expanding on his idea. He died in 1882 and is buried in Westminster Abbey.

The ideas of evolution and survival of the fittest have become the most important criticisms of the teleological arguments. From 1831 Darwin spent five years on HMS *Beagle*, during which time he studied a range of species found in the Galapagos Islands. He noticed slight differences between species on the different islands – his most famous example being the finches, which had slight variations according to which island they were found on, such

continued overleaf

as how the shape of the beak varied according to the type of food they ate. Darwin realised that small changes became even bigger changes as the generations of finches followed each other. This idea was partly influenced by Sir Charles Lyell's *Principles of Geology* (1830–33), which described how the landscape had come about through a series of small changes over thousands of years. Darwin was also influenced by the ideas of Thomas Malthus (1766–1834).

Aquinas the man (1225–1274)

Thomas Aquinas

World History Archive / Alamy

Thomas Aquinas was born in 1225. As a young man he joined the Dominican Order. He was a brilliant academic and studied under Albert the Great. He is renowned

continued opposite

AQUINAS' COSMOLOGICAL ARGUMENT: THE FIVE WAYS

In the first part of his *Summa Theologiae* Aquinas attempted to show that belief in the existence of God is completely rational. Aquinas considers a number of ways of showing the existence of God and these are known as the five ways. It is the first three that are considered to be a cosmological argument.

WAYS 1 AND 2: THE ARGUMENTS FOR AN UNMOVED MOVER AND UNCAUSED CAUSER

Thomas Aquinas' first way – first or Prime Mover

1   We can observe that things in the world are in a process of motion.
2   Everything that is in motion is in the process of changing from a potential state to an actual state.
3   The same thing cannot be at the same time potentially and actually the same thing.
4   For example if something is actually cold, it cannot be potentially cold, but it can be potentially hot.
5   So, everything that is in a state of motion must be moved by another thing.
6   But the chain of movers '*cannot go on to infinity, because then there would be no first mover, and, consequently no other mover*' (Aquinas, *Summa Theologiae*).
7   Conclusion: '*It is necessary to arrive at a first mover, put in motion by no other; and this everyone understands to be God*' (Aquinas, *Summa Theologiae*).

Thomas Aquinas' second way – first cause

1   Nothing can be its own efficient cause.
2   Efficient causes follow in order: a first cause causes a second, a second a third and so on.
3   It is not possible for efficient causes to go back to infinity, because if there is no efficient first cause, there will not be any following causes.
4   Conclusion: '*It is necessary to admit a first efficient cause to which everyone gives the name of God*' (Aquinas, *Summa Theologiae*).

Aquinas argued that there could not be an infinite regress of causers (movers) and there must be something which is the source of all causation, but does not have a cause itself. For Aristotle this would be the unmoved mover, whereas for Aquinas this is God.

POINTS TO NOTE ABOUT AQUINAS' FIRST AND SECOND WAYS

Motion, potentiality and actuality: Aquinas considered things being acted upon as being changed or moved – this is what he meant by motion. Motion is the way that something becomes something else – for example a glass of water is actually cold but it is also potentially hot if it is heated. Something has to change the water – in this case the heat. The efficient cause is whatever is used to heat the water. Aquinas suggested that there is a *first efficient cause* of everything – that is a cause of everything. This idea comes from Aristotle.

INFINITE REGRESSION

An infinite regression is a chain of events that goes back for ever – for example a domino rally where each domino is made to fall by the one before it. This chain could continue backwards an infinite number of times – this is an example of an infinite regression.

Aquinas said that to explain a chain of events, such as a domino rally, there needed to be an actual cause that is not a potential cause. If the cause of everything is only potential, then it needs something to act on it to achieve its potential and this would mean that the chain of regression would begin again. Aquinas said that the chain is caused by pure act and not potential act, and he concluded that the being that is pure act is God.

EXTRACT FROM THOMAS AQUINAS' *SUMMA THEOLOGIAE*, 1A, 2, 3

Way 1

'[W]hatever is in motion must be put in motion by another. If that by which it is put in motion be itself in motion, then this also must needs be put in motion by another and that by another again. But this cannot go on to infinity because then there would be no first mover, and, consequently no other mover.'

Way 2

'In the world of sense we find there is an order of efficient causes . . . Now to take away the cause is to take away the effect. Therefore, if there be no first

both in the Catholic Church and the history of philosophy for his writings. His most famous work was the *Summa Theologiae*, which he began in 1256. He died before completing it. He was later made a Doctor of the Church in recognition of the quality of his theological and philosophical writings.

The five ways

Way 1 – argument for an unmoved mover

Way 2 – argument for an uncaused causer

Way 3 – argument from contingency

Way 4 – argument from gradation

Way 5 – argument from teleology

cause among efficient causes, there will be no ultimate, nor any intermediate cause.'

Beware of the domino example

Aquinas' argument is often illustrated, as earlier, using the example of a domino rally, claiming that God starts the domino rally off. In the same way a football moves because someone kicked it – but the footballer need not necessarily still be there once he has kicked the ball – he could have been replaced while the ball is still moving.

Aquinas did not make this type of claim, as it would allow the possibility that God no longer exists, like the football kicker who was replaced.

What Aquinas really means

Aquinas meant that the first mover is the reason anything exists at all, not simply the person who begins a chain of events, like the domino rally.

Aquinas was concerned with why there is any motion or causation at all and why there continues to be motion and causation. The philosopher F.C. Copleston called this an 'ontologically ultimate cause'.

Copleston (Copleston, *Aquinas*) explained this point by explaining the difference between:

1   Winding up your watch at night, and
2   Writing on a piece of paper.

Copleston pointed out that the watch once wound would continue to work on its own, whereas the writing stops when you stop writing. He explains that Aquinas' arguments are more like the writing on the piece of paper, which depends on the movement of the hand, which is in turn dependent on other factors. Copleston said that Aquinas was talking about a *'first mover'* or *'first efficient cause'* that is the reason for there being motion or causation at all. An example may help to illustrate this point: According to the Big Bang theory our universe began around 15 billion years ago. Scientists have discovered a lot about its origins and development. However, that does not explain why there is and continues to be a universe.

Is Aquinas correct to say that you cannot have an infinite regression of causes?

It is true that in mathematics it is possible to think of an endless series of numbers, such as: . . . – 3,–2,–1,0,1,2,3. . . This series of positive and negative numbers could continue forever, which means that infinite regressions are possible. So, if God is considered to be the explanation of why there is something rather than nothing, then if someone supported infinite regressions it is perfectly logical for him or her to ask who caused God.

Additionally, if there was a time when every contingent being did not exist, then nothing would come to exist. However, this view can be criticised by considering that it is quite possible for all contingent things at different points in time to not exist and later exist. However, this does not mean that at some time nothing existed.

DAVID HUME'S CRITICISMS OF ARGUMENTS SUCH AS AQUINAS' FIRST AND SECOND WAYS

The philosopher David Hume questioned whether every event has a cause. Hume said that people simply assume that every event has a cause, but this cannot be proved. The following example may help to illustrate this view.

Thought point

The bus

If you are waiting at a bus stop and you want the bus to stop, you put your hand out and the bus should come to a stop (providing the driver does not ignore you or does not see you).

What causes the bus to stop?

If you had never seen a bus before, or a person requesting a bus to stop, why would it be wrong to conclude that the person putting out his or her hand caused the bus to stop?

People can make assumptions about cause and effect which can be completely wrong – for example a snooker ball may strike another, which is then pocketed. We may think that striking the ball caused it to move and be pocketed, but there could be any number of other causes which we do not see, such as a sudden hush in the room, lights being turned on, somebody entering the room and so forth. Hume argued that we assume that cause follows effect, because our minds habitually see causes and automatically link effects to them. Hume argued that just because there is an explanation for every event in a series there may not necessarily be a cause for the whole

Contingent

Philosophers use the word 'contingent' to mean that something is not immortal but depends on something else for its existence. For example human beings are caused to exist by their parents. They do not just exist. So, philosophers would say human beings are contingent beings.

Necessary

The word used in philosophy to say that something has to be that way and cannot be any different (e.g. if a philosopher was discussing necessary existence he or she would be talking about something which has to exist and could not fail to exist).

Cause and effect

The word 'cause' is used in philosophy to refer to something which brings about an effect or result. For example the cause of a football flying through the air could be the person who kicked it. The effect is the result of the action – in this case the ball moving. For more information about cause and effect see the sections on Aristotle.

series. According to Hume we simply consider that every event must have a cause as that is the way we make sense of things.

Hume concluded that we expect all future experiences to somehow conform to past experiences, and this reinforces our belief that A causes B. We see 'uniformity of nature' because our minds work that way, and we simply think that A and B must be connected.

However, according to Hume we cannot always assume that every effect has a cause. If Hume is correct, this is a serious criticism of Aquinas' first two ways. For Hume it is not certain that the beginning of existence has a cause and so the argument for a first cause fails.

The fallacy of composition and David Hume

David Hume also considered whether it is necessary for the whole universe to have a cause just because everything that is within the universe was caused by something. According to Hume there is no reason why God is the first cause as the first cause could simply be the universe itself.

This idea fits in with what we now know about the world as it evolved from primordial matter and so effectively actualises itself, and so it is completely possible that there was no cause of the universe, or that it had always existed and so had no beginning.

Bertrand Russell said that because every man has a mother this does not prove that the human race has a mother. Russell's claimed that 'Obviously the human race hasn't a mother, that's a different logical sphere' (Russell, *Why I Am Not a Christian*). According to the fallacy of composition, just because contingent things in the universe have a cause it is not possible to simply conclude that the universe has a cause.

Is David Hume correct?

In spite of Hume's ideas on the links between cause and effect, people do generally believe that effects have a cause.

Anscombe (1974) criticised Hume's argument by pointing out that you could conclude that '*existence must have a cause*' without believing or knowing that '*such particular effects must have such particular causes*'. She gave the example of a magician pulling a rabbit out of a hat, and said that it is possible to imagine a rabbit '*coming into being without a cause*', but this does not tell us anything about '*what is possible to suppose "without contradiction or absurdity" as holding in reality*' (Anscombe, *Whatever Has a Beginning of Existence Must Have a Cause*).

Anscombe also suggested that even though it is possible to imagine something coming into existence without a cause this tells you nothing about what is possible in reality. You can imagine something, such as the rabbit in Anscombe's example, coming into existence without a cause. However, 'from my being able to do *that*, nothing whatever follows about what is possible to suppose "without contradiction or absurdity" as holding in reality' (ibid.).

REALITY AND SPECULATION

When considering causation and infinite regression, the difference between speculation and reality is an important factor.

> *Reality* means our experience of the universe and the way it works.
> *Speculation* means thinking about the various logical possibilities regarding any issue. For example it is possible to speculate about the possibility of time travel, but in reality this is currently impossible.

Analysis of Aquinas' first and second ways

It could be argued that God as first cause could have existed at one time, but no longer does so and is no longer active in the world.

On the other hand, it is possible to argue that God could be a sustaining cause of the universe, keeping everything going.

Additionally, the first and second ways appear to be based on a contradiction: not only must everything have a cause but also something must exist that caused itself. He is simply saying that God must exist.

Ultimately, the first and second ways only point to the possibility of God as an explanation, and the argument fails if God is not considered to be a being that requires no further explanation.

Way 3: the argument from contingency

Aquinas' third way is called an argument from contingency or necessity, and it could be put as follows:

1   There was a time when nothing existed and in the future nothing will exist. Existence is contingent.
2   If there was a time when nothing existed then nothing would exist.

3   If this is the case then nothing could exist as there would be nothing to bring anything into existence.

4   Interim conclusion: *'There must exist something the existence of which is necessary'* (Aquinas, *Summa Theologiae*).

5   But every necessary thing either has its necessity caused by another or not.

6   An infinite regression of necessary things is impossible, as shown in Way 2.

7   Final conclusion: There exists *'some being having of itself its own necessity . . . causing in others their necessity. This all men speak of as God'* (Aquinas, *Summa Theologiae*).

POINTS TO NOTE ABOUT AQUINAS' THIRD WAY

Contingent existence

Aquinas claimed that a necessary being had to exist or else there could be no contingent beings at all. If it is possible that there was a time when no contingent beings existed, then none could even come into existence as contingent beings need other contingent beings to cause them to exist. Aquinas, therefore, concluded that there must be a necessary being – one which cannot not exist.

Links with Ways 1 and 2

Note that Aquinas links Way 3 with the rejection of infinite regression in Ways 1 and 2.

Analysis of the third way

Immanuel Kant criticised the third way as he said that the argument worked from empirical evidence (our observations of causality) to the non-empirical idea that there is a God. According to Kant the conclusion that there is a God cannot be supported as it moves from the known to the unknown. Kant appeared to think that the cosmological argument depended on the ontological argument as it presupposes necessary existence.

However, the cosmological argument does not depend on first assuming that necessary existence is possible. Instead, the argument tries to show that necessary existence is actual, from which we can infer that it must be possible. Additionally, the cosmological argument is a posteriori, states that the universe exists and then goes on to ask why it exists, but the ontological argument starts for the idea that God exists.

J.L. Mackie (Mackie, *The Miracle of Theism*) also criticised Aquinas' argument for a necessary being, and he does not give any clear reason why God should be that necessary being.

Russell also suggested that the argument appeared to suggest that because everyone has a mother, then the universe must have a parent. While this might be true for each human being, it does not follow for the universe.

The cosmological argument does not prove that God's existence is beyond doubt, but it still remains an important question to ask: 'Why is there something rather than nothing?' Additionally, Aquinas was already a believer in God and was not giving some sort of scientific proof of God, but simply showing that God is true.

Thought point

Look at the picture. When this child is older how would you explain to her why there are stars in the sky? Would you want to give an ultimate explanation – one that a philosopher like Copleston would call a sufficient explanation?

THE RUSSELL-COPLESTON DEBATE

The BBC broadcast a debate entitled *The Existence of God – A Debate* in 1948. This debate was between two great philosophers of their day: Bertrand Russell and Frederick Copleston. Their approaches to the cosmological argument are very different; that of Russell provides useful criticisms while that of Copleston can be used in support of the argument.

Copleston reworked Aquinas' argument and focused on contingency. This is a summary of his argument:

1 Things in the world are contingent – they might not have existed ----- for example we would not exist without our parents.
2 Everything in the world depends on something else for its existence.
3 Therefore, something that exists outside the universe must have caused everything in the universe.
4 This cause has to be a necessary being – one which contains the reason for its existence within itself.
5 This necessary being is God.

Russell rejected the idea of a necessary being as one that cannot be thought not to exist and concluded that the regress of causal events did not lead to the existence of everything in the universe: 'what I am saying is that the concept of cause is not applicable to the total.' The fact that each human has a mother does not mean the entire human race has a mother. He said that the universe is a mere, brute fact, and its existence does not demand an explanation. 'I should say that the universe is just there, and that's all.' Russell thought that the argument for a cause of the universe was meaningless He said it was a 'question that has no meaning' and thus proposed, 'Shall we pass on to some other issue?' Copleston's response to Russell's refusal to accept the importance of the issue was to claim, 'If one refused to sit at the chess board and make a move, one cannot, of course, be checkmated.'

Thought point

The chess problem

With a chess set, try to think of as many strategies as you can to prevent losing. Then read the next section of the textbook about the Copleston-Russell debate and try to work out the link with the debate.

Copleston defended the cosmological argument by reformulating some of the ideas found in the Thomas Aquinas' third way. Russell rejected these arguments and suggested that the universe could not be explained in this way. At the heart of their debate is the issue of contingency and necessity, and what is a sufficient reason to explain why anything exists.

THE PRINCIPLE OF SUFFICIENT REASON

In order to understand the debate between Russell and Copleston it is important to understand the *principle of sufficient reason*. The principle comes from the philosopher G.W. Leibniz, who developed a version of the cosmological argument.

Leibniz defined the principle of sufficient reason as that 'in virtue of which we hold that no fact could ever be true of or existent, nor statement correct, unless there were a sufficient reason why it was thus and not otherwise' (Leibniz, *Philosophical Texts*). By this he meant that you should be able to give an explanation of why, for example, a chair exists that includes how it came to exist. This idea of explaining how a thing came to exist he called the principle of *sufficient reason*.

A *sufficient reason* to explain the universe's existence would thus explain how and why the universe exists.

Thought point

1   Who do you agree with most? Why?
2   What does Copleston mean by a *sufficient* reason?
3   Which person's argument do you think is stronger in this extract?
4   Do you think it will ever be possible to prove your own point of view regarding the cosmological argument in such a way as to end debate about it?

SUMMARY

1   The teleological argument

Thomas Aquinas
Way 5 is a design argument.

> Aquinas argued that everything in the natural world has a purpose and follows natural laws set up by an intelligent being (i.e. God).
> Aquinas uses the example of an archer to show regularity of succession.
> Aquinas was influenced by Aristotle's theory of the Four Causes; he links Aristotle's final cause to God.

Weaknesses in Aquinas' argument

> Does everything follow a general law set down by a designer?
> Anthony Flew suggests there is no purpose in nature.
> Swinburne claims that Aquinas assumes that God imposes regularity and laws on the universe.

William Paley
Paley presents a purpose argument.
Paley compares a rock and a watch, and notes that the watch demonstrates:

* fitness for a purpose
* parts work together/fit for a purpose
* the parts are ordered.

> Part 2 of the argument
> Imaginary function of the watch: producing other watches

A watch like this suggests the existence of something conscious and intelligent.

Argues by analogy that nature requires a much greater designer than the watch.

The complexity of nature is illustrated by the human eye.

Challenges to design arguments

David Hume

Nothing to which a universe can be satisfactorily compared

Hume's analogy of the house builder and an architect; challenge about the design's quality (the problem of evil)

There are other possible explanations than God for apparent design in the universe.

Is there evidence that the world has a single designer? The analogy of a great ship

Random activity can lead to orderliness rather than disorder (supported by the discovery of natural selection).

J.S. Mill

Questioned the goodness of nature given the apparent cruelty to be found within nature (e.g. the behaviour of a digger wasp)

Natural selection

Natural selection can explain the emergence of complex living organisms without any need to refer to design, a designer or purpose.

2   Cosmological arguments

Aquinas' cosmological arguments

Ways 1 and 2: The arguments for an unmoved mover and uncaused causer

Concerned with why there is any motion or causation

Argues that there is a first mover which causes all existence; this first mover is God, who is the first efficient cause of the universe.

Infinite regression is rejected.

Criticisms of Ways 1 and 2

Hume questioned the idea that every event has a cause: it is not possible to claim that every effect has a cause – it may just be the way we see things.

The fallacy of composition

Hume questioned whether it is necessary for the whole universe to have a cause just because everything that is within the universe could be explained by reference to a preceding cause.

Way 3: The argument from contingency

Aquinas argues that God has necessary existence.

Criticisms of Way 3

Immanuel Kant rejected Aquinas' third way for the same reason that he rejected the concept of necessary existence with respect to the ontological argument.

Mackie questioned the assumption that there is a necessary being and that God should be the necessary being.

REVIEW QUESTIONS

Look back over the chapter and check that you can answer the following questions:

1 Richard Dawkins entitled a book The Blind Watchmaker. What point do you think he was making?
2 Outline Paley's analogy of the watch.
3 In what way is Aquinas' teleological argument different from Paley's?
4 Can you explain the difference between a teleological argument based on order and a teleological argument based on regularity?
5 Read the sections on Paley and Hume again. Which argument is stronger?
6 Review the information in this chapter about infinite regression. Do you think that the idea of infinite regression is a serious weakness in Aquinas' argument or just philosophical speculation? Justify your answer with reasons.
7 Outline the main steps of Ways 1 to 3.
8 Do Hume and Mackie's criticisms fatally wound the cosmological argument?
9 The philosopher Anthony Kenny once used the phrase 'the God of the Philosophers' to refer to the way God is spoken of in arguments such as the five ways. What do you think he meant?
10 Is Aquinas' God of the five ways the same as the Christian God? Justify your answer with reasons.

Terminology

Do you know your terminology?

- Variation
- Paley's watch analogy

continued overleaf

- Natural selection
- Three reasons why Hume rejects Paley's watch analogy
- Necessity and contingency
- Infinite regression
- First efficient cause.

 # Examination questions practice

SAMPLE EXAM-STYLE QUESTION

'Hume's criticisms of the cosmological argument do not succeed.' Discuss.

AO1 (15 marks)
- You need to explain Aquinas' ways 1 and 2 as this is where Hume directs his criticisms.
- You need to explain Hume's criticisms and why he held them:
  - Hume's discussion of infinite regression
  - Hume's claim that you cannot move from a thing within the universe existing to the universe itself existing (the fallacy of composition)
  - Hume's argument that you cannot prove that any being is necessary
  - Hume's suggestion that some things might be uncaused or have other causes than God
  - Hume's suggestion that the universe may not have a cause even if things within it are caused
- Hume criticised the cosmological arguments in many ways. You should give a selection of points in your argument. Avoid the trap of spending all your time describing Hume's ideas and not leaving enough time for the other part of the question.

AO2 (15 marks)
- You could discuss the criticisms of Hume's arguments – for example by the philosopher G.E. Anscombe.
- You could discuss some modern philosophers' use of Hume's arguments and whether the modern philosophers approach Hume's ideas positively or negatively. Bertrand Russell would be an example of a person who presents a view similar to that of Hume; Mackie also puts forward arguments that agree with some of Hume's points. Copleston and Anscombe are philosophers who would disagree with some of Hume's ideas.

Further possible questions

- **'No convincing explanation for the existence of the universe has yet been found.' Discuss.**
- **'Darwinism shows that Paley's argument is false.' Discuss.**
- **Critically assess whether the universe shows evidence of design.**

FURTHER READING

Anscombe, G.E.M. 1974. *Whatever Has a Beginning of Existence Must Have a Cause: Hume's Argument Exposed in Philosophy of Religion a Guide and Anthology* (ed. Davies, B.). Oxford: OUP.

Davies, B (ed.). 2003. *Philosophy of Religion*, ch. 2. London: Continuum.

Dawkins, R. 1995. *River Out of Eden*. New York: Basic Books.

Dawkins, R. 2006. *The Blind Watchmaker* (new edition). London: Penguin.

Mackie, J.L. 1982. *The Miracle of Theism*. Oxford: OUP.

Palmer, M. 2001. *The Existence of God*. London: Routledge.

Swinburne, R. 1996. *Is There a God*. Oxford: OUP.

Swinburne, R. 2004. *The Existence of God*. Oxford: OUP.

The existence of God

5 Arguments based on reason

The ontological argument

THE ISSUES

1   If someone has an idea of what God is, can his existence be proved?
2   Is it part of the definition of God that God has to exist in reality, not just in people's minds?
3   Whether a posteriori or a priori is a more persuasive style of argument
4   Whether existence can be treated as a predicate
5   Whether the ontological argument justifies belief
6   Whether there are logical fallacies in the argument that cannot be overcome.

WHAT YOU WILL LEARN ABOUT IN THIS CHAPTER

The ontological argument with details of this argument with reference to:

*   Anselm
*   Guanilo's criticisms
*   Kant's criticisms

THE OCR CHECKLIST

Arguments based on reason

The ontological argument – details of this argument, including reference to:

- Anselm
- Gaunilo's criticisms
- Kant's criticisms

Learners should have the opportunity to discuss issues related to arguments for the existence of God based on reason, including:

- whether a posteriori or a priori is the more persuasive style of argument
- whether existence can be treated as a predicate
- whether the ontological argument justifies belief
- whether there are logical fallacies in this argument that cannot be overcome.

Thought point

Look at the following statements. How would you prove the truth of each of these statements?

1 Father Christmas has a white beard.
2 Unicorns are silver.
3 All war is evil.
4 God exists.
5 Rape is wrong.
6 Three plus three equals six.
7 All dwarves are small.

INTRODUCTION

This chapter examines the ontological argument, which claims to demonstrate that the statement 'God exists' is analytically true – meaning that it would be make no sense to doubt God's existence. The ontological argument claims that once someone has understood what the word 'God' means he must recognise that God exists. This argument is a priori and tries to show that it is possible to argue for God's existence without making any reference to sense experience, as the definition of God means that he exists necessarily.

Thought point

Analytic and synthetic statements

Anselm wanted to show that the statement 'God exists' cannot be doubted. This is an analytic statement.

Look at the following statements and consider which of these statements are true and which need to be proved with evidence.

1   A triangle has three sides and the internal angles add up to 180 degrees.
2   Mount Everest is the highest mountain in the world.
3   Unicorns are silver and have a horn on their head.

Analytic statements

An analytic statement is a statement which it is ridiculous and impossible to think is false. For example a triangle having three internal angles adding up to 180 degrees is an analytic statement, because it is ridiculous and impossible to think of a triangle in any other way. Richard Swinburne gives the following example: 'An analytic or logically necessary proposition is one which it would be incoherent to suppose to be false; "all squares have four sides" and "red is a colour" are logically necessary, because it would be incoherent, make no sense to suppose that red could be anything except a colour, or that a square could have only three sides' (Swinburne, *The Existence of God*).

Synthetic statements

A synthetic statement is a statement in which the statement's truth or falsity depends on evidence which has to be collected. An example of a synthetic statement is statement 2 above. The truth or falsity of this statement depends on evidence one collects.

ANSELM'S ONTOLOGICAL ARGUMENT

For medieval theologians, the existence of God was a 'given' – they did not need to debate it. However, as Aristotle's philosophy and his Muslim commentators were introduced into the universities, they were seen as threatening traditional Christian belief. A debate raged between the supporters of the new philosophy and the 'orthodox' traditionalists. Anselm wanted to reconcile the two approaches.

Anselm wrote *The Monologion* as a meditation on the Divine Being, saying that he wanted to find a single argument which would show that God exists. His argument came to him after a long period of contemplative prayer – it is said that he was at vespers when the idea hit him.

He explained his argument in *The Proslogion*. He based his argument on a quotation from Psalm 14:1, which says, 'Fools say in their hearts, "There is no God."' Anselm argued that it is possible for anyone to conceive of 'that than which nothing greater can be thought'.

Anselm's thoughts on this passage have become known as the ontological argument for God's existence. The name for this argument comes from two Greek words – *ontos* (being) and *logos* (reason or word: the ontological argument is concerned with the being or nature of God).

ANSELM'S FIRST ONTOLOGICAL ARGUMENT

The Proslogion is written as a prayer:

> Therefore, Lord, you who give knowledge of the faith, give me as much knowledge as you know to be fitting for me, because you are as we believe and that which we believe. And indeed we believe you are something greater than which cannot be thought. Or is there no such kind of thing, for 'the fool said in his heart, "there is no God"' (Ps. 13:1, 52:1)? But certainly that same fool, having heard what I just said, *'something greater than which cannot be thought,'* understands what he heard, and what he understands is in his thought, even if he does not think it exists. For it is one thing for something to exist in a person's thought and quite another for the person to think that thing exists. For when a painter thinks ahead to what he will paint, he has that picture in his thought, but he does not yet think it exists, because he has not done it yet. Once he has painted it he has it in his thought and thinks it exists because he has done it.
>
> Thus even the fool is compelled to grant that something greater than which cannot be thought exists in thought, because he understands what he hears, and whatever is understood exists in thought. And

Anselm of Canterbury (1033–1109), scholastic philosopher and saint

St Anselm of Canterbury

Pictorial Press Ltd/Alamy

Anselm was born in Aosta (Piedmont), Italy. As a young man he became a monk at the famous monastery of Bec, in Normandy, France. Eventually he became abbot of the monastery and in 1093 he was chosen as archbishop of Canterbury. During his life he wrote a large number of works examining both the nature of God and the relationship between the Church and the state in medieval Europe. Anselm's writings were influenced by the philosophy of Plato and he was an important early figure in the scholastic movement.

For example once you have understood what

continued overleaf

is meant by 'a square' you understand that by a square you mean something with four sides and four internal right angles, which add up to 360 degrees.

certainly that greater than which cannot be understood cannot exist only in thought, for if it exists only in thought it could also be thought of as existing in reality as well, which is greater. If, therefore, that than which greater cannot be thought exists in thought alone, then that than which greater cannot be thought turns out to be that than which something greater actually can be thought, but that is obviously impossible.

Therefore something than which greater cannot be thought undoubtedly exists both in thought and in reality.

(www.fordham/edu/halsall/source/anselm.html)

What does this mean?

1 This 'something greater than which cannot be thought' must exist, at least in the mind.
2 However, if it exists only in the mind then it is inferior to anything that exists both in the mind and in reality.
3 It must therefore be that the thing than which nothing greater can be thought exists both in the mind and in reality.
4 The most perfect conceivable being must exist in reality as well as in the mind.

Anselm's argument is based on the following points:

• The real will always be greater than the imaginary.
• God is the 'greater thing' that Anselm is talking of.
• This leads to the second stage of Anselm's argument, that if God is the greatest thing imaginable, he must exist – if he did not, something greater could be imagined which actually did exist! God, then, must exist in reality and in the mind.

Anselm based his argument on his reply to the fool who said there is no God, as in order for the fool to say 'there is no God' the fool has to have had some idea in his mind of what God 'is'. Anselm put forward a definition that he thought the fool would accept: that God is the 'greatest possible being'. According to Anselm God is the greatest possible being that can be 'conceived' – meaning 'thought of'.

Anselm then pointed out that it is greater to exist in reality than in the mind alone. For example people have an idea of what a fairy is and can give a description of it. However, while we can happily talk about the idea of a fairy and its nature or qualities (e.g. a small imaginary being of human form with wings that has magical powers), that does not make it exist. Fairies may be brought to life using computer animations in films or in books, such as Tinker Bell in *Peter Pan*, but they do not exist in reality. What was important for Anselm was that what exists in reality as well as in the mind is greater than something that is only an idea in the mind.

Anselm's argument hinges on the assumption that something that really exists is greater than something which is only imaginary. An idea that exists in reality and in the mind has the extra quality of existence that something which exists only in imagination can never have.

Thought point

Watch the film *The Matrix* (1993) and ask yourself whether it supports Anselm's claim that existence in reality is better than existence in the mind alone.

Existence is a predicate

The word 'predicate' is used in philosophy to mean intrinsic property or quality of something. For example a predicate of a particular breed of dog might be its form or its colour. In other words, predicates tell us something about the nature of a thing.

Anselm says that it is part of God's nature that God exists, so in philosophical terms: *a predicate of God is God's existence*.

Philosophers say that the predicates of something are included in the subject itself so a bachelor refers to an unmarried man. The predicate of being a bachelor is that *'you are unmarried.'* This is part of the nature of being a bachelor. It is unnecessary to say: *Mr Brown is a bachelor who is unmarried.*

Anselm claimed that existence is a predicate of God (i.e. a property or quality of God's nature). Therefore, God, being the greatest possible being, must exist, since an imaginary idea is not as great as an idea that exists in reality. To be the greatest possible being, God must, necessarily, have his property of existence.

Anselm concluded that because God is the greatest being that can be thought of, part of being a 'being' or 'thing' of any sort is that you exist. So God must exist. For Anselm, God's existence is therefore analytic.

ANSELM'S SECOND VERSION OF THE ARGUMENT (*PROSLOGION 3*, 1078)

In the third chapter Anselm argues that for God existence is necessary.

In fact, it so undoubtedly exists that it cannot be thought of as not existing. For one can think there exists something that cannot be thought of

Analytic

A proposition or statement that it is incoherent to doubt (e.g. triangles have three sides).

Synthetic

Usually refers to a proposition or statement the truth or falsity of which has to be verified. Predicates of synthetic propositions are not intrinsic to the subject of the proposition (e.g. the car is green – this may or may not be true; check to be sure of your answer).

Predicate

A quality or property of an object or subject. For example the concept of a triangle has the predicates of three sides and three internal angles adding up to 180 degrees.

as not existing, and that would be greater than something which can be thought of as not existing. For if that greater than which cannot be thought can be thought of as not existing, then that greater than which cannot be thought is not that greater than which cannot be thought, which does not make sense. Thus that than which nothing can be thought so undoubtedly exists that it cannot even be thought of as not existing.

And you, Lord God, are this being. You exist so undoubtedly, my Lord God, that you cannot even be thought of as not existing. And deservedly, for if some mind could think of something greater than you, that creature would rise above the creator and could pass judgment on the creator, which is absurd. And indeed whatever exists except you alone can be thought of as not existing. You alone of all things most truly exists and thus enjoy existence to the fullest degree of all things, because nothing else exists so undoubtedly, and thus everything else enjoys being in a lesser degree. Why therefore did the fool say in his heart 'there is no God,' since it is so evident to any rational mind that you above all things exist?

Why indeed, except precisely because he is stupid and foolish?

(www.fordham/edu/halsall/source /anselm.html)

Anselm aims to define God in such a way as to make it impossible to conceive of him as *not* existing. What we cannot conceive of as not existing must be greater than what we can conceive of as not existing. It would make no sense to propose that the greatest thing that can be thought of did not exist, because there would be something greater in reality than the thought first proposed.

Assuming Anselm's definition of God as 'the greatest thing that can be thought' can be accepted. If we can hold the concept of God in our minds, God must exist in reality, since that which exists in reality is always greater than that which exists only in the mind. Therefore, it is impossible to think that God cannot exist. God, then, has necessary existence – he has to exist, unlike dogs, which are contingent, as they might exist or they might not: it just depends if the mating was successful or not!

It is impossible for God not to exist, so if a person claims that God does not exist, this, according to Anselm, is a contradiction as it is part of God's nature to exist. Additionally, if God existed only contingently, like the dogs, he would depend on something else for his existence and so could not be a great a being as one which had to exist and could not fail to exist: one whose existence is necessary.

Necessary

In philosophy 'necessary' is used to refer to something which has to be that way and cannot be different, whatever the circumstances.

Contingent

Something which is not necessary, which depends on something else for its existence.

CRITICISMS OF ANSELM'S ARGUMENT

Gaunilo's criticism of Anselm's argument

There have been many criticisms of Anselm's argument, the most famous one being that of a Benedictine monk called Gaunilo. His argument was entitled *On Behalf of the Fool* and it is a defence of the fool against Anselm's ideas.

Gaunilo argued that Anselm's conclusion, that God cannot fail to exist, is *'unintelligible'* – it cannot show that God necessarily exists. Gaunilo suggests that the fool mentioned in Psalm 14 might reply to Anselm by saying that if what Anselm said was true, then the same could be said to prove the existence of an imaginary island.

1   Gossip

First, the fool could imagine sorts of things that do not exist in reality. Gaunilo gave the example of someone hearing about a person from gossip. However, gossip is notoriously unreliable, and the person and event in question need not be true at all.

2   Defining things into existence

Additionally, Gaunilo argued that you cannot prove the existence of something by just having an idea about it; you cannot define the idea into existence. Philosophers in the Middle Ages would say you cannot prove that just because something is said (*de dicto*) it exists in reality (*de re*).

3   Gaunilo's island

Gaunilo's most famous argument against Anselm's ontological argument was that of a perfect island. He suggested that anyone can imagine a most perfect island and argued that while the most perfect island can be conceived of, this does not mean that it exists.

Gaunilo's island analogy implies that it makes no sense to say that just because you have an idea of something it must exist. Following Gaunilo's argument you can also have, for example, a clear idea of what a perfect car is; it does not mean that the car exists. This led Gaunilo to claim either that the argument about the perfect island is a joke or that the man making the argument is a fool, or that the person believing the argument is a fool.

According to Gaunilo, Anselm was unable to prove that the idea of God as the greatest possible being means that God exists in reality.

Gaunilo's own words

On gossip!

The being is said to be in my understanding already, only because I understand what is said. . . . For, suppose that I should hear something said of a man absolutely unknown to me, of whose existence I was unaware. Through that special knowledge by which I know what man is, or what men are, I could conceive of him also, according to the reality itself . . . And yet it would be possible if the person who told me of him deceived me, that the man himself, of whom I conceived, did not exist. (Deane, trans., *St Anselm: Basic Writings*)

The island analogy

For example: it is said that somewhere in the ocean is an island. . . [and] that this island has an inestimable wealth of all manner of riches and delicacies that is told of the island of the Blest . . . it is more excellent than all other countries . . . Now if someone should tell me that there is such an island, I should easily

continued overleaf

Incoherent
A philosophical argument which fails because it is illogical.

Thought point

A newspaper story reports that 'Princess Diana was seen in London yesterday.' What problem with Anselm's argument might this highlight?

Anselm's reply to Gaunilo

Anselm himself provided a reply, pointing out that an island is a finite, limited thing. When somebody imagines a perfect island, there will always be other perfect islands. The 'that than which nothing greater can be thought' is unique. Anselm believed that Gaunilo's argument was defeated by his own proposition of 'necessary existence'.

Anselm pointed out that whereas the greatest possible island is contingent – it does not have to exist – God's existence is necessary. Gaunilo's argument, he claimed, is totally different from his own. Anselm rejected Guanilo's argument that it is possible to prove a perfect island exists simply because it is possible to imagine it.

Alvin Plantinga added to this by saying that Anselm could also say that however marvellous an island is there could always be a better one as Gaunilo's island has no 'intrinsic maximum' or limit to its marvels. Plantinga concluded that any idea of a greatest possible island is, therefore, an incoherent idea (Plantinga, *God, Freedom and Evil*).

Plantinga considered that God is maximally great according to Anselm – nothing greater can be possible so it is impossible to compare the greatest possible being with the greatest possible island.

Why Thomas Aquinas rejected Anselm's argument

Aquinas did not consider that the existence of God is self-evident to humans, as humans are unable to understand God's nature. So even saying that God exists is beyond human understanding.

'God exists,' of itself is self-evident, for the predicate is the same as the subject, because God is His own existence as will be hereafter shown . . . Now because we do not know the essence of God, the proposition is not self-evident to us; but needs to be demonstrated by things that are more known to us.

(*Summa Theologia* 1a q2 a1)

Aquinas concluded that it is possible to understand God only indirectly through the world and his actions in it. Aquinas' cosmological or design arguments are synthetic arguments that look for evidence to prove God's existence.

SOME FINAL THOUGHTS ABOUT ANSELM'S ARGUMENT

Anselm's argument is not meant as proof of God's existence like Aquinas' cosmological argument, as Anselm does not question God's existence. Instead Anselm is simply showing what he believes to be true.

BOETHIUS AND ANSELM

It has been said by some philosophers that the development of Anselm's ontological argument was influenced by Boethius' book the *Consolation of Philosophy*.

In particular, Boethius suggested that

The universally accepted notion of men proves that God, the fountainhead of all things, is good. For nothing can be thought of better than God, and surely He, than whom there is nothing better, must without doubt be good. Now reason shows us that God is so good, that we are convinced that in Him lies also the perfect good. For if it is not so, He cannot be the fountain-head; for there must then be something more excellent, possessing that perfect good, which appears to be of older origin than God: for it has been proved that all perfections are of earlier origin than the imperfect specimens of the same: wherefore, unless we are to prolong the series to infinity, we must allow that the highest Deity must be full of the highest, the perfect good.

(Boethius 1902, *Consolation of Philosophy*)

According to Boethius God is perfect and nothing can be better than God. This shares some similarities with Anselm's ontological argument. However, there are differences as Anselm's ontological argument stresses that God is the greatest conceivable being, whereas Boethius seems to suggest that God is the most perfectly good being that exists.

Descartes the man (1596–1650)

René Descartes

GL Archive/Alamy

René Descartes was born in La-Haye, France. He joined a Jesuit school in Anjou and later studied at the University of Poitiers. He joined the army of the Prince of Orange in 1618, but did not actually fight in any battles. From 1628 to 1649 he lived in Holland. In 1649 he became the tutor of Queen Christina of Sweden. He died of pneumonia in 1650.

Descartes wrote widely on philosophy, and he is significant because many philosophers see him as the founder of modern philosophy; he developed new approaches to philosophy which differed from the traditional philosophies of Europe that came from the great Greek philosophers of

continued opposite

DESCARTES' ONTOLOGICAL ARGUMENT

Descartes' version of the ontological argument is not required for the examination, but it is important as Kant's criticisms of Descartes' argument can also be applied to Anselm's version.

Descartes wrote about the existence of God in Meditations 3 and 5 of his *Meditations on Philosophy*. Meditation 5 is a version of the ontological argument.

The background to Descartes' ontological argument

Before he even presented his form of the ontological argument Descartes wrote that God had already placed in everyone the idea of God. He also stated that God's existence cannot be doubted – just as mathematics is a truth that cannot be doubted as it has been demonstrated clearly. Thus he suggested that showing that God exists is not intended to prove that God exists but it is simply showing that there is no reason to doubt that fact. This is what his version of the ontological argument is intended to demonstrate.

Descartes' ontological argument

Descartes considered that God was perfect, as an imperfect being could not be God. One property of perfection is existence so it was part of God's nature to exist – in other words existence is a predicate of God and thus tells us something about God. He used the example of a triangle and said that the nature of a triangle is to have three sides and three interior angles which add up to 180 degrees, and it could not be different in any way. Descartes used the word 'immutable' to describe the nature of the triangle – it was incapable of change.

According to Descartes, God, like the triangle, has an 'immutable' nature and part of this nature is that God exists; thus existence is a predicate of God.

Descartes' argument

1 God is a supremely perfect being.
2 A property of perfection is existence.
3 Therefore, God exists.

Thought point

Think of the characteristics of your dream car. Could your dream car be described as the 'perfect' car? What would Descartes say?

the ancient world. He wrote many books, but the most famous is his *Meditations on Philosophy* (1641), which examines the nature of reality and God. It is this book which contains his version of the ontological argument.

KANT'S OBJECTION TO THE ONTOLOGICAL ARGUMENT

Kant objected to Descartes' version of the ontological argument, but his objections also apply to Anselm's ontological argument.

Kant argued that the statement 'God does not exist' is not self-contradictory, in the same way that to say that fairies do not exist is not a contradiction. Some statements do contradict themselves, such as 'a dwarf is a tall being,' but denying something is not a contradiction. Therefore, the denial of God's existence isn't self-contradictory. And because the ontological argument rests on God's non-existence being self-contradictory, it is not sound.

Furthermore, Kant argued that existence is not a 'predicate'. For example one can have an idea of what a fairy is. However, that does not mean it exists in reality, even though we can think about fairies as living creatures. It is possible to consider that a predicate of a fairy is that it is a small being of human form with wings, but that does not mean that it is necessary to believe that fairies exist.

Therefore, for Kant existence is not a real predicate as it does not tell us what something is like. Kant felt that 'exist' merely meant that a concept had actuality and it did not add anything to the concept.

To say that something exists does not add to our understanding of that thing. Kant puts it in terms of a sum of money:

If, now, we take the subject (God) with all its predicates (among which is omnipotence), and say 'God is', or 'There is a God', we attach no new predicate to the concept of God, but only posit the subject in itself with all its predicates, and indeed posit it as being an object that stands in relation to my concept. The content of both must be one and the same; nothing can have been added to the concept, which expresses merely what is possible, by my thinking its object (through the expression 'it is') as given absolutely. Otherwise stated, the real contains no more than the merely possible. A hundred real thalers* do not contain the least coin more than a hundred possible thalers.

* A thaler was a German silver coin.

Kant said that an idea of a pile of 100 coins that exist in my mind and the pile of 100 coins that exist in reality will have the same worth. Thus adding existence to the idea will not make it any better but will only affirm what is. Thus existence is not a predicate, or existence in reality is not a special attribute of God, because it virtually adds nothing to the idea of God. For example in the statement 'the plant is green' the word 'green' is a predicate. The concept of something existing does not change our concept of the thing itself, just the world in which it now exists.

Therefore, according to Kant, existence is not a predicate. And if it's not a predicate, it can't be a perfection. Thus, God can be defined as perfect regardless of whether he exists.

Replies to Kant

Is Kant correct in saying that existence is not a predicate? For example one can have an idea of what the fairy is and list the particular properties of the fairy, such as size, human-like, with wings and magical powers and so forth. However, if I have actual evidence that fairies exist, that adds something to the idea. It can, therefore, be argued that asserting that an object exists can change the way that we conceive of it. For example if someone read about Socrates in the works of Plato, and then discovered that he was a real historical figure – that is that he existed – then this extra information will change the way that the person thinks about him. In the same way it could be suggested that to say that God is not a mere figment of believers' imaginations, but actually exists, does add something to the concept of God. Perhaps, then, Anselm's comparison between a God that exists and a God that does not is possible, and the ontological argument survives Kant's criticism.

Norman Malcolm (Malcolm, 'Anselm's Ontological Argument') suggested that *necessary existence* could be a predicate of God. He argued that the existence of God is either impossible or necessary. Following Anselm's second formulation of the ontological argument, Malcolm claimed that God cannot contingently exist; otherwise God would not be the greatest possible being. According to Malcolm God's existence is impossible only if God's existence is both self-contradictory and illogical.

However, the problem with Malcolm's claim that God *necessarily exists* is that you cannot prove God exists by stating what is not the case. Even if God's existence is not impossible or contradictory, this shows only that God's existence is possible, not that God necessarily exists.

SUMMARY

1   Anselm's ontological argument
Anselm started with a response: *'Fools say in their hearts, "there is no god"'* (Psalm 14: 1).

2   Anselm's first ontological argument

- Something which exists in reality and in the imagination is greater than something which exists as an idea in the mind alone. Therefore, God must exist in reality and in the mind.
- Anselm claimed that existence is a predicate of God.

3   Anselm's second version of the argument

- God has necessary existence – he cannot be thought not to exist.
- The greatest possible being is meant by God.

4   Gaunilo's criticism of Anselm's argument

- Necessary existence is 'unintelligible'. You cannot define the idea into existence.
- Gaunilo argues that while the most perfect island can be conceived of, that does not mean that it exists; the same reasoning applies to Anselm's ontological argument.

5   Anselm's possible reply to Gaunilo

- The comparison does not work as the greatest possible island is contingent – it does not have to exist.

  Thomas Aquinas rejected Anselm's argument as God's existence is not self-evident, and human beings are not in a position to understand God's nature.

6   Descartes' ontological argument

- There is the idea of God in every person.
- Some things cannot be doubted, such as the truths of mathematics or God's existence.
- God and triangles have an 'immutable' nature/essence. Part of God's essence is existence.
- God is the supremely perfect being.

7   Kant's objections to the ontological argument

- Kant argues that existence is not a 'predicate'.

REVIEW QUESTIONS

Look back over the chapter and check that you can answer the following questions:

1   Briefly explain Gaunilo's criticism of the ontological argument.
2   What are the two most serious weaknesses of the ontological argument in your opinion? Justify your choice.
3   Summarise Anselm's and Descartes' version of the ontological argument.
4   What is the difference between an analytic and a synthetic statement? Explain with reference to an example.
5   Explain what Kant means when he says existence is not a predicate.
6   Descartes says that existence is a perfection of God. What does this mean?

Examination questions practice

In order to achieve a high mark when answering questions about the ontological argument, you must make sure you understand the different forms of the argument. It is all too easy to achieve a low mark if you confuse the different writers, ideas and terminology of this topic.

SAMPLE EXAM-STYLE QUESTION

To what extent can logic prove the existence of God?

AO1 (15 marks)
- This question is asking you to consider whether the existence of God is an analytic claim that can be shown to be true by deductive argument. The word 'logic' in the question tells you this. It also asks you to examine to what extent this statement is true and consider all the merits and flaws in the ontological argument.

- You will need to explain the ontological argument briefly in order to examine the question.

AO2 (15 marks)
- You will need to present and assess some differing views. For example you could discuss and evaluate whether the existence of God is an analytic statement and use ideas from the ontological argument to support this. You could include Kant's criticisms here.
- You could argue that the existence of God is an analytic proposition, using Descartes.
- You could argue that the only way to prove the existence of God is by using the cosmological or teleological argument – like Aquinas arguing that the only way to prove God's existence is through evidence: synthetically.

Further possible questions

- **'The ontological argument will never be of any use in trying to prove God's existence.' Discuss.**
- **'The ontological argument will convince only those who already believe in God.' Discuss.**
- **To what extent are criticisms of the ontological argument successful?**

FURTHER READING

'The Ontological Argument' (J. Frye, in *Dialogue* 20, April 2003) provides an excellent overview of the mistakes students often make when answering questions about the ontological argument. It is written for advanced students and is well worth reading.

Mackie, J.L. 1982. *The Miracle of Theism: Arguments for and Against the Existence of God*. Oxford: OUP.

Swinburne, R. 2004. *The Existence of God*. Oxford: OUP.

God and the world

6 Religious experience

WHAT YOU WILL LEARN ABOUT IN THIS CHAPTER

The nature and influence of religious experience, including:

- mystical experience
- conversion experience
- examples of mystical and conversion experiences and views about these, including:
- views and main conclusions of William James.

THE OCR CHECKLIST

Religious experience

- the nature and influence of religious experience, including:
  - mystical experience
  - conversion experience
- examples of mystical and conversion experiences and views about these, including:
  - views and main conclusions of William James
- different ways in which individual religious experiences can be understood
  - as union with a greater power
  - psychological effect, such as illusion
  - the product of a physiological effect.

continued opposite

Learners should have the opportunity to discuss issues related to arguments for the existence of God based on reason, including:

- whether personal testimony or witness is enough to support the validity of religious experiences
- whether corporate religious experiences might be considered more reliable or valid than individual experiences
- whether religious experience provides a basis for belief in God or a greater power.

Read this account of a person's religious experience and then discuss the questions which follow:

One day, when I was at prayer, the Lord was pleased to reveal to me nothing but His hands, the beauty of which was so great as to be indescribable. This made me very fearful, as does every new experience that I have when the Lord is beginning to grant me some supernatural favour. A few days later I also saw the divine face, which seemed to leave me completely absorbed. I could not understand why the Lord revealed Himself gradually like this since He was later to grant me the favour of seeing him wholly, until at length I realised that His Majesty was leading me according to my natural weakness.

(St Teresa of Ávila)

- What do you think is the origin of an experience like this?
- How would you explain why experiences like this happen?

Personal experiences of God for many people show that God does exist. This is shown in the lives of both St Paul in Christianity and Mohammad ﷺ in Islam. Many people see evidence of God in their everyday lives and in ordinary events or many interpret some event as having religious significance. Often these experiences have lasting effects on how people lead their lives. However, in order to argue that these experiences can be used to argue that God exists and acts in people's lives it is necessary to explain what exactly is meant by a religious experience and what exactly caused that experience.

WHAT IS A 'RELIGIOUS EXPERIENCE'?

The Oxford Religious Experience Research Unit found that between about 30% and 45% of the population of Britain, irrespective of age, geographical position or even of belief, say that they have been aware of a presence or power beyond themselves. David Hay's book *Inner Space* records that many of the people interviewed had never previously spoken about their experiences because they thought that others would make fun of them or would not understand. So what exactly are they experiencing?

A religious experience is when a person has, or believes that he has had, an encounter with God. Religious experiences are divided into two groups: *direct* and *indirect experiences*.

Direct experiences mean that someone experiences God directly and seems to observe God in some way. This may take different forms – for example Rudolph Otto (Otto, *The Idea of the Holy*) said that what was experienced was beyond human understanding and beyond the physical world in which we live. Otto called this the 'numinous' and said that experiencing God was experiencing the 'wholly other'. God was something that was outside our own experiences and used the Latin words 'mysterium tremendum et fascinans' to try to explain an experience that was so completely outside our ordinary lives. This is experienced on the emotional level and leaves the person aware of his or her own smallness in the face of an all-powerful God. Albert Einstein also said that the most beautiful thing that we can experience is the mysterious and that this knowledge and feeling are the centre of true religiousness. Kant, however, rejected the possibility of such experiences as he argued that we do not have the senses to experience God as God belongs to the noumenal realm and is not an object in space and time.

Alternatively, Martin Buber (1878–1965) explained religious experiences as intimate and intensely personal – he called them I-thou relationships. This does not involve a sense of awe or wonder as Otto thought, but rather a personal relationship that the individual has with God.

These writers and others, when commenting on direct religious experiences of God, do separate them from ordinary everyday experiences and say that they are in some sense ineffable –they are too great to be described in words.

Indirect experiences are when something leads the person to think about God. For example a beautiful sunset might lead a person to think of God as the creator of such beauty. God does not directly reveal himself to someone, but the person gives a religious meaning to the experience and so learns something about God from the experience.

Direct religious experiences

Refer to events where God reveals her-/himself directly to the person having the experience. The religious experience is not chosen or willed by the person; the person experiences or observes God in some way.

Ineffable

Used to refer to experiences which it is beyond human powers and abilities to fully describe and communicate.

Indirect religious experiences

Experiences, thoughts or feelings about God that are prompted by events in daily life – for example observing the stars in the sky and having thoughts about the greatness of God the Creator.

Thought point

Religious experience and ordinary experience

Think of an event that was very important to you. Try to describe and explain the feelings created by this event. Was this experience religious? If so, what made it religious?

Thought point

Ordinary and ineffable

Can you think of events or incidents in everyday life, or in your life, which are ineffable?

TYPES OF RELIGIOUS EXPERIENCES

According to Richard Swinburne (*The Existence of God*) religious experiences are varied and wide-ranging, and he considers that there are five types of religious experiences. He divides these into two groups: public experiences and private experiences.

Public experiences

1   *Ordinary experiences*: This is when a person will give religious meaning to a perfectly natural event such as a beautiful sunset.
2   *Extraordinary experiences*: This is when the experience seems to go against the normal laws of nature. Experiences that appear to violate normal understanding of the workings of nature, such as Moses seeing a bush that burned but was not consumed.

Private experiences

3   *Describable in ordinary language*: This is when a person might claim to experience God in a dream or a vision.

4   *Non-describable experiences*: This is when a person experiences God in a way that is ineffable and cannot be described in ordinary words.
5   *Non-specific experiences*: This is when a person's experience of God is not mediated by any particular sensation; it may be through meditation or by simply the way the individual sees the world as showing something of the divine.

Thought point

Types of religious experience

In which of Swinburne's categories would you put the following?

- Awe at the beauty and intricacies of God's creation, such as DNA.
- A young girl called Bernadette seeing a vision of Mary, the mother of Jesus.
- John Wesley feeling that his heart had been 'strangely warmed' and his sins 'removed' by Jesus.
- The Qur'an being revealed to Muhammad by Allah.
- Moses receiving the Ten Commandments from God.
- Siddhartha Gautama achieving enlightenment.
- The story of Pope John Paul II's life.

Vision

An event in which God, or something about God, is seen or observed. Visions are usually divided into three types: corporeal, intellectual and imaginative.

Thought point

Paul's conversion

Look up the different accounts of Paul's conversion (Acts 9: 4–8, 22: 6–10, 26) and try to explain what happened to him. In particular, think about how the event is described.

Visions and voices as religious experiences

The religious experience of visions and voices is often described in terms of ordinary perceptions, using the phrases 'I saw' or 'I heard'. However, usually the sights and sounds are not public or shared by others.

There are three types of visions:

1   *Imaginative visions*: There are many accounts of these in the Bible, such as the dream described in Matthew 2:12, when the wise men were warned not to return to King Herod as he would attempt to kill the infant Jesus.

2   *Intellectual visions*: An experience rather than an observation as of a physical object – this is how St Teresa of Ávila described her vision: '*I saw Christ at my side – or, to put it better, I was conscious of Him, for neither with the eyes of the body or of the soul did I see anything*' (*The Life of Teresa of Jesus*). This type of vision is not the same as seeing an external object with the eyes. It is instead a clear vision in the mind's eye. Religious believers who have these types of visions would argue that they are far too profound to be confused with the imagination.

3   *Corporeal visions*: This is a vision as of a physical object, an experience where some kind of knowledge is gained. An example of these are the visions of St Bernadette at Lourdes, where she saw several visions of the Virgin Mary and was told to uncover a stream. Many people today continue to make pilgrimages to Lourdes to bathe in this stream. In her vision Bernadette said that she both saw and talked to Mary.

Thought point

Vision experiences

There are a number of good examples of visions in the Bible. What characteristics can be found in the visions of these verses?

*   Exodus 3:1–15
*   1 Kings 19:1–18
*   Isaiah 6: 1–13
*   Ezekiel 1:1–28
*   Amos 7:1–9
*   Mark 9:2–13
*   Luke 24:13–35.

Voices

One dramatic type of religious experience is the hearing of voices. These experiences carry authority, but it is worth noting that the voice may not be an audible voice but usually communicates knowledge of some sort. The conversion of Augustine is an unusual example of voices.

> I was asking myself these questions, weeping all the while with the most bitter sorrow in my heart, when all at once I heard the sing-song voice of a child in a nearby house . . . it repeated the refrain 'Take it and read, take it and read.' At this I looked up, thinking hard whether there was any kind of game in which children used to chant words like these. I stemmed my flood of tears and stood up telling myself that this could only be a divine command to open my book of scripture.

Augustine, Confessions

The voice may have been the natural voice of a child playing (even Augustine is uncertain); however, Augustine interprets this to be a means of God communicating with him. This shows that religious experiences may not always be supernatural, but are interpreted as such.

Mystical experiences

Used in many ways by writers on religious experience. In general, it is used to refer to religious experiences where God is revealed directly and the person having the experience is passive. William James identified four characteristics that are typical of mystical and other religious experiences: *noetic, passive, transient and ineffable.*

Noetic

Refers to something which gives knowledge, such as a revelation from God in which God reveals something.

Thought point

The voice of God

Read the accounts of Jesus' baptism (Mark 1: 1–9), Paul's conversion (Acts 9: 4–8, 22: 6–10, 26) and the calling of the prophet Samuel (Samuel 1).

- What might be learned about God from these stories?
- What does the voice reveal to the hearer?

Thought point

Some thinkers have observed that experiences such as visions and voices are often linked to physical factors, such as fasting. Could putting the body into a weakened state lead a person to have an authority or visual experience they believe to be a genuine religious experience?
Voices have three aspects:

1 Revelatory – the voice reveals something about God.
2 Authoritative – to those who have the experience the message communicated has God's authority.
3 Disembodied – the voice appears to come from no particular body.

How might one prove that an experience is from God? Some schizophrenics might even believe they have a message from God to kill people.

St Teresa of Ávila offered two tests to determine whether the experience was genuine.

1   Does it fit with Christian teaching?
2   Does the experience leave the individual feeling at peace?

Corporate religious experiences

Obviously, if an individual claimed to have experienced God it is possible to doubt that what he or she claims to have experienced is true. However, if several people claim to have had the same experience, or many people witness the experience, it becomes more difficult to doubt it. There are two examples of group or corporate experiences which could strengthen the argument from religious experience.

In 1916, in the small village of Fatima in Portugal, a group of three children aged 10, 8 and 7 started seeing visions of a being that claimed to be an angel of God. Then, on 13 May 1917, the children saw a vision of who they believed to be the Virgin Mary. She told them to return on the same day each month. The children told other people and on the 13th of each month, large crowds started to gather at the spot where Mary had first appeared to the children.

On 13 October 1917, about 70,000 people gathered to see the vision of the Virgin Mary. Mary appeared only to the children, but a miracle is reported to have happened on the same day, which was apparently witnessed by many:

> One could see the immense multitude turn towards the sun, which appeared free from clouds and at its zenith. It looked like a plaque of dull silver and it was possible to look at it without the least discomfort. It might have been an eclipse which was taking place. But at that moment a great shout went up and one could hear the spectators nearest at hand shouting: 'A miracle! A miracle!' Before the astonished eyes of the crowd, whose aspect was Biblical as they stood bareheaded, eagerly searching the sky, the sun trembled, made sudden incredible movements outside all cosmic laws – the sun 'danced' according to the typical expression of the people . . .
>
> People then began to ask each other what they had seen. The great majority admitted to having seen the trembling and dancing of the sun; others affirmed that they saw the face of the Blessed Virgin; others, again, swore that the sun whirled on itself like a giant Catherine wheel

and that it lowered itself to the earth as if to burn it with its rays. Some said they saw it change colours successively.

(www.theotokos.org.uk/pages/approved/appariti/fatima.html)

This was likely to have been an eclipse, but the crowds reported it as a miracle.

Another form of corporate religious experience happens every Sunday in churches across the world. Charismatic worship is a form of Christian worship that takes its name from the word 'charismat' or gift of the spirit. This is inspired by the events of Pentecost, where the Holy Spirit visited the 11 remaining disciples and gave them the 'gift of tongues' – they could speak any language in order to spread the message of the life of Jesus to the world.

Charismatic worship, also known as Pentecostalism, really became famous in 1994, when Pastor Randy Clark preached at Toronto Airport Vineyard Church on 20 January 1994. Following the sermon people began to laugh hysterically, cry, leap, dance and even roar. Some saw this as the result of the Holy Spirit and numerous people went to Toronto to participate. The 'Toronto Blessing' has spread to evangelical congregations around the world.

As far as charismatic worship goes, it is clear that the people present at those services do experience profound emotional and spiritual moments. However, many of the congregations where these events take place see these experiences almost as necessary to be a member of the group. It is possible that many people feel pressured into having these kinds of experiences, simply to fit in. Also, many of the pastors who lead these services are extremely charismatic and use powerful readings from the Bible promising hellfire for sinners and rapture for the righteous. When in a group, people often get carried away by the emotions of the people around them, such as at football matches or protest marches that turn into riots. If the pastor is whipping people up into a frenzy, it is not surprising that there are extreme and hysterical reactions.

However, the supporters of the 'Blessing' point to the changes that people have experienced. Healings, both physical and spiritual, are claimed. Communities have been rejuvenated by the 'Blessing', families reconciled, relationships improved and non-believers converted. These claims are not unique to the Toronto Blessing – other charismatic communities have experienced similar benefits from far less spectacular (and controversial) experiences. Its supporters believe that the 'Blessing' is a sign from God that some new manifestation of God's power is about to be released on the world. People's lives are being transformed by this power. The barking, laughing and other strange manifestations are simply a sign of the sheer power of the experience.

To the outsider, the whole thing may seem bizarre. People behaving in a completely undignified way is alien to the traditional view of worship, even allowing for contemporary developments. More disturbing is the answer given to the cautious who suggest care and biblical study before accepting the experience. Such people are told that they should 'stop thinking about it and simply allow the experience to happen'. Such non-analytical approaches seem to be similar to those employed by cults.

So, even the charismatic Christian community is divided. However, applying the various tests to the experience might help the observer to make some judgement about the validity of the claims. How suggestible are the people who demonstrate these manifestations? How far do the preachers engineer the situation so that people are coerced into the experience? Do people who feel spiritually starved in a bewilderingly materialist world make easy targets for induced 'religious' experiences? One could, therefore, ask whether the people who demonstrate these manifestations are simply suggestible. Equally, it has to be asked: how far are these genuine religious experiences?

Finally, it is worth asking whether the experiences match the various arguments, such as the test offered by Teresa of Ávila.

1 Are the experiences in line with scriptural teachings concerning the manifestations of the gifts of the spirit?
2 Do the experiences have precedent in Christian history, and how do they compare? For example are the experiences similar to those of the Shakers, who underwent experiences that caused them to tremble violently?
3 Have the experiences led to significant and lasting changes in the lives of the people who experienced them? Are these changes in line with the strong religious traditions throughout history?

It is also worth noting that the experiences of charismatic Christians have not all been as controversial.

Conversion experiences

Conversion experiences traditionally lead a person to change to a religious way of life as a result of some experience of divine truth (whether directly or indirectly). This can be sudden and dramatic, such as the conversion of St Paul, which completely changed his life, from being a persecutor of Christians to spreading the Christian message. This experience was transformative and all his previously held priorities and beliefs were changed. This type of conversion can be considered to be an involuntary and unconscious experience.

> Pentecostal Christians emphasise the importance of 'Pentecost', the fiftieth day after Passover, when the Disciples experienced the events recorded in Acts 1:1–11. The story states that the Disciples were given the gifts of the Holy Spirit.
>
> **Evangelical** – taken from the Greek *euangelion*, meaning 'good news'. An evangelical seeks to share the 'good news' with others.
>
> Charismatic worship tends to be contemporary in style. There is no set liturgy, and no prayer books. Modern multimedia technology is used to maximise the experience for the worshippers, who are encouraged to clap, sing and dance, and to become involved in worship.

St Paul

Niday Picture Library/Alamy

However, conversion experiences are not always so sudden and may simply be gradual realisation, a conscious and voluntary experience. This volitional type features a gradual change and consists of the slow development of new moral and spiritual habits. It may be that the person suddenly 'becomes aware' of the change one day.

While a majority of conversions are clearly gradual, the sudden experience would appear to be the most significant and profound. It often affects people who have no religious faith whatsoever before the experience.

Religious conversion is likely to include a change in belief on religious top-ics, which in turn leads to changes in the motivation for people's behaviour so that they act in a way they believe to be right.

Bernard Lonergan distinguished three types of conversions: intellec-tual, moral and spiritual or religious. He explained that this is a process which takes place in incremental steps throughout a person's life.

How permanent is conversion? In some instances, people experienc-ing sudden conversion may know very little about what they have come to believe in. Their knowledge may amount to little more than what they have read in a series of leaflets, or what they have heard from a local preacher, and as Lonergan points out, if this knowledge is not developed the individ-ual may decide at some future point that there are inherent problems in what the preacher has told them, or that there are flaws in the literature they have based their new beliefs and outlook upon. Gradual conversion always seems more likely to be permanent than sudden conversion, prob-ably because a slower procedure is more likely to be more thorough. For example a well-planned essay will always be more thorough than a quickly scribbled effort.

Thus, although conversion experiences do lead the individuals to change their beliefs and the way they lead their lives and have a great effect on the person concerned, this would not necessarily convince others. How-ever, evangelical Christians do believe in the importance of conversion and the idea of being a 'born-again Christian'.

William James argued that there are two basic types of conversions: the *volitional* type and the type by *self-surrender*. The volitional type is where people decide that they wish to make spiritual changes in their life and they go about doing the things necessary to bring this about. James argued that in the second case, there are two things in the mind of the candidate for con-version: first, the wrongness or sinfulness of their life and secondly the ideal form of life which they long to achieve (i.e. living life as a religious person). James argues that conversion is not something that we can strive after; it is something that just happens, almost as if it is given to us as a gift. James likens this situation to those moments when you are trying desperately to remember the name of someone, perhaps an actor in a film, and you know it is going to keep you awake. The mind seems 'jammed' in these situations and it is not until later on, when we have forgotten our search for the name, that it seems to miraculously pop into our head. James argues that there are two ways of understanding this process: either as the work of God or as the work of the subconscious mind.

James argues that there are several features of a conversion experience:

1   A loss of worry: the certainty of God's activity in a person's life and a feeling of overwhelming harmony and completeness.

2   Perceiving truths not known before: the mysteries of life become lucid and clear.
3   The world appears to go through a change: 'an appearance of newness beautifies every object.'
4   Ecstasy of happiness: 'no words can express the wonderful love that was shed abroad in my heart. I wept aloud with joy and love.'
5   Saintliness: living a life of moral goodness.

The question that remains is whether these feelings are caused by God or by psychological processes that take place in the brain. James comes up with no clear answer on this, as neuroscience (the study of the workings of the brain) was very much in its infancy at the time. However, experiments conducted since James wrote his book (see ahead) have suggested possible 'naturalistic' explanations for conversion (and other) religious experiences.

One of the key features of conversion that points to the reality of these experiences is saintliness: when a person's life is completely changed by the experience that he or she has had. This is also often referred to as the 'fruits' of the experience. It is common for people who have had conversion experiences, either sudden like Saul or more gradually, to bring about serious changes to their life: they devote themselves more fully to religious practice and live more moral lives. This is very strong evidence that the people who have conversion experiences see what they have experienced as real: if they were in any doubt, they might not have made the significant changes to their lives that for most people require real efforts of the will. This idea is similar to dedicated smokers who say that they will never give up, or indeed, smokers who try over and over again to give up, but cannot and keep relapsing: when they develop cancer or heart disease, very often they stop smoking and never smoke again; it is a form of conversion experience.

WILLIAM JAMES' ARGUMENT FROM RELIGIOUS EXPERIENCE

In his book, *The Varieties of Religious Experience: A Study in Human Nature*, William James investigated many accounts of religious experiences. He wanted to explore the nature of the wide variety of religious experiences people have. James thought that religious experience was how religious institutions, such as churches, came into being. Churches, for James, were secondary to each individual person's religious experiences. James did not consider church communities as all that important and thought that religious experiences were 'solitary' events in which individuals experienced the divine or God.

He saw that religious experiences have great importance for the person who has them and often affect and change a person's life, with religious beliefs assuming a great importance. It was this great change in people's behaviour as a result of religious experiences that led James to think that they were the inspiration and source of religious institutions.

James saw that there were a great variety of religious experiences and examined what they had in common. William James argued that there are four 'marks' of mystical religious experience:

1 **Ineffability**: that the experiencer finds it very difficult to put their experience into words. In many accounts of mystical experiences, we read the words 'I cannot express what took place.'
2 **Noetic quality**: that when the mystic unites with God, he or she becomes aware of truths not previously known.
3 **Transiency**: the experience is over quickly.
4 **Passivity**: the experiencers have no control over the experience; it happens to them and they are unable to stop it.

Pragmatism

Pragmatism originated in the late nineteenth century. However, today it has a number of meanings.

The most common use of pragmatism is to describe an approach to political decision making which focuses on getting results – that is using the method and approach to get the job done in the most efficient manner. Political pragmatists reject ideological approaches to decision making.

In philosophy, pragmatism suggests that the meaning of a concept or idea is derived from looking at the consequences that come from the original idea or concept.

In order to ascertain the meaning of an intellectual conception one should consider what practical consequences might conceivably result by necessity from the truth of that conception; and the sum of these consequences will constitute the entire meaning of the conception.

(Peirce, CP 5.9, 1905)

Pragmatism was put forward by Charles Peirce and later developed by philosophers, such as William James and John Dewey.

William James did a lot of work in exploring how our psychology affects our understanding of religious experiences. One of his key arguments is the difference between what he called the 'healthy minded' and the 'sick soul.' People who are healthy minded are basically optimistic: if something goes wrong for them they take active steps to improve the situation. The person

James the man (1842–1910)

William James

Mary Evans Picture Library/ Alamy

William James was a philosopher and psychologist. He was a pragmatist. He studied medicine at Harvard University and was initially a lecturer in anatomy. Later he became a professor of philosophy and then professor of psychology. He wrote a large number of books on both psychology and philosophy.

Authority

When applied to religious experience the word 'authority' indicates that the person who has the religious experience has some new insight or knowledge about the world and God's relationship with the world. This gives the person authority. Many authors argue that the authority is limited to the individual who has the experience; it is not about authority and power over other people.

with the sick soul is basically pessimistic, seeing life as a constant struggle. This person may feel as if he has a 'divided self': the person may not feel worthy of being loved or of achieving success because he or she feels like a sinner who is constantly fighting to keep on top of sinful urges. James gives the example of St Augustine to illustrate the sick soul:

> The new will which I have begun to have was not yet strong enough to overcome that other will strengthened by long indulgence. So these two wills, one old, one new, one carnal, the other spiritual, contended with each other and disturbed my soul.
>
> (St Augustine, *Confessions*; quoted in James, p. 172)

James argued that mystical experiences mostly happen to sick souls who need to be 'twice-born' in order to achieve happiness and unite the divided self. By this he meant that many people are happy and content for most of the time and their religious beliefs simply enhance this happiness. Others, however, are generally unhappy and some sort of radical change must take place in their life in order for them to be happy. For a number of religious people, this has been a mystical experience: the mystical experience is their 'second birth' into a new life of happiness.

James did make it clear, however, that conversion or mystical experiences are just examples of the many ways that unity can be reached. However, he thought that the only sign that a religious experience could be from God was that it resulted in a 'good disposition', but this would have value and meaning only for the person concerned. James said that religious experiences were real for those who experienced them, but he also looked at how they were similar to other experiences, such as dreams and hallucinations.

In the concluding chapter of *The Varieties of Religious Experience* he suggests that the cause of religious experiences lies in a deep and as yet not understood part of the subconscious mind:

> It is one of the peculiarities of invasions from the subconscious region to take on objective appearances and to suggest to the Subject an external control . . . it is primarily the higher faculties of our own hidden mind which are controlling, the sense of union with the power beyond us is a sense of something, not merely apparently, but literally true.
>
> (James, *Varieties of Religious Experience*)

James concluded that religious experiences on their own do not prove God's existence, although they can suggest the existence of '*something larger*':

> I feel bound to say that religious experience, as we have studied it, cannot be cited as unequivocally supporting the infinitist belief. The only

thing that it unequivocally testifies to is that we can experience union with something larger than ourselves and in that union find our greatest peace.

(James, *Varieties of Religious Experience*)

Thus, although James thought that religious experiences were 'psychological phenomena', he did not consider that this was an argument against the existence of God – this possibility he leaves open. He does, however, conclude that religious experiences lead to a new enthusiasm for life and often lead to profound and significant changes, such as a sense of peace and security, and of great love for others.

Responses to James' ideas

- It is true that religious experiences are very similar to the effects of hallucinogenic drugs. William James himself recorded examples of people who experienced mystical states after having taken anaesthetic drugs, such as ether. Many these experiences sounded similar to experiences of God had by people who had spent years meditating or in deep states of prayer. However, Robert Charles Zaehner, former MI6 agent and taker of psychoactive drugs, argued that there is a difference between theistic mysticism and non-theistic mysticism. The former is where the mystic returns to the ground of his being, God. The latter is where the mystic simply unites with his or her own self: in other words, the mystic achieves the unity of the divided self, not union with God.
- Abraham Maslow went further: he attempted to prove spiritual experiences were just a fact of the human mind. Maslow described something called 'peak experience' and he collected examples from a wide range of different people from different cultures and times. Maslow argued they have common features, such as a feeling of transcending the universe, loss of sense of space and time and the person being flooded with feelings of awe, wonder, joy, love and gratitude. For Maslow, these feelings were generated by the mind and were then interpreted as spiritual by the person having them or by the society around them.
- James argued that religious experiences are the main source of religious belief. However, many psychologists and sociologists say that religious experiences happen only to people who are already members of a religious tradition. However, this does not explain why some people who have no connection with any religious tradition also have religious experiences.
- J.L. Mackie argued that religious experiences have no authority if they can be explained psychologically. Mackie also argued that people

interpret experiences in the light of 'cultural conditioning'. In other words, people believe that something is what they have been taught to believe it is. One of the key problems in religious experience is that people in 'Christian countries' tend to experience God/Jesus/the Virgin Mary and people in 'Hindu countries' tend to experience Brahma/Vishnu/Shiva and so forth. Either these different gods are appearing to people, or one spiritual reality is appearing and the experiencers are interpreting their experience through what they have been taught.

- In his book *Easter in Ordinary*, Nicholas Lash attacks William James' whole conception of religious experience. Lash rejects the idea that God can be experienced directly in the way that James claims. To hold this, he says, is to make religion depend on a few privileged 'pattern setters'. He wrote,

> In action and discourse patterned by the frame of reference provided by the creed, we learn to find God in all life, all freedom, all creativity and vitality, and in each particular beauty, each unexpected attainment of relationship and community . . . To speak of 'spirit' as 'God' is to ascribe all creativity and conversion, all fresh life and freedom, to divinity.
>
> (Lash, *Easter in Ordinary*, p. 267)

This view could support an understanding of religious experience whereby one learns to see the world in a religious way as a result of schooling and 'formation' into a religious tradition.

CAN RELIGIOUS EXPERIENCE BE VERIFIED?

It would appear that religious experience is far more widespread than either James or his critics would allow.

In 1969 Alister Hardy founded the Religious Experience Research Centre, which now has an archive at Lampeter University, holding 6,000 accounts of religious experiences. Hardy collected people's spiritual or religious experiences, asking what is known as 'the Hardy question': 'Have you ever been aware of or influenced by a presence or power, whether you call it God or not, which is different from your everyday self?'

Since Hardy's time there has been a growing amount of research. Surveys indicate that between a third and a half of British people claim to have had direct personal awareness of 'a power or presence different from everyday life'. Much depends on exactly what question is asked, but the figure seems to be going up: a study by David Hay in 2001 found 76% of the British population claimed awareness of a transcendent reality. Some believe the rise may reflect a change in culture: perhaps more people feel able to admit that they had spiritual experiences without thereby identifying themselves with belief systems they do not hold.

Also in 2001 Olga Pupynin and Simon Brodbeck in London asked passers-by in Trafalgar Square, 'Have you ever had an experience that you would describe as sacred, religious, spiritual, ecstatic, paranormal or mystical?' Sixty-five per cent not only answered 'yes' but also were also willing to answer further questions. The following discussion showed that these had been important events in their lives, often life-changing events, and they were grateful for the opportunity to talk about them. The top three categories were 'spiritual, religious and mystical'.

However, the question remains as to whether these are actually experiences of God, or simply the results of the human mind or even drugs. Can we simply accept it when someone says that he or she has had a religious experience? If religious experiences are 'all in the mind' they are still real experiences, just as someone feels pain, the pain is real, but those experiences might not necessarily point to anything: just as there is not always a physical cause of pain. In other words, someone might feel as if he or she has had an experience of God, but God might not exist and the experience might be all in the mind.

There are several main ways of trying to check that the experience is real:

1   If it results in the person's life changing for the better;
2   Whether our experiences are normally reliable;
3   Whether the religious experience is similar to other experiences we know to be religious in nature.

Richard Swinburne has in *The Existence of God* suggested the principles of credulity and testimony to add support to believing in other people's stories of religious experience.

The *principle of credulity* states,

> if (in the absence of special considerations) it seems to a subject that x is present, then probably x is present. And similarly I suggest that . . . if it seems to a subject that in the past he perceived something or did something then (in the absence of special considerations) probably he did.

In other words, if it seems to people that they have experienced something (including God) then they probably did. Swinburne argued that, in general, we have good reason to believe what a person tells us is correct. So if someone tells us that he or she can see a robin in the garden, we believe them, even if we have not seen the robin.

We do, however, need to consider what Swinburne means by 'special considerations'. He suggests five reasons why we might not believe someone:

1   The person claiming to have experienced God has a generally faulty perception, or his or her perception is generally faulty when under the influence of hallucinogenic drugs.
2   The person claiming to have experienced God cannot reproduce the claim in similar circumstances. For example the person claims to have read normal-sized print at 100 metres, yet in all other circumstances where the person tries to read normal print at 100 metres, he or she cannot do so.
3   The person claiming to have experienced God has not had the type of experience necessary to show that the person knows what he or she is talking about. For example someone who claims to be tasting tea who has never tasted tea before might be argued to be making false testimony: how could this person possibly know what tea is?
4   The object the person claims to have perceived, based on other evidence, probably was not present.
5   Although the person claiming to have experienced God believed that God was there, God was probably not the cause of the experience: Swinburne gave the example of seeing twins: you could think you saw John and later discover it was his identical twin brother.

It could be argued that Swinburne's principle of credulity does not overcome the problem that even though we might think that we are experiencing God, we are in fact having another type of experience and claiming that it is God: the arguments from psychology you will look at later can be used here. Also, Swinburne uses our experience of everyday objects, such as tables and chairs, and people to argue that if something seems to be there, it probably is. That said, it is one thing to move from testimonies about things that we have regular interaction with in the physical world to testimonies about beings possibly beyond it. If someone claimed that there was a robin in the garden and that the person making the claim is quite sane and is basing the testimony on regular experiences of robins, but if that same person claimed to have experienced God, I would wonder how someone could do that, given that he may have had little or no direct experience of God at all in his life and, even so, would have precious little to verify his experience against, apart from the teachings of religion.

To strengthen his case, Swinburne has also developed the *principle of testimony*. This is the principle that '(in the absence of special considerations) the experiences of others are (probably) as they report them.' In other words, when people tell us that something happened, it probably did. In other words, it is reasonable to believe people unless they are known liars.

With the principles of credulity and testimony, Swinburne is arguing that the two variables within a report without an event: the person telling us the story and the events that make up that story are both, probably, reliable.

Swinburne suggests that a good way of making sure of the truthfulness of someone's claim to have had a religious experience is to look at whether there are changes in that person's life. If someone claims to have witnessed or experienced God, you would think that this would change his or her life, such as St Paul's encounter with Jesus on the road to Damascus, which led to him becoming a follower of Jesus.

Swinburne does account for the fact that not everyone has religious experiences and those who do are likely to be religious as they are capable of using their religious beliefs to recognise the experience. According to Swinburne, if other evidence for God's existence is taken into account, then religious experience makes it likely that God exists. Swinburne concludes, 'On our total evidence, theism is more probable than not.'

Swinburne makes a cumulative argument and says that, taken with other evidence of God's existence, religious experience makes it likely that God exists. Flew rejects the accumulation of arguments by his 'ten leaky buckets' analogy. He claimed (30 years before Swinburne) that ten deeply flawed arguments do not make one good one. However, Caroline Franks Davies suggested that the buckets could be stacked in such a way that the holes were covered! The issue is whether the various arguments are deeply flawed or whether, taken together, they do serve to make what Basil Mitchell called a 'cumulative case'. It is important to recognise that the religious experience argument does not stand on its own – it depends on the prior probability of God's existence being established.

The fruits of the experience are one way of verifying that it is genuine. Another way that philosophers argue that the experience has genuinely taken place is that as William Alston stated, 'beliefs formed on the basis of experience possess an initial credibility by virtue of their origin.' In other words, when we believe we have experienced something, we are usually right about that belief.

Alston argues, similarly to James, that unless we can prove otherwise, experiences are generally accurate. 'Unless we accord a prima facie credibility to experiential reports, we can have no sufficient reason to trust any experiential source of beliefs' (Alston, 'Why Should There Not Be Experience of God?'). Alston concentrates on direct experiences of God which exclude, for instance, being aware of God 'through the beauties of nature, the words of the Bible or a sermon'. These experiences are most likely to be plausibly regarded as presentations of God to the individual (St Teresa says that God 'presents Himself to the soul by a knowledge brighter than the sun'). Alston also considers non-sensory experiences as, since God is held to be purely spiritual, a non-sensory experience has a greater chance of presenting God as God is than a sensory experience.

Alston rejects the limitation of the five senses suggested by Kant: 'Why should we suppose that the possibilities of experiential givenness, for human beings or otherwise, are exhausted by the powers of our five senses?' Animals, he claims, have senses wider than ours so 'why can't we envisage presentations that do not stem from the activity of any physical sense organs, as is apparently the case with mystical perception?' Alston ('Perceiving God') also discussed whether it made sense to talk about a person experiencing God and gaining knowledge from the experience. Alston argued that in normal life knowledge is gained from experience. For example if you say, 'There's a robin in the garden', then you are referring to things you have observed using your sense of sight. You are not doubted as others have had a similar experience using their sense of sight. Alston therefore asked that if many people have had a religious experience using their minds, is it right to immediately doubt what they claimed to have experienced? He claimed that if our *sense perceptions* are generally reliable, why should we not believe our senses if we have a religious experience? He said that just because an experience is unusual there is no reason to reject it as we would not reject other sense perceptions.

Alston rejected the argument that religious experiences cannot be verified, and suggested that we check things are true by making other sense observations. He suggested that other people's religious experiences are also sense observations. Alston advocates a 'perceptual model' of mystical experience – something presents itself to us. We may 'see' it differently depending on our perceptual schemes and prior assumptions, but he claims there is something that presents itself to us. Alston accepts that believers make use of their prior frameworks but claims we do this with normal experience. If he sees his house from 50,000 feet, he sees his house and he may learn something new but it would basically be as he expected his house to look. Similarly, God is experienced as believers expect God to be experienced – there is no difference between ordinary experiences and religious ones.

These arguments do not show that religious experiences are experiences of God, but they do show that religious experiences cannot be rejected out of hand as illogical and irrational. Alston's argument does not seek to prove God exists, but rather to show that if one believes in God, then it is reasonable to accept that religious experiences are from God.

However, the key problem is the word 'if' – in other words, the conclusion that God is experienced depends on one's prior beliefs. Antony Flew took up this point and proposed the vicious circle argument in opposition to the argument from religious experience. He argued that everything which we are is based on something else; x leads to y, which in itself enforces x. A religious belief, Flew said, enforces a religious experience, and vice versa.

However, this does not account for either people of one religion having religious experiences relating to different religions or people converting to a religion without having a religious experience

John Hick also supported religious experiences, claiming that they are a different way of experiencing the world from non-religious experiences. He distinguishes between the transcendent as it is in itself and the way we think of it and experience it. In itself the transcendent is outside our concepts. Whatever concept we have of God is inadequate. There is an inbuilt human capacity to be aware that the transcendent is there, but we experience it in ways which are conditioned by our culture. It all depends on the interpretation, as events which one person considers to be ordinary or natural another person may experience as showing the presence and activity of God. The religious person simply interprets things differently and so experiencing God in the world is not irrational.

Thought point

Strange experiences

- Have you ever had an experience or feeling of some power outside of yourself and your normal way of observing the world?
- If a trusted friend told you any of the following, how would you respond?
- What would you think? Explain your answers:

   ○ I experienced God last night;
   ○ I felt God's presence with me last night;
   ○ I saw an alien spacecraft fly past last night;
   ○ I saw a Martian in the field;
   ○ I saw a Yeti on the mountain;
   ○ I learned that human beings are genetically related to earthworms;
   ○ I was abducted by an alien last night;
   ○ The dream I had three months ago came true yesterday.

Thought point

Recognising religious experiences

Look up 1 Samuel 3 in the Bible. What can be learned from this story about possible difficulties in recognising a religious experience?

CHALLENGES TO RELIGIOUS EXPERIENCE ARGUMENTS

Philosophical challenges

Another philosophical problem with religious experiences is the lack of evidence that they have happened, beyond what a person says. Religious experiences may lead to noticeable changes in a person's lifestyle (think of Paul) but this shows only that the person has changed; it does not give any insight into the nature and origins of religious experience.

Religious experiences may be challenged on philosophical grounds, by simply arguing that God is not the sort of being that may be experienced. If I have an experience of something like the wind, a table or a robin, unless my senses have been impaired I know that I have experienced it. Many philosophers, such as Kant, Aquinas and Maimonides, have argued that God is simply beyond our experience, so much so that for Aquinas and Maimonides our ability just to speak of God is strictly limited. However, this did not lead them to claim that God does not exist: all three believed in God, even though Aquinas argued that in this life, it is not possible to have direct acquaintance with God, because God is ultimately beyond the world in which we live – God is transcendent. Aquinas argued that we could become acquainted only with the products of God's existence –- that is the universe and its contents. This is known as general revelation.

However, if we admit that the existence of God is possible, we should also admit that it could be possible to have some experience of God. If we argue, as Brian Davies has done in the introduction to *Philosophy of Religion*, that it is reasonable to believe that God exists, then we must *logically* accept that it is reasonable to believe that God may be experienced, or that some of his nature or attributes may be experienced, such as goodness or power, either directly (e.g. witnessing God's power in a miracle) or indirectly (e.g. witnessing God's goodness through the work of someone inspired by God to help the homeless).

Physiological challenges

An argument against religious experiences says that they have a physiological cause and are the result of physical changes in the body. It is possible that St Paul had epilepsy, which could possibly explain his experience of bright light, or that experiences claimed by teenage girls are caused by the hormonal changes at puberty.

However, much work in the last 20 years has focused on the function of various areas of the brain. Some scientists suggest that there are neuropsychological mechanisms which underlie religious experiences. They refer to the 'causal operator' and the 'holistic operator' within the brain. These seem to show up on brain scans done on meditating Buddhist monks. Just because there is a physical dimension to religious experience need not lead us to reject the experience completely. All experiences can be reduced to a series of neurological blips that show on brain scans, yet we do not doubt the reality of objects we see. Some thinkers have suggested our brains are constructed in such a way that we are almost wired up to experience God.

Richard Dawkins rejects this approach, and in his book *The God Delusion*, he tells a story from his student days. He recalls that a fellow undergraduate was camping in Scotland and claimed to have heard 'the voice of the devil – Satan himself'. In fact, it was just the call of the Manx Shearwater (or 'Devil Bird'), which has an evil-sounding voice.

For Dawkins, this highlights the key problem with personal experiences. They are often used in an appeal to God because people are ignorant of more straightforward physical or psychological explanations for what they perceive. According to Dawkins it is an argument based on ignorance.

However, it is one thing to say, 'Some religious experiences can be explained physiologically' and another to say that *all* religious experiences can be explained like this. There is no evidence that every person who has had a religious experience had an illness that can cause side effects, such as hallucinations, visions and delusions, in those who suffer.

Additionally, all experience has a biological basis. So just the fact that vision has a basis in the brain does not mean that it should be disbelieved. If religious experience has neural correlates, it could still be accurate.

Also, a religious believer can claim that if there is a God, God could work through one's physiology.

Psychological challenges

William James did believe that religious experiences could in some way come from the human subconscious; he did not believe this was an argument against God's existence.

Additionally, the work of Sigmund Freud has led some to suggest that religious experiences are a result of human psychology. This could explain why religious experiences occur in different cultures and throughout history.

Freud considered religion to be a neurosis as he observed that mentally ill patients displayed obsessive behaviour. These he thought were similar to religious practices and worship.

For Freud religion was an *illusion* – it simply expressed what people wanted to believe and met their psychological needs. Religion, he thought, came from a childlike desire for a God who resembles a father figure. This would suggest that religious experiences are a product of desire for a father figure. Religious experiences are hallucinations. Just as dreams are caused by deep desires we are unaware of, religious experiences are caused by the desire for security.

Replies to Freud

- Even today medical professionals do not completely understand the relationship between the mind and the body, let alone the conscious and unconscious mind.
- Again a religious believer can claim that if there is a God, God could work through one's psyche.
- Michael Palmer criticises Freud, asking how the Oedipus complex applies to religions where people believe in multiple gods. He says that in Freud's argument '*All evidence is discredited*.'
- Not all psychologists reject religious experience. Carl Gustav Jung accepted the reality of numinous experiences and argued that development of the spiritual aspect of us was essential to psychological wholeness. He claimed that each of us has the archetype (idea) of God within a shared collective unconscious.

Sociological challenges

Some sociologists claimed that the origins of religion and religious experience are to be found in society. A religious experience thus reflects the society and religious tradition in which someone lives.

Karl Marx challenged religious claims and considered that religion was a form of 'alienation' from one's true self. Religion simply took people away from the reality of their own lives – he called religion 'the opiate of the people' – it was like a drug that stopped people facing the reality of their lives and was a form of oppression and control.

For Marx the institution of the Church controlled people's behaviour and was part of the class-divided society that kept working people oppressed and exploited. He considered the teaching of reward in heaven and punishment in hell gave people comfort of a better life and punishment for those who oppressed them.

Marx's views were obviously shaped by the realities of life in the nineteenth century, arguing that the poverty of so many people was exacerbated by the Church as it encouraged people to keep to the status quo of society.

According to Marx, religious experience is simply the result of the society in which a person lived and his or her religious beliefs – it was not something that came from God but from the beliefs and teachings of the Church.

Replies to Marx

- Karl Marx never really understood that religion is not merely a product of society and for many religion is not simply a drug but a relationship with God.
- Religion has not been just a method of control but also a force for change in society. Martin Luther King Jr fought for black people's civil rights in the USA and his belief in equality came from his Christian faith.
- Marx's argument was proposed in a time in which many religious organisations were corrupt, which arguably does not always apply to modern world religion.

CONFLICTING CLAIMS

David Hume's argument that the conflicting claims of miracles in different religious traditions cancel each other out can be used to oppose religious experience as well. He simply argued that two opposing religious experiences cancel one another out and discredit them. He called this 'A triumph for the sceptic'.

Believers from many different religions claim to have experienced God, and while there are some similarities between these experiences, there are also differences – for example a Christian may claim to see Mary and a Hindu to see Lakshmi.

These differences can be explained by the prior beliefs of the person, and in any attempt to describe an ineffable experience the individual will naturally use his or her own culture and belief system. It could be argued that all religious experiences come from the same God but are simply interpreted differently.

Also, two conflicting religious experiences still leave the possibility of one being correct.

CONCLUSION: DO RELIGIOUS EXPERIENCES DEMONSTRATE THE EXISTENCE OF GOD?

Many people have religious experiences, which are similar despite occurring to very different people in very different circumstances. The best explanation of these experiences, and their common nature, is that they are genuine experiences of something divine. Therefore, God exists.

Many philosophers have argued that, taken with other arguments for God's existence, religious experience suggests that it is likely that God exists. It is true that the argument for the existence of God based on religious experience works better as a probability rather than a proof (which Swinburne would have agreed with). The existence of the world, and the way in which it is fine-tuned and ordered, as well as the existence of human consciousness and the apparent experience by so many of the presence of God, all make it more probable than not that there is a God (Swinburne, *Is There a God?*).

Religious experiences are a clear proof of God's existence for those who have direct experience. However, as James said, this does not extend to other people and so a philosophical proof of God's existence based on religious experience is not possible.

Religious experiences seem to depend so much on a person's prior beliefs. As Alston pointed out, if someone believes in God then it is rational to believe that people have religious experiences of God. Additionally, Swinburne argued that an account of a direct religious experience of God should be accepted for what it is, unless there is a good reason to not believe what the person is saying.

In the light of all this, it is very difficult to argue conclusively that the object of a religious experience is an objectively existing supernatural power that many people call God. However, we must take James' point seriously that religious experiences are absolutely authoritative for the subject. For people who claim to have had religious, spiritual or mystical experiences, whether the result of prayer, discipline or psychoactive drugs, these people very often believe the experiences to be life-changing, and for many, their lives do permanently change for the better. As St Francis of Assisi said, 'for every tree is known by its fruits'.

It would seem that religious experience as an 'argument for the existence of God' is applicable only for the individual concerned. As with all philosophical arguments that attempt to prove the existence of God, this argument may well do much to strengthen the existing faith of the believer.

SUMMARY

1   Types of religious experience

Classification

Direct experiences
> Rudolph Otto – the 'numinous', mysterium tremendum et fascinans, wholly other
> William James – the individual's experience of the 'divine'

Indirect experiences
Experiences where the mind of an individual focuses on God

Richard Swinburne

Public experiences
> Ordinary experiences
> Extraordinary experiences

Private experiences
> Describable in ordinary language
> Non-describable experiences
> Non-specific experiences

Vision experiences

God is 'seen' or 'observed'
Three types of visions:
Intellectual vision
Corporeal vision
Imaginative vision

Voices

The communication of knowledge from God
Characteristics:
> The voice is disembodied
> The voice is authoritative

2   Corporate religious experiences

Several people have the experience or witness it – for example Fatima,
> Toronto Blessing

3   Conversion

Can be dramatic – for example St Paul
Can be gradual
Leads to a change of beliefs and lifestyle

Teresa of Ávila's criteria for assessing the validity of a religious experience

Does the religious experience fit in with Christian Church teaching?
Does the experience leave the person feeling at peace with the world
> and God?

William James

Characteristics of mystical experience:
> Ineffable
> Noetic

Karl Marx
Everett Historical/ Shutterstock

Transient
Passive

Authority of the experience: only for the individual who has it

4 Challenges to religious experience arguments

Richard Swinburne

Principle of credulity
Principle of testimony

Philosophical challenge
God is transcendent and cannot be experienced by humans.

Physiological challenges
Caused by biology – comes from the brain or from illness

Psychological challenges

Suggestion that religious experiences are a product of human psychology

Freud
Religion is an illusion.
Religion expresses people's desires.
Religion originates from a childlike desire for a God who resembles a father figure.

Sociological challenges

The origins of religious experience are to be found in society.

Karl Marx
Religion is about mythological beliefs and an unreal god that distracted people from the real world.
Religion is 'the opiate of the people'.
Religious experiences create alienation.
A religious experience could be the product of the desperate situation in which a person lived.

REVIEW QUESTIONS

1   Outline William James' understanding of religious experience.
2   Why would a follower of Freud or Marx reject religious experience as evidence of God's existence?

continued opposite

3 If a friend told you he or she had seen God, how would you react to and assess what this friend told you?

4 Do you think religious experiences are veridical? Explain your answer with reasons.

Terminology

Try to explain the following ideas without looking at your books and notes:

- Noetic
- Transient
- Ineffable
- Authority
- Passive
- Indirect and direct experiences
- The principle of testimony
- The principle of credulity.

Examination questions practice

'ARGUMENTS FROM RELIGIOUS EXPERIENCE ARE NEVER CONVINCING.' DISCUSS.

AO1 (15 marks)

You would need to explain the types of religious experiences using the work of Swinburne and William James. You might consider conversion, mystical experiences and/or corporate religious experiences.

AO2 (15 marks)

- You might begin by asking for whom are the religious experiences supposed to be convincing – the individual concerned or other people?

- You could discuss the fact that religious experiences have validity only for the person involved or that that the most likely people to have religious experiences are those who are already religious.

- You could evaluate the challenges to religious experience given by Freud and Marx. You could also evaluate the physiological challenges.

- You could argue in favour of religious experience arguments by referring to the arguments of philosophers such as Alston and

Swinburne. You could also discuss the fact that religious experiences lead many people to lead better lives or to completely change them.

Further possible questions

- 'A human being cannot have an experience of God.' Discuss.

- 'Religious experiences are simply delusions.' Discuss.
- Critically assess the idea of William James in explaining religious experiences.

FURTHER READING

Alston, W.P. 1999. 'Perceiving God', in *Philosophy of Religion: The Big Questions*, Stump, E., et al. (eds). Oxford: Blackwell.

Alston, W.P. 2000. 'Why Should There Not Be Experience of God?' in *Philosophy of Religion, a Guide and Anthology*, Davies, B. (ed.). Oxford: OUP.

Davies, B. 1997. *God, Reason and Theism*. Edinburgh: Edinburgh University Press.

Hay, D. 1990. *Religious Experience Today*. Mowbray: Continuum International.

Hick, J. 1964. *The Existence of God*. New York: Palgrave Macmillan.

James, W. *The Varieties of Religious Experience: A Study in Human Nature*. London: Penguin Classics.

Mackie, J. 1982. *The Miracle of Theism*. Oxford: OUP.

Palmer, M. 2001. *The Question of God*. London: Routledge.

Swinburne, R. 1991. *The Existence of God*. Oxford: OUP.

Vardy, P. 1990. *The Puzzle of God*. London: Fount Paperbacks.

God and the world

7 The problem of evil

WHAT YOU WILL LEARN ABOUT IN THIS CHAPTER

The problem of evil and suffering:

- logical and evidential aspects
- the theodicies of Augustine, Irenaeus and Hick's use of original perfection and the Fall.

THE OCR CHECKLIST

The problem of evil

- the problem of evil and suffering:
  - different presentations
    - including its logical (the inconsistency between divine attributes and the presence of evil) and evidential (the evidence of so much terrible evil in the world) aspects
  - theodicies that propose some justification or reason for divine action or inaction in the face of evil
    - Augustine's use of original perfection and the Fall
    - Hick's reworking of the Irenaean theodicy which gives some purpose to natural evil in enabling human beings to reach divine likeness.

Learners should have the opportunity to discuss issues related to the problem of evil, including:

- whether Augustine's view of the origins of moral and natural evils is enough to spare God from blame for evils in the world

continued overleaf

○   whether the need to create a 'vale of soul-making' can justify the existence or extent of evils
○   which of the logical or evidential aspects of the problem of evil pose the greater challenge to belief
○   whether it is possible to successfully defend monotheism in the face of evil.

For many people, acts of wickedness and evil in the world and the suffering caused by natural disasters are the strongest arguments against belief in God. Discuss with others what the problem of evil is for a religious believer like a Jew, Christian or Muslim.

1   Write up your answer as a set of questions.
2   Can you think of any answers or solutions to the questions you have thought of?

Some clues:

1   Think about what the traditional qualities of God are.
2   Study the pictures on this page. Use the pictures to help you work out what the problem of evil is.

One major problem faced by most of the world's most well-known religions is the question of how the particular God that they worship can allow the amount of evil that is in the world and whether that God should take responsibility for it. This has gradually become known as the problem of evil, and is often presented as an argument against the existence of God, although it is more properly an argument concerning the nature of God.

The problem of evil says that God, being all-powerful (omnipotent), all-knowing (omniscient) and also all-places (omnipresent), has the ability to end evil. God should want to put an end to evil and suffering as he is also all-god – omnibenevolent. Thus God has the motive and the ability to ensure that there is no suffering or evil taking place under His ever watchful eye. But evil still exists.

Theodicy

A philosophical attempt to solve the problem of evil.

A DEFINITION OF THE PROBLEM OF EVIL

A definition of the problem of evil was put forward by the Greek philosopher Epicurus over 2,000 years ago and again by David Hume:

Is God willing to prevent evil, but not able to? Then he is not omnipotent.
Is God able to prevent evil, but not willing to? Then he is malevolent (evil).
Is God able to prevent evil and willing to? Then why is there evil?

Mackie called this the *inconsistent triad*, which shows that it appears impossible to marry both the existence of evil with the existence of God, bearing in mind his characteristics.

Evil exists

God is all-powerful   God is all-loving

The same problem still challenges human beings today.

The problem, as set out by Epicurus, highlights the difficulties that the problem of evil raises for the religious believer. It questions God's omnipotence, God's goodness and God's omniscience.

There are possible solutions to this problem, but they also cause problems:

- weakening the status of God makes the existence of evil easier to account for, but also makes it harder to ascribe the name 'God'.
- God exists only in the language of believers. Talk of God is a way of affirming religious belief. God is not therefore an external reality, so God cannot take responsibility for evil.
- Rather than change God's goalposts, move evil's. Christian Scientists claim that evil is an illusion of the mind – the problem of evil is only an apparent problem.

Evil can be categorised as follows:

- *Natural or physical evil*, such as natural disasters and cruelty in the natural world. Most philosophers today would argue that natural evils are caused by the way the natural world works.
- *Moral evil* is the evil that comes from the actions of humans. People are free agents, responsible for their actions and the consequent results.

Omnipotent

Literally means 'all-powerful'. It is used as a characteristic of God.

Omniscient

Literally means 'all-knowing'. Like omnipotent, it is used as a characteristic of God.

Thought point

Are the terms 'natural evil' and 'moral evil' easy to apply?

Study the list ahead and decide which ones are natural evils and which ones are moral evils. Make a bullet point list of the causes of each event referred to.

1   A hurricane flooding a town, leading to hundreds of people drowning
2   An earthquake destroying a city
3   A man robbing a bank
4   A paranoid schizophrenic stabbing a woman
5   Becoming infected with HIV after receiving a tainted blood transfusion
6   Killing a person when he or she steps out in front of your car. It was impossible to foresee the accident happening
7   A person dying of hunger because he or she has no money
8   and no one gave them food or help
9   Suffering from hepatitis caught from injecting yourself with heroin using a dirty needle.

WHY THE EXISTENCE OF EVIL CHALLENGES BELIEF IN GOD

The whole 'problem of evil' is based on some basic religious assumptions:

- that the world can be understood rationally
- that there is an overall meaning and purpose to everything that happens
- that there is a single underlying reality – a good or loving God
- that God has a direct and absolute control over individual events.

Now, the problem only really applies to theism – the belief in one God who is the creator of the world, infinite, perfect, omnipotent and omniscient.

For many people evil and suffering in the world are the greatest challenges to belief in the existence of this God. This argument has been proposed by many philosophers, including J.L. Mackie and Anthony Flew.

If God is all-powerful why does God not prevent evil?

This challenge to the existence of God is sometimes called the *'logical problem'*. J.L. Mackie said it was a logical problem because theists have to show that their beliefs make sense and are logical. Mackie said that if God is actually omnipotent then God has power over 'causal laws' (Mackie, *The Miracle of Theism: Arguments for and Against the Existence of God*) – by this he means the physical laws of the universe. Why then does God not stop evil if he has the power to do so?

The amount of evil in the world appears to challenge the goodness of creation

Richard Dawkins pointed out that there is a tremendous amount of suffering in the natural world, and even religious believers find it difficult to defend that the natural world is good in the face of the existence of evil and suffering. Nature is neither good nor evil – it simply exists to pass on genes to the next generation and is used to support ideas of creation being good and having been made by God.

Humans also inflict great evil and suffering on one another – for example war, rape, torture and other forms of abuse.

How can an omnipotent God allow such actions? These challenges are put forward by Dostoevsky in his book *The Brothers Karamazov*. One of the characters, Ivan, rebels against God because of the suffering of innocent young children, which he says cannot be justified. He says,

> Listen! If all must suffer to pay for the eternal harmony, what have children to do with it, tell me, please? It's beyond all comprehension why they should suffer, and why they should pay for the harmony. Why should they, too, furnish material to enrich the soil for the harmony of the future?
>
> (Dostoevsky, *The Brothers Karamazov*)

For Ivan it is never right to allow evil so that good may come, so he is saying that nothing can justify God allowing evil, nor is it possible to believe in a good God who allows evil and the suffering of the innocent. He concludes that it would be better if the world did not exist at all than have a world which included the suffering of children.

It could be argued that children learn by making mistakes and sometimes this causes suffering, such as learning not to touch hot things because they burn you, but this does not mean we need all the range of suffering that occurs in the world.

Free will

The ability to make one's own decisions and choose freely between different possible courses of action.

Thought point

The Brothers Karamazov

If you have the time, read *The Brothers Karamazov*, by Dostoevsky. Alternatively, an good discussion of the passages of the book which concern the problem of evil may be found in *The Puzzle of Evil* by Peter Vardy.

Mackie argues that evil committed by humans is the price of having free will. However, he then suggests that if God is omnipotent, he could have made humans who always freely choose what is good (Mackie, *The Miracle of Theism: Arguments for and Against the Existence of God*). However, Mackie's view means that free will is limited if people cannot choose what is bad.

An additional problem is that evil and suffering seem to affect both good people and bad people. This again does not support the belief in a just and good God.

Thought point

Is suffering of any benefit?

A rare genetic condition causes children to be born with an inability to feel pain. What are the possible advantages and disadvantages of such a condition?

Thought point

Nature: good, bad or indifferent

Read the passages ahead and then answer the questions which follow.

Text 1

And God said, 'Let the earth bring forth living creatures of every kind: cattle and creeping things and wild animals of the earth of every kind.' And

continued opposite

it was so. God made the wild animals of the earth of every kind, and the cattle of every kind, and everything that creeps upon the ground of every kind. And God saw that it was good . . .

So God created humankind in his image, in the image of God he created them; male and female he created them . . .

God saw everything that he had made, and indeed, it was very good. And there was evening and there was morning, the sixth day.

(Genesis 1:24, 25, 27, 31a)

Text 2

As we shall see, nature is not cruel, only pitilessly indifferent. This is one of the hardest lessons for humans to learn. We cannot admit that things might be neither good nor evil, cruel nor kind, but simply callous – indifferent to all suffering, lacking all purpose.

(Richard Dawkins, *River Out of Eden: A Darwinian View of Life*)

Questions

- Which text presents a more accurate picture of the world?
- Make a list of any evidence that supports the claims of each text.
- Which text appeals more to you?
- Would you teach the ideas presented in these texts to your children (if you had any)?
- In your opinion:
  - Did God make the earth?
  - Is nature pitilessly indifferent?

THEODICY

Theodicy is the word used by religious believers for their explanations of how belief in a good, omnipotent God can be maintained in the face of all the evil and suffering present in the world. The word 'theodicy' comes from two Greek words: *theos* (meaning 'God') and *dikaios* (meaning 'justification'). So a theodicy is about justifying belief in God, even though evil and suffering exist.

Evil: a problem to be endured or solved?

The problem of evil as expressed by Epicurus, Hume and the Inconsistent Triad is often explained as follows:

1   Evil is caused by people's free will.
2   Evil is a means by which people develop moral qualities, such as compassion.
3   Evil can be explained if we have a different understanding of the nature of God.

Attempting to justify a good God in the face of evil is known as a theodicy, and the approaches that are studied in this chapter focus on the first two foregoing explanations. The third solution is not studied in this chapter but can be found in the further reading section.

Theodicies are intellectual and rational explanations of how evil exists and God remains good, but these responses are very different from actually facing and coping with evil and suffering.

AUGUSTINE'S THEODICY

The creation stories in Genesis 1–3 influenced Augustine's theodicy. It is often claimed that Augustine interpreted the creation stories literally, but in *The Literal Meaning of Genesis*, Augustine argued that the first two chapters of Genesis were written to suit the understanding of the people at that time. In order to communicate in a way that all people could understand, the creation story was told in a simpler, allegorical fashion. Augustine was influenced by the Platonists and believed that God created everything in an instant, but also that this creation was not static; the world has the capacity to develop, a view that is harmonious with biological evolution. Augustine understood the stories as mythological, communicating values and meaning.

McGrath sums up Augustine's Creation thoughts thus:

First, Augustine does not limit God's creative action to the primordial act of origination. God is, he insists, still working within the world, directing its continuing development and unfolding its potential. There are two 'moments' in the Creation: a primary act of origination, and a continuing process of providential guidance. Creation is thus not a completed past event. God is working even now, in the present, Augustine writes, sustaining and directing the unfolding of the 'generations that he laid up in creation when it was first established.'

(McGrath 2011a, p. 219)

Much of Augustine's writing was a rejection of Manichaeism, which had fascinated him in his youth. Manichaeism had no problem with the existence of evil as it saw the whole of matter as evil and the purpose of salvation was to redeem humans from this evil matter and transfer to a spiritual realm. Augustine could not accept this approach and saw both creation and redemption as actions of God, and so it was not possible to blame creation for the existence of evil as God created a good world. Evil, according to Augustine, was a consequence of the misuse of human free will.

Free will

Augustine's explanation of the problem of evil centres on free will and attempts to account for the suffering brought about by natural disasters and diseases as well as the evil that humans choose to do. According to Augustine the story of the Fall in Genesis when Adam and Eve chose to turn against God and sinned had two key consequences:

- It meant that human nature became corrupted so that every generation would inherit their sin. This is the doctrine of original sin.
- It also corrupted God's creation. Natural evil, such as disease and natural disasters, did not exist before the Fall and so they are also a result of the misuse of free will.

Augustine believed literally that human beings are made in the image and likeness of God, which meant that human beings are not just physical creatures but also spiritual. Christians usually interpret this as meaning that human beings are capable of rational thought (unlike animals), and this is a God-like quality. However, all suffering is a result of human sin and God could have prevented this only by denying free will. Augustine considered that it is better to have free will despite the consequences, but God also offers humans redemption and release from the suffering they have caused. Jesus' death atones for the misuse of free will. Christ freely chose ultimate goodness to redress the balance after humans chose evil. God experiences suffering through Jesus Christ to identify with humans and to suffer in our place. At the end of time, we will be judged. Good will be rewarded and evil punished, both in an afterlife. The good will experience eternal happiness, and the evil will receive their just punishment.

However, the question remains as to how humans could have chosen evil if God had not made it possible for humans to choose it. Augustine attempts to solve this dilemma by saying that it all originated from Satan – a fallen angel who was originally created good but chose to rebel against God. Augustine did not explain the original fall of this good angel. Additionally, if Augustine considered the biblical creation stories to be mythical, so that Adam and Eve never existed and the Fall never literally happened, then they cannot be used to explain the suffering caused by natural diseases and disasters.

Sharing in Adam's sin

Augustine argued that all human beings were present in Adam's sin. This idea comes from Paul, who wrote that 'Therefore, just as sin came into the world through one man, and death came through sin, and so death spread to all because all have sinned' (Romans 5:12). What Augustine meant is that all human beings are descended from Adam and Eve and all share in the consequences of Adam and Eve's sin. In Christian theology all people are said to share in Adam's sin because they were 'seminally present' in Adam; thus everyone is born into this disharmonious world.

THE THEODICY OF AUGUSTINE: KEY IDEAS

1   *God*: God the Creator is omnipotent and good.
2   *Good creation*: Creation is good and reflects the perfection of God.
3   *Hierarchy of beings*: Angels, humans, animals.
4   *Privation*: Evil is a privation or lack of goodness in something.
5   *The Fall*: Angels and human beings fall through their own free choice. Adam and Eve are tempted and as a result sin and death enter the world.
6   *Moral and natural evil*: Adam and Eve's disobedience brought about 'disharmony' in both humanity and Creation.
7   *Original sin*: The whole of humanity experiences this disharmony because we were all 'seminally present' in the loins of Adam.
8   *Free will*: Free will is valuable so God sustains a world within which moral and natural evil occurs. God is justified in not intervening because the suffering is a consequence of human action.
9   *Aesthetic value*: The existence of evil highlights the goodness of creation because of the contrast between good and evil.

Privation and evil

Augustine solves the problem of saying God is responsible for evil in the world by defining evil as a 'privation'. Augustine did not want to say that God was the cause of evil. Neither did he wish to say that evil was not some kind of a reality. He knew very well from his own experience that evil was a real factor in his own life as well as in the lives of others. Disharmony is introduced into creation by the choice to rebel. This introduces evil. Augustine believed that since everything in Creation was created by God, evil could not be a substance. If evil were a substance, God would have had to create it, and this would not be logical. For Augustine, evil was therefore 'privation', or a lack of something – evil comes about when a part of creation leaves its proper path and ceases do what it was created to do. For example the eye is created to be perfectly good and blindness is a malfunction of the eye. Blindness is therefore not a 'thing' but a state or a condition. Free will, good in itself, has been corrupted by choosing evil.

Augustine's idea of evil as a privation also applies to human beings: if you say that a human being is evil, or that his or her actions are evil, you are saying that the way he or she behaves does not match expectations about how a human being should behave. For example if someone racially abuses, robs or tortures people, he is not living up to the standards expected of humans. It is falling short of what a human should be that is wrong.

By this solution Augustine affirmed that God was the creator of good while at the same time affirming that evil is a kind of reality. It is not a full reality or being; rather it is a privation whose cause is the will of man.

Thus, Augustine said that *'evil comes from God'* because God causes to exist and keeps in existence human beings who have free will and, of course, human beings can become evil through their free choices.

Augustine stated that nobody can be completely evil because to be evil you have to lack goodness, which means you had goodness to start with. Even the devil has some good in him. Talking about all God had created, Augustine said, *'It was obvious to me that things which are liable to corruption are good . . . If there were no good in them there would be nothing capable of being corrupted'* (Augustine, *Confessions*).

Augustine's theodicy

Augustine did not write a book that he called a 'theodicy'. Instead, many of his writings include comments relevant to this topic. So although people refer to the Augustinian theodicy, what they are really referring to is a collection of ideas linked to the writings of Augustine.

Privation

Means something is lacking a particular thing that it should have. Augustine gave the example of 'blindness'. He called this a privation, because if you are blind it means that you are unable to see – in other words you lack the attribute of sight.

Thought point

Evil and privation

Is evil a 'privation' or 'lack' of something? What do you think?

Thought point

What does the word 'inhuman' mean?

Describing someone as inhuman, or his or her behaviour as inhuman, comes from the idea of evil being a privation. Consider what the link is.

Thought point

Is God to blame for evil?

Augustine made the following comment about evil:

> 'I thought it better to believe that you had created no evil . . . rather than to believe that the nature of evil, as I understood it, came from you' (Augustine, *Confessions*).

Discuss:

1   What Augustine believed at first (in italics in the foregoing quote)
2   What he believed later (underlined in the foregoing quote)
3   Why do you think he changed his mind?

Harmony

Refers to objects existing in an ordered way together or living creatures existing in a state of peace and happiness with each other.

The Fall

Refers to the story of Adam and Eve in the Garden of Eden and their disobeying of God. It can be read in Genesis 2:4 to 3:1 of the Bible.

Original sin

A reference to the first sin of Adam in the Garden of Eden and its effects, according to traditional Christian beliefs.

Thought point

The Genesis stories

Read the two creation stories in Genesis, chapters 1–3, and make a comparison of them.

Thought point

Experiment

Buy a packet of sweets and eat one of them. Try to describe the sweets to people without giving them a sweet. Then give them a sweet. How accurate was your description?

Why create creatures with free will?

Augustine believed that free will matters so much that he argued that allowing evil to happen is a price worth paying for human freedom. This means that God allows evil and suffering.

Additionally, if there was no free will it would remove not only the bad choices that people make but also their good choices.

Augustine also argued that when the creation (universe) is viewed as a whole, the contrast between what is good and what is bad highlights the beauty of goodness. This is called the *aesthetic principle* by some philosophers.

To complete his ideas on the existence of evil, Augustine's writings also suggest that evil is evil only from a human perspective. In God's sight everything is good. Augustine said the universe is like a work of art – some might not look too good when seen in isolation, but they are a necessary part of the whole work and contribute to its beauty. Thus, what humans see as evil is necessary for the beauty of the whole world as God sees it.

CRITICISMS OF AUGUSTINE'S THEODICY

- How can something perfect go wrong? Why should creatures living in a perfect world choose to rebel? There is also the problem of the existence of angels, for whom there is no convincing evidence. In his book *Evil and the God of Love*, John Hick suggests that Augustine's theodicy is implausible for modern people.

  Augustine explained that what went wrong was less than perfect. But creating a universe with imperfections makes evil God's fault, and humans are therefore being punished for what is God's fault.
- Modern theories of creation, such as the theory of evolution, seem to disprove Augustine. There is no room for the development of a moral sense. Natural disasters shaped the planet long before there were humans to punish. By the same token, the stories of the Garden of Eden and the fall of the archangel Lucifer appear to have no place in a modern view of the world.

  Augustine's belief in a perfect world that is then spoilt by evil cannot be accepted as true in any literal sense. Is Augustine speaking in mythological terms? This does not make his theodicy untrue: a myth seeks to give understanding to a spiritual truth. The apparent lack of historical truth in the story of Adam and Eve does not mean that the principle is not true. There is room for evolution in the myth of Adam and Eve.

  Augustine claimed that everyone shares in the effects of the Fall because they were 'seminally present' in the loins of Adam. Modern science

Augustine and free will

Augustine's theodicy emphasises the fact that human beings and angels choose whether to live in harmony with God. This is a free will defence of the problem of evil.

Original sin

Original sin is defined in many ways by Christian thinkers, but one interpretation is to define it as the inbuilt tendency humans have to do things wrong despite their good intentions. The concept of original sin comes from interpretations of the Genesis story.

indicates that each person is a unique individual who inherits half of his or her DNA from his or her mother and half from his or her father. Augustine's ideas rely on an ancient understanding of biology according to which people existed before conception. Given today's understanding, it would appear unjust if God then punishes later human beings for the first human being's sin as they could not have been 'seminally present' in Adam.

- Over the centuries, philosophers such as Schleiermacher (1768–1834) have questioned why a perfect world would go wrong. If angels were created to live in the presence of God, why would one turn against him?

- Also there seems to be something illogical in the account – if God is all-knowing, he surely knew that Adam and Eve would 'fall'. It is therefore hard to accept the role of an all-loving God in a brutal universe given this point.

  The classic response to this argument is to say that God wishes to enter in a 'loving relationship' with people and this is possible only in a situation of total freedom – there can be no compulsion. A world populated by people compelled to love God would be a world of robots – a non-moral world.

  However, if everything depends on God for its existence, then God must be causally involved in free human actions. Do we really have free will?

- Augustine argued for a world in which God is responsible for everything and that suffering is a punishment for the sin of Adam, but Christians believe in a merciful and kind God. Augustine's response was that God was merciful because he sent Jesus to save people. Mackie responded that God could have made people who freely chose the good. Or he could have created a world with less suffering.

  Alvin Plantinga (*God, Freedom and Evil*, 1974) argued that it is logically impossible for God to create another being that always freely performs only good actions. If God to caused them to do good they would not be free. Others have argued along different lines, pointing out that even if it is logically possible, not everything logically possible is equally achievable. Love cannot be programmed. The fact that heaven is pictured as containing people who will never sin suggests that perhaps God could have created such beings on earth. However, people have chosen to be in heaven, which may mean some restrictions on free will as a result.

- Augustine's view of evil as a privation can also be challenged. It is not sufficient to say that it is a lack or absence of good. Many would argue that it is a real entity.

THE IRENAEAN THEODICY

Irenaeus was a bishop during the earliest stages of the development of Christian theology, and one of the most important Greek fathers of the early Church. He is one of the first Christians to attempt to explain Christian beliefs in an organised way. His greatest work is called *On the Detection and Overthrow of the So-called Gnosis – 'Against the Heresies'*, which explains Christian beliefs. Like Augustine, Irenaeus was keen to refute what he saw as heretical ideas. The Gnostics believed that matter was inherently evil and so it would be impossible for a good God to create it. Additionally, Jesus could not have had a physical body as this also would be inherently evil. Irenaeus intended to show that everything came from God and, therefore, he had to explain the existence of evil in the role and even give evil a purpose. Like Augustine, Irenaeus argued that evil is the consequence of human free will and disobedience. However, unlike Augustine, Irenaeus believed that God was partly responsible for evil and suffering.

In general terms, the Augustinian theodicy is a *soul-deciding* theodicy. In contrast, the Irenaean theodicy is *soul-making*. In the writings of Irenaeus (130–202), there appears the idea that humans were not created perfect but are developing towards perfection.

He uses Genesis 1:26 – 'Let us make humankind in our image, according to our likeness' – to show that the purpose of humans is to develop their own soul. Creation is not yet finished. We have been made in the image of God with the potential to be like God. Irenaeus said that God had given human beings free will. This free will entailed the potential for evil. He understands Adam and Eve as almost like children who do wrong because they have not yet developed the wisdom to choose what is right. Irenaeus believed in the story of the Fall. He saw Genesis 3 as literally true and believed it showed that humans were not ready to accept God's grace or goodness as we were spiritually and morally immature. However, Irenaeus did not consider this to be original sin in the same way that Augustine did; people were simply led astray by the devil, because they were distant from God spiritually. People are like Adam and Eve in that they go astray morally because they have not yet gained the wisdom to do what is right. This is how Irenaeus approaches the problem of moral evil:

- *Natural evil* has the divine purpose to develop qualities such as compassion through the soul-making process.
- *Moral evil* is derived from human free will and disobedience.

Perfection
Another traditional characteristic or quality of God. It means that God is lacking nothing and can be no different or better.

THE IRENAEAN THEODICY: KEY IDEAS

Irenaeus the man (c. CE 130–200)

Irenaeus originated from Smyrna in Asia Minor. He was a Christian preacher and later became the bishop of Lyon, France. He died in the year 200.

1   *God*: God the Creator is omnipotent and all-good.
2   *Creation develops*: The universe and earth develop over time.
3   *Human beings are created immature*: Human beings grow from the 'image' of God into the likeness of God.
4   *Soul-making world*: The world is an environment where people grow and develop into the likeness of God. Hence, natural evil is present in it.
5   *Epistemic distance*: There is an epistemic distance between God and people so that human beings can choose freely to grow into relationship with God.
6   *Eschatological aspect*: All will come to be in the likeness of God eventually, but this will not be in physical life.
7   *Free will*: Free will is important, so God sustains a world within which moral evil and natural evil occur.

Growing into the likeness of God

Irenaeus said that Adam and Eve in the Garden of Eden are created in the 'image' and 'likeness' of God, which meant that they had free will (making them in the image of God) and are spiritual as well as physical beings (making them in the likeness of God). However, Irenaeus claimed that human beings were separate from God because they are mortal. He believed that God's gift of free will was better than receiving ready-made goodness. To back up this point he uses the example of a mother not being able to give a child 'substantial nourishment' as a baby requires milk and not solid food because he or she is immature, and in the same way humans could not be given complete goodness as they were spiritually immature and so are given free will to develop their own goodness. Humans are made in the image of God (with the potential for good) and moving towards the likeness of God (becoming good). Irenaeus believed that the gift of moral perfection would not have meant anything to human beings if they did not learn to value it for themselves. People become like God or move towards the likeness of God by freely choosing the good, but when people choose to do evil and sin then they are creating evil in the world. According to Irenaeus moral evil is caused by humans' misuse of free will. God allowed us to have this free will as it was seen as more beneficial than making ready-made perfection. The fall of humanity is seen as an inevitable part of growing up and maturing. The presence of evil helps people to grow and develop. Thus the emphasis in this theodicy is soul-making.

Irenaeus argues that

For, while promising that they [human beings] should be as gods, which was in no way possible for him [Adam] to be, he wrought death in them; wherefore he [the serpent] who had led man captive, was justly captured in turn by God; but man who had been captured, was loosed from the bonds of condemnation.

(*Against the Heresies*, Book 3; 23)

The role of suffering and evil

According to Irenaeus Adam and Eve go astray but it is not a rebellion as Augustine thought, where Adam and Eve deliberately turn away from God. Irenaeus said that God did not curse Adam and Eve in Genesis 3, but cursed the ground and the serpent. Instead Adam and Eve must suffer by working the ground and Eve will have pain in childbirth. Punishment was necessary so that Adam and Eve would not 'despise' God. Irenaeus saw punishment as educative.

Irenaeus thought that throughout their lives people changed from being human animals to 'children of God'. This is a choice made after struggle and experience as people choose God rather than their baser instincts. There are no angels or external forces at work here. God brings in suffering for the benefit of humanity, and from it humans learn positive values. Suffering and evil are:

- useful as a means of knowledge – hunger leads to pain and causes a desire to eat and to feed others. Knowledge of pain prompts humans to seek to help others in pain.
- character building – evil offers the opportunity to grow morally. If people were programmed to 'do what is good' there would be no moral value to their actions.
- the result of a predictable environment – the world runs according to a series of natural laws. These laws are independent of human needs and operate regardless of anything. Natural evil is when these laws come into conflict with humans' perceived needs. There is no moral dimension to this. However, we can be sure of things in a predictable world.

According to Irenaeus all history is overseen by God and the world has to be a hard place in which people experience suffering, so that humans can come to know God. The Old Testament prophets pointed out the right path to God, and the incarnation of God in Jesus unites humans with God once again.

Irenaeus argued that Jesus is the Saviour and the new Adam who obeys God and dies on the cross (the tree), and thus he undoes the fault of Adam, who took the forbidden fruit from the tree. As the words of the Easter Proclamation (the Exultet) say, '*O happy fault, O necessary sin of Adam, which gained for us so great a Redeemer*!'

Recapitulation

According to Irenaeus it is clear that humans cannot get to God by their own means, but need assistance. He used the example of a potter and clay to explain this and suggested in *Against Heresies* (Book 4:39–42) that humans should enable God to mould them through the existence of natural evil. It is the experience and contact with natural evil that mould people into the image of God from the likeness. Natural evil, he claims, enables people to develop good moral qualities or virtues and so grow into the 'likeness' of God.

It is therefore necessary for God to help humans achieve moral and spiritual perfection. The term 'recapitulation' is often used to describe this theodicy. It means to bring something back to the beginning – in other words people are being brought back into a relationship with God. For Irenaeus Jesus is the second Adam who makes this recapitulation possible. Jesus allows us to create a relationship with God that we were not ready to enter into at the beginning of creation; through his death on the cross Jesus links God and humans as he is both divine and human.

God, therefore, is justified in allowing moral and natural evil because natural evil is seen as an instrument for God's purpose in enabling humans to move into the likeness of God. However, while Irenaeus did seem to suggest that salvation is open to all, he did believe that only those who accepted God would be saved and the others would be damned. He did believe some form of soul-making would continue in the next life so that souls could complete their transformation into the likeness of God, but not for the damned who rejected God and followed the devil, who will be punished:

> It is therefore one and the same God the Father who has prepared good things with Himself for those who desire His fellowship, and who remain in subjection to Him; and who has the eternal fire for the ring-leader of the apostasy, the devil, and those who revolted with him, into which [fire] the Lord has declared those men shall be sent who have been set apart by themselves on His left hand. And this is what has been spoken by the prophet, 'I am a jealous God, making peace, and creating evil things'; thus making peace and friendship with those who repent and turn to Him, and bringing [them to] unity, but preparing for the

impenitent, those who shun the light, eternal fire and outer darkness, which are evils indeed to those persons who fall into them.

(Against the Heresies, Book 4, 60)

The idea of universal salvation is a more modern interpretation of Irenaeus and not part of his original thought.

Thought point

Irenaeus' own words

'[U]nless God had freely given salvation, we would not now possess it securely. And unless man had been joined to God, he could never have become a partaker of incorruptibility. For it was incumbent upon the Mediator between God and men, by his relationship to both, to bring both to friendship and accord, and present man to God, while he revealed God to man' (Irenaeus, 'The Ante-Nicene Christian Library').

1   What do you think Irenaeus means by the word 'mediator'?
2   Does salvation come only from God? What did Irenaeus think? What do you think?

Thought point

Criminal tendencies

1   Do people assume that children's attitudes and behaviour reflect those of their parents? Is it right to assume this link and then act on this basis?
2   Does an assumption such as this affect the way people relate to the children of:

- Doctors
- Cleaners
- Lawyers
- Teachers
- Criminals
- Prostitutes?

Recapitulation

The word 'recapitulation' is often applied to the ideas of Irenaeus concerning the problem of evil. Recapitulation literally means to 'bring something back to the head or beginning'; it also means to 'summarise or sum something up'. Irenaeus' theodicy is about bringing people back into relationship with God; hence it is called a theory of recapitulation.

CRITICISMS OF IRENAEUS' THEODICY

- It is not orthodox Christianity as it denies the Fall.
- Do natural disasters actually provide opportunities to do good in practice?
- Why do some people get more than would seem to be their fair share of suffering?
- Hume is critical: 'Could not our world be a little more hospitable and still teach us what we need to know? Could we not learn through pleasure as well as pain?'
- Swinburne argues that our suffering is limited, by our own capacity to feel pain and by our lifespan.

MODERN IRENAEAN THEODICIES

The Irenaean theodicy as set out by modern philosophers, such as John Hick, starts from a belief that God exists and attempts to explain why there is evil in the world.

Augustine's theodicy claimed that the world was perfect and good until evil came into it through people's choices. Augustine's theodicy presents a free will defence.

Irenaean theodicies reject these ideas and the work of modern defenders of the free will defence, such as Alvin Plantinga.

According to John Hick, Augustinian theodicies are unconvincing to scientifically educated people because:

- The story of Adam, Eve and the Fall is a myth, and so is not literally true.
- The idea that fallen angels cause natural disasters, such as earthquakes, is rejected as simply unbelievable.

JOHN HICK'S IRENAEAN THEODICY

The problem to be solved

In his book *Evil and the God of Love* Hick wrote that the role of mythology is to examine some of the great problems of human life, such as evil. According to Hick, however, although the imagery used in a myth, such as that of the Garden of Eden, might be memorable, it is not the most important part of the myth. It is what the imagery tries to examine that matters, such as the problem of the existence of evil.

Human beings

Hick, like Irenaeus, thought that human beings were not created perfect as in Augustine's theodicy, but develop in two stages.

Stage 1: 'Image'

According to Hick, humans are created in the image of God, which means they evolve into rational, 'intelligent and religious animals' (Hick, 'Encountering Evil' in *Live Options in Theodicy*). He stressed the fact that humans are one of many life forms on earth and are not unique, nor did they evolve from the Garden of Eden, but from a struggle for survival.

Humans, therefore, are not perfect but spiritually immature. And they evolve into spiritually mature beings through their struggle for survival. 'A world without problems, difficulties, perils and hardships would be morally static, for moral and spiritual growth comes through responses to challenges; and in a paradise there would be no challenges' (Hick, *Evil and the God of Love*, p. 372).

Stage 2: 'Likeness'

Hick said that when humans have achieved 'likeness' with God, they will, sometime in the future, grow into a relationship with God.

The Fall

The Fall for Irenaeus is not as important as it is for Augustine, as he saw it as simply a mistake made by immature humans who are only in the 'image of God'. Hick thought that the Fall symbolised the distance between God and humans.

Humans, according to Hick, were not created in the presence of God, as he thought that if humans were in God's presence, all their free will would be removed. The all-powerfulness of God would mean that humans could not make any choices; thus he considered that there is an *epistemic distance* between God and human beings.

This is not a spatial 'distance', for God is omnipresent. It must be an epistemic distance: a distance of knowledge – in other words if God interfered or became too close, humans would be unable to make a free choice and thus would not benefit from the developmental process. This *epistemic distance* or knowledge gap between humans and God maintains their identity but

Epistemic distance

The phrase used by John Hick and other philosophers to express the idea that God's existence is not obvious and thus human begins are not overwhelmed by God's presence into believing in God.

allows humans to seek knowledge of God and have a choice as to whether to believe in him. Suffering is a necessary condition of being finite.

Peter Vardy gave a modern example to explain this idea: a king falling in love with a peasant girl. And rather than forcing her to marry him, he tries to win her heart. Thus, for Hick, the idea of an epistemic distance makes belief in an all-loving and all-powerful God completely rational and God is not obviously present in the world in order to protect human free will. He argued that the world is religiously ambiguous – it can be seen as the creative work of God or as completely secular as God's presence is not evident. This leaves people free to either accept God or reject him. Hick argued that this freedom is vital if humans are to develop into the 'likeness' of God.

God, according to Hick, uses evil and suffering to bring about the greatest good – which means that evil and suffering are positive, not negative.

Thought point

Free choice?

Think about your time in school. Have you ever misbehaved? If you have, would you have behaved in the same way if your mother or father had been sitting next to you in class?

In some schools teachers ask the parents to come into class with their child if the child misbehaves. Can you think of any disadvantages of this system of discipline?

Thought point

Evil actions

Can anything good come from evil actions?

Soul-making

According to Hick this world is one of soul-making – in other words it is a world in which people can make choices about how to behave and these choices enable them to develop virtuous characters and good habits. For example virtues, such as compassion and charity, can be developed only in a world where there is suffering, which in turn enables people to become more moral.

Thus it is people's choices that are important, not the abilities and personality they were born with. Humans can become like God but sometimes it is easier simply to respond to their own instincts and desires.

Why are there natural disasters?

Hick claimed that the *'challenging environment'* caused by natural disasters stimulates human intellectual and imaginative development. He wrote,

> In a world devoid both of dangers to be avoided and rewards to be won we may assume that there would have been virtually no moral development of the human intellect and imagination, and hence of either the sciences or the arts, and hence of human civilisation or culture.
>
> (Hick, 'Encountering Evil' in *Live Options in Theodicy*)

People need to face real dangers and real suffering in order for us to develop into the likeness of God. Natural evil is not, as Augustine thought, the result of human moral evil but part of the creative work of God.

In response to challenges from people such as Dostoevsky about the sheer amount and depth of evil in the world, Hick suggests that the only answer may be that in heaven all will be well. This is called an *'eschatological answer'*. He sees that from the point of view of the person suffering this is not always a helpful response, but says that people simply have to trust God that evil and suffering are necessary to create an environment in which all can develop. This also explains the random nature of evil: why it is that good people seem to suffer and evil people do not, as if only evil people suffered, we would not live in an environment in which we could develop.

Universal salvation

In the Irenaean theodicy humans become like God after death. An essential part of this theodicy is that this process is worthwhile because of the eventual outcome. If the process is not completed in this life, then Hick argued that there is another life in another realm to which we go, until the process is complete. However, unlike Irenaeus, Hick maintains that everyone will eventually be saved and go to heaven: all humans are on a journey towards God and eventually this journey will be completed and people will, after death, develop for the image of God into his likeness.

Hick believes in universal salvation – God saves everyone after death; for Hick there is no hell. The fact that everyone will eventually achieve salvation justifies the amount of evil and suffering in the world.

Eschatological

This is a word used by Christians to refer to what will happen at the end of time or in the last days of the universe. Traditionally it is linked with the idea of an afterlife.

Purgatory

Purgatory is a state of existence post-death in which people are purified by punishment after death. This is a different state from hell and the nature of punishment is purification, unlike hell. Belief in purgatory is most commonly associated with Roman Catholic Christianity, though some other Christians also share this belief.

Thought point

Daylight robbery

Would you steal what you liked if you knew that in the end you would go to heaven anyway?

Thought point

If you will be saved – whatever

Would you behave differently if you knew that eventually you would go to paradise with God despite whatever you did?

CRITICISMS OF HICK'S THEODICY

- Hick rejected Augustine's theodicy as implausible in a scientific age, but his own theodicy can also be considered implausible, particularly its eschatological aspect. However, Hick was a Christian, and he asks that his argument be viewed as a reasonable interpretation.
- Traditionally, Christianity taught that humans are responsible for their own actions and God will judge them. Justice is understood as treating people as they deserve, so many Christians believe that universal salvation is unjust, as whatever you do in life will not matter in the end.
- According to Hick, God is responsible for creating a world in which there are natural disasters and, therefore, is responsible for the resulting suffering. This seems plainly to contradict the belief in a good and loving God.
- Is it necessary for there to be so much evil and suffering in the world? What about the suffering of children and the innocent?
- Do the ends justify the means? Can it be possible to justify evil so that people can grow into the likeness of God? Many Christians would deny any idea of God creating evil for the greater good.

- The epistemic distance may simply be a way of hiding the fact that God does not exist – why is God not more visible?
- How do we know that the purpose of existence is to grow into loving and compassionate people in the likeness of God?

CONCLUSION

The Augustinian and Irenaean theodicies do attempt to address the problems presented by the existence of evil and the amount in the world. Both theodicies stress the importance of free will as an explanation of much evil in the world.

Additionally, people do learn from their mistakes: the idea of soul-making does support this.

There are criticisms of both theodicies, but whether this means that the problem of evil is an argument against the existence of God is another matter. There are many challenges to the theodicies, but maybe this means that, in our complex world, it can be said only that evil is a mystery that humans cannot solve, and that it is not simply an academic problem but that people need to choose to stand up against it.

Swinburne's theodicy

Swinburne (*Existence of God*, 1979) also addressed the problem of the sheer quantity of evil in the world. Swinburne argued that some evil is necessary in order for us to achieve higher-order goods. He pointed out that a genuinely free person must be allowed to harm himself and others. God could intervene to stop it, or let the person learn from the consequences of his or her actions. He argued that it was better to live in a world where evil and suffering existed than in a 'toy world' where the consequences of human actions did not matter and humans would not need to make moral decisions.

He thought that the exercise of moral freedom was important even if these free choices bring about death. Swinburne argued that death is good in that it brings an end to suffering. It would surely be immoral for God to allow human beings to have unlimited power to do harm. Also actions matter more when there is a limited life. Death makes possible the ultimate sacrifice and it makes possible fortitude in the face of absolute disaster. When it comes to the Holocaust he says, 'the less God allows men to bring about large scale horrors, the less the freedom and responsibility he gives them.' In other words, we can make real choices.

For Swinburne, natural evil is necessary so that humans have a knowledge of how to bring about evil. Rational choices can be made only in the light of knowledge of the consequences of alternative actions. He cites the example of earthquakes. A choice of building on earthquake belts, and so risking destruction of whole populations, is available only if earthquakes have already happened due to unpredicted causes (*Existence of God*, p. 208). However, if the purpose of evil is to teach, what about those who never learn?

Swinburne thought that God created a 'half-finished' universe, which gives humans the possibility to choose to make it better. This idea depends on humans having free will.

THE FREE WILL DEFENCE

The theodicies of Augustine and Irenaeus depend on human free will. For Augustine the misuse of free will led to evil – humans are responsible for evil, not God. For Irenaeus, Hick and Swinburne free will is necessary in order for humans to improve both themselves and the world. Both approaches see evil as the result of human free will; however, free will is necessary so that humans can have a free, loving relationship with God.

Criticisms of the free will defence

Anthony Flew asked what free will actually meant. Flew claimed that freely chosen actions cannot have external causes; they have to be internal to the person in order to be really freely chosen. Flew said that God could have created a world in which humans could always freely choose to do the right thing – they would be naturally good, but still make free choices according to Flew's definition of free choice.

This approach, however, means that God manipulates his creation in order to bring about certain results, whereas the free will defence depends on humans being free to love and worship God and free to reject him.

J.L. Mackie adds to this argument, claiming that God could have created a world in which humans were really free but would never have chosen to do evil. Mackie's argument is logical: if it is possible for a person who is free to do the right thing on one occasion, then it is possible for a person to do the right thing on every occasion, so God could have created a world in which everyone is genuinely free, and yet chooses always to do the right thing. Mackie concluded that as God failed to do this he cannot be omnipotent and omnibenevolent.

Additionally, it could be argued that humans have no free will as everything that they do is determined by events in the past, by sociological and psychological factors. Thus, choices which appear to be free may be determined by factors of which the individual is completely unaware. Logically, this means that there is no point in talking about good and evil actions, as if these actions are determined, there is no difference between good and evil.

PROCESS THEODICY

Evil is a problem only if one maintains the traditional God of classical theism. Process theodicy, developed by Alfred North Whitehead and David Griffin, states that God is not omnipotent and is not separate from his creation. God is part of creation and can, therefore, influence what happens in the world but cannot determine it.

Everything is in process. Every actual event is a momentary event, charged with creativity. God continually offers each event the best possible outcome, but every event is free to conform (or not) to God's will. Evil comes from events that fall short of God's purpose. God can try to influence humans to do what is good, but humans can ignore this and God cannot stop them. However, when evil is committed God suffers with those who suffer as he is part of the world and consequently is affected by it. This is similar to the ideas of Jürgen Moltmann, who wrote in *The Crucified God* (1973) that any Christian response to the problem of evil and suffering should be rooted in the death of Christ. Through the Crucifixion people are offered the promise that God is not detached from suffering because he died on the Cross. God is suffering alongside the world.

Process theodicy limits the power of God – he cannot stop evil, which is not explained but simply seen as simply part of the natural processes of the world. According to Griffin, there is more good than evil in the universe and so it is better to have this universe than no universe: '*Should God, for the sake of avoiding the possibility of Hitler, and horrors such as Auschwitz, have precluded the possibility of Jesus, Gautama, Socrates, Confucius, Moses?*' (David Griffin, 2004, *God, Power and Evil, a Process Theology*). Is this limited God actually worthy of worship? Is the suffering God any help to someone who is really suffering and faced with the most appalling evil?

Thought point

The problem of evil – *final task*

1   How does the following quotation relate to the problem of evil?
2   Is the quotation a satisfactory conclusion to the problem of evil? Give reasons to explain your answer.

continued overleaf

> Where were you when I laid the foundation of the earth?
> Tell me, if you have understanding.
> Who determined its measurements – surely you know!
> Or who stretched the line upon it? (Job 38:4–5)

SUMMARY

1   The problem

Epicurus: Is God willing to prevent evil, but not able to? Then he is not omnipotent. Is God able to prevent evil, but not willing to? Then he is malevolent (evil). Is God able to prevent evil and willing to? Then why is there evil?

Inconsistent triad

2   Why the existence of evil challenges belief in God

If God is all-powerful why does God not prevent evil?

The sheer amount of evil in the world challenges the goodness of creation.

Dostoevsky: *The Brothers Karamazov*

Huge amount of suffering in nature (J.S. Mill, Richard Dawkins)

3   Theodicy

'Theodicy' comes from *theos* (meaning 'God') and *dikaios* (meaning 'justification').

4   Types of evil

Moral evil – caused by humans

Natural evil – suffering caused by natural disasters, disease and so forth

5   Possible solutions

Evil is caused by humans using their free will.

Evil is necessary as a means for humans to develop moral qualities, such as compassion.

The nature of God needs to be understood differently.

6   The theodicy of Augustine

Key ideas

God the Creator is omnipotent and all-good.

Creation is good and harmonious.

Hierarchy of beings: angels, humans, animals.

Evil is a privation – a lack of goodness.

Angels and human beings fall through their own free choices.

Natural evil is a result of the Fall.

Free will is important so God allows moral and natural evil to occur.

Soul-deciding world.

Criticisms of Augustine's theodicy

The earth evolved very slowly over billions of years. Life has developed
through evolution by natural selection. There was no instantaneous
creation.

How could a perfect world go wrong?

If the world was perfect and there was no knowledge of good and evil,
how could Adam and Eve have the freedom to disobey God if goodness and evil were as yet unknown?

Augustine's view that every human in seminally present in the loins.
Adam is biologically inaccurate and the question can be raised, is God
really justified in allowing punishment of one human being for the
sin of another human being? How could the perfect world go wrong?

God's responsibility for natural evils

7   Theodicy of Irenaeus

Key ideas

God the Creator is omnipotent and all-good.

The universe and the Earth develop over time.

Human beings are created in an imperfect state, evolving from 'image'
into 'likeness' of God.

Soul-making world

Value of free will

8   Criticisms of the theodicy of Irenaeus

It denies the Fall.

Do natural disasters actually provide opportunities to do good in
practice?

Why do some people get more than would seem to be their fair share of
suffering?

9   Hick's theodicy

Key ideas

God the Creator is omnipotent and all-good.

The universe and the Earth develop over time.

Human beings are created in an imperfect state, evolving from 'image' into 'likeness' of God.
Soul-making world
Epistemic distance
Universal salvation
Value of free will

10 Criticisms of Hick's theodicy

Is suffering a price worth paying?
Is so much suffering necessary?
Do the ends justify the means?
The epistemic distance
Why is God not more clearly visible?

REVIEW QUESTIONS

Look back over the chapter and check that you can answer the following questions:

1 List the positive and negative features of Augustine's and Irenaeus' theodicies. Do you think either theodicy is adequate? Justify your answer with reasons.

2 Aristotle famously stated that *'we become just by doing just acts, temperate by doing temperate acts, brave by doing brave acts'* (Aristotle, *Nichomachean Ethics*). How could this support the ideas of Christian theodicies?

3 Would you say that 'the existence of evil' is a mystery? If it is a mystery, can 'the existence of evil' be used as an argument against the existence of God?

4 Desmond Tutu wrote in 1977 about South Africa under the apartheid system of discrimination against black people:

[T]he burning question is not 'Why is there suffering and evil in the universe of a good God?' but the more immediately pressing one of *'Why do we suffer so?' 'Why does suffering seem to single out us blacks to be the victims of a racism gone mad?'* (Tutu, *African Theology en Route: Papers from the Pan-African Conference of Third World Theologians*; emphasis added)

continued opposite

(a) Do you agree with Desmond Tutu about what the key question is (italics)?

(b) Do the ideas of the Irenaean and Augustinian theodicies answer Desmond Tutu's question?

Terminology

Do you know your terminology?

Try to explain the following ideas without looking at your books and notes:

- Theodicy
- The Fall
- Epistemic distance
- Privation.

Examination questions practice

SAMPLE EXAM-STYLE QUESTIONS

'Reasoned arguments cannot account for the amount of evil in the world.' Discuss.

AO1 (15 marks)
- You might begin by explaining the problem of evil, possibly using the version put forward by Epicurus.
- You would need to explain the important points of the theodicies – of Augustine, Irenaeus and Hick – and be able to explain points which focus on the question.
- You could explain the different approaches to humanity.
- You could explain the role God as creator, of free will and soul-deciding versus soul-making.

AO2 (15 marks)
- There are many ways to approach this question. You need to put forward an argument that either supports or disagrees with the statement in the question.
- You could discuss whether theodicies provide a rational defence of belief in God even though evil exists.
- You could discuss the logical problem with believing in a good, omnipotent, omniscient God in the light of all the evil in the world. For example you could discuss the particular problem of God being all-knowing: would that mean that God always knows what humans will choose to do? If so why does he not prevent it? You need to consider whether either Augustinian or Irenaean theodicies can answer such questions and justify the amount of evil in the world.
- You could assess whether the sheer amount of evil in the world means that human freedom is too high a price to pay. You could

discuss the criticisms from *The Brothers Karamazov*.

- You could also argue that there is so much evil in our world that no benevolent God could possibly exist. Views expressed by thinkers such as Richard Swinburne, J.L. Mackie, John Hick or Richard Dawkins could be used in your argument.
- You would need to evaluate whether any or none of the theodicies provide a satisfactory answer.

Further possible questions

- 'There is too much evil in the world for there to be a God.' Discuss.
- Critically assess the theodicy of Augustine.
- 'There is no justification for evil.' Discuss.
- 'Moral evil may be humanity's fault but natural evil is God's fault.' Discuss.

FURTHER READING

Hick, J. 1985. *Evil and the God of Love*. Basingstoke: Palgrave Macmillan.
Philips, D.Z. 2004. *The Problem of Evil and the Problem of God*. London: SCM Press.
Swinburne, R. 1979. *The Existence of God*. Oxford: OUP.
Swinburne, R. 1998. *Providence and the Problem of Evil*. Oxford: OUP.
Vardy, P. and Arliss, J. 2003. *The Thinker's Guide to Evil*. Arelsford: John Hunt.

RELIGIOUS ETHICS

PART II

8 What is ethics?

Ethics is the philosophical study of good and bad, right and wrong. It is commonly used interchangeably with the word 'morality' and is also known as moral philosophy. The study of ethics requires you to look at moral issues, such as abortion, euthanasia and cloning, and to examine views that are quite different from your own. You need to be open-minded, use your critical powers and above all learn from the way different ethical ethics need to be applied with logic so that we can end up with a set of theories to approach the issues you will study for AS and A level. Ethics needs to be applied with logic so that we can end up with a set of moral beliefs that are supported with reasons, are consistent and reflect the way we see and act in the world. Ethical theories are constructed logically, but give different weights to different concepts.

However, it is not enough to prove that the theory you agree with is true and reasonable; you must also show where and how other philosophers went wrong.

FALLACIES

With the possible exception of you and me, people usually do not have logical reasons for what they believe. This is especially true for ethical issues. Here are some examples of how not to arrive at a belief. We call them fallacies.

Here are some common beliefs; you may recognise your own reasons for holding a particular view:

- A belief based on the mistaken idea that a rule which is generally true is without exceptions – for example 'Suicide is killing oneself – killing is murder – I'm opposed to euthanasia.'
- A belief based on peer pressure, appeal to herd mentality or xenophobia – for example 'Most people don't believe in euthanasia, so it's probably wrong.'
- A belief in fact or obligation simply based on sympathy – for example 'It's horrible to use those poor apes to test drugs, so I'm opposed to it.'

- An argument based on the assumption that there are fewer alternatives than actually exist – for example 'It's either euthanasia or long, painful suffering.'
- An argument based on only the positive half of the story – for example 'Animal research has produced loads of benefits – that's why I support it.'
- Hasty generalisation: concluding that a population has some quality based on a misrepresentative sample – for example 'My grandparents are in favour of euthanasia, and I would think that most old people would agree with it.'
- An argument based on an exaggeration – for example 'We owe all of our advances in medicine to animal research, and that's why I'm for it.'
- The slippery slope argument: the belief that a first step in a certain direction amounts to going far in that direction – for example 'If we legalise euthanasia this will inevitably lead to killing the elderly, so I'm opposed to it.'
- A subjective argument that truth varies according to personal opinion – for example 'Euthanasia may be right for you, but it's wrong for me.'
- An argument based on tradition: the belief that X is justified simply because X has been done in the past – for example 'We've done well without euthanasia for thousands of years, and we shouldn't change now.'

IS–OUGHT FALLACY

David Hume (1711–1776) observed that often when people are debating a moral issue they begin with facts and slide into conclusions that are normative – that is conclusions about how things ought to be. He argued that no amount of facts taken alone can ever be sufficient to imply a normative conclusion: the is-ought fallacy. For example it is a fact that slavery still exists in some form or other in many countries – that is an 'is'. However, this fact is morally neutral, and it is only when we say we 'ought' to abolish slavery that we are making a moral judgement. The fallacy is saying that the 'ought' statement follows logically from the 'is', but this does not need to be the case. Another example is to say that humans possess reason and this distinguishes us from other animals – it does not logically follow that we ought to exercise our reason to live a fulfilled life.

AREAS OF ETHICS

Ethics looks at what you ought to do as distinct from what you may in fact do. Ethics is usually divided into three areas: *meta-ethics*, *normative ethics* and applied ethics.

1   *Meta-ethics* looks at the meaning of the language used in ethics, and includes questions such as: are ethical claims capable of being true or false, or are they expressions of emotion? If true, is that truth relative only to some individual, society or culture? What does it mean to say something is good or bad, and what do the words 'good' and 'bad' mean? (This is studied in Year 2.)

2   *Normative ethics* asks the question 'what ought I to do?' and attempts to arrive at practical moral standards (or norms) that tell us right from wrong and how to live moral lives. These are what we call ethical theories. This may involve explaining the good habits we should acquire and looking at whether there are duties we should follow or whether our actions should be guided by their consequences for ourselves and/or others. There are various ethical theories that are described as normative:

   - *Teleological or consequential ethics*, where ethical decisions are based on the consequences of an action
   - *Deontological ethics*, which is based on duty and obligation
   - Ethics based on *God-given laws (divine command)*.

3   *Applied ethics* is the application of theories of right and wrong and theories of value to specific issues, such as abortion, euthanasia, cloning, foetal research, and lying and honesty.

Ethics is not just giving your own opinion, and the way it is studied at AS and A level is very like philosophy: it is limited to facts, logic and definition. Ideally, a philosopher is able to prove that a theory is true and reasonable based on accurate definitions and verifiable facts. Once these definitions and facts have been established, a philosopher can develop the theory through a process of deduction, by showing what logically follows from the definitions and facts. The theory may then be applied to controversial moral issues. It is a bit like baking a cake.

THE DEFINITIONS OF THE MAIN THEORIES IN NORMATIVE ETHICS

Deontological ethics is concerned with the acts that are right or wrong in themselves (intrinsically right or wrong). This may be because these acts go against some duty or obligation or they break some absolute law – for example a deontologist may say that killing is wrong as the actual act of killing another human being is always wrong. Deontologists are always certain in their moral decisions and can take strong moral positions, such as being totally against war. On the other hand they do not take into account the circumstances, or different cultures or different religious views.

Teleological ethics is concerned with the ends, results or consequences of an action. Followers of teleological ethics consider the consequence of an ethical decision before they act. The action is not intrinsically good (good in itself) but good only if the results are good – the action produces happiness and love. However, the main problem with teleological ethics is that it can never be sure what the result or consequence of an action might be – it is possible to make an educated guess but not to be absolutely sure, and sometimes we can tell if the consequences of an action are right only with hindsight. Another problem with teleological ethics is that some actions are always wrong – rape for example – and can never be justified by the consequence.

Moral objectivism claims that there are certain universal and absolute values. Modern moral objectivists do not believe that these universal values hold forever, but they hold until they are proven to be false.

Moral subjectivism claims that moral statements are simply a matter of personal opinion. We simply make our own morality according to our own experiences and see our moral views as true for ourselves or our society and not necessarily applying to others.

Intrinsic good means something is good in itself: it has value simply because it exists without any references to the consequences. This applies to deontological ethics.

Instrumental good means something is good because of the effects or consequences it has, or as a means to some other end or purpose. To explain this Peter Singer (*Practical Ethics*, 2011, p. 246) uses the example of money – it has value because of the things we can buy with it, but if we were marooned on a desert island we would not want it.

ETHICAL THEORIES

If we are to have valid ethical arguments then we must have some normative premises to begin with. These normative premises are either statements of ethical theories themselves or statements implied by ethical theories. The ethical theories that will be examined in this book are as follows:

Utilitarianism: An action is right if it maximises the overall happiness of all people.

Kantian ethics: Treat other people the way you wish they would treat you, and never treat other people as if they were merely objects.

Cultural relativism: What is right or wrong varies according to the beliefs of each culture.

Divine command: Do as the creator tells you.

Natural law: Everything is created for a purpose, and when this is examined by human reason a person should be able to judge how to act in order to find ultimate happiness.

Situation ethics: Based on agape, which wills the good of others.

REVIEW QUESTIONS

Look back over the chapter and check that you can answer the following questions:

1   What is the 'Is-ought fallacy'?
2   Name the three areas of ethics.
3   Explain what is meant by 'Cultural relativism'?

9 Moral absolutism and moral relativism

Essential terminology

Absolute
Consequentialism
Cultural relativism
Descriptive relativism
Moral absolutism
Moral objectivism
Moral relativism
Subjectivism

This chapter introduces some of the main ethical theories that are looked at in more detail in later chapters. You should read this chapter again once you have studied them. Although there is not a particular section on absolutism and relativism in the specification, you will need this information to help you understand the ethical theories you will be studying in this course.

Key scholars

Protagoras (c. 480 – c. 411 BCE)
Socrates (c. 470 – c. 399 BCE)
Plato (428–347 BCE)
Aristotle (384–322 BCE)
Joseph Fletcher (1905–1991)

WHAT YOU WILL LEARN ABOUT IN THIS CHAPTER

*   What it means in ethics to call a system 'relativist'.
*   Moral relativism as distinct from cultural relativism.
*   Situation ethics as an example of relative ethical systems.
*   What is meant by moral absolutism.
*   Absolute and relative ways of understanding 'right' and 'wrong'.
*   The skills to decide whether there are any moral absolutes, or whether morality is completely relative, or whether there is an in-between position.
*   The strengths and weaknesses of moral absolutism.
*   The strengths and weaknesses of moral relativism.

WHAT IS ETHICAL RELATIVISM?

We all make ethical judgements about what we consider to be right and wrong, and we often have different views about ethical issues. We make judgements about actions or behaviour as being absolutely wrong in all circumstances – this is absolute ethics, which takes a deontological approach. An ethical relativist, on the other hand, believes that there are circumstances and situations in which actions or behaviour that are usually considered to be 'wrong' can be considered to be 'right'.

Moral relativism
There are no universally valid moral principles and so there is no one true morality.

Sophists

This was a name originally applied by the ancient Greeks to learned men. In the fifth century, the Sophists were travelling teachers. They concluded that truth and morality were matters of opinion and emphasised skills, such as rhetoric.

Protagoras (c. 480 – c. 411 BCE)

Protagoras was a Greek philosopher, born in Thrace. He taught in Athens for money. He said that nothing is absolutely good or bad and that each individual is his or her own final authority when making decisions. Like Socrates, he was charged with impiety and fled to Sicily, but drowned on the journey.

There are basically two sorts of ethical relativism: cultural relativism, which says that right and wrong, good and evil are relative to a culture, to a way of life that is practised by a whole group of people; and individual relativism, which says that right and wrong, good and evil are relative to the preferences of an individual. Both cultural and individual relativism hold that there are no universally valid moral principles. All principles and values are relative to a particular culture or age. Ethical relativism means that there is no such thing as good 'in itself', but if an action seems good to you and bad to me, that is it, and there is no objective basis for us to discover the truth.

The problem today is that relativism tends to lead people into thinking that truth depends on who holds it, or that there is only one truth – their own. We often hear people say, 'Well, that's your point of view, but it's not mine,' and this can actually be a way of stopping thinking. Truth then no longer matters, as everything depends on the community to which one belongs, or one's own perspective. Where there is no agreed set of values, relativism can seem very attractive.

Each person's values are relative to that person and so cannot be judged objectively.

THE ORIGINS OF RELATIVISM

We can trace the origins of Western ethical thinking to the city states of ancient Greece. At the time of Homer (c. eighth century BCE), being good meant being a heroic warrior, and the type of person you were – noble, courageous, strong – was the most important thing. This became further developed in the ethical theories of Socrates, Plato and Aristotle, who looked at the ideas of character and virtue.

However, everything began to change, and by the sixth century BCE there was no longer any moral certainty. *Alasdair MacIntyre* in his book *A Short History of Ethics* (1985) says this was due to the discovery of other civilisations with different ideas of what it meant to be good and changes within Greek society itself. The discovery of these different cultures led the Greeks to question the absoluteness of their own moral ideas; also, as the city states expanded, it became less clear what a person's role in society was and so more difficult to know how to live a virtuous life.

Eventually a series of wise men, known as Sophists, appeared and argued that all morality was relative – right and wrong varied from place to place, from time to time and from person to person. Protagoras famously said, 'Man is the measure of all things.' All they saw as important was getting on in life, taking part in political life and fitting in – 'truth' was a variable concept. Socrates and later Plato and Aristotle worked on proving this view to be wrong.

Socrates

It is difficult to distinguish between the views of Socrates and Plato, as Socrates left no writings and everything we know about him we know through his pupil Plato. However, Plato's dialogues have Socrates as the main protagonist, who argues that all humans share a common, innate understanding of what is morally good.

Plato

Plato explained how this moral knowledge was acquired with his theory of the Forms – moral knowledge came from the highest of the forms: the Form of the Good. According to Plato, there are objective and universal moral truths – the complete opposite of the view of the Sophists.

Aristotle

Aristotle approached ethics from a completely different angle, and although he thought universal truths could be discovered, he rejected Plato's idea of the world of the Forms as he thought that understanding of goodness and wisdom could be found in this world. According to Aristotle, we can find out how to be virtuous by looking at virtuous people and by discovering how we can better develop our character.

Socrates, Plato and Aristotle all oppose complete relativism from different angles and ask people not to just blindly follow what everyone else is thinking and doing, to consider what they believe and why they believe it, to dialogue with others and to look for truths that are not limited by their own time and culture.

It cannot be assumed that relativism means the same thing to everyone and this chapter will explore some of the different approaches.

CULTURAL RELATIVISM

You do not need to be an anthropologist to know that throughout the world there are many different ideas about how to behave and there always seem to be clashes of moral codes between one culture and another. To many people it seems obscene to chop off a person's hand as punishment for theft or to stone somebody for adultery, yet to many Muslims this is simply the required punishment, and they on their part

**Socrates
(c. 470–399 BCE)**

Socrates did not leave any writings of his own but, as a Greek philosopher, he shaped Western philosophy. His pupil Plato wrote dialogues which claim to describe Socrates' views. He is also mentioned in the works of Xenophon and others. At the age of 70 he was tried for impiety and sentenced to death by poisoning (probably hemlock).

**Plato
(428–347 BCE)**

Plato is one of the most famous philosophers in history. His writings influenced the development of philosophy throughout the Western world and a large number of his books survive. Plato was taught by the first great Western philosopher, Socrates. Most of the books he wrote have Socrates as the leading character. His early books are about Socrates' philosophy, but the later ones present arguments from Plato's own thinking. Plato wrote about many issues, ranging from the existence of

continued overleaf

the soul and the nature of beauty to who should run a government. Plato founded his own school of philosophy, like a university, called the Academia, from which we get the word 'academy' in English. He died in 347 BCE, aged 81.

Aristotle (384–322 BCE)

Aristotle was born in Macedonia. At the age of 17 he moved to Athens, where he joined Plato's Academy. In 347 BCE he moved to Turkey due to the growing political tensions between Macedonia and Athens. He spent his time there investigating science and particularly biology. In 341 BCE he moved with his family back to Macedonia to become tutor to the son of King Philip II of Macedonia, Alexander (who would later become Alexander the Great). After Alexander became king, Aristotle returned to Athens and founded a school called the Lyceum. He remained in Athens teaching until 323 BCE, when Alexander the Great died. After Alexander's death it became

continued opposite

may condemn what they see as the excessive liberalism and immorality of Western societies.

This is what is known as the *diversity thesis* – because of the diversity across and within cultures there can be no one true morality.

Many other examples of this clash of cultures may be found. Some societies practise polygamy, others monogamy; some have arranged marriages and others are free to make their own choice of spouse; we put our elderly in homes, whereas in other cultures they are valued for their wisdom and have an important place in the family home. For the relativist such differences present no problems – different tribes, different customs. Rules of conduct differ from place to place, as was noted by the ancient Greek historian Herodotus, who recounts an episode in which the king of Persia induced horror on the part of both the Greeks and the Callatians by asking them to adopt each other's funeral practices. What the Greeks took to be right and proper (e.g. burning their dead), the Callatians saw as absolutely abhorrent – Herodotus implied that since fire burned just as well in Greece as in Persia, moral practices are relative to cultural contexts. By implication there is nothing right or wrong universally. This is what is known as the dependency thesis – what is right or wrong depends upon the nature of the society. No one can judge the morality of other cultures, as different cultures create different values, and we cannot be objective about another culture since we are all the product of our own culture.

However, for the absolutist these different forms of behaviour cause a major dilemma. Absolutism implies that forms of behaviour are universally right or wrong – an example of this is that when the nineteenth-century British missionaries went to Africa and Asia they imposed their Western *absolutes* as being more right than local customs. Thus, for example, female converts to Christianity were made to cover their breasts – surely more a sign of Victorian prudery (and the cold British climate) than any universal moral code.

Historically we can also find support for the relativist position – forms of behaviour that were condemned in the past are now considered acceptable and vice versa. We no longer allow acts of cruelty for public entertainment as in the Roman games; homosexuals can enter into same-sex marriages or civil partnerships; unmarried mothers are no longer put in mental institutions; slavery is no longer legal and so on. The attitudes of society have changed on many issues.

Morality then does not exist in a vacuum, what is considered right or wrong must be considered in context, and morality is seen as just a set of common rules and customs that over time have become socially approved and differ from culture to culture. If all morality is rooted in culture, there can be no universal moral principles valid for everyone at all times.

Thought point

1   Jesus is quoted as saying, 'The sabbath was made for humankind, and not humankind for the sabbath; so the Son of Man is lord even of the sabbath' (Mark 2:27b–28).

   • Does this mean that all rules are relative in human relationships? Or are there some rules that cannot be broken?

2   Winston Churchill's physician, Lord Moran, once remarked of the French president General de Gaulle 'He's so stuffed with principles that he has no room for Christian charity.'

   • How relevant is this comment to the discussion on moral relativism?

3   There are many areas of human behaviour about which attitudes have changed.

   • Add to this list: hire purchase; cockfighting; the role of women in society.
   • Are the changes all for the better?
   • What accepted practices today do you think people will look back at in horror in the future (e.g. pollution and gas-guzzling cars; the breeding and slaughter of animals for food; the use of nuclear power for energy)?

difficult for Aristotle to stay in Athens, as he was a Macedonian. Worried that he would die like Socrates, Aristotle and his family moved to Chalcis, where he died a year later.

Aristotle was a remarkable person. He tutored students on most traditional subjects that are taught at universities today. He was fascinated with understanding the physical world around him and the universe. His biology books were not superseded by anything better until 2,000 years later. Aristotle also wrote about other areas of study, including drama, rhetoric (public speaking), meteorology, sport and physics.

THE REASONS FOR RELATIVISM

• The decline of religious authority has meant that people look for other reasons to be ethical.
• A greater understanding of other cultures, particularly from anthropology, has led to an understanding that morality is not absolute and simply means ways of acting that are approved by a particular society.
• Relativism simply explains the differences between one time and another – for instance slavery was acceptable in the past and no longer is.
• The unacceptable effects of interfering with other cultures.
• The influence of meta-ethical analysis – asking what the terms 'ought', 'right' and 'wrong' mean. If there is no agreement about what the words

Descriptive relativism

Different cultures and societies have differing ethical systems and so morality is relative.

Cultural relativism

What is right or wrong depends on the culture.

mean, then this implies conceptual relativism – what an intuitionist thinks is good is different from what an emotivist thinks.
- The development of competing theories – utilitarian, intuitionist, egoist, emotivist.

THE WEAKNESSES OF RELATIVISM

Absolute
A principle that is universally binding.

Moral objectivism
Truth is objectively real regardless of culture.

Consequentialism
The rightness or wrongness of an act is deter-mined by its consequences.

- It implies that there can be no real evaluation or criticism of practices such as the burning of witches, human sacrifice, slavery, the Holocaust or the torture of the innocent.
- Relativism does not allow societies to progress (e.g. the realisation that slavery was unacceptable was slow to develop – but no one would doubt that we have made progress).
- Relativism seems to give little reason for behaving morally except to be socially acceptable.
- Although relativism is not subjectivism, it is only a step away and may come to this problematic position.
- Some statements are true absolutely (e.g. 'It is wrong to torture innocent people'; 'It is right for parents to be responsible for their children').
- The fact that cultures vary does not mean that there is no objective 'good'.
- Ethical beliefs can change when challenged – primitive practices do stop.

Note: Relativists do not reject moral principles. They say that all the different moral principles in the world are valid relative to the culture. Believing that moral values are relative does not mean that a person does not have any moral values.

NORMATIVE RELATIVISM

Normative ethics is where actions are assessed according to ethical theories – it is about what is actually right or good and not simply about cultural diversity and cultural dependency. A relativist will normally hold at least one absolute principle: that it is wrong to impose absolute moral rules.

Both utilitarianism and situation ethics are thought of as examples of normative theories, but they are different in the way they understand this. However, it is important to note that neither theory is completely relativist as they have one absolute each – love for situation ethics and the greatest happiness principle for utilitarianism. Utilitarians recognise 'happiness', 'pleasure' or 'well-being' as the result of good actions, but accept that this may differ from culture to culture. Situationists, like Fletcher, reject the use of words like 'never', 'always' and 'absolute' and adopt a pragmatic approach to decision making. The only exception is that love should be seen as the absolute. 'Love relativises the absolute.' Fletcher described his theory as relativistic.

Normative relativists reject the principle of objectivity or absolutism and see morality as something that evolves and changes.

WHAT IS ETHICAL ABSOLUTISM?

An ethical absolute is a command that is true for all time, in all places and in all situations. Certain things are right or wrong from an objective point of view and cannot change according to culture. Certain actions are intrinsically right or wrong, which means they are right or wrong in themselves.

According to moral absolutism, there are eternal moral values applicable everywhere. Absolutism gives people clear guidelines for behaviour and accepts a universal set of absolutes. This is a popular position for those who believe in a God who establishes moral order in the universe. This approach is deontological. The consequences of an action are not taken into consideration.

Central Criminal Court
Kenneth Grant/Alamy

Moral absolutism

There is only one correct answer to every moral problem.

This ethical system is easy and simple to apply – a crime is a crime, regardless of circumstances. If we take murder as an example – is it all right to kill someone for no reason? Both the ethical relativist and the ethical absolutist would say no. Now if we assume the murderer is a doctor who could kill one patient to save another – again both the ethical relativist and the ethical absolutist would still say this was not right. However, if we consider killing one person to save many lives, the ethical relativist will feel it is all right to kill, but for the ethical absolutist it is still wrong.

Absolute ethics allows judgements to be made about the actions of others – we can say the Holocaust was absolutely wrong. Absolute ethics allows courts of law to exist and order to be maintained.

Where do these absolute laws come from? For a theist the answer is simple – they come from God. For the agnostic or atheist the answer is more complicated – they just seem a priori in nature. They fit into Plato's world of the Forms, as there are some things we just seem to know are wrong without being taught: do you remember your parents ever telling you not to sleep with your sister? So to some extent moral absolutes can be seen as inherent: the nature of man.

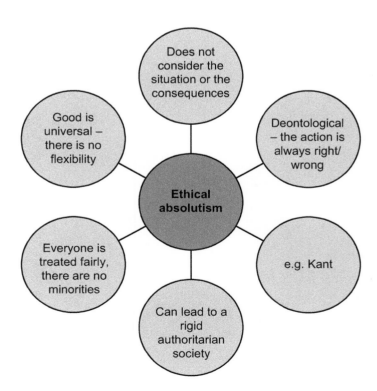

NORMATIVE ABSOLUTISM

The absolutist theory that is dealt with elsewhere in this book is Kantian ethics, which is based on reason. Natural law has a strong absolutist element in the primary precepts but it is also goal-oriented and so teleological. Thus Kantian ethics can be considered to be completely deontological, whereas natural law has a teleological element in the sense that it understands everything as being oriented towards a final purpose, but this does not simply mean that the consequences or results of an action are considered as in situation ethics or utilitarianism. However, even theories that are relativist in practice contain an absolute core – the greatest good for the greatest number in utilitarianism and agape in situation ethics.

Strengths of absolutism

- Absolutism gives a fixed ethical code by which to measure actions.
- One culture can judge that the actions of another are wrong (e.g. genocide) and then act on that judgement.
- Absolutism can support universal laws, such as the United Nations Declaration of Human Rights.

Weaknesses of absolutism

- Absolutism does not take into account the circumstances of each situation.
- Absolutists can seem intolerant of cultural diversity.
- How do we actually know what absolute morals are, as all sources of morality are open to human interpretation?
- Absolutism may often be seen as an impossible ideal.

THE DIFFERENCES BETWEEN ABSOLUTISM AND RELATIVISM

Absolutism

- There is an objective moral truth.
- Absolute ethics are deontological, concerned with the action, not the results.

- Moral actions are intrinsically right or wrong – right or wrong in themselves regardless of culture, time, place, opinion or situation. Moral truth is universal and unchanging.
- Absolutism gives clear guidelines for behaviour and so it is easy to make ethical decisions.
- Absolutism cannot take into account the circumstances.
- Absolutism can seem intolerant of cultural diversity.

Relativism

- There is no objective moral truth.
- Moral values vary according to culture, time, place and religion.
- Morals are subject to culture, time, place and religion – morals are subjective.
- The existence of different views does not mean they are all equal.
- Relativism explains why people hold different values and it is a flexible system that can fit a variety of lifestyles.
- Relativism cannot condemn different cultural practices.
- If the ideas of relativism were accepted universally, relativism would become an absolute moral code.

REVIEW QUESTIONS

Look back over the chapter and check that you can answer the following questions:

1   In ten bullet points explain what is meant by cultural relativism, including the difference between the diversity thesis and the dependency thesis.
2   List the main weaknesses of relativism.
3   What is the historical background of situation ethics?
4   List the principles on which situation ethics is based.
5   List the strengths of absolutism.

continued opposite

Terminology

Do you know your terminology?

Try to explain the following ideas without looking at your books and notes:

- Consequentialism
- Moral absolutism
- Moral relativism
- Moral objectivism

SUMMARY

- Relativists believe that moral truth can vary depending on time, culture, religion and so forth.
- Relativists believe that moral reality is not fixed and morals are subjective.
- Relativism does explain why people hold different values.
- Situation ethics was described by Fletcher as relativist.
- Absolutists believe that moral truths are universal and so are the same for everyone at all times and places.
- Absolutists believe that moral actions are right or wrong in themselves.
- Absolutists consider the act, not the end result, as most important.
- Absolutism gives clear guidelines but does not consider individual situations.
- Kantian ethics is an example of absolute deontological ethics.
- Both situation ethics and utilitarianism have an absolute core.
- Natural law has both absolute and teleological elements.

Essential terminology

Absolutism
Apparent good
Deontological ethics
Divine law
Eternal law
Intrinsically good
Natural law
Phronesis
Primary precepts
Purpose
Real good
Secondary precepts
Synderisis
Telos

Normative ethical theories: religious approaches

10 Natural moral law

WHAT YOU WILL LEARN ABOUT IN THIS CHAPTER

- The origins of natural moral law.
- Aquinas' theory of natural moral law.
- The doctrine of double effect.
- The strengths and weaknesses of natural moral law.
- How to apply natural moral law to ethical dilemmas.

Key scholars

Aristotle (384–322 BCE)
Thomas Aquinas (1225–1274)

THE OCR CHECKLIST

Aquinas' natural law, including:

- telos
  - origins of the significant concept of telos in Aristotle and its religious development in the writing of Aquinas
- the four tiers of law – what they are and how they are related:
  1. Eternal law: the principles by which God made and controls the universe and which are fully known only to God
  2. Divine law: the law of God revealed in the Bible, particularly in the Ten Commandments and the Sermon on the Mount
  3. Natural law: the moral law of God within human nature that is discoverable through the use of reason
  4. Human law: the laws of nations
- the precepts – what they are and how they are related
  - the key precept (do good, avoid evil)
  - five primary precepts (preservation of life, ordering of society, worship of God, education of children, reproduction)
  - secondary precepts.

Learners should have the opportunity to discuss issues raised by Aquinas' theory of natural law, including:

- whether natural law provides a helpful method of moral decision making
- whether a judgement about something being good, bad, right or wrong can be based on its success or failure in achieving its telos
- whether the universe as a whole is designed with a telos, or human nature has an orientation towards the good
- whether the doctrine of double effect can be used to justify an action, such as killing someone as an act of self-defence.

(From *OCR AS Level Religious Studies Specification H173*)

WHAT IS NATURAL MORAL LAW?

Natural moral law includes those ethical theories which state that there is a natural order to our world that should be followed. This natural order is determined by some supernatural power. Natural law as we understand it originated in the philosophy of the ancient Greeks, especially that of Aristotle, and was developed by Thomas Aquinas. It is an absolute theory of ethics but it is not rooted in duty, or in an externally imposed law, but in our *human nature* and our search for genuine *happiness* and *fulfilment*. Aquinas considered that by using our reason to reflect on our human nature, we could discover our specific end telos or purpose and, having discovered this, we could then work out how to achieve it. This understanding of God's plan for us, built into our nature at creation, Aquinas called natural law.

- Natural law is not just about 'doing what comes naturally' – it is not about what nature does in the sense of being observed in nature. Natural law is based on nature interpreted by human reason.
- Natural law is not exactly a law in that it does not give you a fixed law – it is not always straightforward and there is some flexibility in its application.

THE ORIGINS OF NATURAL LAW

The earliest theory of natural law first appeared among the Stoics, who believed that God is everywhere and in everyone. Humans have within them a divine spark which helps them find out how to live according to the will of God, or in other words to live according to nature. Humans have a choice

Deontological ethics
Ethical systems which consider that the moral act itself has moral value (e.g. telling the truth is always right, even when it may cause pain or harm).

Purpose
PhotoAlto sas/Alamy

whether to obey the laws that govern the universe, but they need to use their reason to understand and decide whether to obey these cosmic laws.

Thomas Aquinas linked this idea of a cosmic natural law with Aristotle's view that people, like every other natural object, have a specific nature, purpose and function. Aristotle considered that not only does everything have a *purpose* (e.g. the purpose of a knife is to cut) but also its supreme good is found when it fulfils that purpose (e.g. the knife cuts sharply).

The supreme good for humans is *eudaimonia*, which is usually translated as happiness but includes the idea of living well, thriving and flourishing with others in society. Aristotle saw this as the final goal for humans but this is to be achieved by living a life of reason. Aristotle saw reason as the highest of all human activities: 'Reason is the true self of every man, since it is the supreme and better part . . . Reason is, in the highest sense, a man's self' (*Nichomachean Ethics*).

Reason is seen not just as the ability to think and understand but also as how to act: ethics is reason put into practice.

Purpose
The idea that the rightness or wrongness of an action can be discovered by looking at whether the action agrees with human purpose.

THE NATURAL LAW OF THOMAS AQUINAS

Thomas Aquinas was very influenced by Aristotle's writings, which had been lost as far as European philosophy was concerned, but preserved by Islamic scholars. Aristotle's philosophy had been 'rediscovered' just before Aquinas took up his position at the University of Paris.

Aquinas used the ideas of Aristotle and the Stoics as an underpinning for natural law:

1   Human beings have an essential rational nature given by God in order for us to live and flourish – from Aristotle and the Stoics.
2   Even without knowledge of God, reason can discover the laws that lead to human flourishing – from Aristotle.
3   The natural laws are universal and unchangeable and should be used to judge the laws of particular societies – from the Stoics.

THE PURPOSE OF HUMAN BEINGS

Like Aristotle, Aquinas concludes that humans aim for some goal or purpose – but he does not see this as *eudaimonia*. Humans, for Aquinas, are above all made 'in the image of God' and so the supreme good must be the development of this image – perfection. However, unlike Aristotle, Aquinas did not think that this perfection, or perfect happiness, was possible in this life. Aquinas sees happiness as beginning now and continuing in the next life. The purpose of morality is to enable us to arrive at the fulfilment of our natures and the completion of all our desires.

THE FOUR TIERS OF LAW

In his book *Summa Theologiae*, Aquinas attempts to work out what this perfection actually is by examining the 'reflections' of natural moral law as revealed by the following.

Eternal law – the principles by which God made and controls the universe and which only God knows completely. We know these only as 'reflections'; in other words, we have only a partial and approximate understanding of the laws which govern the universe. God's wisdom is reflected in nature and shown in the way he sustains his creation, but humans cannot know this directly. We cannot have any real understanding of why God chose to make the universe the way he did, but as God is God he cannot act irrationally or contradict himself. As Copleston pointed out, '*The eternal law is thus the plan of divine wisdom directing all things to the attainment of their ends*' (Aquinas, p. 220). Humans cannot know the eternal law in God's mind but can work out by reflection and the use of reason so that they are able to pursue good and avoid evil. By the use of reason humans can come to know the natural law: 'The natural law is nothing else but a participation of the eternal law in a rational creature' (*Summa Theologica*, 1a, 11ae, 91, 2).

NASA/ Alamy

Divine law – this is the Bible, which Aquinas believed 'reflects' the eternal law of God. However, this 'reflection' can be seen only by those who believe in God and only if God chooses to reveal it. The revelation of Scripture adds to our understanding of God's purpose, and although divine law cannot contradict natural law, it does affirm it and make it clear. However, Aquinas does not consider that divine law will apply in all circumstances, and so both natural law and human law will supplement it. Aquinas did, however, recognise that humans, including the greatest philosophers, are not free from prejudices and passions that will influence their powers of reason, and so it was necessary that God should reveal certain binding moral laws, even if they could be discovered through reason. The Ten Commandments would be such a revelation.

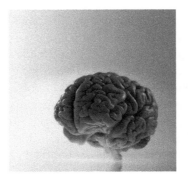

Alamy

Natural law – this refers to the moral law of God, which has been built into human nature; it is also a 'reflection' of the eternal law of God. However, it can be seen by everyone as it does not depend on belief in God or God choosing to reveal it – we simply need to use our reason to understand human nature. Humans, he considers, will naturally avoid anything that goes against their human nature. This natural moral law is not something imposed from above but something humans recognise as rational and binding and so choose to follow. Humans intuitively know that good should be done and evil avoided.

Science History Images/ Alamy

Human law – this refers to the fact that humans live and function in society, and this is part of human nature, ordained by God. In order for humans to flourish this society needs to be organised, but Aquinas does not mean by this that God proposed the organisation of humans into countries and states. There does need to be governance but not simply in order to keep control and punish those who step out of line. Unlike Augustine, Aquinas did not see the state as a result of the Fall and the necessity for some method of control of human's evil tendencies, but simply as a natural institution. Aquinas saw the state as the promoter of a full and good human life. Human laws must, therefore, agree with natural law, and so it is logical to say that just laws are binding in conscience, whereas unjust laws, which do not help the common good or contravene divine law, are not binding in conscience. Aquinas did not seem to hold that any form of government was divinely ordained for all people, but the ruler should promote the good of all and care for all – tyrants and those who enact unjust laws could be removed from power as long as the result would promote the common good and not make the situation worse. According to Aquinas the state and the human law it enacted must enable humans to fulfil the purpose for which they were created.

Good actions should conform to all of these forms of law, but ultimately it is our own powers of reason that confirm whether the law is right. Every action which goes against reason is wrong, even if that reason is mistaken. Aquinas argues that it is the end or purpose of an act that confirms whether

Thomas Aquinas (1225–1274)

Aquinas was born in Roccasecca, Sicily. He died in Fossanova, in the Papal States. His feast day is 28 January (originally 7 March).

He studied under the German philosopher Albertus Magnus. He was an Italian Dominican theologian and the foremost medieval scholar. He worked on his own ideas from the basis of Aristotle, particularly in the metaphysics of personality, creation and Providence.

Aquinas wished to reconcile faith and intellect. His philosophical works were aimed at a synthesis of the works of Aristotle and Augustine; of the Islamic scholars Averroës and Avicenna; and of Jewish scholars, such as Maimonides and Solomon ben Yehuda ibn Gabirol. His most important theological works are the *Summa Theologiae* and the *Summa Contra Gentiles*. His own system of doctrine, developed by his followers, is known as Thomism.

Eternal law

The principles by which God made and controls the universe, which are fully known only by God.

Divine law

The Bible – this reflects the eternal law.

Edward Olive/ Alamy

it is right or wrong, and this purpose is in fact revealed by divine law and confirmed by natural law.

Natural moral law

The theory that an eternal, absolute moral law can be discovered by reason.

Human law

This refers to the fact that humans live and function in society, and this is part of human nature, ordained by God.

Thought point

1   What is the difference between Aristotle's idea of the purpose of humans and that of Aquinas?
2   How did Aquinas view the importance of scripture?
3   How do you think the state could help humans achieve their purpose as Aquinas saw it?
4   Is philosophical reflection based on common experience?

AQUINAS' NATURAL LAW

Natural inclinations

Aquinas thought that God had instilled in all humans inclinations to behave in certain ways which lead us to the highest good and, by using our reason, we can discover the *precepts* (laws) which express God's natural law built into us.

Real and apparent goods

The most fundamental inclination, according to Aquinas, is to act in such a way as to achieve good and avoid evil. He thought this because we are designed for one purpose – perfection – and so we would not knowingly pursue evil. Aquinas saw that in fact humans do not always behave like this and explained this by saying that we get things wrong and follow *apparent good* – something we think is good but in reality does not fit the perfect human ideal. For example if people have affairs they do not do so with the express purpose of hurting their partner but because they think they are 'in love' and it is a good thing to do. In order to work out what is a *real good* and what is an *apparent good* we need to use our reason correctly and choose the right thing to do. There is an 'ideal' human nature that we can all live up to or fall away from, and our moral actions determine whether we achieve this.

Telos

For both Aristotle and Aquinas the universe and everything in it have a purpose. The potential of everything within the universe would be fulfilled when it was directed towards its purpose or telos. Aquinas' teleological approach to nature was based on Aristotle's theory of causality. The telos comes from the nature (form, design) of a thing. The efficient cause is anything that brings about the final cause – for Aristotle the telos of humans is eudaimonia: the good, flourishing life within the community. Aquinas, however, believed that we fulfil our telos not in this life but in the next, when we achieve the union with God for which we were created.

When humans act in accordance with their true nature, they act in accordance with their final purpose, so both the intention (interior act) and the act (exterior act) are important and need to be correct. However, Aquinas did believe that acts were good or bad in themselves and we need to use our reason correctly ('right use of reason' as Aquinas called it) to work out what acts to do.

We can get actions wrong: if the object is evil – for example reproduction if the purpose of the action is ignored – for example masturbation ignores the purpose of reproduction; if a voluntary choice is made to break natural law – for example choosing to sleep with someone else's wife. Aquinas recognised that we can also be influenced by our emotions, bad opinions or habits to do wrong actions.

The synderisis principle

According to Aquinas good is the very first thing understood by practical reason and all rational people will pursue good as it is the way we have been designed by God. The starting point for natural law is, therefore, the *synderesis* rule: do good and avoid evil. Synderesis is the innate, God-given tendency that, according to Aquinas, all people have to pursue good ends and avoid evil ones. Synderesis can also be seen as another word for conscience; then *phronesis*, or practical wisdom, enables us to make moral choices. However, our inclinations to do good are good only in so far as they are subject to reason. We need to deliberate and make responsible decisions and also make

Apparent good
Something which seems to be good or the right thing to do but which does not fit the perfect human ideal.

Real good
The right thing to do – it fits the human ideal.

Study hint

Aquinas thought that all humans share a single nature and so there should be a single aim or purpose for all humans. If we do not believe that there is a final purpose for all humans, then natural law makes no sense.

Primary precepts

The fundamental principles of natural moral law.

Secondary precepts

These are worked out from the primary precepts.

sure that these decisions agree with the eternal law that is also revealed in the natural world. This means that natural law is not unchanging: as our reason is constantly discovering new things in the world our findings may lead to a development of natural law.

So, looked at in this way, natural law is not so much a theory or a way of making moral decisions but rather a way of stressing that our nature is knowable and that we need to use our reason to know and understand it. This becomes clearer as Aquinas explains the fundamental primary principles of natural law, which he believes are fixed.

Thought point

1   How does Aquinas use and change Aristotle's ideas?
2   Explain how natural law, according to Aquinas, can lead us to the supreme good.
3   Explain where natural law may be found and how it can show us how we ought to behave.

Primary and secondary precepts

Aquinas saw the *primary precepts* of natural law as always true and applying to everybody without exception, as they are a direct 'reflection' of God's eternal law. These primary precepts or primary goods can be worked out by observing natural human tendencies and then using our reason so that we fulfil our natural inclination to do good. The primary precepts are as follows:

- the preservation of life
- reproduction
- the nurture and education of the young (to learn)
- living peacefully in society
- worship of God.

These primary precepts are always true in that they point us in the right direction and are necessary for human flourishing.

The *secondary precepts*, on the other hand, are dependent on our own judgements of what actually to do in a given situation, are open to faulty reasoning and may lead to completely wrong choices. The secondary precepts require experience, the use of reason and the exercise of practical wisdom (phronesis); they may change as we reflect on how to achieve our true purpose. The following diagram shows some applications, but be wary of taking this as some sort of absolute list.

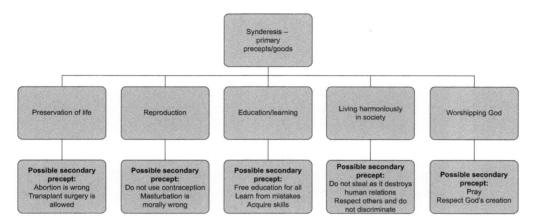

Using excellent reason is vital and its role is to guide us towards those 'goods' that will enable us to thrive and flourish as people. You cannot simply read the secondary precepts from the primary precepts like a list of instructions; so, for example, the primary precept of reproduction might need secondary precepts that explain what is acceptable sex and what is an acceptable way to have children (e.g. in vitro fertilisation). You need to apply practical wisdom, which is an ability to work out what is good and what will lead humans to perfection – this needs imagination and creativity, not blanket rules.

The secondary precepts make Aquinas' understanding of natural law realistic and quite flexible. It does not imply a body of principles from which we simply work out our moral decisions, but takes account of our human limitations and weaknesses. Natural law may seem rigid, but the secondary precepts have to be interpreted in the context of the situation and, according to Aquinas, the more detailed you try to make it, the more the general rule allows exceptions.

What is good for us depends on our natures, not on our decisions – this allows for right and wrong decisions as we have to decide what really leads to human fulfilment, and here lies the problem. *Gerard Hughes* says that we tend to see human fulfilment through our own life experiences and from what we have learned is human fulfilment, and forget to apply reason – both reason and practical wisdom are necessary.

There are modern natural law thinkers whose lists of primary goods differ somewhat from that of Aquinas. *Germain Grisez* includes self-integration, practical reasonableness, authenticity, justice and friendship, religion, life and health, knowledge of truth, appreciation of beauty and playful activities

John Finnis includes life, knowledge, aesthetic appreciation, play, friendship, practical reasonableness and religion. Finnis also changes procreation to marital good. *Joseph Boyle* refers to actions that 'contribute towards communal well-being and flourishing', and his list of goods is very similar to the previous two, except that he stresses that nobody has the right to take away one of these basic goods from another person – so as life is a basic good, euthanasia is an immoral act.

Absolutism

An objective moral rule or value that is always true in all situations and for everyone, without exception.

THE DOCTRINE OF DOUBLE EFFECT

Aquinas saw the primary precepts as objectively true for everyone, and he believed that by using our reason we can discover the right action in every situation by following this principle. In this he is absolutist.

There are times when we have moral dilemmas in which we cannot do good without a bad consequence. To solve this dilemma the doctrine of double effect was devised, roughly saying that it is always wrong to do a bad act intentionally in order to bring about good consequences, but that it is sometimes all right to do a good act despite knowing that it will bring about bad consequences. However, these bad consequences must be only unintended side effects – the bad consequences may be foreseen but not intended. So, if a pregnant woman has cancer she could have a hysterectomy, even though this would result in the death of the foetus – but any other pregnancy-related life-threatening condition whereby deliberately killing the foetus is the only way of saving the woman would not be allowed.

It is the intention that is important. The bad consequence must not be intended for itself, and there must be a proportionately grave reason for allowing the bad consequence. In general people should not do things to deliberately cause harm and should always act with a good intention to find the best outcome in the circumstance.

THE CATHOLIC CHURCH AND NATURAL LAW

Aquinas' natural law is the basis for the morality of the Catholic Church, and it is also considered to be the morality of reason, based on the Bible and our understanding of the natural world, which can be understood by all regardless of whether they are believers.

The Magisterium of the Catholic Church (the teaching authority, usually the pope and cardinals meeting together) claims to be following in the footsteps of Peter and sees itself as an interpreter of both divine law (the Bible) and natural moral law. The *Catechism of the Catholic Church* states, 'The natural law, present in the heart of each man and established by reason, is universal in its precepts and its authority extends to all men. It expresses the dignity of the person and determines the basis for his fundamental rights' (§1956). This view of natural law stresses that we need to exercise responsible moral choices in order to follow the objective moral order established by God. This view was made most clear in two papal encyclicals: *Humanae Vitae* (1968) and *Veritas Splendor* (1993). *Veritas Splendor* moves away from the focus of Vatican II (*Gaudium et Spes* §16) and stresses the act and the personal dimension of conscience and the dignity of the person, which were objective law, which makes actions good or bad according to their object.

The encyclical states that God is the true author of moral law, and human reason can never supersede the elements of the moral law that are of divine origin. The motives and the circumstances do not count if acts are intrinsically evil; as an example, *Veritas Splendor* reiterates the teaching against the use of contraception found in *Humanae Vitae*.

Thought point

1   The Catholic Church has a number of secondary precepts on issues such as abortion. Would the prohibition of the abortion of a foetus growing in the fallopian tubes represent incorrect reasoning?
2   The biological purpose of sex is procreation, but it may have a secondary purpose of giving pleasure and showing love. Does sex always need to be open to the possibility of procreation? How far should the secondary purpose be considered?
3   The doctrine of double effect is often used in war. Is it possible to bomb a military command base in the centre of a civilian population and next to a hospital if the deaths of the civilians are not intended but simply foreseen?
4   'All human beings have a common human nature, and homosexuality is against human nature.' Consider arguments for and against this statement.

Intrinsically good
Something which is good in itself, without reference to the consequences.

SUMMARY OF NATURAL LAW

Natural law underpins the ethics of the Catholic Church, but in reality it attempts to establish a standard for morality which is independent of God's will (see the Euthyphro dilemma, 21) and does this by claiming the following.

STRENGTHS OF NATURAL LAW

- It allows for a clear-cut approach to morality and establishes common rules.
- It is an autonomous, rational theory which makes as much sense to believers as to non-believers – the primary precept of the preservation of life fits in with the Darwinian idea of survival.
- The basic principles of preserving human life, reproduction, learning and living in society are common in all cultures and so natural law is reasonable.

- Natural law does not simply dictate what should be done in individual cases from general moral principles.
- Natural law concentrates on human character and its potential for goodness and flourishing rather than on the rightness or wrongness of particular acts, and so it allows for some measure of flexibility. The doctrine of double effect is also a way through moral dilemmas when two rules conflict.
- Moral decision making is not done by reason alone. Aquinas also involves the imagination – the body, the emotions and passions – and practical wisdom. However, we are not restricted by our emotions or our genes, and it enables us to fulfil our purpose, which is inherent in our make-up and leads to both personal and societal growth.
- All those things that we require for happiness – health, friends – are morally good. The purpose of morality is the fulfilment of our natures.

WEAKNESSES OF NATURAL LAW

- Natural law finds it difficult to relate complex decisions to basic principles in practice (e.g. should more money be spent on schools than on hospitals?).
- Natural law depends on defining what is good, but according to *G.E. Moore*, this commits the naturalistic fallacy. Moore argues that goodness is unanalysable and unnatural, and so cannot be defined by any reference to nature. Aquinas argues that humans are social animals and it is part of our nature to want to live peacefully in the company of others and to care for them. He then goes on to argue that as this 'property' of caring for others is part of our human nature, it must be good. Moore criticises this by saying, 'You cannot derive an ought (value) from an is (fact)' – so it may be a fact that I have within me the natural inclination to care for others, but that does not mean that I ought to care for them. In reality we do not make divisions between facts and values in the way we experience the world – because we are moral beings we unite these together.
- Others argue that natural law is based on assumptions about the world and the inbuilt purpose of things that are questioned by modern science. Darwin shows that nature has particular characteristics due to natural selection. The world has no rational system of laws governing it, but the laws of nature are impersonal and blind, with no intention of moving towards particular purposes. There is no divine purpose – it is simply the way things are.

- Kai Neilsen argues against Aquinas' belief in a single human nature common to all societies. Differing moral standards and cultural relativism challenge the idea of a common natural law. Maybe people have changeable natures (e.g. some are heterosexual and some are homosexual), and natural law is more complex than Aquinas thought.
- Karl Barth thought that natural law relies too much on reason, as human nature is too corrupt to be trusted, and not enough on the grace of God and revelation in the Bible.
- Some Catholic scholars also distrust philosophical theories, such as natural law, and insist it must be supplemented by revelation or by Church teaching – this has led to some rigid interpretations of natural law.
- Vardy and Grosch criticise the way Aquinas works from general principles to lesser purposes and see his view of human nature as unholistic and too simplistic.

REVIEW QUESTIONS

Look back over the chapter and check that you can answer the following questions:

1   Where did natural law come from?
2   What did Aquinas see as the purpose of human beings?
3   How do we discover the primary and secondary precepts and what are they?
4   Make a chart of the strengths and weaknesses of natural law.

Terminology

Do you know your terminology?

Try to explain the meaning of the following ideas without looking at your books and notes:

- Apparent good
- Deontological ethics
- Intrinsically good/bad
- Primary precepts
- Secondary precepts.

Examination questions practice

Read the question carefully – many candidates know all about the weaknesses of natural law, but not so much about its strengths. Answer the question set, not the one you would like to have been set.

To help you improve your answers look at the AS Levels of Response.

SAMPLE EXAM-STYLE QUESTION

Assess the view that natural law is not the best approach to ethical decision making.

AO1 (15 marks)

- This question requires you to either evaluate natural law itself or compare it with other ethical theories, such as Kantian ethics, utilitarianism or situation ethics. However, the focus of the question must always be on natural law.
- You need to show your knowledge of natural law, but pick only those parts of natural law which are pertinent to the question – for example there is no need to go into detail about the origins of natural law.
- You could explain the main principles of natural law and how Aquinas developed the theory.
- You could explain that natural law is God's law revealed through nature and discoverable through reason. The application of practical wisdom is especially important to this question.
- You could then explain the primary precepts and how the secondary precepts are derived from them and put into practice.
- You could explain that practical wisdom should be applied so that the secondary precepts do not lead to wrong decisions. You could explain real and apparent goods.
- Use examples to illustrate your answer.

AO2 (15 marks)

- It is a good idea to set criteria as to what makes natural law a good or bad approach to ethical decision making.
- You could evaluate all the disadvantages of natural law – how it is impossible to define what is good (the naturalistic fallacy), the uncertainty of any divine purpose or common human nature. You could say that natural law relies too much on human reason, which cannot be trusted – or on the other hand that it is too religious and rigid compared to utilitarianism.
- You would need to contrast this with some of the advantages of natural law and discuss how it is clear-cut in its establishment of common rules. You could again contrast it with utilitarianism and say that it avoids the problems of minorities and unforeseen consequences.
- You could consider that both the act and the intention are important when making ethical decisions or alternatively you could argue that it is only natural to consider consequences when making ethical decisions.
- Whichever way you argue it is important to have a clear conclusion which gives a reason as to whether natural law is or is not a good approach to ethical decision making.

Further possible questions

- 'Natural law theory faces serious challenges.' Discuss.
- Discuss the claim that it is too optimistic to believe the view of natural law that humans naturally incline to doing good and avoiding evil.

- 'The absolutism of natural law leads to negative consequences.' Discuss.
- Assess the view that the doctrine of double effect is useful in determining the right ethical decision.
- 'If natural law is applied rigidly to ethical problems there will be obvious injustices.' Discuss.

SUMMARY

- The natural law of Thomas Aquinas is based on that of Aristotle.
- Natural law is a deontological theory which is based on a teleological view of the world.
- Natural law is living in accordance with our true nature, and our purpose is to discover this through reason. In so doing we will fulfil our natures and so achieve perfection and unity with God in the next life.
- The natural inclination of humans is to do good and avoid evil – the synderisis rule.
- Humans sometimes make mistakes and choose apparent goods over real goods. Both the intention and the action are important.
- For Aquinas there are four tiers of laws which help us work out what this purpose is:

  ○ Eternal law
  ○ Divine law
  ○ Natural law
  ○ Human law

- The primary precepts enable people to achieve their true purpose. The primary precepts are:

  ○ the preservation of life
  ○ reproduction
  ○ the nurture and education of the young (to learn)
  ○ living peacefully in society
  ○ worship of God.

- The secondary precepts are derived from the primary precepts using reason and are more flexible, but they must not contradict the primary precepts.

FURTHER READING

Aquinas, T. 1997. 'Summa Theologiae', in *Basic Writings of Thomas Aquinas*, Pegis, A.C. (ed.), Hackett, IN: Random House.

Aristotle Physics II 3. http://classics.mit.edu/Aristotle/physics.2.ii.html (accessed 5th August 2017)

Copleston, F.C. 1955. *Aquinas*, ch. 5. Middlesex: Penguin.

Hughes, G. 1998. 'Natural Law', in *Christian Ethics: An Introduction*, Hoose, B. (ed.), London: Cassell.

Macquarrie, J. and Childress, J. 1986. *A New Dictionary of Christian Ethics*. London: SCM.

Pojman, L.P. 2002. *Ethics: Discovering Right and Wrong*. Toronto: Wadsworth.

Catechism of the Catholic Church 1954–1960. http://www.vatican.va/archive/ENG0015/_INDEX.HTM (accessed 5th August, 2017)

Stanford Encyclopedia of Philosophy. 2005 rev. 2011. *Aquinas' Moral, Political and Legal Philosophy*. http://plato.stanford.edu/entries/aquinas-moral-political/

Normative ethical theories: religious approaches

11 Situation ethics

WHAT YOU WILL LEARN ABOUT IN THIS CHAPTER

- The situation ethics of Joseph Fletcher
- The role of authority, tradition and conscience in Christian ethics
- The link between religion and morality
- Absolutism and relativism in Christian ethics
- The relationship between situation ethics and utilitarianism
- The relationship between situation ethics and Kantian ethics
- The relationship between situation ethics and contemporary moral thought

THE OCR CHECKLIST

Fletcher's situation ethics, including:

- agape
  - origins of agape in the New Testament and its religious development in the writing of Fletcher
- the six propositions
  - what they are and how they give rise to the theory of situation ethics and its approach to moral decision making:
    1 Love is the only thing that is intrinsically good.
    2 Love is the ruling norm in ethical decision making and replaces all laws.
    3 Love and justice are the same thing – justice is love that is distributed.
    4 Love wills the neighbour's good regardless of whether the neighbour is liked.

continued overleaf

5   Love is the goal or end of the act and that justifies any means to achieve that goal.

6   Love decides on each situation as it arises without a set of laws to guide it.

- the four working principles
  - what they are and how they are intended to be applied:
    1   pragmatism: it is based on experience rather than on theory.
    2   relativism: it is based on making the absolute laws of Christian ethics relative.
    3   positivism: it begins with belief in the reality and importance of love.
    4   personalism: persons, not laws or anything else, are at the centre of situation ethics.
- conscience
  - what conscience is and what it is not according to Fletcher – that is a verb and not a noun; a term that describes attempts to make decisions creatively

Learners should have the opportunity to discuss issues raised by Fletcher's theory of situation ethics, including:

- whether situation ethics provides a helpful method of moral decision making
- whether an ethical judgement about something being good, bad, right or wrong can be based on the extent to which, in any given situation, agape is best served
- whether Fletcher's understanding of agape is really religious or whether it means nothing more than wanting the best for the person involved in a given situation
- whether the rejection of absolute rules by situation ethics makes moral decision making entirely individualistic and subjective

(From *OCR AS Level Religious Studies Specification H173*)

Natural law

The theory that an eternal, absolute, moral law can be discovered by reason.

Situation ethics

The morally right thing to do is the most loving in the situation.

WHAT IS CHRISTIAN ETHICS?

There is no easy answer to this question, as there is so much diversity within Christianity. Some Christians will base their ethics solely on the Bible and its teachings, others will base their ethics on the biblical teachings but also on Church tradition and natural law, others will follow a situation ethics approach and others will look to their conscience as a guide. As a result of this diversity, Christians have different responses to ethical issues. It is important to understand not only what Christians think on different ethical issues but also why they think as they do and the basis of their ideas. 'In everything do to others as you would have them do to you' (Matthew 7:12a). The ultimate Christian ethical teaching seems to centre on love: 'Love is the fulfilling of the law' (Romans 13:10b). This New Testament ethical teaching is part of the relationship with God – what makes Christian ethics different is the 'faith' element; Christian ethics comes from a need to interpret, understand and respond to ethical issues from the point of their particular relationship with God. This relationship is one of love and, in particular, agape. Agape is selfless, sacrificial, unconditional love, the highest of the four types of love in the Bible. Agape is a Greek word that is frequently found throughout the New Testament and describes the kind of love that Jesus has for his followers and the love that God has for humans – it is unconditional and self-sacrificing, serving others regardless of the circumstances.

Agape – the highest form of love, sacrificial love

Phila – brotherly love

Eros – sexual love

Storge – family love

Thought point

Look up some of the following texts to see how Jesus' ethics is based on, yet seems to reinterpret, the Jewish law:

- Matthew 5–7
- Mark 2:23 to 3:6
- Mark 7:1–23

This idea of the special relationship with God is carried on in the idea of the Kingdom of God. What the Kingdom of God actually means has been debated endlessly, but it seems to be a state which has arrived, but not yet – a little like a visitor who has arrived at a friend's house and rung the doorbell, but the door has not yet been opened. The problem is how this paradox is to be maintained as far as ethics is concerned. Jesus' ethics can be connected with the idea of the Kingdom of God only by seeing entry into the Kingdom as a result of responding to the appeal to the desire to be children of God – a joyful acceptance of forgiveness and a desire to do God's will. This is no blind obedience, nor is it a morality of law, command, duty and obligation; nor is it motivated by the promise of reward in heaven or punishment in hell, but by a desire to follow God's will – the love commandment. Jesus appeared to be moving away from the legalistic interpretations of the Torah that seemed to be current at the time and asking people to consider their true motives. Following these ideas, relativist forms of Christian ethics arose in the twentieth century – one example being situation ethics. However, the idea of Christian ethics based on love is not new:

> Love, and do what you will. If you keep silence, keep silence in love; if you speak, speak in love; if you correct, correct in love; if you forbear, forbear in love. Let love's root be within you, for from that root nothing but good can spring.
>
> (Augustine, *Epistola Joannis* 7.8)

Relativism

Nothing may be said to be objectively right or wrong; it depends on the situation, culture and so on.

Teleological ethics

The morally right or wrong thing to do is determined by the consequences.

Love, according to Thomas Aquinas, is the reason why we were and love alone leads to happiness and fulfilment. It unites us with God, and to love is to share his life. Without love no virtue is possible, and love alone leads to happiness and fulfilment.

Although Aquinas followed the early Christian idea of morality as love and grace, not law, it is true that legalism has justifiably been associated with Christian ethics, both in theory and in practice. Peter Singer criticises this legalism and accuses Christianity of obscuring the true nature of morality: human fulfilment – happiness. He thinks that the end of the Christian influence on our moral standpoints will open up a 'better way of life for us' and the Judaeo-Christian ethic is 'an empty shell, founded on a set of beliefs that most people have laid aside'. Christian ethics have been seen as deontological and authoritarian, with an emphasis on certain acts as being either right or wrong.

Actions are right or wrong depending on whether they follow God's commands.

> ## Joseph Fletcher (1905–1991)
>
> Fletcher was an American professor who founded the theory of situation ethics in the 1960s. He was a pioneer in bioethics and was involved in the areas of abortion, infanticide, euthanasia, eugenics and cloning. Fletcher was an Episcopalian priest, but later renounced his belief in God and became an atheist.

SITUATION ETHICS

Joseph Fletcher developed situation ethics in the 1960s in reaction to Christian legalism and antinomianism (which is the belief that there are no fixed moral principles, but that morality is the result of individual spontaneous acts).

Situation ethics presumes that it is not necessary to abandon moral autonomy, nor is it necessary to allow everything (antinomianism) or to be totally legalistic. In any situation people need to avoid subjectivism and individualism, and to use in each situation the moral rules of the community, but they should also be prepared to set these aside if love is better served by doing so. Reason, then, is to be used, but based on the Christian principle of agape. This centralisation of love is explained most clearly by Joseph Fletcher in his book *Situation Ethics* (1966) – nothing is intrinsically good except love. Rules can help us, but they cannot tell us what to do – they are subservient to love. Love wills the good of our neighbour, regardless of whether we like him; love is to be the only motive for action, and consequences need to be taken into account and only the end justifies the means.

There is just one absolute – love.

Fletcher argues that each individual situation is different and absolute rules are too demanding and restrictive. The Bible shows what good moral decisions look like in particular situations, but it is not possible to know what God's will is in every situation. Fletcher says, 'I simply do not know and cannot know what God is doing.' As it is not possible to know God's will in every situation, love or agape is situation ethics' only moral 'rule'.

So it is not just the situation that guides what you should do, but the principle of agape and the guiding maxims of the Christian community: 'Do not commit murder,' 'Do not commit adultery,' 'Do not steal,' 'Do not lie.' Situation ethics is midway between legalism and antinomianism, and Fletcher's book, which was published in 1966, reflected the mood of the times – Christians should make the right choices without just following rules and by thinking for themselves.

Christians should base their decisions on one single rule – the rule of agape. This love is not merely an emotion but involves doing what is best for the other person, unconditionally. This means that other guiding maxims could be ignored in certain situations if they do not serve agape; for example Fletcher says it would be right for a mother with a 13-year-old daughter who is having sex to break the rules about underage sex and insist her daughter use contraception – the right choice is the most loving thing and it will depend on the situation. However, the situation can never change the rule of agape, which is always good and right regardless of the circumstances.

According to Fletcher's situation ethics, this ethical theory depends on four working principles and six fundamental principles.

The four working principles

Pragmatism – what you propose must work in practice and bring about a good consequence. This does not involve any rules but the highest good in the situation must be considered. The highest good is always that love should be served in the situation, but the solution must always be practical.

Relativism – words like 'always', 'never', 'absolute' are rejected. There are no fixed rules, but all decisions must be relative to agape. Fletcher wrote that situation ethics 'relativizes that absolute, it does not absolutize the relative'. Thus moral laws and rules may guide people towards the right action, but it is not possible to know in advance what love will require in any situation. According to Fletcher, 'Love's decisions are made situationally, not prescriptively.'

Positivism – a value judgement needs to be made, giving the first place to love. Situation ethics requires the Christian believer to freely choose that God is love and to respond by loving others. This is the opposite from the natural positivism of Kant and natural law, which use reason to deduce the right course of action. Situation ethics starts with a positive choice – the person needs to want to do good. Love provides justification, not proof for an ethical decision: agapeic love is morally right without question and faith in God as love is important.

Personalism – people are put in first place, and morality is personal and not centred on laws. The aim is to achieve the most loving outcome, so a woman stealing food to feed her starving children would be considered right according to this principle.

The six propositions

1 *'Only one thing is intrinsically good; namely love: nothing else at all.'*

Love (agape) is the only absolute. It is the only thing that is intrinsically 'good' and 'right', regardless of the situation. Love decides which actions are good and which are not, but it all depends on the circumstances.

2 *'The ruling norm of Christian decision is love; nothing else.'*

This love is self-giving love, which seeks the best interests of others but allows people the freedom and responsibility to choose the right thing for themselves. The law is to be followed only if it serves love; as Jesus said, 'The Sabbath is made for man not man for the Sabbath.'

3 *'Love and justice are the same, for love is justice distributed, nothing else.'*

Justice will follow from love, because 'justice is love distributed.' If love is put into practice, it can result only in justice. Justice is concerned with giving everyone their due – its concern is with neighbours, not just our neighbour. Justice works out the right action to carry out in a situation, taking everyone's interests into account. This is very similar to utilitarianism, with the greatest happiness simply changing to the principle of agape, so when working out the morality of an action the loving consequences should be spread to as many as possible.

4 *'Love wills the neighbour's good whether we like him or not.'*

Love has no favourites and does not give those whom we like preferential treatment – it is good will which reaches out to strangers, acquaintances, friends and even enemies. Love is not the same as liking nor does it rely on our emotions or personal feelings; it is totally distinct from sentimentality. It is the idea of love written about by St Paul in his letter to the Corinthians:

Love is patient; love is kind; love is not envious or boastful or arrogant or rude. It does not insist on its own way; it is not irritable or resentful; it does not rejoice in wrongdoing, but rejoices in the truth. It bears all things, believes all things, hopes all things, endures all things.

Love never ends. But as for prophecies, they will come to an end; as for tongues, they will cease; as for knowledge, it will come to an end.

(1 Corinthians 13:4–8)

5 *'Only the end justifies the means, nothing else.'*

Love must be the final end, not a means to an end – people must choose what to do because the action will result in love, not be loving in order to achieve some other result. For Fletcher without having an end in sight means an act is simply meaningless, random or pointless. There would be no reason for doing anything. However, this does not mean that any action is permissible as that would lead to anarchy. The action has to fit the situation and the means to an end could vary from one situation to another. If an action causes harm it is wrong, but if good is the result then it is right. According to Fletcher it is not possible to follow a rule such as do not lie if it is obvious that it will cause great harm. Only a good outcome can justify any action.

6 *'Love's decisions are made situationally, not prescriptively.'*

The loving thing to do will depend on the situation – and as situations differ, an action that might be right in one situation could be wrong in another. This is quite different from traditional Christian ethics and is far more relativistic, having just one moral rule – agape.

Some of Fletcher's examples

Fletcher developed his theory by drawing on a wide range of cases that could not be resolved by applying fixed rules and principles. Examples include the burning house and time to save only one person; your father or a doctor with the formulae for a cure for a killer disease in his head alone; the woman who kills her crying baby to save a party from massacre by Indians on the Wilderness Trail; the military nurse who deliberately treated her patients harshly so they would be determined to get fit and able to leave the hospital; and the famous case of Mrs Bergmeier:

> Mrs Bergmeir was imprisoned by the Russians at the end of the Second World War and therefore separated from her husband and three children. The only reason the Russians would release prisoners was if they were too ill for the camp's doctor to deal with or if they were pregnant. Mrs B persuaded a guard to sleep with her; she conceived a child and was packed off home to Germany. A child was born, called Dietrich, who was loved dearly.

The insurance problem

'I dropped in on a patient at the hospital who explained that he only had a set time to live. The doctors could give him some pills (that would cost $40 every three days) that would keep him alive for the next three years, but if he didn't take the pills, he'd be dead within six months. Now he was insured for $100,000, double indemnity and that was all the insurance he had. But if he took the pills and lived past next October when the insurance was up for renewal, they were bound to refuse the renewal, and his insurance would be cancelled. So he told me that he was thinking that if he didn't take the pills, then his family would get left with some security, and asked my advice on the situation.'

The honey trap

'I was reading *Biblical Faith and Social Ethics* (Clinton Gardner's book) on a shuttle plane to New York. Next to me sat a young woman of about 28 or so, attractive and well turned out in expensive clothes of good taste. She showed some interest in my book, and I asked if she'd like to look at it. "No," she said, "I'd rather talk." What about? "Me." I knew this meant good-bye to the reading. "I have a problem I'm confused about. You might help me to decide," she explained . . . There was a war going on that her government believed could be stopped by some clever use of espionage and blackmail. However, this meant she had to seduce and sleep with an enemy spy in order to lure him into blackmail. Now this went against her morals, but if it brought the war to an end, saving thousands of lives, would it be worth breaking those standards?'

The mental hospital

An unmarried female patient with schizophrenia is raped by another patient and becomes pregnant. State law permits abortion only on 'therapeutic grounds' – that is to avoid risk to the mother's life. Should the patient be given an abortion?

What would a follower of situation ethics say about these cases? William Barclay in his book *Ethics in a Permissive Society* (1971) criticised situation ethics by saying that Fletcher's cases were all extreme and people rarely have to make these sorts of decisions. As Barclay puts it, 'It is much easier to agree that extraordinary situations need extraordinary measures than to think that there are no laws for ordinary everyday life.'

He also considers that Fletcher puts too much emphasis on being free from rules as they do protect us from crime and so forth, and as a result people are forced to be constantly making ethical decisions.

Do you agree with Barclay's views? Situation ethics has been criticised for being utilitarian and simply substituting love for pleasure, and Fletcher is thought to be rather vague; values and situations are so variable that we cannot easily see all the ramifications, past, present and future. Can situation ethics be considered Christian? It certainly puts love at the centre, but there are many differences among Christians about what exactly love is and how it is shown. Fletcher's examples are all exceptional cases: Mrs Bergmeier; dropping the atomic bomb on Hiroshima; a man considering stopping his medication so that he would die and his family would receive his life insurance; and a woman who has to seduce and sleep with an enemy spy to end a war. Fletcher's idea of love is not exactly the same as that of Jesus, who individualised love; take, for example, the woman with the haemorrhage, or the healing of the centurion's servant – not a very popular act of love. Fletcher either reinterprets Jesus' actions or dismisses them, so it is hardly surprising that in later life religion played no part in his life and he ceased to describe himself as a Christian situationist.

Thought point

1   Do you think Fletcher's ethics are Christian?
2   Analyse Fletcher's view that 'the end of love justifies the means.'
3   Is situation ethics a useful guide for everyday ethical decisions?
4   Are moral rules totally useless in moral decision making or can you see a role for them?
5   Is the choice for Christian ethics just between legalism and situationism?

Strengths of situation ethics

Situation ethics is easy to understand and can be constantly updated for new problems and issues as they arise, such as genetic engineering and foetal research.

It is flexible and can take different situations into account, but it is based on the Christian concept of love, and so seems to follow the teachings of Jesus.

It does not rely just on consequences to decide if an action is good. Motive is also important.

It focuses on humans and concern for others – agape. It puts people before rules. Agape motivates people to change things for the better – for example to get rid of racism.

Situation ethics allows people to take responsibility for their own decisions and make up their own minds about what is right or wrong. Bishop John Robinson called it 'an ethic for humanity come of age'. It also allows for more flexible decisions to be made when vulnerable people are faced with seemingly harsh rules.

Note: Robinson later changed his mind, arguing that people could not take the responsibility of deciding the morality of their actions, and remarked that 'It will all descend into moral chaos.'

Weaknesses of situation ethics

This method of decision making was condemned in 1952 by Pope Pius XII, who said it was wrong to make decisions based on individual circumstances if these went against the teaching of the Church and the Bible. He said it was too individualistic and too subjective.

Additionally, if the individual is expected to act independently, then all Church teaching is left out and all the teaching of the past ignored. Situation ethics gives the individual person more authority than the Bible, the Church and even God.

It is not possible to determine the consequences of actions – how do we know that the result will be the most loving for all concerned? Situation ethics can be vague as it is almost impossible to work out what is the most loving thing to do – it changes from situation to situation.

Situation ethics has just one moral rule – agape or unconditional love – and it is relative in that it accepts that different decisions will be right or wrong according to the circumstance. Rules, as Paul Ramsay (*Deeds and Rules in Christian Ethics*, 1967) pointed out, do help people when faced with two seemingly contradictory actions, both of which seem to be the loving thing to do. He suggested that instead of looking for agape in each action there should be 'rules of practice' based on agape. Is it ever possible for people to agree on which action shows the most love?

Humans do need some absolute and clear rules – such as against genocide or child abuse – or every action simply becomes dependent on the situation, which may allow wrong actions. Justice does require that people follow the law and treat everyone equally, but situation ethics allows people to treat others differently, break rules and even steal and lie if the circumstance seems to require it. This is not treating people fairly. As William Barclay pointed out, people cannot be trusted to always do the right thing and situation ethics would work only 'if all men were like angels'.

Thought point

These examples are taken from William Barclay's *Ethics in a Permissive Society* (1971). Barclay wants you to agree with the actions; can you see other ways of acting?

1   Suppose in a burning house there is your aged father, an old man, with the days of his usefulness at an end, and a doctor who has discovered a cure for one of the world's great killer diseases and who still carries the formulae in his head, and you can save only one – whom do you save? Your father, who is dear to you, or the doctor, in whose hands there are thousands of lives? Which is love?

2   On the Wilderness trail, Daniel Boone's trail, westward through Cumberland Gap to Kentucky, many families in the trail caravans lost their lives to the Indians. A Scottish woman had a baby at the breast. The baby was ill and crying, and the baby's crying was betraying her other three children and the rest of the party; the party clearly could not remain hidden if the baby continued crying; their position would be given away. Well, the mother clung to the baby; the baby's cries led the Indians to the position, the party was discovered, and all were massacred. There was another such occasion. On this occasion there was a black woman in the party. Her baby too was crying and threatening to betray the party. She strangled the baby with her own two hands to stop its crying – and the whole party escaped. Which action is love?

3   What about the commandment that you must not kill? When T.E. Lawrence was leading his Arabs, two of his men had a quarrel and in the quarrel Hamed killed Salem. Lawrence knew that a blood feud would arise in which both families would be involved, and that one whole family would be out to murder the other whole family. What did Lawrence

continued overleaf

do? He thought it out and then with his own hands he killed Hamed and thus stopped the blood feud. Was this right? Was this action that stopped a blood feud and prevented scores of people from being murdered an act of murder or of love?

4   Ethically, has humanity come of age, as Bishop John Robinson suggested in 1966?

5   To what extent is love compatible with human nature?

6   Why might critics of situation ethics argue that it is really utilitarianism under a different name?

7   Explain why some critics have questioned whether situation ethics is really Christian.

Conscience

Our sense of right and wrong.

CONSCIENCE

Many Christians consider that conscience plays an important part in Christian ethical decision making. There have been many interpretations of what conscience actually is, varying from Newman's voice of God to Aquinas' reason making informed decisions. But conscience as the 'voice of God' can easily become what we mean by 'right' and 'wrong' – so men persecute 'heretics', slaughter enemies and become suicide bombers in the name of God.

Aquinas did not see conscience as some inner voice or oracle that will point us in the right direction – conscience is not about feelings but about reason and judgement, and is reason making moral decisions.

However, conscience does not make the law; it recognises law and uses it to assess conduct. So, for religious ethics, conscience is not so much the voice of God as a response to God's voice. Conscience can be mistaken; doing a bad action when following the guidance of conscience does not make that action good. Conscience is just a way of using reason to come to a decision, but it needs to be informed, and in following conscience we need to be prepared to accept the costs, not just do what we want.

Fletcher does not agree with these approaches, but understands conscience in a far more pragmatic way. Fletcher considers that all ways of understanding conscience are wrong because they treat conscience as a thing, which Fletcher believes is a mistake as conscience is a process, not a thing. For him, conscience is a *verb* rather than a noun – it is something you *do* when you make decisions, as he puts it, 'creatively'. 'There is no conscience; "conscience" is merely a word for our attempts to make decisions creatively, constructively, fittingly' (Joseph Fletcher).

According to Fletcher conscience does not examine and judge our past actions, but simply works out the best action to take – it is proactive and is focused on the future, not the past. 'There are no easy solutions. After careful consideration of all values involved, the Christian chooses what he believes to be the demands of love in the present situation' (Joseph Fletcher). This takes account of the complex and varied situations which people find themselves faced with.

Finally, for Fletcher conscience is simply the act of doing situation ethics; it is the process of ethical decision making.

This view can be criticised as the literal meaning of conscience, 'knowing together', does not support Fletcher's idea of individual judgements in particular situations. Critics might also consider whether individuals can really choose the right course of action without reference to rules and to a collective understanding of morality.

REVIEW QUESTIONS

Look back over the chapter and check that you can answer the following questions:

1   What is agape?
2   What are Fletcher's Six propositions?
3   Do you think Situation ethics is really a Christian ethical theory? Explain your answer?
4   Make a chart of the strengths and weaknesses of natural law.

Terminology

Do you know your terminology?

Try to explain the meaning of the following ideas without looking at your books and notes:

- Antinominalism
- Personalism
- Positivism
- Pragmatism
- Relativism

SUMMARY

- Situation ethics rejects legalism and antinomianism in favour situationalism
- Situation ethics considers each situation on its merits before applying the Christian principle of agape – love.
- Situation ethics is based on four working principles:

  - Pragmatism – it has to work in practice.
  - Relativism – there are no absolutes; every decision depends on the situation.
  - Positivism – statements of faith are accepted freely and reason is then used to work within faith.
  - Personalism – a concern for people rather than things.

- There are six propositions:

  - Only one thing is intrinsically good – namely love.
  - The ruling norm of Christian decision is love.
  - Love and justice are the same.
  - Love wills the neighbour's good.
  - Only the end justifies the means.
  - Love's decisions are made situationally, not prescriptively.

- Situation ethics is an attempt to link Christianity with a new ethics for 'man come of age' (Robinson).

Examination questions practice

SAMPLE EXAM-STYLE QUESTION

Assess the view that situation ethics cannot be considered a Christian approach to ethics.

AO1 (15 marks)
- You could discuss what a Christian approach to ethics actually is. You could briefly explain that some Christians stress biblical commands and values, while others look to Church councils and key thinkers and leaders or look to the individual conscience.
- You could explain how situation ethics is based on agape (love) as found in the teachings of Jesus and briefly explain the main principles of the theory.

AO2 (15 marks)

- You could argue that situation ethics is clearly compatible with other Christian approaches to ethics as agape makes it compatible with any Christian approach that sees love as central. You could point out that Jesus himself broke the Sabbath law in favour of a person-centred approach. In addition, you could consider how Christian views have changed on issues such as slavery, war and equality, and so Christian ethical approaches are not absolute.
- On the other hand, you could discuss the Catholic Church's rejection of situation ethics as relative and subjective. You could also use the views of William Barclay in support of this.
- Moreover, you could say that there are clear fundamental laws and absolutes in the Bible that many Christians adhere to when making moral decisions. You could argue that the approach of natural law that we can work out a definitive course of action through reason is certainly not compatible with situation ethics.
- You may conclude either way but need to make sure that your arguments are clear and consistent, and that you have considered whether situation ethics can be considered a Christian approach as it encourages freedom from moral rules.

Further possible questions

- 'Situation ethics is simply utilitarianism with a different name.' Discuss.
- 'Good consequences are the most important aspect of situation ethics.' Discuss.
- Assess Fletcher's teaching that the ends always justify the means.

FURTHER READING

Cook, D. 1983. *The Moral Maze*. London: SPCK.

Fletcher, J. 1997. *Situation Ethics*. Westminster: John Knox Press.

Gill, R. 2001. *The Cambridge Companion to Christian Ethics*. Cambridge: Cambridge University Press.

Macquarrie, J. and Childress, J. 1986. *A New Dictionary of Christian Ethics*. London: SCM.

Messer, N. 2006. *Christian Ethics*. London: SCM.

Normative ethical theories
12 Kantian ethics

WHAT YOU WILL LEARN ABOUT IN THIS CHAPTER

- Kant's understanding of pure reason, a priori knowledge and objectivity.
- Kant's Copernican Revolution.
- Practical moral reason – the hypothetical and categorical imperatives.
- Kant's ideas of the moral law, good will, duty and the summum bonum.
- The strengths and weaknesses of Kant's theory of ethics.
- The theory of W.D. Ross.
- How to apply Kantian ethics to ethical dilemmas.

THE OCR CHECKLIST

Kantian ethics, including:

- duty
  - origins of the concept of duty (acting morally according to the good regardless of consequences) in deontological and absolutist approaches to ethics
- the hypothetical imperative
  - what it is (a command to act to achieve a desired result) and why it is not the imperative of morality
- the categorical imperative and its three formulations
  - what it is (a command to act that is good in itself regardless of consequences) and why it is the imperative of morality based on:

1   Formula of the law of nature (whereby a maxim can be established as a universal law)

2   Formula of the end in itself (whereby people are treated as ends in themselves and not means to an end)

3   Formula of the kingdom of ends (whereby a society of rationality is established in which people treat each other as ends and not means)

- the three postulates
  - ○ what they are and why in obeying a moral command they are being accepted:
    1   Freedom
    2   Immortality
    3   God

Learners should have the opportunity to discuss issues raised by Kant's approach to ethics, including:

- whether Kantian ethics provides a helpful method of moral decision making
- whether an ethical judgement about something being good, bad, right or wrong can be based on the extent to which duty is best served
- whether Kantian ethics is too abstract to be applicable to practical moral decision making
- whether Kantian ethics is so reliant on reason that it unduly rejects the importance of other factors, such as sympathy, empathy and love, in moral decision making.

(From *OCR AS Level Religious Studies Specification H173*)

WHAT IS KANT'S THEORY OF ETHICS?

Immanuel Kant believed in an objective right and wrong based on reason. We should do the right thing just because it is right and not because it fulfils our desires or is based on our feelings. We know what is right not by relying on our intuitions or facts about the world but by using our reason. To test

---

Immanuel Kant (1724–1804)

GL Archive/Alamy

Immanuel Kant was born in Königsberg, Prussia, on 22 April 1724. He was educated at the Collegium Fredericianum and the University of Königsberg. He studied classics and, at university, physics and mathematics. He had to leave university to earn a living as a teacher when his father died. Later, he returned to university and studied for his doctorate. He taught at the university for 15 years, moving from science and mathematics to philosophy. He became a professor of logic and metaphysics in 1770. He held unorthodox religious beliefs based on rationalism rather than revelation, and in 1792 he was forbidden by the king from teaching or writing on

continued overleaf

religious subjects. When the king died in 1797, Kant resumed this teaching, and in 1798, the year after he retired, he published a summary of his religious views. He died on 12 February 1804.

a moral maxim, we need to ask whether we can always say that everyone should follow it and we must reject it if we cannot.

Kant opposed the view that all moral judgements are culturally relative or subjective so that there are no such things as moral absolutes. Kant's approach to ethics was deontological, where the right takes precedence over the good, and basic rights and principles guide us to know which goods to follow.

Modern deontology avoids too close a link with Kant and rejects his absolutism and complete disregard for consequences; however, his moral theory has been and continues to be influential.

KANT'S COPERNICAN REVOLUTION

Kant's main area of study was to investigate the formal structures of pure reasoning, causality, a priori knowledge (knowledge not based on experience) and the question of objectivity. He wrote these ideas in the *Critique of Pure Reason* (1781; 2nd edn 1787). He then went on to demonstrate the formal structure of practical-moral reasoning in the *Critique of Practical Reason* (1788) and to study the conditions of the possibility of aesthetics and religion in the *Critique of Judgement* (1790).

Kant's work was a reaction against the rationalists and empiricists, and he was concerned with the problem of objective knowledge: can I have any knowledge of the world that is not just 'knowledge of the world as it seems to me'? He is asking, 'How do we know what we know and what does it mean to know?'

The views of other philosophers about knowledge:

René Descartes (1596–1650)

René Descartes is often called the founder of modern philosophy. He was born in Touraine and was educated at a Jesuit school – La Flèche in Anjou. There he studied mathematics and scholasticism. He then studied law at Poitiers and later took up a military career. He went to Italy on pilgrimage in 1623–24 and then, until 1628, he studied philosophy in France. He moved to the Netherlands in 1628 and in 1637 published his first major work: *Essais Philosophiques* (Philosophical Essays). This book covered geometry, optics, meteors and philosophical method. He died from pneumonia in 1650.

- *Descartes* (1596–1650) – the foundation of knowledge is the knowledge of one's own existence: 'I think therefore I am.' Kant criticised this, as he said it did not tell us what 'I' is, or even that it is.
- *Leibniz* (1646–1716) – thought that we can have knowledge untouched by the point of view of any observer.
- *Hume* (1711–1776) – argued that we cannot have any objective knowledge at all.

Kant is closer to the rationalist views of Descartes and Leibniz and opposed to the empiricist views of Hume, which spurred him to explain his own view. Kant considers that our knowledge is not of the world as it is in itself but of the world as it *appears* to us. If our sense organs were different, our languages and thought patterns different, then our view of the world would be different. Kant is saying that humans can never know the world as it really is (the thing in itself) because as it is experienced it is changed by our minds – the world we now see is a *phenomenon* (like a reflection in a mirror). Kant argued that various structures or categories of thought (space, time and causality) were built into the structure of our minds – we have been preprogrammed. This means that all we can really know about scientifically are our own experiences and perceptions, which may or may not correspond to ultimate reality.

Kant called this analysis the *Copernican Revolution*, as its implications for us are just as vital as the implications of believing that the solar system revolves around the sun. Science then can never give us any knowledge of objective reality, as it can never move beyond the view of the world given to us by the categories of our mind. However, Kant did think that these categories could be described as objective, as they are the objective laws of our mind – this is *pure reason* and tells you what is the case.

KANT'S MORAL THEORY

Practical reason looks at evidence and argument and tells you what ought to be done. This sense of the moral 'ought' is something which cannot simply depend on external facts of what the world is like, or the expected consequences of our actions. Kant saw that people are aware of the moral law at work within them – not as a vague feeling but a direct and powerful experience. 'Two things fill the mind with ever new and increasing admiration and awe the oftener and more steadily we reflect on them: the starry heavens above me and the moral law within me' (*Critique of Practical Reason*). Kant's moral theory is explained in the 'Groundwork of a Metaphysics of Morals' (1785) and tries to show the objectivity of moral judgement and the universal character of moral laws and attempts to base morality on reason as opposed to feelings, inclinations, consequences or religion. He roots his view of morality in reason to the exclusion of everything else, and rejects especially Hume's idea that morality is rooted in desires or feelings. He does not reject desires and feelings, but says that they have nothing to do with morality. Only reason is universal. Kant approached morality in the same way as he approached knowledge (looking at the a priori categories through which we make sense of the world) – he looked for the categories we use: what makes a moral precept moral? Kant declared that these were rooted in rationality, were unconditional or categorical and completely unchanging and presupposed freedom.

Freedom

For Kant, if I am to act morally then I must be capable of exercising *freedom* or *autonomy of the will*. The opposite of this is *heteronomy* – that something

Gottfried Wilhelm Leibniz (1646–1716)

Gottfried Wilhelm Leibniz was a German philosopher, mathematician and statesman. He was born in Leipzig and studied at the universities of Leipzig, Jena and Altdorf. In 1666 he began work for Johann Philipp von Schönborn, who was archbishop elector of Mainz. In 1673 Leibniz went to Paris. From 1676 until 1716 he was librarian and privy counsellor at the court of Hanover. His work comprised diplomacy, history, law, mathematics, philology, philosophy, physics, politics and theology.

Copernican Revolution
Belief that the solar system revolves around the sun.

Autonomy

Self-directed freedom, arriving at moral judgement through reason.

A posteriori

A statement which is knowable after experience.

A priori

A statement which is knowable without reference to any experience.

Absolute

A principle that is universally binding.

Absolutism

There is only one correct answer to every moral problem.

Good will

Making a moral choice expresses good will.

Duty

A motive for acting in a certain way which shows moral quality.

is right because it satisfies some desire, emotion, goal or obligation. Our reason must not be subservient to something else even if this is the happiness of the majority.

Good will

The idea of a 'good will' is Kant's starting point for his morality.

> It is impossible to conceive of anything at all in the world, or even out of it, which can be taken as good without qualification, except a good will. Intelligence, wit, judgement and any other talents of the mind we care to name, or courage, resolution, and constancy of purpose, as qualities of temperament, are without doubt good and desirable in many respects; but they can also be extremely bad and hurtful when the will is not good expresses good will. which has to make use of these gifts . . . Good will, then, like a jewel, it would still shine by its own light, as a thing which has its whole value in itself. Its usefulness or fruitfulness can neither add to nor take away anything from this value.

('Groundwork of a Metaphysics of Morals')

It is only the 'good will' which counts and which is the starting point for ethics. Abilities, talents and even virtues count for nothing, as do consequences. Only the will is within our control and so only the will can be unconditionally good and can exercise pure practical reason. This will means the total effort involved in making a conscious moral choice. The good will is when someone acts rationally and ignores inclinations, desires and emotions when making an ethical decision. This requires freedom, as a moral agent needs the ability to choose to act with the right intention.

This is the opposite of Hume's argument that morality is based only on making people happy and fulfilling their desires – it is just a servant of the passions, and morality is founded on our feelings of sympathy for others and depends on our human nature.

Duty

Duty is what makes the good will good. It is important that duty be done for its own sake, and it does not matter whether you or others benefit from your action – our motives need to be pure. Doing duty for any other reason – inclination, self-interest, affection – does not count. The good will chooses duty for duty's sake.

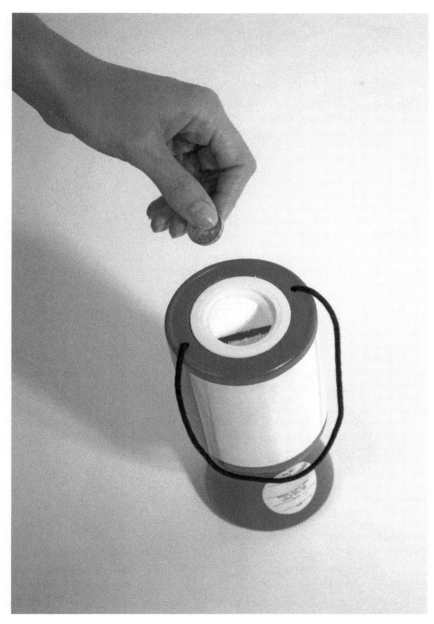

Duty

Richard Warburton/Alamy

Acting according to good will is doing one's duty and is acting without any personal motive or from any hope of gain, such as personal pleasure. Kant does not rule out pleasure in doing one's duty, but pleasure will not help us to know what duty is or the morality of our actions. According to

Kant, there is no moral worth in the feeling of satisfaction we get from doing our duty – if giving to charity out of love for others gives you that warm glow of having helped others, it is not necessarily moral. If I give to charity because duty commands it, then I am moral. So, even though the act of giving to charity has the same result, according to Kant one way is moral and the other is not. *We are not moral for the sake of love but for duty's sake only*. He is arguing against Hume that duty and reason can help us guide our emotions so that we are not dominated and ruled by them.

Kant

Kant was looking for some sort of objective basis for morality – a way of knowing our duty. Practical reason, therefore, must give the will commands or imperatives. He makes the distinction between two kinds of imperatives – non-moral (hypothetical) and moral (categorical).

Hypothetical imperative
An action that achieves some goal or end.

THE HYPOTHETICAL IMPERATIVE

Hypothetical imperatives are not moral commands to the will, as they do not apply to everyone. You need to obey them only if you want to achieve a certain goal – that is why a hypothetical imperative always begins with the word 'if'.

For example: if I want to lose weight I ought to go on a diet and exercise more. A hypothetical imperative depends on the results and aims at personal well-being.

Categorical imperative
A command to perform actions that are absolute moral obligations without reference to other ends.

THE CATEGORICAL IMPERATIVE

Categorical imperatives, on the other hand, are *moral commands* and do not begin with an 'if', as they tell everyone what to do and do not depend on anything, especially desires or goals. According to Kant these categorical imperatives apply to everyone (like the categories of pure reason, which apply to everyone) because they are based on an objective a priori law of reason, which Kant calls the categorical imperative. This is a test to judge whether an action is in accordance with pure practical reason.

There are a number of different forms of this, but they are variations on three basic ones:

1   The universal law.
2   Treat humans as ends in themselves.
3   Act as if you live in a kingdom of ends.

1 Act only according to that maxim whereby you can at the same time will that it should become a universal law

Kant calls this the formula of the law of nature. This first formulation of the categorical imperative asks everyone to universalise their principles or *maxims* without contradiction. In other words, before you act ask yourself whether you would like everyone in the same situation to act in the same way. If not, then you are involved in a contradiction and what you are thinking of doing is wrong because it is against reason.

Kant always wants to universalise rules, as he wants everyone to be free and rational, and if rules are not universalisable then others will not have the same freedom to act on the same moral principles as I use. However, Kant does not claim that everyone should be able to do the same thing as I choose to do in order for it to be moral – but rather everyone should be prepared to act on the same maxim.

Kant uses promise-keeping as an example. I cannot consistently will that promise-breaking for my own self-interest should be a universal law. If I try to make a universal law of the maxim 'I may always break my promises when it is for my benefit,' the result will be that there is no point in anyone making promises – this is inconsistent and so cannot be a moral imperative.

To make his argument as clear as possible Kant uses four examples, including the one of promise-keeping:

- A man feels sick of life as a result of a series of misfortunes that have mounted to the point of despair, but he is still so far in possession of his reason as to ask himself whether taking his own life may be contrary to his duty to himself. He now applies the test 'Can the maxim of my action really become a universal law of nature?' His maxim is 'From self-love I make it my principle to shorten my life if its continuance threatens more evil than it promises pleasure.' The only further question to ask is whether this principle of self-love can become a universal law of nature. It is then seen at once that a system of nature by whose law the very same feeling whose function is to stimulate the furtherance of life should actually destroy life would contradict itself, and consequently could not subsist as a system of nature and is therefore entirely opposed to the supreme principle of all duty.
- Another finds himself driven to borrowing money due to need. He well knows that he will not be able to pay it back; but he sees too that he will get no loan unless he gives a firm promise to pay it back within a fixed time. He is inclined to make such a promise; but he still has enough conscience to ask: 'Is it not unlawful and contrary to duty to get out of difficulties in this way?' Supposing, however, he did resolve to do so; the maxim of his action would be: 'Whenever

Law
Objective principle, a maxim that can be universalised.

Maxim
A general rule in accordance with which we intend to act.

I believe myself short of money, I will borrow and promise to pay it back, though I know that this will never be done.' Now this principle of self-love or personal advantage is perhaps quite compatible with my own entire future welfare; only there remains the question 'Is it right?' I therefore transform the demand of self-love into a universal law and frame my question thus: 'How would things stand if my maxim became a universal law?' I then see straightaway that this maxim can never rank as a universal law of nature and be self-consistent, but must necessarily contradict itself. For the universality of the intention not to keep it would make promising, and the very purpose of promising, itself impossible, since no one would believe he was being promised anything, but would laugh at utterances of this kind as empty shams.

- A third finds in himself a talent whose cultivation would make him a useful man for all sorts of purposes. But he sees himself in comfortable circumstances, and he prefers to give himself up to pleasure rather than bother about increasing and improving his fortunate natural aptitudes. Yet he asks himself further: 'Does my maxim of neglecting my natural gifts, besides agreeing in itself with my tendency to indulgence, agree also with what is called duty?' He then sees that a system of nature could indeed always subsist under such a universal law, although (like the South Sea Islanders) every man should let his talents rust and should be bent on devoting his life solely to idleness, indulgence, procreation and, in a word, to enjoyment. Only he cannot possibly will that this become a universal law of nature or should be implanted in us as such a law by a natural instinct. For as a rational being he necessarily wills that all his powers should be developed, since they serve him, and are given to him, for all sorts of possible ends.

- Yet a fourth is himself flourishing, but he sees others who have to struggle with great hardships (and whom he could easily help); and he thinks: 'What does it matter to me? Let everyone be as happy as heaven wills or as he can make himself; I won't deprive him of anything; I won't envy him; only I have no wish to contribute to his well-being or to support in distress!' Now admittedly, if such an attitude were a universal law of nature, mankind could get on perfectly well – better no doubt than if everyone prates about sympathy and good will and even takes pains on occasion to practise them, but on the other hand cheats where he can, traffics in human rights, or violates them in other ways. But although it is possible that a universal law of nature could subsist in harmony with this maxim, it is impossible to will that such a principle should hold everywhere as a law of nature. For a will which decided in this way would be in conflict with itself, since many a situation might arise in which the man needed love and sympathy from others, and in which by such a law of nature sprung from his own will he would rob himself of all hope of the help he wants for himself.

('Groundwork of a Metaphysics of Morals')

Kant's followers disagree about how to apply this universal law test. *R.M. Hare* suggests an alternative approach to test a proposed moral maxim:

- Try to understand the consequences of following it on affected individuals.
- Try to imagine yourself in the place of these individuals.
- Ask yourself whether you want the maxim to be followed regardless of where you imagine yourself in the situation. This is the role of reason in choosing only maxims that can be universalised.

The challenge then is to distinguish right maxims from wrong ones. This is the role of reason in choosing only maxims that can be universalised.

2 So act as to treat humanity, whether in your own person or in that of any other, never solely as a means but always as an end

Kingdom of ends
A world in which people do not treat others as means but only as ends.

Kant calls this the *formula of end in itself*. He means that we should not exploit others or treat them as things to achieve an end, as they are as rational as we are. To treat another person as a means is to deny that person the right to be a rational and independent judge of his or her own actions. It is to make oneself in some way superior and different. To be consistent we need to value everyone equally.

Kant saw the first two formulations as two expressions of the same idea. He summed this up as follows: 'Principles of action are prohibited morally if they could not be universalised without contradiction, or they could not be willed as universal laws' ('Groundwork of a Metaphysics of Morals'). The third formulation follows from the other two.

3 Act as if a legislating member in the universal kingdom of ends

This he calls the *formula of a kingdom of ends*. Everyone should act as if every other person was an 'end' – a free, autonomous agent. Kant believed that each person is autonomous, and moral judgements should not be based on any empirical consideration about human nature, human flourishing or human destiny. However, this idea of the autonomy of the individual does not mean that everyone can just decide their own morality, but rather that each individual has the ability to understand the principles of pure practical reason and follow them. Pure practical reason must be impartial and so its principles must apply equally to everyone. Kant's kingdom of ends is an ideal community in which all members are both the authors and subjects of all laws. In this community the only possible laws are those which could apply to all rational beings. This means that the categorical imperative demands that we follow only those principles that could be laws in the kingdom of ends. Thus the kingdom of ends can be achieved only if each individual follows the categorical imperative unfailingly; so helping to achieve the kingdom of ends is a duty, and people must hold each other accountable for helping achieve it.

In more modern times a good application of Kant's thoughts on the kingdom of ends can be found in Rawls' theory of justice as fairness (Rawls, 1971). Rawls' approach is that the correct rules of justice are those that are conducive to harmony in society. This means that our fundamental obligation is to act only on principles that would be accepted by a community of fully rational autonomous agents who all share in legislating these principles for their community. This adds a social dimension to Kantian ethics.

4 Any action that ignores the individual dignity of a human being in order to achieve its ends is wrong

Thought point

1   Why does Kant believe that the 'good will' is the only thing that is good without qualification? Can you think of anything else that is good without qualification? What are Kant's supporting reasons? Do you agree with him?

2   How would Kant suggest that where there is a clash of duties, we know what takes precedence by following the categorical imperative. Does this work? Discuss the following:

   (a)   It is your turn to make a presentation in class and you are running late. On the way you witness a car crash and are asked to wait to make a statement to the police.

continued opposite

(b) If only actual persons are ends in themselves, how would a Kantian approach a student who accidentally becomes pregnant and decides to have an abortion so as to continue her studies?

(c) E.M. Forster wrote, 'If I had to choose between betraying my country and betraying my friend I hope I should have the guts to betray my country.' Do you agree?

3   Kant could be criticised for having an homogenous view of people. How might his views make sense in a society with multiple cultures, religions and values?

4   Would the kingdom of ends be a model society? Is it like a modern democracy?

THE THREE POSTULATES OF PRACTICAL REASON

Apart from making the individual the sole authority for moral judgement, Kant's theory of ethics seems to grant freedom to do anything that can be consistently universalised. This morality sets limits but does not give direct guidance; therefore, in order for it to make sense Kant has to postulate the existence of *God, freedom and immortality*.

Kant's ethical theory could, in fact, be said to be a religious morality without God but he seems to take for granted God as lawgiver and he argues that there must be a God and an afterlife, as there has to be some sort of reward.

Kant has already explained that happiness is not the foundation or reason for acting morally, but he claims that it is its reward. Kant's ideas seem to be really twisted with regard to happiness. In the 'Groundwork of a Metaphysics of Morals' he writes,

> The principle of personal happiness is the most objectionable not merely because it is false and because its pretence that well-being always adjusts itself to well-doing is contradicted by experience; not merely because it contributes nothing to morality (since making a man happy is quite different from making him good) but because it bases morality on sensuous motives.

However, he also says that we have a duty to make ourselves happy, not because we want to be happy but because it is necessary for us to do our other duties. Kant seems to put duty in a sort of vacuum, totally separate from our everyday lives.

Summmum bonum
The supreme good that we pursue through moral acts.

To solve this dilemma Kant looks at the postulates of *God* and *immortality*: after death, in the next world, there is no conflict between 'duty' and 'happiness', as 'duty' is part of the natural harmony of purposes created by God. Kant thought that our aim in acting morally is not to be happy but to be worthy of being happy. The *summum bonum* or highest good is a state where happiness and virtue are united – but for Kant it is the virtuous person who has a 'good will' which is vital for morality; happiness is not guaranteed. The summum bonum, however, cannot be achieved in this life, and so there must be life after death where we can achieve it – thus for Kant, morality leads to God.

STRENGTHS OF KANT'S THEORY OF ETHICS

- Kant's morality is very straightforward and based on reason.
- There are clear criteria to assess what is moral.
- The moral value of an action comes from the action itself.
- Kant's categorical imperative gives us rules that apply to everyone and command us to respect human life.
- It makes clear that morality is about doing one's duty and not just following feelings or inclinations. This means that we cannot assume that what is good for us is morally good and so good for everyone else. This is Kant's equivalent of the Golden Rule of Christian ethics.
- It aims to treat everyone fairly and justly and so corrects the utilitarian assumption that the minority can suffer so long as the majority are happy.
- Kant sees humans as being of intrinsic worth and dignity as they are rational creatures. Humans cannot be enslaved or exploited. This is the basis of the Universal Declaration of Human Rights.

WEAKNESSES OF KANT'S THEORY OF ETHICS

- Kant's theory is abstract and not always easily applied to moral situations – it tells you what *types* of actions are good, but it does not tell you what is the right thing to do in particular situations. As Alasdair MacIntyre points out, you can use the universalisability principle to justify practically anything: 'all I need to do is to characterise the proposed action in such a way that the maxim will permit me to do what I want while prohibiting others from doing what would nullify the action if universalised' (*A Short History of Ethics*).
- Kant's emphasis on duty seems to imply that an action is made moral by an underlying *intention* to do one's duty. However, it is not always possible to separate 'intentions' from 'ends', as intentions are closely linked with what we do (e.g. intending to come to the help of a friend who is

being beaten up is not the same as actually doing so). In addition, our motives are not always pure and people seldom act from pure practical reason; we more often help others because we like them or we feel sorry for them. Some philosophers think that putting duty above feeling is cold and inhuman. Kant's theory severs morality from everyday life and everyday feelings and emotions.

- Many people would consider that thinking about the result of an action is an important part of ethical decision making, and if the outcome hurts another person, most people would feel guilty.
- Kant's system seems to work only if everyone has the same view of the final purpose and end of humans. It depends on some notion of God to justify this rationally ordered world. We do not all even have the same views on life and obeying the moral law could put one at a real disadvantage when dealing with people who are wicked, amoral or simply less rational.
- Kant is clear when explaining the conflict between duty and inclination, but he does not help us understand the conflict between different duties, each of which could be justified.
- In addition, though Kant tells us in general terms to respect others and not treat them as ends, this does not tell us what to do in individual cases. What about the terminally ill patient who wants help to die? What about protecting the innocent victim from murderers? What about stealing a drug to help a loved one to live? What about conscription in time of war? Kant's theory here seems to lead either to a position where no decision can be made or to a situation where I may consider doing my duty as just plain wrong.

Universalisability

If an act is right or wrong for one person in a situation, then it is right or wrong for anyone in that situation.

THE THEORY OF W.D. ROSS

These problems with Kant's theory of ethics led W.D. Ross to make certain changes.

Ross said that there were two kinds of duties:

- Prima facie duties
- Actual duties.

Prima facie duties

Ross argued that exceptions should be allowed to Kant's duties – he called these *prima facie duties* (first sight duties). These duties are conditional and can be outweighed by a more compelling duty (e.g. 'Never take a life' could be outweighed by 'Never take a life except in self-defence').

> I suggest *'prima facie duty'* or 'conditional duty' as a brief way of refer-
> ring to the characteristic (quite distinct from that of being a duty proper)
> which an act has, in virtue of being of a certain kind (e.g. the keeping of
> a promise), of being an act which would be a duty proper if it were not at
> the same time of another kind which is morally significant. Whether an
> act is a duty proper or actual duty depends on all the morally significant
> kinds it is an instance of.
>
> (*The Right and the Good*, pp. 19–20)

Ross lists seven prima facie duties:

1   fidelity or promise-keeping
2   reparation for harm done
3   gratitude
4   justice
5   beneficence
6   self-improvement
7   non-maleficence.

These stress the personal character of duty. The first three duties look to the
past and the last four to the future, but they do not need to be considered
in any particular order, but rather as to how they fit the particular situation.
For example who should I save from drowning: my father or a famous doctor? A utilitarian would save the doctor because he could help more people.
Ross says we have a special duty of gratitude to our parents which outweighs
any duty to a stranger. Ross shows that there are possible exceptions to any
rule and these exceptions depend on the situation in which I do my duty,
the possible consequences of doing my duty and the personal relationships
involved.

However, calling these 'duties' may be a bit misleading, as they are
not so much duties as 'features that give us genuine (not merely apparent)
moral reason to do certain actions'. Ross later described prima facie duties
as 'responsibilities to ourselves and to others' and he went on to say that our
actual duty is determined by the balance of these responsibilities.

> Every act therefore, viewed in some aspects, will be *prima facie* right,
> and viewed in others, *prima facie* wrong, and right acts can be distin-
> guished from wrong acts only as being those which, of all those possible
> for the agent in the circumstances, have the greatest balance of *prima
> facie* rightness, in those respects in which they are *prima facie* right,
> over their *prima facie* wrongness, in those respects in which they are
> *prima facie* wrong . . . For the estimation of the comparative stringency

of these *prima facie* obligations no general rules can, so far as I can see, be laid down.

(*The Right and the Good*, p. 41)

Actual duties

This is the duty people are left with after they have weighed up all the conflicting prima facie duties that apply in a particular case.

Problems with Ross' theory:

- How do we know what a prima facie duty is?
- How do we know which one is right where there is a conflict between them?

Ross says that we simply *know* which acts are right by consulting our deepest moral convictions, but is this an adequate response? Can we be sure that Ross' list of duties is correct? How can we compare and rank them in order to arrive at a balance which will guide us to our actual duty?

Ross thought that people could solve problems by relying on their intuitions.

REVIEW QUESTIONS

Look back over the chapter and check that you can answer the following questions:

1   What did Kant mean by 'good will'?
2   Why is duty important to Kant?
3   Spider diagram or mind map the categorical imperative, with examples.
4   Make a chart of the strengths and weaknesses of Kantian ethics.

Terminology

Do you know your terminology?

Try to explain the following terms without looking at your books and notes:

- The categorical imperative
- The hypothetical imperative

continued overleaf

- Duty
- Good will
- The kingdom of ends
- Maxim
- The summum bonum
- Universalisability.

SUMMARY

- Deontological ethics are concerned with actions, not consequences. Kant's theory is deontological because it is based on duty. To act morally is to do one's duty and so obey the moral law.
- Moral actions must be free autonomous actions that are freely decided upon.
- People seek the highest good – the summum bonum, which is virtue plus happiness. Morality, therefore, leads to God. And God is necessary for morality.
- The good will is intrinsically good and means acting in accordance with the moral law, out of duty and not out of any emotion. Kant's ethics are based on reason.
- Moral statements are categorical – they prescribe and the result is not important.
- Kant rejects hypothetical imperatives as they are not universal and do not apply to everyone. A hypothetical imperative can be good but not moral as it depends on the result.
- Moral actions follow the categorical imperative:

  ○ Universal law
  ○ Treat humans as an end in themselves
  ○ Live in a kingdom of ends.

Examination questions practice

It is a good idea always to use examples to explain the categorical imperative. Do not use phrases like 'a priori' if you cannot remember what they mean.

To help you improve your answers look at the AS Levels of Response.

SAMPLE EXAM-STYLE QUESTION

Critically assess the claim that Kant's theory of universalisability provides a sound basis for ethical decision making.

AO1 (15 marks)
- You could include some of the following in your answer:
- An explanation of Kantian ethics, including Kant's ideas about the importance of duty and the categorical imperative, playing particular attention to the idea of universalisability.

AO2 (15 marks)
- Here you need to think about whether Kant's theory works in practice when making ethical decisions.
- You may argue that Kant's theory is abstract and not easily applied to ethical situations.
- You may consider that Kant's approach does not consider outcomes, that there are conflicts between duties and that there is no room for emotions.
- On the other hand, you may consider that Kant's theory of universalisation can provide a good basis for ethical decision making as it gives clear criteria to know which actions are moral, it respects human life and the idea of duty means that we will always do what is right and not be swayed by emotions and feelings. They may say that his rules are fair as they apply to everyone, and so universalisability does give a sound basis for making ethical decisions.
- In considering these issues and reaching a conclusion you might also argue that utilitarianism, which does consider consequences but cannot be universalised to everyone, is a better approach.

Further possible questions

- **Critically assess Kant's defence of an absolute morality.**
- **'Kant's theory of ethics has serious weaknesses.' Discuss.**
- **To what extent is doing one's duty the most important part of ethics?**

FURTHER READING

Kant, I. 2005. 'Groundwork of a Metaphysics of Morals', in *The Moral Law*, Paton, H.J. (trans.), London: Routledge.

MacIntyre, A. 1968. *A Short History of Ethics*. London: Routledge.

Norman, R. 1998. *The Moral Philosophers*. Oxford: Oxford University Press.

O'Neill, O. 2013. 'Kantian Approaches to Some Famine Problems', in *Ethical Theory: An Anthology*, Shafer-Landau, R. (ed.). Chichester: Wiley-Blackwell.

Pojman, L.P. 2002. *Ethics: Discovering Right and Wrong*. Toronto: Wadsworth.

Ross, W.D. 1930, 2002. *The Right and the Good*. Oxford: Oxford University Press.

Scruton, R. 1982. *Kant*. Oxford: Oxford University Press.

Ward, K. 1972. *The Development of Kant's View of Ethics*. Oxford: Blackwell.

13 Utilitarianism

Essential terminology

Act utilitarianism
Consequentialist
Hedonic calculus
Hedonism
Preference
Utilitarianism
Principle of utility
Qualitative quantitative
Rule utilitarianism
Teleological
Universalisability

Key scholars

Epicurus (341–270 BCE)
Richard Brandt (1910–1997)
Jeremy Bentham (1748–1832)
R.M. Hare (1919–2002)
John Stuart Mill (1806–1873)
John Rawls (1921–2002)
W.D. Ross (1877–1971)
Bernard Williams (1929–2003)
Karl Popper (1902–1994)
Peter Singer (1946–)

WHAT YOU WILL LEARN ABOUT IN THIS CHAPTER

- The principle of utility, the hedonic calculus, act and rule utilitarianism.
- Classical forms of utilitarianism from Bentham and Mill; modern versions from Popper, Hare, Singer and Brandt.
- The strengths and weaknesses of utilitarianism.
- How to apply utilitarianism to ethical dilemmas.

THE OCR CHECKLIST

Utilitarianism, including:

- utility
  - the use of the significant concept of utility (seeking the greatest balance of good over evil, or pleasure over pain) in teleological and relativist approaches to ethics
- the hedonic calculus
  - what it is (calculating the benefit or harm of an act through its consequences) and its use as a measure of individual pleasure
- act utilitarianism
  - what it is (calculating the consequences of each situation on its own merits) and its use in promoting the greatest amount of good over evil, or pleasure over pain
- rule utilitarianism
  - what it is (following accepted laws that lead to the greatest overall balance of good over evil, or pleasure over pain) and its use in promoting the common good

continued opposite

Learners should have the opportunity to discuss issues raised by utilitarianism, including:

- whether utilitarianism provides a helpful method of moral decision making
- whether an ethical judgement about something being good, bad, right or wrong can be based on the extent to which, in any given situation, utility is best served
- whether it is possible to measure good or pleasure and then reach a moral decision.

(From *OCR AS Level Religious Studies Specification H173*)

WHAT IS UTILITARIANISM?

You have probably heard someone justify their actions as being for the greater good. Utilitarianism is the ethical theory behind such justifications.

Utilitarianism is a teleological theory of ethics. It is the opposite of deontological ethical theories that are based on moral rules, on whether the action itself is right or wrong. Teleological theories of ethics look at the consequences – the results of an action – to decide whether it is right or wrong. Utilitarianism is a consequentialist theory.

The theory of utilitarianism began with *Jeremy Bentham* as a way of working out how good or bad the consequence of an action would be. Utilitarianism gets its name from Bentham's test question: 'What is the use of it?' He thought of the idea when he came across the words 'the greatest happiness of the greatest number' in *Joseph Priestley's An Essay on the First Principles of Government*, on the nature of political, civil and religious liberty (1768). Bentham was very concerned with social and legal reform and he wanted to develop an ethical theory which established whether something was good or bad according to its benefit for the majority of people.

Bentham called this the *principle of utility*. Utility here means the usefulness of the results of actions. The principle of utility is often expressed as 'the greatest good of the greatest number'. 'Good' is defined in terms of pleasure or happiness – so an act is right or wrong according to the good or bad that results from the act and the good act is the most pleasurable. Since it focuses on the greatest number, Bentham's theory is quantitative.

Principle of utility
The theory of usefulness – the greatest happiness for the greatest number.

Consequentialist
Someone who decides whether an action is good or bad by its consequences.

Teleological
Moral actions are right or wrong according to their outcome or telos (end).

Hedonism
The view that pleasure is the chief 'good'.

THE ORIGINS OF HEDONISM

The idea that 'good' is defined in terms of pleasure and happiness makes utilitarianism a *hedonistic* theory. The Greek philosophers who thought along similar lines introduced the term *eudaimonia*, which is probably best translated as 'well-being'. Both Plato and Aristotle agreed that 'good' equated with the greatest happiness, while the Epicureans stressed 'pleasure' as the main aim of life. The ultimate end of human desires and actions, according to Aristotle, is happiness, and although pleasure sometimes accompanies this, it is not the chief aim of life. Pleasure is not the same as happiness, as happiness results from the use of reason and cultivating the virtues. It is only if we take pleasure in good activities that pleasure itself is good. This idea of Aristotle's is taken up by John Stuart Mill, as we will see later.

JEREMY BENTHAM'S APPROACH

Jeremy Bentham developed his ethical system around the idea of pleasure, and it is based on ancient hedonism, which pursued physical pleasure and avoided physical pain. There is, therefore, no consideration of the natural rights of humans, which Bentham rejected as 'nonsense on stilts'. An individual's right to life or to freedom is granted by society and is the result of legislation, and logically for a utilitarian, such as Bentham, it could be removed if the result was greater social utility and greater pleasure and well-being for the majority.

According to Bentham, the most moral acts are those that maximise pleasure and minimise pain. This has sometimes been called the 'utilitarian calculus'. An act would be moral if it brings the greatest amount of pleasure and the least amount of pain.

Pain versus pleasure

Bentham said,

> The principle of utility aims to promote happiness which is the supreme ethical value. Nature has placed us under the governance of two sovereign masters, *pain* and *pleasure*. An act is right if it delivers more pleasure than pain and wrong if it brings about more pain than pleasure.

By adding up the amounts of pleasure and pain for each possible act we should be able to choose the good thing to do.

Happiness = pleasure minus pain

Jeremy Bentham (1748–1832)

Jeremy Bentham was born in London on 15 February 1748. He could read scholarly works at age 3, played the violin at 5 and studied Latin and French at 6. At age 12 he went to Oxford and trained as a lawyer. Bentham was the leader of the Philosophical Radicals, who founded the *Westminster Review*. He died in London on 6 June 1832. His body was dissected and his clothed skeleton is in a glass case in University College, London. Bentham advanced his theory of utilitarianism as the basis for general political and legal reform.

Hedonic calculus
Bentham's method for measuring the good and bad effects of an action.

The hedonic calculus

To help us choose the good thing to do and work out the possible consequences of an action, Bentham provided a way of measuring. This is the *hedonic calculus*.

It has seven elements:

1 the intensity of the pleasure (how deep)
2 the duration of the pleasure caused (how long)
3 the certainty of the pleasure (how certain or uncertain)
4 the propinquity (remoteness) of the pleasure (how near or far is the pleasure)
5 the fecundity of the pleasure – chance of a succession of pleasures (how fertile will it be in producing other pleasures?)
6 the purity of the pleasure (how secure – or will it lead to pain for others?)
7 the extent of the pleasure (how universal – how many will be affected?).

The quantity of happiness
Jordi Clave Garsot/Alamy

This calculus gave Bentham a method of testing whether an action is morally right, in that if it was good it would result in the most pleasurable outcome, all the elements having been weighed up. Whatever is good or bad can be measured in a *quantitative* way. Bentham's utilitarianism stresses that each person's pleasures count equally – so public interest is more important than the individual's own happiness or pleasure. Sentience – the ability to feel pleasure and pain – is also important for Bentham: 'The question is not,

Can they reason? Nor Can they talk? But Can they suffer?' (Bentham, *An Introduction to the Principles of Morals and Legislation*). Overleaf there is an example of how the hedonic calculus might be applied to a young totally paralysed man who is deciding whether to have euthanasia.

It is actually quite difficult to decide which decision would bring the most pleasure and the least pain, and this is one of the problems when using the hedonic calculus as it is not possible for us to see into the future; we can only make educated guesses, and these are often clouded by our emotional state at the time.

Hedonism

Bentham's utilitarianism is a universal hedonism – the highest good is the greatest happiness for the greatest number. Actions are judged as a means to an end. What is right is that which is calculated to bring about the greatest balance of good over evil, where good is defined as pleasure or happiness.

Bentham's view is described as *act utilitarianism*.

Quantitative
Looking at the quantity of the happiness.

Act utilitarianism
A teleological theory that uses the outcome of an action to determine whether it is good or bad.

Hedonic calculus	Have euthanasia	Do not have euthanasia
Intensity	He could be at peace and his family would not have to devote their lives to caring for him. However, his death could bring intense feelings of pain to his family and friends.	His continuing existence gives intense feelings of joy to his family and friends, but may also lead to resentment in those who care for him.
Duration	Death is permanent but the grieving of family and friends might last a long time.	The young man will need looking after for a lifetime.
Certainty	The freedom from the pain of his situation is certain.	It is uncertain what pleasures continuing to live totally paralysed will bring.
Remoteness	The relief from his situation is immediate.	Any possibility of a cure or of learning to live successfully with his situation is a long way off.
Succession	There will be no more choices. The relief that he is no longer suffering may help his family and friends to accept his death.	Pleasure that he is still living but pain that he is still suffering will cancel each other out.

continued opposite

Hedonic calculus	Have euthanasia	Do not have euthanasia
Purity	If he regrets his decision it will be too late.	May live a miserable life stuck on a bed or in a wheelchair, totally dependent on others.
Extent	The young man and his family and friends are the most directly affected.	His continuing existence will bring both pain and pleasure for a lifetime.

Bentham argued that we should be guided by the principle of utility and not by rules. However, it may be necessary to use rules of thumb based on past experience, especially if there is no time to work out the consequences. However, it is the consequences that are the most important for Bentham as they can be easily predicted.

Thought point

1 What would be the problems if everyone acted as an act utilitarian all the time?
2 Are all actions good only because they have good results?
3 Suppose a rape is committed that is thought to be racially motivated. Riots are brewing that may result in many deaths and long-term racial antagonism. You are the police chief and have recently taken a man into custody. Why not frame him? He will be imprisoned if found guilty and this will result in peace and safety. Only you, the innocent man and the real rapist (who will keep quiet), will know the truth. What is the morally right thing to do? Look at all the consequences of any action.
4 Suppose a surgeon could use the organs of one healthy patient to save the lives of several others. Would the surgeon be justified in killing the healthy patient for the sake of the others?
5 You are an army officer who has just captured an enemy soldier who knows where a secret time bomb is planted. If it explodes it will kill thousands. Will it be morally permissible to torture the soldier so that he reveals the bomb's location? If you knew where the soldier's children were, would it also be permissible to torture them to get him to reveal the bomb's whereabouts?

John Stuart Mill (1806–1873)

John Stuart Mill was born on 20 May 1806, the son of James Mill, who had a significant influence on nineteenth-century British thought in philosophy, economics, politics and ethics. From 1822 he worked for his father in India House and stayed there until 1858, when the company closed and he retired. Mill then lived in St Véran, France, until 1865, when he became a member of Parliament. He went back to France in 1868, and lived there until his death on 8 May 1873. He is most famous for his essay *On Liberty* (1859).

Qualitative
Looking at the quality of the pleasure.

JOHN STUART MILL'S APPROACH

Mill was also a hedonist and accepted that happiness is of the greatest importance. He stressed happiness rather than pleasure.

The greatest happiness principle

Mill said,

> The Greatest Happiness Principle holds that actions are right in proportion as they tend to promote happiness, wrong as they tend to produce the reverse of happiness. By happiness is intended pleasure, and the absence of pain; by unhappiness, pain and the privation of pleasure.

Happiness for Mill is more than just pleasure and also includes having goals and virtues.

The quality of pleasure

Having affirmed his agreement with the principle of utility, Mill then modifies Bentham's approach, especially the quantitative emphasis. He says, 'Some kinds of pleasures are more desirable and more valuable than others, it would be absurd that while, in estimating all other things, quality is not also considered as well as quantity.'

According to Mill, quality of pleasure employs the use of the higher faculties. Here he is answering the objection to Bentham's approach that utilitarians are just pleasure-seekers. For example consider the case of the Christians and the Romans: many Romans got a lot of pleasure from seeing a few Christians eaten by lions – here the greatest happiness (that of the Romans) was produced by an act (Christians being eaten by lions) that is surely quite wrong. Mill says that the quality of pleasure that satisfies a human is different from that which satisfies an animal. People are capable of more than animals, so it takes more to make a human happy. Therefore, a person will always choose higher-quality human pleasures and reject all the merely animal pleasures. As Mill puts it,

> Few human creatures would consent to be changed into any of the lower animals for a promise of the fullest allowance of the beast's pleasures . . . It is better to be a human being dissatisfied than a pig satisfied; better to be Socrates dissatisfied than a fool satisfied. And if the fool or the pig

The quality of happiness
Darren Robb/Getty

are of a different opinion, it is because they only know their side of the question.

(On Virtue and Happiness, 1863)

So since the Romans are enjoying only 'animal' pleasure, it does not matter that they are getting a lot more of it than the Christians – it is the quality and not the quantity of the pleasure that really counts. For Mill, it is intellectual pleasures (e.g. reading poetry or listening to music) that really count and are more important than such pleasures as eating, drinking or having sex.

Happiness, he argues, is something that people desire for its own sake, but we need to look at human life as a whole – happiness is not just adding up the units of pleasure but rather the fulfilment of higher ideals. In order to distinguish between these higher and lower pleasures Mill proposed the idea of competent judges who had experienced both higher and lower pleasures and so were able to say with authority that the higher pleasures were to be preferred.

Universalisability

Mill next develops the argument that in order to derive the principle of the greatest good (happiness) for the greatest number we need the principle of universalisability. He says, 'Each person's happiness is a good to that

Universalisability

If an act is right or wrong for one person in a situation, then it is right or wrong for anyone in that situation.

Rule utilitarianism

Establishing a general rule that follows utilitarian principles.

person, and the general happiness, therefore, is a good to the aggregate of all persons.'

As you can see, the last proposition does not follow logically from the previous one. To move from each person to everyone is a fallacy. Mill makes this move because he wants to justify 'the greatest number'. This can mean that utilitarianism demands that people put the interests of the group before their own interests, and Mill compares this to 'the Golden Rule of Jesus of Nazareth'. Mill has a positive view of human nature and thinks that people have powerful feelings of empathy for others, which can be cultivated by education and so on.

Mill also separates the question of the motive and the morality of the action. There is nothing wrong with self-interest if it produces the right action.

Happiness
Mint Images Limited/Alamy

Rule utilitarianism

Another aspect of Mill's approach is the idea that there need to be some moral rules in order to establish social order and justice – but the rules should be those which, if followed universally, would most likely produce the greatest happiness. Mill has been seen as a *rule utilitarian* in contrast to Bentham's act utilitarianism – although Mill never discussed act or rule utilitarianism in these terms. Also, like many philosophers, Mill's approach was not consistent throughout his writings – at first Mill appears to be an act utilitarian, saying that pleasures can be described as either higher or lower, and later he writes that rights and rules are principles of utility. He argues that some rights need to be guaranteed in order to ensure general happiness and the greater good. Mill considers that people have interests that ought to be defended, such as protection from harm, so rule utilitarianism can protect human rights if they make everyone's lives happier. He seems to assert that when one is uncertain as to which action to take, the rules of justice and rights (life, liberty and property) must be considered as most important.

As Mill's position is unclear it is perhaps better to describe him as a weak rule utilitarian, as when a strong utilitarian reason exists to break the rule, the rule should be disregarded. This is also the case when two utilitarian rules conflict – for example should Robin Hood break the rule 'do not steal' or the rule 'help the poor'? In this dilemma the only possible solution is to consider which action will maximise utility. However, this still leaves the possibility of injustice, lack of consideration for minorities and so forth, which rule utilitarianism was designed to avoid.

Comparing Bentham and Mill

Bentham	Mill
'The greatest good [pleasure] for the greatest number'	'The greatest happiness for the greatest number'
Focused on the individual alone	We should protect the common good, universalistic
Quantitative – hedonic calculus	Qualitative – higher/lower pleasure
Act utilitarianism	Rule utilitarianism
In search of maximisation of happiness	
Consequentialist	Consequentialist

Jeremy Bentham
World History Archive/Alamy

ACT AND RULE UTILITARIANISM

The distinction between act and rule utilitarianism is to do with what the principle of utility is applied to.

*   According to act utilitarianism the principle is applied directly to a particular action in a particular circumstance.
*   According to rule utilitarianism the principle is applied to a selection of a set of rules which are in turn used to determine what to do in particular situations.

John Stuart Mill
Everett Collection Historical/Alamy

ACT UTILITARIANISM

You must decide what action will lead to the greatest good in the particular situation you are facing and apply the principle of utility directly. You need to look at the consequences of a particular act and what will bring about the greatest happiness.

Flexibility

Since the same act might in some situations produce the greatest good for the greatest number, but in other situations not, utilitarianism allows moral rules to change from age to age, from situation to situation.

There are no necessary moral rules except one: that we should always seek the greatest happiness for the greatest number in all situations.

Act utilitarianism is linked to Bentham's form of utilitarianism.

Weaknesses of act utilitarianism

- It is difficult to predict the consequences.
- There is potential to justify any act.
- There is difficulty in defining pleasure.
- There is no defence for the minorities.
- It is impractical to say that we should calculate the morality of each choice.
- *Teleological* – aims for a maximisation of pleasure for the majority. It has an end aim or goal.
- *Relative* – no notion of absolute right/wrong. No external source of truth. Nothing in itself is right or wrong.
- *Consequential* – the consequences of an act alone determine its rightness/wrongness.

RULE UTILITARIANISM

Rule utilitarians believe that rules should be formed using utilitarian principles for the benefit of society. Your action is judged right or wrong by the goodness or badness of the consequences of a rule that everyone should follow in similar circumstances. Rule utilitarianism enables us to establish universal rules that will promote the happiness of humanity and will generally be right in most circumstances (e.g. telling the truth, keeping your promises). This avoids the difficulty of the negative consequences which could result if act utilitarianism were to be universalised – if everyone acted according to their own personal knowledge of the situation without considering general rules or excepted behaviour, the result could lead to injustice, disorder and unpredictable actions. So for a rule utilitarian it is better to follow general rules based on the principle of utility than try to work out the best action to take in every situation. This can also protect human rights as in general having rights makes everyone's lives happier.

Strong rule utilitarians believe that these derived rules should never be disobeyed.

Weak rule utilitarians say that although there should be generally accepted rules or guidelines, they should not always be adhered to indefinitely. There may be situations where the better consequence might be achieved by disregarding the rule (e.g. where it might be better to tell a lie).

Weak rule utilitarianism is commonly linked with Mill; however, it is not clear whether Mill was an act or a rule utilitarian. For Mill it seems that experience teaches us the best consequences of our actions, so in utilitarianism he advocates that it could be a duty to steal medicine or food in order to save a life.

Weaknesses of rule utilitarianism

- It is difficult to predict the consequences.
- It is difficult to define what constitutes happiness.
- There is no defence for the minorities.
- To invoke rules means that the approach becomes deontological, not teleological.
- Followers of rule utilitarianism can be either strict rule-followers or rule-modifiers, but neither seems satisfactory. Strict rule-followers can be irrational: obeying the rule even when disobeying it will produce more happiness. Rule-modifiers can end up being no different from act utilitarians.
- *Deontological* – rules take priority.
- *Relative* – what is right/wrong is established as the maximisation of pleasure for the particular community/society within which it operates.
- *Consequential* – the overall consequences determine its rightness/ wrongness.

Thought point

1   Suppose that you were God, and because you are omnibenevolent, you want your creatures to be as happy as possible across time (i.e. you believe in utilitarianism). If you were choosing a moral code to teach your created people that would make them all happy, what code would you teach them?
2   Explain the distinction between act and rule utilitarianism and why rule utilitarianism came about.
3   The country is threatened with drought, so people are urged to conserve water, and hose-pipe bans are in force. Joe lives in an isolated part of the country and nobody ever drives past his house. The water company has forgotten Joe exists and so he is never billed for his water. Joe knows about the hose-pipe ban, but he really wants a green lawn. His lawn is tiny, so he knows he will not be harming anyone if he waters it and the small amount he uses will not affect the drought. Joe continues to use water. What would an act utilitarian say about this? What would a rule utilitarian say? Give reasons.

Preference utilitarianism
Moral actions are right or wrong according to how they fit the preferences of those involved.

SOME MORE MODERN APPROACHES TO UTILITARIANISM – STRETCH AND CHALLENGE

Preference utilitarianism

Preference utilitarianism is a more recent form of utilitarianism and is associated with *R.M. Hare*, *Peter Singer* and *Richard Brandt*.

An act utilitarian judges right or wrong according to the maximising of pleasure and minimising of pain, a rule utilitarian judges right or wrong according to the keeping of rules derived from utility, but a preference utilitarian judges moral actions according to whether they fit in with the preferences of the individuals involved. This approach to utilitarianism asks, 'What is in my own interest? What would I prefer in this situation? Which outcome would I prefer?' However, because utilitarianism aims to create the greatest good for the greatest number, it is necessary to consider the preferences of others in order to achieve this. This requires an equal consideration of the interests of everyone else affected by an ethical decision.

R.M. Hare's approach

Hare argues that in moral decision making we need to consider our own preferences and those of others. He says that 'equal preferences count equally, whatever their content'. People are happy when they get what they prefer, but what we prefer may clash with the preferences of others. Hare says we need to 'stand in someone else's shoes' and try to imagine what someone else might prefer. We should treat everyone, including ourselves, with impartiality – he also argues for universalisability.

Peter Singer's approach

Singer also defends preference utilitarianism and suggests that we should take the viewpoint of an impartial spectator combined with a broadly utilitarian approach. He says that 'our own preferences cannot count any more than the preferences of others' and so, in acting morally, we should take account of all the people affected by our actions. Ethical judgements must be made from a universal point of view. This view accepts that our own wants, needs and desires cannot count for more than those of anyone else. Singer uses the example of sharing the abundance of nature's fruits – everyone is entitled to an equal share. These have to be weighed and balanced, and then we must choose the action that gives the best possible consequences for those affected. Singer says society is made up of a collection of individuals, each with their own preferences; trade-offs, however, have to be made for the general welfare – in other words some preferences have to be accepted and others rejected so that the good of all may be achieved.

For Singer, the 'best possible consequences' means what is in the best *interests* of the individuals concerned – this is different from Bentham and Mill, as he is not considering what increases pleasure but what diminishes pain. In *Practical Ethics* (1993) Singer wrote that *'an action contrary to the preference of any being is wrong, unless this preference is outweighed by contrary preferences'* The more preferences satisfied in the world, the better – so killing someone like Hitler, which would save the lives of many others and lead to many preferences being fulfilled, would be the right thing to do.

This principle of equal consideration of preferences or interests acts like a pair of scales – everyone's preferences or interests are weighed equally. So, in Singer's view, killing a person who prefers to go on living would be wrong and not killing a person who prefers to die would also be wrong. Racism is wrong, as it goes against the principle of acknowledging other people's interests or preferences and gives greater value to the preferences of one's own race.

If Singer's principles were put into practice, they would prove radical – for example he argued that since $1,000 can keep several children alive for years, each of us is obligated not to spend it but to donate it to Oxfam or the Red Cross. Singer's principle is 'If it is in our power to prevent something bad from happening, without thereby sacrificing anything of comparable moral importance, we ought, morally, to do it' ('Famine, Affluence, and Morality').

Peter Singer (1946–)

Peter Singer was born on 6 July 1946 in Melbourne. He studied at Melbourne and Oxford. In 1999 he was appointed DeCamp Professor of Bioethics at the University Center for Human Values at Princeton University. Singer's system is based on reason and not on self-interest or social conditioning. His work deals with issues such as embryo experimentation, genetic engineering, surrogacy, abortion and euthanasia. Singer's best-known work is *Animal Liberation* (1975). He is a vegetarian and donates the royalties from his books to international aid and animal liberation. He gives between 10% and 20% of his income to the poor.

A moment's reflection on the implications of this principle should convince you of its radicalness. If we were to follow it, we would be left just slightly better off than the worst off people in the world (who would be much better off). People would have to turn in their second cars and second homes and share the ones they already have.

(Pojman, *Ethics: Discovering Right and Wrong*, 2002)

There are always going to be issues with this as one could argue that it is not always possible to know people's true preferences, as these change over time as our knowledge and understanding change, and according to Singer's principle of equal consideration this shows that the ties of love and kinship do not count.

Some of Singer's approaches seem difficult to accept for many people – he argues that some animals have a higher moral status than some humans. He begins this argument by observing that many animals prefer to avoid pain and enjoy pleasure. Singer argues that causing animals pain by killing them for food, caging them, separating them from their mates and families and so forth is against their preferences and is therefore wrong. He does not consider humans to be above animals and states that an intelligent adult ape has more conscious preferences than a newborn infant. To think otherwise is to be guilty of speciesism. He approves of Bentham's dictum 'the question is not, Can they *reason*? nor, Can they *talk*? but, Can they *suffer*?', and follows Mill's idea when he talks of extending 'the standard of morality so far as the nature of things permits, to the whole of sentient creation' (*utilitarianism*). Singer accords animals rights as sentient (feeling) beings; they have valid interests. So according to Singer's preference utilitarianism, it is preferences rather than human life that we should value.

This view obviously brings out the problem of those people who are unable to express preferences – the newborn, the severely mentally disabled and those who have no rational self-consciousness, such as people suffering from Alzheimer's. Also, according to Singer, an early foetus would have no preferences as it cannot feel pain, and even a late foetus would have its limited preferences outweighed by those of the parents: for Singer the worth of human life varies. The same philosophy applies to the dying or those with Alzheimer's – they may have no preferences left, but the family and friends who love them do.

Richard Brandt's approach

Richard Brandt was one of the leading utilitarian philosophers of the twentieth century. He defended a version of rule utilitarianism, but later, in his book *A Theory of the Right and the Good* (1979), he talks about the preferences you would have if you had gone through a process of cognitive psychotherapy, explored all the reasons for your preferences and rejected any you felt were not true to your real values. He argued that the morality you would then accept would be a form of utilitarianism – with your preferences free from any psychological blocks and you in full possession of all the facts. Such a person would not, therefore, be influenced by advertising.

STRENGTHS OF UTILITARIANISM

- It is straightforward and based on the single principle of minimising pain and maximising pleasure and happiness. A system which aims to create a happier life for individuals and groups is attractive.
- It relates to actions that can be observed in the real world (e.g. giving to charity promotes happiness for poor people and is seen to be good, whereas an act of cruelty is condemned as bad).
- Its consequentialism is also a strength, as when we act it is only natural to weigh up the consequences.
- Utilitarianism's acceptance of the universal principle is essential for any ethical system. It is important to go beyond your own personal point of view.
- The idea of promoting the 'well-being' of the greatest number is also important – this is the basis of the healthcare system: care is provided to improve the health of the population and if more money is spent on the health service, people are healthier and therefore happier.
- Preference utilitarianism also gives us the valuable principle of being an impartial observer or, as Hare puts it, 'standing in someone else's shoes'. It is important to think about others' interests or preferences as long as one also includes behaving justly.

Weaknesses of utilitarianism

- It is good to consider the consequences of our actions, but these are difficult to predict with any accuracy.
- Utilitarianism can also be criticised because it seems to ignore the importance of duty. An act may be right or wrong for reasons other than the amount of good or evil it produces. The case of the dying millionaire illustrates this. The millionaire asks his friend to swear that on his death he will give all his assets to his local football club. The millionaire dies and his friend sets about fulfilling his last wishes, but he sees an advertisement to save a million people who are dying of starvation. Should he keep his promise or save a million people?

> **Bernard Williams (1929–2003)**
>
> Bernard Williams was born in Southend-on-Sea and studied at Balliol College, Oxford. In 1967 he was made Knightsbridge Professor of Philosophy at the University of Cambridge. In 1988 he moved to the USA. He was a professor at Berkeley, California, and White's Professor of Moral Philosophy at Oxford until his retirement in 1996. He was very interested in politics and sat on several government committees, including those on gambling, drugs and pornography.

However, some promises may be bad and should not be kept. Duty does not stem from self-interest and is non-consequential – is motive more important than outcomes? Should promises be kept, the truth told and obligations honoured? *W.D. Ross* thought that the role of duty had some importance and advocated prima facie duties as more acceptable.

- Utilitarianism can also advocate injustice, as in the foregoing case where the innocent man is unjustly framed for rape to prevent riots.
- Another weakness is the emphasis on pleasure or happiness. If I seek my own happiness it is impossible for me to seek general happiness and to do what I ought to do. The qualitative and quantitative approaches also pose problems, as all we can really do is guess the units of pleasure – how do we measure one pleasure against another? Should we try to maximise the average happiness or the total happiness (e.g. should the government give tax cuts for the minority with the lowest income or spread the cuts more thinly across all tax payers?). Bentham would allow an evil majority to prevail over a good minority and the exploitation of minority groups – does this not go against what we would consider ethical behaviour?
- Utilitarianism does not consider motives and intentions and so rejects the principle of treating people with intrinsic value. Utilitarianism does not take any notice of personal commitments but considers only the consequences of an action. *Bernard Williams* said that we should not ignore integrity and personal responsibility for moral actions, and he uses the story of Jim and the Indians, where Jim is asked to choose between killing 1 Indian and letting 19 go free, or refusing and having all 20 shot, to illustrate this and argues that people need to retain their integrity even if this leads to unwelcome consequences.
- *John Rawls* also argues that utilitarianism is too impersonal and does not consider the rights of individuals in its attempt to look for the 'greater good'.

Utilitarianism has some major weaknesses as far as duty, justice, motives, intentions and consequences are concerned, and the principles of 'the greatest good for the greatest number' and 'treating people as a means to an end' are rather dubious moral principles. The principles of seeking to act in a benevolent way and trying to apply universality and a consideration of consequences (even if only estimated) are principles that may be used with other, more deontological principles, such as duty and integrity. Perhaps we need to combine the best principles from both the teleological and deontological approaches to ethics.

John Rawls (1921–2002)

John Rawls was known for his theory of 'justice as fairness'. He taught at Cornell University and Massachusetts Institute of Technology, and then moved to Harvard. He is known for *A Theory of Justice* (1971) and *Political Liberalism* (1993).

REVIEW QUESTIONS

Look back over the chapter and check that you can answer the following questions:

1   Explain the main principle of utilitarianism.
2   Explain the utilitarianism of Bentham.
3   Explain the utilitarianism of Mill.
4   Explain the differences between act and rule utilitarianism.
5   Complete the following diagram:

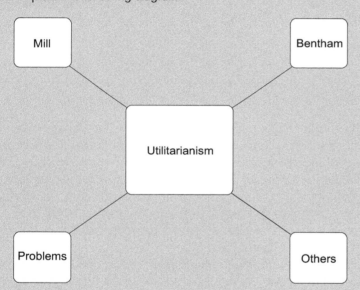

Terminology

Do you know your terminology?

Try to explain the following key ideas without looking at your books and notes:

- Consequentialist
- Teleological ethics
- Act utilitarianism
- Rule utilitarianism
- Preference utilitarianism.

SUMMARY

- Utilitarianism is teleological – the consequences determine whether an action is good.
- The principle of utility – the greatest good for the greatest number – will show if an action is good or not. A good action is shown by the amount of pleasure or happiness which results from the action.
- Bentham's utilitarianism is quantitative and uses the hedonic calculus to check if an action is the right one to take. The hedonic calculus weighs up the pain and pleasure using the following criteria:

  - Intensity
  - Duration
  - Certainty
  - Propinquity
  - Fecundity
  - Purity
  - Extent.

- Mill focused on qualitative pleasures and divided pleasures into higher pleasures (intellectual) and lower pleasures (bodily). Higher pleasures are to be preferred and competent judges will know the difference.
- Act utilitarianism says that good actions are those which lead to the greatest good and produce the most pleasure in a given situation.
- Act utilitarianism seems flexible as it takes account of different circumstances, but it can potentially justify any action if it benefits the majority. The minority are ignored.
- Rule utilitarianism aims to apply general rules that are based on the principle of utility and will give the best result for all. However, it still does not protect the minority.
- The modern version of preference utilitarianism considers the preference of all involved and aims to minimise pain. However, this could lead to a popular decision rather than a moral one.

Examination questions practice

When writing answers to questions on utilitarianism, make sure you can explain clearly the different types, as utilitarianism is more a family of theories than one simple theory.

SAMPLE EXAM-STYLE QUESTION

'Utilitarianism will always lead to wrong ethical decisions.' Discuss.

AO1 (15 marks)
- You will need to begin by giving an explanation of utilitarianism – the rightness or wrongness of an action is determined by its 'utility' or usefulness, which is the amount of pleasure or happiness caused by the action. An action is right if it produces the greatest good for the greatest number.
- You could also consider the different approaches of Bentham and Mill, act and rule utilitarianism.
- It would be a good to illustrate this with specific examples.

AO2 (15 marks)
- You could consider the fact that we cannot accurately predict the future, and can, therefore, make mistakes. You could discuss that there is potential to justify any act and so there is no defence for minorities.
- You could consider that it is impractical to calculate the morality of each choice, and so people simply will not bother. You might argue that having general rules based on the principle of utility would be a better approach.
- On the other hand, you might consider that utilitarianism is democratic and practical, and so can deal with most moral situations. You might consider Mill's ideas about defending rights and the application of general rules based on the principle of utility.
- Use examples of practical ethical decisions to support your arguments and make sure that you justify the points that you make.

Further possible questions

- **Assess the main differences between act and rule utilitarianism.**
- **To what extent is utilitarianism a useful method of making ethical decisions?**
- **'Utilitarianism is not a good guide for resolving ethical dilemmas.' Discuss.**

FURTHER READING

Bentham, J. 1948. *An Introduction to the Principles of Morals and Legislation* (ed. Harrison, W.). Cambridge: Cambridge University Press.

Gensler, H., Earl, W. and Swindal, J. 2004. *Ethics: Contemporary Readings*. New York: Routledge (contains original writings of many classic and contemporary philosophers).

Mill, J.S. [1861, 1863], 2002. *Utilitarianism*. Indianapolis: Hackett.

Norman, R. 1998. *The Moral Philosophers*. Oxford: Oxford University Press.

Pojman, L.P. 1989. *Ethical Theory*. Toronto: Wadsworth.

Pojman, L.P. 2002. *Ethics: Discovering Right and Wrong*. Toronto: Wadsworth.

Pojman, L.P. 2006. *Ethics: Inventing Right and Wrong* (5th ed.). Belmont, CA: Thomson/Wadsworth.

Singer, P. 1993. *Practical Ethics*. Cambridge: Cambridge University Press.

Smart, J.J.C. and Williams, B. 1973. *Utilitarianism: For and Against*. Cambridge: Cambridge University Press.

Applied ethics

14 Euthanasia

WHAT YOU WILL LEARN ABOUT IN THIS CHAPTER

- Definitions of the different types of euthanasia.
- The idea of the sanctity of life and how it applies to euthanasia.
- Personhood.
- Suicide.
- Ideas of autonomy.
- The difference between killing and letting die/acts and omissions.
- The approaches of natural moral law and situation ethics to euthanasia.

THE OCR CHECKLIST

Key ideas, including:

- sanctity of life
    - the religious origins of this concept (that human life is made in God's image and is therefore sacred in value)
- quality of life
    - the secular origins of this significant concept (that human life has to possess certain attributes in order to have value)
- voluntary euthanasia
    - what it is (that a person's life is ended at his or her request or with his or her consent) and its use in the case of incurable or terminal illness
- non-voluntary euthanasia
    - what it is (that a person's life is ended without his or her consent but with the consent of someone representing his or

continued opposite

her interests) and its use in the case of a patient who is in a persistent vegetative state.

Learners should have the opportunity to discuss issues raised by euthanasia, including:

the application of *natural law* and *situation ethics* to euthanasia

- whether the religious concept of sanctity of life has any meaning in twenty-first-century medical ethics
- whether a person should or can have complete autonomy over his or her own life and decisions made about it
- whether there is a moral difference between medical intervention to end a patient's life and medical non-intervention to end a patient's life.

(From *OCR AS Level Religious Studies Specification H173*)

WHAT IS EUTHANASIA?

'Euthanasia' comes from the Greek *eu*, meaning 'well' and 'easy', and *thanatos*, meaning 'death'. Euthanasia is the intentional premature ending of another person's life either by direct means (active euthanasia) or by withholding medical treatment, food and hydration (passive euthanasia), because the patient asks for it (voluntary euthanasia) or without his or her express request (involuntary euthanasia).

Active euthanasia involves an actual act of mercy killing. For example, if a doctor decides that it is in the patient's best interest that the patient die, and so kills the patient for that reason, this is active euthanasia. This may be done by lethal injection by another person, but the patient would not die as quickly on his or her own. It is illegal in this country and many others.

Passive euthanasia involves helping someone die because it is judged that it is better for the person to be dead. This may be when a doctor withholds life-saving treatment with the intention that the patient dies – but it has to be done because of concern for the patient, not to free up hospital beds and so forth. It is practised in the UK, and many of those who oppose active euthanasia see no problem with it.

The ethical question that these two forms of euthanasia raises is whether it is the same thing to kill someone as it is to let someone die.

Study hint

Many of the issues of medical ethics are progressing all the time as science and technology move forward. To stay abreast of these issues it is a good idea to keep a folder of relevant newspaper cuttings and annotate them with how you think the different ethical theories would react to the issues.

Active euthanasia

The intentional premature termination of another person's life.

Passive euthanasia

Treatment is either withdrawn or not given to the patient in order to hasten death. This could include turning off a life-support machine.

Voluntary euthanasia

The intentional premature termination of another person's life at his or her request.

Involuntary euthanasia

This term is used when someone's life is ended to prevent his or her suffering, without the person's consent, even though he or she is capable of consenting.

PVS (persistent vegetative state)

When a patient is in this condition, doctors may seek to end the patient's life. The relatives have to agree and usually the patient must be brainstem-dead.

Voluntary euthanasia is carried out at the request of the person. This is illegal in the UK, but it is legal in the Netherlands under medical supervision. There is campaigning in this country for the same law here. In this country there are Do Not Resuscitate orders – DNRs – which can be seen as a chosen form of passive euthanasia. However, they are controversial as there have been cases of DNRs being written into a patient's notes without his or her consent. Guidelines issued by the British Medical Association say that DNR orders should be issued only after discussion with the patient and/or the patient's family.

Involuntary euthanasia occurs when it is impossible to get the patient's consent – perhaps he or she has lost the ability to make a decision or is still an infant. Involuntary euthanasia is carried out against the wishes of the patient and few people would defend this approach. However, it is possible for someone to be the victim of involuntary euthanasia – such as having a DNR order applied regardless of the patient's wishes.

The ending of a life by euthanasia may thus be either through acts of omission or through intentional acts. Note: the active/passive distinction cuts across the voluntary/non-voluntary, involuntary distinctions. There can be passive and active versions of each.

The debate about euthanasia includes the following issues:

- The sanctity of life and the idea that it is God-given.
- The maintenance of life as an absolute.
- Is the act in itself wrong or do the consequences make it wrong?
- The question of personal autonomy.
- The motives that lead to euthanasia.
- The difference between killing and letting die.

EUTHANASIA, PERSONHOOD AND THE SANCTITY OF LIFE

Human life is recognised by most people as 'something sacred', and believers also see it as a 'gift from God'. There are, however, different views on what it is that makes us human: many believers would say that we are human from conception or at the latest from birth, whereas others might say that we can be considered human only when we think and act as conscious human beings. According to the first viewpoint, we are fully human regardless of whether we are embryos or comatose patients. Immature or damaged, we are still persons, whereas others may argue that a patient who is in a persistent vegetative state (PVS) may be a human but is not really a person because he or she is unable to be so; thus in all important aspects he or she is already dead. If this view of personhood is taken to its logical conclusion, all sorts of people, including the mentally disabled and the paralysed, could also be considered as incomplete persons and so already dead.

The sanctity of life is central to the Catholic position, set out in the *Declaration on Euthanasia* (Sacred Congregation for the Doctrine of the Faith, 1980), which defines euthanasia as 'an act or an omission which of itself or by intention causes death, in order that all suffering may in this way be eliminated'. To do this to another or to ask it for oneself is not allowed – in accordance with natural law; the first primary precept is self-preservation and so death should not be hastened by euthanasia. The document does, however, recognise that while a time to prepare for death is useful, suffering can be so great both physically and psychologically that it can make a person wish to remove it whatever the cost. It accepts that very few can follow the path of Mother Teresa of Calcutta and limit the dose of painkillers so as to unite themselves with the sufferings of Christ, but it also says that 'suffering has a special place in God's plan of salvation.'

The doctrine of double effect plays an important part in Catholic thinking about euthanasia according to the teaching of Pope Pius XII, which distinguishes between painkillers that have a secondary effect of shortening life and drugs used to hasten death with a secondary effect of killing pain. It is the intention which is all important. The document says that it is 'important to protect, at the moment of death, both the dignity of the human person and the Christian concept of life against a technological attitude that threatens to become an abuse'. The document refers to 'ordinary' and 'extraordinary' pain – ways of attempting to save life which are disproportionate to the pain suffered. A major problem here is how 'extraordinary' means are to be measured; there is a lack of clarity here, as 50 years ago a patient kept alive today on a life-support machine would have died. Issues of quality of life are now being seen as important, and when death is imminent a patient may refuse unnecessary treatment so long as 'the normal care due the sick person is not interrupted'. The introduction of proportionalism is significant, but not all Catholic scholars would agree with this.

Most Christians are in fact against euthanasia as they believe in the sanctity of life and see human life as created by God and made in God's image. This makes human life worthy of respect and reverence and intrinsically worthwhile. Yet humans often see some lives as being more valuable than others, and even within Christian tradition views can be roughly divided into strong sanctity of life arguments and weak sanctity of life arguments.

Strong sanctity of life

Those who hold strong sanctity of life arguments often appeal to the biblical basis of their ideas: God is the giver and creator of life and people have no right to destroy what he has given. People are created in the 'image of

God' – *imago dei* – and so humans are set apart from other animals and have a 'spark' of divinity within them – the breath of life was breathed into Adam by God. The incarnation, according to Christian teaching, reaffirms the sanctity of human life as God himself became human.

> So God created humankind in his image.
>
> (Genesis 1:27a)

> God blessed them, and God said to them, 'Be fruitful and multiply, and fill the earth and subdue it; and have dominion over the fish of the sea and over the birds of the air and over every living thing that moves upon the earth.'
>
> (Genesis 1:28)

> And the Word became flesh and lived among us, and we have seen his glory. The glory as of a father's only son, full of grace and truth.
>
> (John 1:14)

Additionally, if God is the creator of life it is down to him to say when life should start and end. A person does not have the freedom to decide to end his or her own life or anyone else's life.

> He said, 'Naked I came from my mother's womb, and naked shall I return there; the LORD gave, and the LORD has taken away; blessed be the name of the LORD.'
>
> (Job 1:21)

> I know, O LORD, that the way of human beings is not in their control, that mortals as they walk cannot direct their steps.
>
> (Jeremiah 10:23)

Throughout the Bible there is also the command not to take life, and the biblical writer saw this as part of the covenant with God and his people: 'You shall not murder' (Exodus 20:13). This belief in the sanctity of life applies to all people: 'The rich and the poor have this in common: the LORD is the maker of them all' (Proverbs 22:2).

Weak sanctity of life

Many supporters of euthanasia maintain that they believe in the basic sanctity and dignity of life, but argue that ending the suffering of terminally ill patients at their request is actually a move which respects sanctity of life. For them death with dignity, as opposed to a life of pain and suffering, is more humane. This view accepts that patients can refuse treatment when death is imminent and so considers that in some cases it would cause greater harm to prolong life.

However, such a view seems to be concerned more with the quality of life than its sanctity, and argues that if it is necessary to decide between the two, quality of life is more important than the sanctity of life. Thus the extremely low quality of life of a terminally ill patient outweighs the sanctity of that life and justifies his or her 'mercy' killing.

Germain Grisez and Joseph Boyle stress the importance of personhood and reject the view that one can cease to be a person and yet be bodily alive – they do not accept that a patient in a persistent vegetative state has lost that which makes them distinctively human: a human being is a whole, and bodily life is seen as a good in itself. Grisez and Boyle say that there are certain basic goods necessary for human well-being, including play and recreation, knowledge of the truth, appreciation of beauty, life and health, friendship and integration. They do not require this list to be in any particular order but they would absolutely reject euthanasia, as it attempts to achieve one good, such as freedom and dignity, by putting it in direct conflict with another: life and health. These basic goods cannot be compared or balanced off each other, and the key issue for them where euthanasia is concerned is that it is against the basic good of life.

The question of personhood, however, lies at the heart of the proportionalist position held by Daniel Maguire. This view states that life is a basic but not an absolute good and, while it is important to respect and value life, nobody should always be obliged to prolong it in every situation. Maguire rejects the idea that God alone should decide the time of death for each person; this seems to reject the idea that God alone has the power over life and death and that we belong to God and are his property. He points out that we do, in fact, intervene to save life and to preserve it, and that there is no real difference between ending life and preserving it so long as the principle of achieving a good death is adhered to. Maguire uses the ideas of weighing up the proportional values of living in any condition and choosing a good death in certain specific circumstances. He recognises that this is a departure from the traditional Christian ethic of 'not destroying innocent life', and that making judgements between conflicting values is difficult and can lead to mistakes, but ethical reflection can lead to euthanasia being on some occasions a legitimate moral choice.

Euthanasia may also be seen as legitimate once the dying process has begun – this view still maintains the sanctity of life and respects life, but the dying process shows that life has reached its limit. The use of euthanasia to shorten the time taken to die by not prolonging life is considered legitimate, as humans can still have power over this without denying the sanctity of life.

> **Germain Gabriel Grisez (1929–)**
>
> Germain Grisez is an important and influential Catholic moral theologian. His best-known work is *Way of the Lord Jesus*. He is opposed to utilitarianism and also to those who oppose the teaching of the Magisterium of the Catholic Church. Grisez has developed a version of natural law theory, known as 'new natural law'.

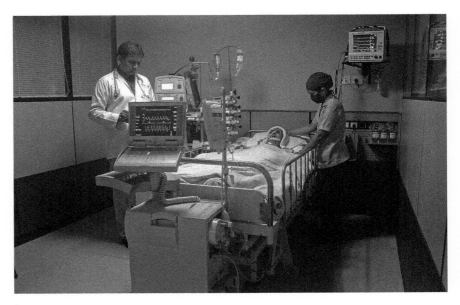

Intensive care unit
Vijaykumar Soni/Alamy

EUTHANASIA AND THE QUALITY OF LIFE

Quality of life

The belief that human life is not valuable in itself; it depends on what kind of life it is.

The quality of life view allows the value of life to vary with its quality and may factor in the immanence of death, constancy of pain, an ability to think and an ability to enjoy life and make rational choices. Today when modern medicine allows people to live longer, but not always profitable or happy lives, the quality of life approach asks whether people should be kept alive at all costs.

This question becomes important for medical practitioners who have limited resources at their disposal, and they assess a person's quality of life using the concept of quality adjusted life years (QALY). This was proposed by NICE (the National Institute for Health and Care Excellence) and considers the patient's level of pain, mobility and so forth. QALYs are used primarily to correct someone's life expectancy based on the levels of health-related quality of life they are predicted to experience throughout the course of their life, or part of it. They are used to assess whether particular treatments will result in an improvement in the patient's quality-adjusted life expectancy. This allows medical practitioners to decide which treatment is best for a particular patient, and how many years of a reasonable quality of life the patient might have as a result of the treatment. The cost-effectiveness of this treatment is then calculated.

QALYs, however, are not without their critics as they assume that the value of a patient's life can be calculated mathematically and are paternalistic as it is the doctor who makes all the decisions. This consideration of the quality of life, which looks at whether the use of extraordinary means would usefully improve the quality of life of the patient, is very different from the Catholic view, which allows the patient to refuse treatment if there is 'an acceptance of the human condition, or a wish to avoid the application of a medical procedure disproportionate to the results that can be expected, or a desire not to impose excessive expense on the family or the community'. No one is obliged to have a medical procedure that is risky or burdensome.

Peter Singer is particularly important in this debate as he believes that the traditional sanctity of life ethic must collapse and we need to develop a new ethic, as people now believe that the low quality of a person's life, as judged by the person, can justify the person taking his or her life or justify someone else doing it for the person. In cases where a person cannot make a judgement or express a view about the quality of his or her own life, someone else should do it for the person.

In his book *Rethinking Life and Death* (1994) Singer presents five commandments of what he calls the old ethic and suggests how they might be rewritten. In his scheme, the first, 'Treat all human life as of equal worth,' becomes 'Recognise that the worth of human life varies'; the second, 'Never intentionally take innocent human life,' becomes 'Take responsibility for the consequences of your actions.' The third and fourth express Singer's views that people have the right to end their own lives and that unwanted children should not be brought into the world. All of these will trigger outrage in various quarters, but perhaps most provocative is his fifth revision: 'Treat all human life as always more precious than any nonhuman life' becomes 'Do not discriminate on the basis of species.' Singer does not in fact completely reject sanctity of life ethics but insists that it applies to all life, not just human life. He states, 'The question is not whether [the Judeo-Christian sanctity of human life ethic] will be replaced, but what the shape of its successor will be.'

However, there is so much more that contributes to the quality of a person's life than that which can be measured medically, and Singer also fails to consider that a person's life has a value to the wider community as well as to the individual.

VOLUNTARY EUTHANASIA AND THE RIGHT TO LIFE

A person's right to life corresponds to the duty of others not to kill that person. The idea of a duty not to kill seems to rule out any form of euthanasia – but we do not see the duty not to kill as absolute, as we think some wars can be justified, or killing in self-defence or in the defence of others can be justified; even capital punishment is justified by some people. It is, in fact, easier to justify killing in voluntary euthanasia, where the person chooses death, than in these other cases, where the person who dies does not choose to do so. Life is a person's most valued and precious possession; can this then be just overturned if the person no longer wishes to live? Can the right to life, like any other right, be overturned or renounced? If that happens, can others say that they have a duty to kill him? If the person asks for voluntary euthanasia, is he then actually asserting his right to be killed in a particular way? However, who then has the duty to kill him? Many doctors who are happy to let people die, withdraw treatment or even assist suicide may not be so happy about having a positive duty to kill at a patient's request.

Thought point

1 Is the sanctity of life ethic out of date? What could replace it?
2 What problems do you see in the doctrine of double effect?
3 Is there any point to suffering and can it help a person to become nearer to God?
4 What problems do you foresee in stressing the quality of life?
5 Is it wrong to help humans to die when they are actually dying? How do we decide when the dying process has begun?

Assisted dying/suicide
When a person takes his or her own life with the assistance of another person. When the other person is a doctor, it is called physician-assisted suicide.

EUTHANASIA AND SUICIDE

Suicide is the deliberate termination of one's own life, and many people, not only those who are religious, are appalled that people could even think of choosing death over life. They feel it demeans life and denies its meaning. All sorts of things give our life meaning – it may be 'God's plan' or it may be family or career – and suicide makes all this meaningless and trivial, as the act is not natural and breaks the timeless cycle of birth and death.

Henry Sidgwick said that only conscious beings can appreciate values and meanings, and so they see life as significant and part of some eternal plan, process or design. Suicide, therefore, is a statement by an intelligent, conscious being about the meaninglessness of life, but it is a statement that society rejects, and in the past suicide was seen as a criminal act.

Suicide, then, breaks the social contract, but it also breaks the bond between God and man – Thomas Aquinas also saw suicide as an unnatural act and a rejection of God's gift of an immortal soul. This view lay at the heart of the old legislation about suicide, which the state had a right to prevent and punish.

Today suicide is no longer illegal but the state still attempts to treat people as possessions and not allow them full autonomy and freedom – so the 'nanny state' protects drug addicts, alcoholics, smokers and the obese from themselves.

However, suicide is subject to a double moral standard: self-sacrifice in the form of martyrdom for either religious or political beliefs is admired, and for a believer such a death is seen as part of a journey leading to life with God; to die on the battlefield is courageous, and many people are involved in life-threatening occupations, such as the fire and rescue service, the armed forces and the police; certain industries, such as the manufacture of cigarettes, alcohol and armaments, increase the mortality rate. Death here is controlled by religion, the state and political parties, whereas suicide is a free act and does not serve any social ends or uphold group values and structures.

- Is it morally justified to commit suicide to avoid forthcoming pain, loss of self-control or coma?
- Is it morally justified to ask others to help you commit suicide if you are incapable of doing it yourself?

Dignitas office
Sean Gallup/Getty

Autonomy
In ethics this means freely taken moral decisions by an individual.

EUTHANASIA AND PERSONAL AUTONOMY

John Stuart Mill (*On Liberty*, 1859) writes that in matters that do not concern others, individuals should have full autonomy. Those who support voluntary euthanasia believe that personal autonomy and self-determination are paramount and any competent adult should be able to decide on the time and manner of his or her death.

The right to have one's life ended by euthanasia is the subject of ethical, social and legal limitations. In some countries, such as the Netherlands and Belgium, it is allowed and socially acceptable to have a doctor end one's life if death is imminent and the quality of life is very poor. However, the patient has to be of sound mind and to request death repeatedly.

But what if the patient's wishes are based on faulty information about his or her illness, or depression clouds his or her judgement? What if a cure is found just after the patient's death? What if the request for euthanasia is easier to respond to than providing good palliative care?

Personal autonomy is an important value but it is often in conflict with other equally important ones – how do we work out which value overrides another and which are the true basic goods?

NON-VOLUNTARY EUTHANASIA

Killing and letting die

Many doctors will argue that euthanasia goes on already, as they will give patients painkillers in such doses that death will be hastened, and in the case of the brain-dead or those in a persistent vegetative state they will withdraw or withhold treatment to bring about death.

However, we do see a difference between killing (taking life) and letting die (not saving life). There is a right not to be killed, but no right to have one's life saved.

James Rachels saw no distinction between active euthanasia (killing) and passive euthanasia (letting die). If anything, he believes that passive euthanasia is worse, as it is cruel and inconsistent and the process of dying may be long and drawn out, bringing about more suffering than is necessary. The result is the same – the patient is dead.

Jonathan Glover also argues for the quality of life, but for him it is consciousness that is the most important factor in determining the quality of life, so his approach supports non-voluntary euthanasia for patients in PVS. His ideas also stress the centrality of personhood in the debate about euthanasia and could possibly point to voluntary euthanasia for patients with

**James Rachels
(1941–2003)**

James Rachels taught at the University of Richmond, New York University, the University of Miami, Duke University and the University of Alabama at Birmingham, USA. Rachels argued for moral vegetarianism and animal rights, preferential quotas and the humanitarian use of euthanasia.

Alzheimer's disease and other forms of severe dementia where the person has no awareness of him- or herself as an individual. Glover seems to give equality and value to some lives but not to all, and to those only on the basis of consciousness as it is this which gives quality to the individual's life.

However, when deciding whether a person's life might not be worth living the judgement is usually made not by the patient but by others. The judgement tends to be made by the competent over the incompetent as medicine itself has become so technological. Often the person who must decide the quality of the life of another is an unwilling judge, whether it is the doctor or a family member. This makes the quality of life position controversial, as when a person is made to judge the quality of another's life his or her judgement could result in death.

Additionally, many arguments concerning euthanasia, whether active or passive, are influenced by the fear that allowing one kind of euthanasia will be the first step on a slippery slope, and the value of human life will be depreciated and made subordinate to economics and personal convenience. Helga Kuhse challenges this 'slippery slope' view and concludes that the situation in the Netherlands is not following the example of Nazi Germany in making some lives valueless for reasons other than mercy or respect for autonomy.

Slippery slope
This means that when one moral law is broken others will also be gradually broken and there will be no moral absolutes.

APPLYING ETHICAL THEORIES TO EUTHANASIA

Natural law

The basic principle of natural law is that everything is created for a purpose and when this is examined by human reason, a person should be able to judge how to act in order to find ultimate happiness.

Natural law does not look at the people involved in a decision about euthanasia, or the consequences of the action – instead natural law considers the act of euthanasia itself. Protection and preservation of life are a primary precept and euthanasia goes against this. It would seem, therefore, that for a follower of natural law euthanasia is always wrong.

Followers of natural law believe in the sanctity of life, as they believe that life itself is given by God and human life is the most important from of life; as humans are made in God's image, killing, including suicide, is not allowed, unless it is in self-defence.

Euthanasia could also be considered to go against the precept of living in a harmonious or ordered society – according to Aquinas we injure the society of which we are a part by killing ourselves. One could argue that a society which does not take care of the terminally ill is not looking after its citizens.

However, the doctrine of double effect will allow a form of indirect euthanasia as it is permissible to give someone pain relief even if the action leads to death. Death in this case is a by-product of another action and seems to be almost proportionate, leading many natural law thinkers to find the doctrine of double effect hard to reconcile with the precepts of natural law.

Natural law does allow a patient to refuse treatment if it is over and above what is needed for existence – extraordinary means. Basic treatment, such as hydration, to sustain life without necessarily prolonging it cannot be refused as that would mean committing suicide, which goes against the primary precept of the preservation of life.

Proportion is important in natural law and actually enables each situation to be looked at individually so that the action that is proportionate to the needs of the patient is chosen. The weak sanctity of life argument says that where death is inevitable the doctor treats the patient with care and compassion: 'Thou shalt not kill; but need not strive officiously to keep alive.' Arthur Clough's poem *The New Decalogue* sums up this view.

Evaluating the natural law approach to euthanasia

Natural law ignores the circumstances and the wishes of the patient. No account is taken of any ideas of personal autonomy, except it allows the patient to refuse treatment. This could be said to accord with John Stuart Mill's ideas of individual sovereignty over his body and mind.

Joseph Fletcher criticised the way that natural law would not allow euthanasia and so prolonged death and suffering. Our age values mercy and so today people use that argument in favour of euthanasia. Euthanasia is, nevertheless, wrong for a follower of natural law, who could argue that in the past people valued honour and dignity and so allowed claims of vengeance or duelling. Duelling and private vengeance are, however, wrong, in the eyes of natural law and many would simply consider them wrong today.

Natural law does not consider that much modern medicine, such as transplants, could be considered as simply extending human life and so as 'playing God' – is this any different from 'playing God' by ending the life of a terminally ill patient?

It is quite legitimate to worry about the consequences of legalising euthanasia. It is logical to wonder to what point a principle will be extended once established. The 'slippery slope' argument is a common one put forward against euthanasia – that it will lead to the elderly being pressurised to end their lives. However, in those countries that have legalised euthanasia this does not seem to be the case.

The doctrine of double effect relies on a distinction between foresight and intention – so for example heavy sedation may have the intention of relieving the patient's pain but at the same time may shorten his life, and this bad side effect must be foreseen but not intended by the doctor. However, it is difficult for a doctor to distinguish between what he intends and what he merely foresees; surely what he foresees becomes an intention and the doctrine of double effect introduces a utilitarian aspect into natural law.

Society today is secular, and many people hold a quality of life view rather than a sanctity of life view and so consider natural law with its basis in religion as simply irrelevant.

Situation ethics

Joseph Fletcher's situation ethics stresses the fact that the ethical decision for any moral dilemma will depend on the situation. Fletcher did not think it was necessary to have a set list of maxims or rules that one should follow when making a moral decision, but believed in agape love and was keen on the idea of making a moral decision depending on what is the most loving thing to do, and what will be best for the person in the situation. Thus doing the most loving thing involves making the decision that will maximise the well-being of another person, whoever that person is and however close your relationship to the person is.

When applying situation ethics to voluntary euthanasia, it is quite clear to see that Fletcher would support it. If a person is suffering from an incurable disease that is putting a person through a huge amount of pain and the person requests help to end his or her life and stop this suffering, Fletcher would say that the most loving thing to do is to allow the person to end his or her life. In this way his or her suffering is ended, and the patient's wishes are being carried out. In this approach, it is presumed that the patient has a terminal disease and that all medical interventions have failed.

When applying situation ethics to non-voluntary euthanasia it is slightly more difficult to come to a clear conclusion. If someone's life is being ended without him or her asking for it, this is not necessarily a loving or right thing to do. However, Fletcher could say that as the person is still suffering an incredible amount of pain and assuming that the person cannot be otherwise cured, it is still a loving thing to do if you are ending his or her pain. On the other hand, it may not be the most loving thing to do as it may be going against the patient's wishes and forcing the patient to end his or her life when the patient may have still wanted to live. Therefore, in this circumstance the principle of situation ethics can be used to make the ethical decision. This principle is that there is not a strict set of moral laws, so the moral decision that you make should depend on the situation.

With situation ethics it is not possible to give clear guidelines, so if you are considering ending a person's life even though the person has not asked, but you genuinely think that the patient is suffering a huge amount of pain and that it would be best for the patient to end his or her life, as there is no way his or her quality of life can improve, then it is acceptable to help the patient end his or her life even if the patient has not or is unable to specifically ask for this. Having said this, if someone wants to force someone to end his or her life for personal benefits, such as receiving money from the will of a deceased person, then euthanasia is not being carried out for a loving purpose or for the person's best interests, meaning that according to situation ethics euthanasia should not be allowed or encouraged in this circumstance. Involuntary euthanasia is right only in circumstances in which you are carrying it out for selfless reasons, and for the patient's best interests.

Situation ethics focuses on the patient as a person and treats each case individually, and patients are treated as autonomous decision-makers. So although Joseph Fletcher was the former president of the Euthanasia Society of America, situation ethics as a theory does not have firm view on euthanasia as it depends on applying agape to the situation. This means that a responsible approach must be taken, not influenced by sentimentality or feelings and fully aware of the consequences of the action. Fletcher presumes this will avoid the 'slippery slope' argument; however, he does consider euthanasia as right when a patient is in incurable pain which destroys the patient as a person and means the patient no longer lives a useful life. This poses a problem as a patient who is comatose and so feels no more pain is in a different situation from that of the person overwhelmed with pain, unless one sees them both as instances of valueless life, with no quality of life.

Evaluating the situation ethics approach to euthanasia

Situation ethics is applied to each individual situation as far as euthanasia is concerned. This is all well and good, but euthanasia concerns all terminally ill as far as law-making is concerned. If clear laws are not made and patients protected, it could lead to a 'slippery slope' as it is not always clear when life ceases to be worthwhile and valuable and also whether a patient in severe pain is capable of making rational decisions about his or her own death.

Situation ethics can be seen as merely a utilitarian approach to euthanasia as it still relies on predicting consequences and it is fundamentally vague, resting on a very ambiguous definition of love, and could in practice be used to justify anything, such as euthanasia for anyone whose life is deemed not to be worth living. It takes relativism in the sense of opposing a plethora of absolute rules to the extreme of relativism in the sense of anything goes, so long as the motive can be described as 'loving'.

Situation ethics ignores the sanctity of life as this is seen as an absolute rule and leaves it to the individual and his or her family or the doctor to make a decision about euthanasia. This approach means that situation ethics no longer follows Christian ethical approaches to the issue.

Thought point

In pairs or groups research one of the following and apply the foregoing ethical theories to it:

1   Tony Bland and his doctor, Jim Howe.
2   Diane Pretty.
3   Mary Ormerod.
4   Annie Lindsell.
5   Baby Charlotte Wyatt.
6   Terri Schiavo.
7   Dr Anne Turner and Dignitas.

Further research

Dr Andrew Fergusson – chairman of Healthcare Opposed to Euthanasia (HOPE)
Dame Cecily Saunders – founder of the modern hospice movement
Baroness Warnock
Euthanasia in the news

REVIEW QUESTIONS

Look back over the chapter and check that you can answer the following questions:

1   (a) Explain the link between euthanasia and the sanctity of life.
     (b) Explain the link between euthanasia and the quality of life.
2   What is the difference between killing and letting die? Does it matter?
3   What are QALYs?
4   Make a chart applying the different ethical theories to euthanasia.

continued overleaf

Terminology

Do you know your terminology?

Try to explain the following ideas without looking at your books and notes:

- Autonomy
- Active euthanasia
- Involuntary euthanasia
- Voluntary euthanasia
- Passive euthanasia
- Slippery slope

SUMMARY

'Euthanasia' comes from the Greek *eu*, meaning 'well' and 'easy', and *thanatos*, meaning 'death'. Euthanasia is the intentional premature ending of another person's life either by direct means (*active euthanasia*) or by withholding medical treatment, food and hydration (*passive euthanasia*), because the patient asks for it (*voluntary euthanasia*) or without his or her express request (*involuntary euthanasia*).

The ending of a life by euthanasia may thus be either through acts of omission or through intentional acts.

The debate about euthanasia includes the following issues:

- The sanctity of life and the idea that it is God-given.
- The maintenance of life as an absolute.
- Is the act in itself wrong or do the consequences make it wrong?
- The question of personal autonomy.
- The motives that lead to euthanasia.
- The difference between killing and letting die.

Other concepts in this chapter include:

- Human life is recognised by most people as 'something sacred', and believers also see it as a 'gift from God'. There are, however, different views on what it is that makes us human.

- The sanctity of life is central to the Catholic position, set out in the Declaration on Euthanasia (1980), which defines euthanasia as 'an act or an omission which of itself or by intention causes death, in order that all suffering may in this way be eliminated'.
- The quality of life view allows the value of life to vary with its quality – it is not valuable in itself. Today modern medicine allows people to live longer, but not always profitable or happy lives.
- Peter Singer believes that the traditional sanctity of life ethic is finished and we need to develop a new ethic, as people now believe that the low quality of a person's life, as judged by the person, can justify the person taking his or her life or justify someone else doing it for the person.
- QALYs consideration of the quality of life looks at whether the use of extraordinary means would usefully improve the quality of life of the patient. This idea is basically utilitarian, as doctors consider the possible length of life of the patient, the patient's state of mind, how the procedure would enhance the patient's life and so forth.
- Refusal of extraordinary means is the Catholic position. No one is obliged to have a medical procedure which is risky or burdensome.
- John Stuart Mill (*On Liberty*, 1859) wrote that in matters that do not concern others individuals should have full autonomy. Those who support voluntary euthanasia believe that personal autonomy and self-determination are paramount and any competent adult should be able to decide on the time and manner of his or her death.
- James Rachels saw no distinction between active euthanasia (*killing*) and passive euthanasia (*letting die*). If anything, he believed that passive euthanasia is worse, as it is cruel and inconsistent and the process of dying may be long and drawn out, bringing about more suffering than is necessary. The result is the same – the patient is dead.
- Natural law considers the act of euthanasia itself. Protection of life is a primary precept and euthanasia goes against this. Natural law does allow a patient to refuse treatment if it is over and above what is needed for existence – extraordinary means.
- The doctrine of double effect plays an important part in Catholic thinking about euthanasia according to the teaching of Pope Pius XII, which distinguishes between painkillers that have a secondary effect of shortening life and drugs used to hasten death with a secondary effect of killing pain. It is the *intention* which is all-important.
- The situation ethics approach to euthanasia applies agape to each individual situation and person. It supports voluntary euthanasia if a person is suffering from an incurable disease. For involuntary euthanasia guidelines are not as clear. Situation ethics does consider the consequences of any action.

Examination questions practice

Read the question carefully – if it asks you to write about voluntary eutha-nasia, do not write about other sorts just because you know about them. Do not just reproduce 'my euthanasia essay'.

SAMPLE EXAM-STYLE QUESTIONS

Assess the view that the concept of the sanctity of life is not helpful in understanding the issues surrounding euthanasia.

AO1 (15 marks)

• You need to explain what is meant by the sanctity of life its biblical links and links to natural law.

• You need to consider the issues surrounding euthanasia – for example voluntary and involuntary, killing and letting die, personhood, autonomy, ordinary and extraordinary means.

AO2 (15 marks)

• A common argument is to contrast the sanctity of life with the argument for autonomy and quality of life.

• You could also argue that the sanctity of life argument leaves no room for compassion and consider a relative theory of ethics, such as situation ethics, as an alternative.

• You might put forward the alternative point of view in favour of the sanctity of life, possibly linking it to the precept to pre-serve life in natural law. You might argue that the sanctity of life respects people and avoids the 'slippery slope'.

Further possible questions

• **'Natural law leaves no room for compas-sionate treatment of the dying.' Discuss.**

• **'From a Christian point of view, situa-tion ethics does not offer an acceptable way of making decisions about euthana-sia.' Discuss.**

• **Assess the view that the concept of personal autonomy is most important when discussing the issues surrounding euthanasia.**

FURTHER READING

Cook, D. 1983. *The Moral Maze*. London: SPCK.

Glover, J. 1990. *Causing Death and Saving Lives*. London: Penguin.

Hinman, L. 'Ethics Updates', http://ethics.acusd.edu/.

Kuhse, H. and Singer, P. (eds.). 1999. *Bioethics – an Anthology*. Oxford: Blackwell (contains articles by Jonathan Glover, Germain Grisez and Joseph Boyle, James Rachels and Helga Kuhse).

Lafollette, H. (ed.). 2002. *Ethics in Practice – an Anthology*. Oxford: Blackwell.

Macquarrie, J. and Childress, J. 1986. *A New Dictionary of Christian Ethics*. London: SCM.

Sacred Congregation for the Doctrine of the Faith. 1980. *Declaration on Euthanasia*. Rome: s.n.

Singer, P. 1993. *Practical Ethics*. Cambridge: Cambridge University Press.

Singer, P. 1994. *Rethinking Life and Death: The Collapse of Our Traditional Ethics*. Oxford: Oxford University Press.

Warnock, M. 1999. *An Intelligent Person's Guide to Ethics*. London: Duckworth.

Wilcockson, M. 1999. *Issues of Life and Death*. London: Hodder & Stoughton.

Applied ethics

15 Business ethics

WHAT YOU WILL LEARN ABOUT IN THIS CHAPTER

- The importance or not of corporate social responsibility.
- The role and importance of whistle-blowing.
- Good ethics as good business.
- Globalisation and whether it encourages good ethics in business.
- The approaches of Kantian ethics and utilitarianism to business ethics.
- How to assess the different approaches and to evaluate their strengths and weaknesses.
- An understanding of the underlying principles and implications of these different approaches for making decisions about business.

THE OCR CHECKLIST

Key ideas, including:

- corporate social responsibility
  - what it is (that a business has responsibility towards the community and environment) and its application to stakeholders, such as employees, customers, the local community, the country as whole and governments
- whistle-blowing
  - what it is (that an employee discloses wrongdoing to the employer or the public) and its application to the contract between employee and employer
- good ethics is good business

continued opposite

- what it is (that good business decisions are good ethical decisions) and its application to shareholders and profit-making
- globalisation
  - what it is (that around the world economies, industries, markets, cultures and policy-making are integrated) and its impact on stakeholders.

Learners should have the opportunity to discuss issues raised by these areas of business ethics, including:

- the application of *Kantian ethics* and *utilitarianism* to business ethics
- whether the concept of corporate social responsibility is nothing more than 'hypocritical window-dressing' covering the greed of a business intent on making profits
- whether human beings can flourish in the context of capitalism and consumerism
- whether globalisation encourages or discourages the pursuit of good ethics as the foundation of good business.

(From *OCR AS Level Religious Studies Specification H173*)

WHAT IS BUSINESS ETHICS?

Business ethics considers the ethical relationship between businesses and consumers, between businesses and their employees. It also considers the impact of globalisation on the environment, and on society at large.

Ethicists do not always agree about the purpose of business in society – some see the main purpose of business is to maximise profits for its owners or its shareholders. In this case, only those activities which increase profits are to be encouraged as this is the only way that companies will survive – this was the view of the economist Milton Friedman. Others consider that businesses have moral responsibilities towards their stakeholders, including employees, consumers, the local community and even society as a whole. Other ethicists have adapted social contract theory (based on the ideas of John Rawls in his *A Theory of Justice*) to business, so that employees and other stakeholders are given a voice as to how the business operates.

However, this view is criticised as businesses are property, not means of distributing social justice.

Times have changed, however, and ethics in business and corporate social responsibility are becoming crucial. There are many reasons for this, driven by the social, political and economic developments in the world. Consumers have shown their dissatisfaction through taking to the streets, and social responsibility is becoming crucial. There are many reasons for this: there have been riots from Genoa to Seattle, bringing together many different types of activists and protesters, campaigning on a variety of business-related issues, from globalisation and human rights to third-world debt. Stakeholders, and especially consumers, are becoming increasingly empowered and vocal, forcing businesses to review their strategies.

Organisations like The Body Shop and The Co-operative have led the way and brought business ethics and social responsibility into the public eye and onto the business agenda, championing key issues, such as human and animal rights, fair trade and environmental impact. Consumers now expect businesses to be socially responsible, and businesses are increasingly thinking about what they can achieve by putting the power of their marketing behind some key social issues so that they can help make a positive social difference.

However, business ethics is not as simple as it looks as there is no longer one agreed moral code and multinationals operate in different parts of the world, employing and serving people from different cultures. Profit will still be the main motivating factor for businesses and this affects all the people who work there, generating its own culture with its own standards, so it becomes difficult for individuals to stand up against any attitudes and decisions they disagree with.

Modern technologies also create ethical dilemmas for businesses that never existed until quite recently – such as medical products and gene technologies: should parents be allowed to alter the genetic profile of their unborn child, and should businesses sell products to do this?

All these issues pull businesses in different directions, so that many now set up their own ethical committees. Businesses that get caught acting unethically are publicised in the press, and pressure groups that oppose the activities of certain businesses are better organised, better financed and so better able to attack such businesses. An extreme example of this is Huntingdon Life Sciences in Cambridgeshire, where the animal liberation movement set up a splinter group called SHAC (Stop Huntingdon Animal Cruelty), which started an international campaign to close the company down, often using ethically dubious methods, threatening employees and employees of shareholders and banks. The opponents of this business understand business and its weak points very well as the company nearly went bust; however, the company changed tactics, the public reacted against the extreme methods of SHAC, and in 2007 the company reported a 5% increase in profits, leading the managing director to plead with the banks to no longer treat the business as 'radioactive' (*Financial Times*, 16 September 2007).

CORPORATE SOCIAL RESPONSIBILITY

Corporate social responsibility is concerned with the sustainability of an organisation's ethics over the long term. At its core, corporate social responsibility seeks to add value to an organisation's activities by ensuring they have a positive impact on society, the environment and the economy. It includes financial as well as social and environmental responsibility.

Areas of corporate social responsibility include:

- *community* – focusing on how the organisation's activities positively or negatively affect the general public
- *employees or labour* – focusing on the rights and well-being of employees and other workers in the value chain
- *environment* – from recycling materials to the whole carbon footprint of the organisation
- *marketplace* – including issues such as fair trading, corporate taxes and anti-bribery.

The need to focus on corporate social responsibility has become increasingly obvious over recent years. There has been much media attention given to environmental disasters, poor labour standards and the responsibility that consumers and companies in developed countries have for global value chains. Equally, reckless lending and opaque financial transactions were clear contributors to the recent global financial crisis.

As a result, businesses are witnessing increasing demands from statutory bodies for detailed information about their corporate standards. At the same time, the widespread loss of trust in business means a genuine focus on corporate social responsibility is vital for restoring and maintaining consumer and investor confidence. This has been shown recently by the Volkswagen and Audi diesel emissions scandal. Thus, for businesses corporate social responsibility is not a luxury that can be avoided but a necessity that has grown in importance through the global recession. However, it will also provide other benefits, such as increased efficiency and reduced waste – for example cutting fuel costs through environmental initiatives, building trust and enhancing brand in the marketplace, and even supporting employee engagement, retention and employer brand.

The foundation of corporate social responsibility is a stakeholder-based view of value creation and an organisation's responsibilities.

Who are the stakeholders? A stakeholder is anyone who has an interest in a business.

THE RELATIONSHIP BETWEEN BUSINESS AND CUSTOMERS

Customer rights – quality, safety, price and customer service – were once the most important ethical concerns in business. Now consumers influence business ethics and have been instrumental in bringing about change: consumers expect businesses to demonstrate ethical responsibility in its widest sense – affecting the treatment of employees, the community, the environment, working conditions and so forth. Some companies have been the focus of consumer criticism and forced to change their practices – Shell over Brent Spar and Ogoniland; Monsanto over GM food; Nike and Gap over child labour. Shell bowed to consumer pressure and did not sink the Brent Spar, and Nike now monitors its factories following the BBC Panorama programme.

One of the first ethical businesses was The Body Shop, pioneered by the late Anita Roddick. The company became a great success in the mid-1980s following a change in consumer awareness of how beauty products were tested, as it began to look for alternative ways. However, an ethical business does not need to be at the level of The Body Shop as even small gestures like participation in community events or collections for charities can improve a company's appearance to consumers.

Consumer action, therefore, can be very effective, as if enough consumers stop buying from a business then the business will be forced to change or go bust. Ethical business practices will give a better image to the consumer and better sales.

THE RELATIONSHIP BETWEEN EMPLOYERS AND EMPLOYEES

Much of the employer/employee relationship now consists of them working together. In 1978 in the UK the Advisory, Conciliation and Arbitration Service (ACAS) was set up to try to create good and harmonious working relationships. It negotiates in disputes and has been very successful, as there have been few major employment disputes, and ACAS has been able to suggest guidelines for better relationships in most situations.

For employer/employee relationships to be successful there has to be a balance of interests: the employer wants to plan for the future of the business, make profits and keep employees motivated; the employee wants the best possible conditions and living standards. If employees are unhappy there will often be high turnover of staff, poor time-keeping and much absenteeism – as a result of this discontent, profits will suffer.

However, relationships between employers and employees do not always work out. The Internet now allows for rapid sharing of information across the world – and multinationals operate across the world. There are a multitude of websites that publicise and discuss the behaviour of businesses. Whistle-blowing is now more acceptable – access to secret information is now better and it is even protected by law in some countries. From 'Deep Throat' (the codename of the informant in the 1972 Watergate scandal) to Dr David Kelly, whistle-blowers have risked their lives to tell what they perceive to be the truth and to make organisations accountable.

The question of whether it is ethical for an employee to blow the whistle, especially in the public domain, raises questions of confidentiality and loyalty – there is no simple answer to cover all cases. However, neither confidentiality or loyalty implies that the unethical conduct of others should not simply be reported, especially when product safety or the severe financial hardship of others is concerned. Whistle-blowers often risk dismissal and may find it difficult to find similar employment in the future; they may be frozen out or ostracised. There are now organisations to protect whistle-blowers, such as 'Freedom to Care', which promotes our 'ethical right to accountable behaviour from large organisations' and argues that employees have an 'ethical right to express serious public concerns' in the workplace and, if necessary, to go public.

Thought point

1 'Business exists to make a profit.' Is it society's task to protect those who are badly affected in the process?
2 Do you think standards of integrity in business are declining? Give reasons and examples.
3 Do you think workers should participate in management?

CASE STUDY

1 There are three area managers in a company: Tom, Steve and Tim. Tom was the latest to join the company and has learned from Tim and from his own observations that Steve is not to be trusted. Steve seems to have no morals and his only goal seems to be his own advantage. He 'manages upwards', always trying to please the director; he lies to cover up difficulties or shortfalls; he tells his staff to take no notice of established policy – but never in writing and never to more than one person at a time. At the same time Steve gives the impression of being a straight-talking man of the people.

Tom finds this really hard to deal with but is unsure how to respond.

- Sinking to Steve's level would not be acceptable, but just putting up with it, like Tim does and Steve's own staff do, really goes against the grain and all that Tom holds dear. How do you accuse a colleague of dishonesty?
- What are the choices facing Tom?
- What principles do you think are relevant when dealing with a colleague of this sort?

2 The head of a department in a medium-sized company with a good profit record is 55 years old and has worked for the company for 20 years. He is married, with two children at university. His life is his work. However, he is becoming less effective and no longer inspires those who work for him. Several of the brightest young people in his department have left because of the situation.

continued opposite

If you were his boss would you:

(a) Declare him redundant with compensation?

(b) Retire him prematurely on a full pension?

(c) Transfer him to an advisory post?

(d) Take corrective action and leave him in his job?

(e) Transfer him to a new executive position on the same pay until he is 60?

(f) Do nothing or take some other course of action?

3 Why is it important for a business to behave in a socially responsible manner?

THE RELATIONSHIP BETWEEN BUSINESS AND THE ENVIRONMENT

Environmental responsibility is a vital component of a business strategy as it not only helps the environment but also wins the trust of communities and gains the respect of the governments of the countries in which the business operates. All businesses impact on the environment: they emit pollution, produce waste and use resources. Businesses, however, are continually being encouraged to improve their approach to environmental issues. Every year there is a prestigious award, the Business Commitment to the Environment Award, and in 2007 the Co-operative was one of the winners for its response to global climate change. Some of its efforts for the environment included: the reduction by 86% of its CO_2 emissions, use of 98% green electricity and an ethical investment policy.

However, balancing business growth and environmental quality is always going to be a challenge for business. Businesses are encouraged to have an environmental policy, just as they do for many other issues – again this has often been a reaction to consumer pressure, and also international pressure from organisations, such as the World Wide Fund for Nature. UK law and the UN Global Compact also provide minimum standards for how businesses treat the environment, and not only the small but also the large multinational businesses will generally seek to operate within the law to protect their reputation.

For example the Anglo American Mining Company is one of the 20 largest UK-based companies, heavily involved in mining and quarrying – activities which have an immediate impact on the environment. When Anglo American carries out its mining operations it tries to have a positive effect in three areas:

1   In the area where the mine is located, it carries out its operations with care and tries to improve the lives of local people – for example minimising noise and other types of pollution.
2   In the area immediately surrounding the mine, it is active in conservation and improvement.
3   In the wider region around the mine, it contributes financially to local communities and helps generate new businesses.

An example of Anglo American's environmental conservation projects is at Tarmac's Langford Quarry in the UK, where the company has created reed beds in streams and ponds surrounding the quarry. Reed beds are an endangered habitat and local people worked with Tarmac to plant the first 10,000 reeds.

Supermarkets have been one of the businesses where the importance of 'green credentials' has become increasingly important. Concerns about 'food miles' and plastic and packaging are growing among consumers. Supermarkets have realised that they must compete on their environmental ethical credentials as well as price, availability, accessibility and so forth, as all these factors influence where consumers shop. Responding to consumer preferences, helping the environment, profitability and corporate social responsibility go hand in hand.

There are four components of corporate social responsibility

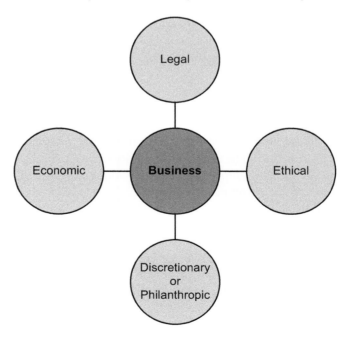

Economic

The economist Milton Friedman wrote that the social responsibility of a business was to increase its profits. A profitable business creates jobs, goods and services that improve life for all. Profitable businesses also buy goods and services from other businesses and provide income for their shareholders or owners. This improves society in general. This is the responsibility on which all the others rest.

Legal

If businesses are to be socially responsible they need to operate within the laws of society. For example the goods they produce must be safe as must the workplaces in which they are produced. There must be no discrimination within the workplace and the business must live up to all its contractual obligations.

Ethical

Ethical considerations often go beyond legal ones. For example a bank could legally foreclose on someone's home, but might instead organise a repayment plan that the customer could afford. On a global scale businesses are supposed to know and do something about issues such as child labour. Such issues now affect the company brand.

Discretionary or philanthropic

This final component involves going beyond ethical expectations to actively engage in programmes that help society; examples include charitable giving, sport sponsorship, aid given to the local community or even staff volunteering projects.

QUESTIONS ARISING ABOUT CORPORATE SOCIAL RESPONSIBILITY

Is corporate social responsibility simply a publicity exercise to enhance a company brand?

A company can have a good corporate social responsibility policy but that does not guarantee good practice, as the case of US energy giant Enron showed. Enron was well-known for its corporate social responsibility and published social and environmental reports on all the good work it was

The invisible hand

[A merchant] intends only his own security; and by directing that industry in such a manner as its produce may be of the greatest value, he intends only his own gain, and he is in this, as in many other cases, led by an invisible hand to promote an end which was no part of his intention. Nor is it always the worse for the society that it was no part of it. By pursuing his own interest he frequently promotes that of the society more effectually than when he really intends to promote it. I have never known much good done by those who affected to trade for the public good.

(Smith, The Wealth of Nations, pp. 26–27)

Discussion

What do you think Smith means when he says that a merchant who strives only for his own gain unwittingly promotes the interests of society? What are society's interests, and how does the merchant promote them?

Do you agree or disagree with this statement by Adam Smith? Why?

Is it true, as Adam Smith suggests, that the market moderates personal selfishness, as customers who are exploited will not continue to use that business?

doing. The trouble is that at the same time it was lying about its profits. When the truth emerged, it led to the company's collapse in 2001, while top executives were jailed for conspiracy and fraud. Enron became a byword for corporate irresponsibility, and all of its community and environmental work was undermined by the fact that it was carried out by a company with dishonest business practices.

Not everyone believes it is the job of big business to address problems in society. Eamon Smith, the director of the free market economics think-tank the Adam Smith Institute, believes that businesses do recognise the responsibility they have to the wider public, but that ultimately they are concerned with business and it is the interference of politicians who try to make businesses pay for welfare projects that should be paid for out of taxes.

So is the business of business only business? Or do all sectors, businesses as well as governments, need to work together to address big issues, such as global warming, and share collective responsibility, knowledge and expertise?

GLOBALISATION

Globalisation means 'the reduction of the difference between one economy and another, so trade all over the world, both within and between different countries, becomes increasingly similar'. This has been going on for a long time, and used to be quite a slow process, but in recent times it has speeded up. The reasons for the increase in the pace of globalisation are:

1   Technological change – especially in communications technology.
2   Transport is both faster and cheaper.
3   Deregulation – an increase in privatisation, and countries now able to own businesses in other countries – for example some UK utilities which were once government-owned are now owned by French businesses.
4   Removal of capital exchange controls – money can now be moved easily from one country to another.
5   Free trade – many barriers to trade have been removed, sometimes by grouping countries together, such as the EU.
6   Consumer tastes have changed and consumers are now more willing to try foreign products.
7   Emerging markets in developing countries.

All of this means that businesses are now freer to choose where they operate from, and can move to countries where labour is cheaper. This has meant, for example, that much manufacturing has moved to countries such as Indonesia, and many telephone call centres have moved to India.

National borders are becoming less important as markets stretch across them, and multinationals have taken advantage of this. Consumers are alike, but not the same, in different countries, and businesses have needed to consider local variations.

However, globalisation also brings problems – especially those of justice towards poorer countries. Trade between countries is not totally fair, and some of the richest countries, such as the United States, have very strong trade barriers to protect their national interests. It could be said that globalisation means that the interests of the shareholders are more important than the interests of the employees or the consumers, and it means that the poorest people have just 1.4% of the global income. The disaster at Bhopal in India is a prime example, as the chemical companies concerned continued to deny responsibility for a long time, and some survivors still await compensation. Toxic waste still pollutes the environment.

Anti-globalisation movements campaign against the bad effects of globalisation and for business based on the UN Norms for Business.

- Amnesty International campaigns for a global human rights framework.
- The World Council of Churches campaigns for responsible lending and unconditional debt cancellation.
- There are also campaigns for ecological farming practices, and against the imposed privatisation of public services, especially water.

In his book *One World: The Ethics of Globalisation* Peter Singer lists the various global problems that we face and challenges us to develop a system of ethics and justice that can be accepted by all people, regardless of their race, culture or religion.

WHISTLE-BLOWING

Whistle-blowers are workers who report wrongdoings or illegal practices at work. The disclosure must affect the general public. Whistle-blowers are protected by law and should not be treated unfairly or lose their jobs as a result of 'blowing the whistle'.

The Public Interest Disclosure Act 1998 is the key piece of whistle-blowing legislation protecting employees who 'blow the whistle' in the public interest. Employees are protected by law if they report any of the following:

- a criminal offence – for example fraud
- a danger to someone's health and safety
- risk or actual damage to the environment
- a miscarriage of justice
- a company's violation of the law – for example not having the right insurance
- a deliberate attempt to cover up a wrongdoing.

Ensuring a working environment that encourages employees to challenge poor or dangerous practice is important for good business ethics. Good leadership and an open and honest culture can enable individuals to feel comfortable about raising concerns with their colleagues or managers. Unfortunately, in some cases the work environment is not so open and employers are not so receptive to concerns about malpractice.

One such example is Terry Bryan, a whistle-blower and former senior nurse at Winterbourne View who was initially ignored by his manager, senior Castlebeck staff and the Care Quality Commission (CQC). His tenacity, however, paid off, and the resulting BBC Panorama exposé resulted in real change for the better. The residents were moved to safety, the abusers were prosecuted, the home was closed and ultimately the provider went out of business. The CQC also changed its practice in relation to whistle-blowers.

This example shows that whistle-blowing is not easy and the employee may not be listened to or may be accused of disloyalty to the organisation or his or her employer. Additionally, whistle-blowers and the media have enjoyed a somewhat symbiotic relationship, and even though they may have different agendas and motives they both aim to expose wrongdoing and bring about change, as in the care homes scandal, where individuals reported for altruistic reasons.

Thought point

Investigate the following 'whistle-blowers':

Sherron Watkins

An executive for the Enron Corp., she helped expose the formidable company in 2001 and 2002 as one constructed on enormous financial lies and frauds. Along with Coleen Rowley and WorldCom's Cynthia Cooper, she was one of three whistle-blowers named *Time* magazine's Persons of the Year in 2002.

Bradley Manning

The Army soldier was court-martialled at Fort Meade, Maryland, in the summer of 2013 for documents provided to WikiLeaks. 'I am sorry that my

continued opposite

actions hurt people. I'm sorry that they hurt the United States,' he said at his sentencing hearing.

Edward Snowden

Snowden was a former technical worker at the CIA who sensationally revealed himself as the whistle-blower behind leaks to the *Guardian* and the *Washington Post* in June 2013 that uncovered secret US government surveillance programmes.

Julian Assange

Founder and editor-in-chief of WikiLeaks, Mr Assange's organisation has been responsible for over 1.2 million leaks to date since the website's creation in 2006. Assange has been staying in the Ecuadorian embassy in London, where he is seeking political asylum from charges against him in Sweden since 2012.

Terry Bryan

A former charge nurse (i.e., head of a ward) at Winterbourne View hospital in Bristol, which is the centre of an abuse investigation, alleges that senior hospital managers and the industry regulator ignored his complaints. Terry Bryan said he earlier reported incidents to managers and the Care Quality Commission but said nothing was done.

Investigate some of these whistle-blowers:

* What do they tell you about the culture of the organisation?
* Are they heroes or villains?
* Do you think they acted out of a Kantian sense of duty?
* Were their actions utilitarian, serving the greater good?
* Consider the consequences of their actions.

BENEFITS OF ETHICS FOR BUSINESS

One of the main benefits for a business of behaving ethically is that a better image is shown to the world at large, and especially to consumers, resulting in greater profit. It also means that expensive and potentially embarrassing public relations disasters are avoided. As far as employees are concerned, if the business is seen to behave ethically – for example with regard to the environment – it will recruit more highly qualified employees, and this leads to better employee motivation as the employees are proud of their jobs.

PROBLEMS OF ETHICS FOR BUSINESS

Being ethical can increase costs for the business – for example they have to pay reasonable wages to all employees. If a business is truly putting its ethics into practice it will have to pass on the same standards down the supply chain and this will mean no longer doing business with suppliers who are not prepared to meet the same standards.

However, businesses are products of the society in which they operate, and if society does not always have clear standards it is not always easy for a business to decide what to do – for example some people in our society are completely opposed to experimenting on animals, but others would argue that it is all right for a business to do so if it benefits human health.

Sometimes a business needs to consider that its role is to make a profit, provide jobs and create wealth for society as a whole, and it may consider that ethics are good if they help achieve these aims, and to be ignored if they do not.

Ultimately to really be ethical a business may have to change its whole business practice and organisational culture.

APPLYING ETHICAL THEORIES TO BUSINESS ETHICS

Utilitarianism

Utilitarianism considers the majority affected by a certain action and as far business is concerned develops Adam Smith's enlightened self-interest – general welfare is important, and this is often seen as good business policy: the general good of the organisation is more important than that of individuals. So, for example, an employee, although qualified for a certain position, will have to give way to another so that the interest of the business as a whole can be preserved. A farmer may have to give up some of his land for a dam project, because it will provide irrigation for lots of farmers and generate electricity for the whole community. However, the best business transactions are the ones in which the best result is achieved, when both business and consumer, employer and employee, shareholders and stakeholders are considered and benefited. This means that when making business decisions all options need considering – no one can act just on intuition if they wish to maximise utility and a cost-benefit approach needs to be taken.

Classical utilitarianism does promote a free market economy, which would approach issues from the viewpoint of the best results for the majority. In addition, John Stuart Mill would consider the harm principle and this would support corporate social responsibility, although this could be tempered by the utilitarian reasoning that the ends justify the means – it would depend on whether the follower of utilitarianism favoured the good of society as a whole or the maximisation of profits.

Globalisation is also favoured by Bentham's emphasis on the greatest good for the greatest number, which means that all stakeholders involved count; however, it must be remembered that this could, for example, maximise the happiness of consumers who want cheap goods at the expense of exploitation of the workers.

Economically, utilitarianism would seem to be a good ethical approach to business; however, in many cases it is not simple and clear-cut. For example closing a polluting factory may be good for the environment, but not for the local community, who may need the jobs. Whatever the business does, it is going to upset one group of people or another. Utilitarianism does not always help here.

Evaluating a utilitarian approach to business ethics

Taking the ends as justifying the means can lead to unjust business practices, such as exploiting workers or neglecting health and safety. However, Singer pointed out that the fact that a person can suffer needs to be considered when making business decisions – a worker in a sweatshop can suffer just as the customer can for having to pay more for goods, so having cheap goods is not a good enough reason to make another person suffer

There is in utilitarianism the continuing problem of the minority who could suffer so that the majority are happy.

Utilitarianism can make business simply a way of calculating consequences which can lead to immoral actions to achieve those ends – but those consequences cannot always be predicted.

Kantian ethics

Kant believed that morality, in all spheres of human life, including business, should be grounded in reason. His categorical imperative held that people should act only according to maxims that they would be willing to see become universal norms, and that people should never be treated as a means to an end. Kant's theory implies the necessity of trust, adherence to rules and fulfilment of promises (e.g. contracts). Kant argued that the highest good was the good will – the importance of acting from duty – so, for example, if a merchant is honest in order to gain a good reputation, then these acts of honesty are not genuinely moral. Kant's ethics are ethics of duty rather than consequence: a business behaving morally in order to impress consumers is not truly moral according to Kant. Kant's ethical theory applies well to both employees and consumers as it does not permit people to be treated as means to an end – even if that end is profit. Kantian ethics would also see a business as a moral community, with all stakeholders – employers and employees, customers and shareholders – standing in a moral relationship with each other, which would influence the way they treat each other. This seems to require that the work that employees are given is meaningful, and that businesses should be organised more democratically.

Kant's universalisation means that business laws would have to be universal – for example no bribery or corruption – and this would have a beneficial effect on international business. However, Kantian ethics has far more to offer to international business ethics as it shows how business can contribute to world peace. N.E. Bowie (*Business Ethics*, 1991) quotes Kant as saying,

> In the end war itself will be seen as not only so artificial, in outcome so uncertain for both sides, in after effects so painful in the form of an ever-growing war debt (a new invention) that cannot be met, that it will be regarded as the most dubious undertaking. The impact of any revolution on all states in our continent, so clearly knit together through commerce will be so obvious that other states, driven by their own danger, but without any legal basis, will offer themselves as arbiters, and thus will prepare the way for distant international government for which there is no precedent in world history.
>
> (Kant, *Idea for a Universal History from a Cosmopolitan Point of View*, 1784)

If business (commerce) brings people together then the chance of peace among nations improves. Bowie considers that Kantian ethics has rich implications for business ethics.

As far as globalisation is concerned Kant's second maxim, never to treat people as a means to an end, implies that businesses have responsibility for their workers' pay, conditions of work and so forth and profits should not be achieved by exploitation, whether it be of the employees, the suppliers or the customers.

A Kantian approach to business ethics would support corporate social responsibility as everyone is treated as an autonomous person and there is consideration for all stakeholders. Kant's third imperative, living in a kingdom of ends, reminds business leaders of the importance of responsibility to all people and to the planet. Kantian views a business as a moral community relationship to all the others, and so Kant points out that humans are worth more than mere profit.

Evaluating a Kantian approach to business ethics

Kantian ethics creates unbreakable duties which apply to all involved in a business. But what if two duties conflict? What if it is necessary to choose between duties to different stakeholders, such as shareholders and employees? Employees' and customers' needs and the need for a business to make a profit can be in conflict – for example with health and safety regulations. Is it better for the workers in a factory in Bangladesh to have no jobs, and good health and safety regulations, or jobs with a poor safety record?

Is it possible to apply absolutes, such as the categorical imperative, to issues in businesses which are spread throughout the world? Also many issues in business which seem to be exploitative have both pros and cons, such as zero hours contracts, which can be abused by the employer or used to advantage by both employer and employee.

Perhaps it is better to use, as W.D. Ross suggests, a hierarchy of prima facie duties: but this is not Kantian deontology but a form of *deontological relativism*.

Kant's universalisation does not consider local cultures and customs, such as a gift offered before a business deal being considered normal in one culture but as a bribe in another.

REVIEW QUESTIONS

Look back over the chapter and check that you can answer the following questions:

1. Explain how consumers can influence business ethics.
2. Why is environmental responsibility a good business strategy?
3. List the benefits and the problems of ethics for businesses.
4. List the strengths and weaknesses of a utilitarian approach to business ethics.
5. How does Kant think business can help world peace?

SUMMARY

Business ethics considers the ethical relationship between businesses and consumers, between businesses and their employees. It also considers the impact of globalisation on the environment, and on society at large.

One of the main benefits for a business of behaving ethically is that a better image is shown to the world at large, and especially to consumers, resulting in greater profit. It also means that expensive and potentially embarrassing public relations disasters are avoided.

Milton Friedman emphasised the importance of maximising profits – 'The business of business is business.'

Corporate social responsibility has become increasingly important for business – good ethics makes for good business. Consumers now expect businesses to be socially responsible and businesses are increasingly thinking about what they can achieve by putting the power of their marketing behind some key social issues so that they can help make a positive social difference.

Corporate social responsibility concerns four main areas:

- *Economic responsibilities*: be profitable. This is the foundation on which all the others rest.
- *Legal responsibilities*: obey the law and play by the rules.
- *Ethical responsibilities*: obligation to do what is right, just and fair. Avoid harm.
- *Philanthropic responsibilities*: be a good corporate citizen. Contribute to the community and improve the quality of life.

Considering *stakeholders* is important for achieving corporate social responsibility.

The main stakeholders are:

- *Customers*: consumer rights – quality, safety, price and customer service were once the most important ethical concerns in business. Now consumers influence business ethics, and have been instrumental in bringing about change: consumers expect businesses to demonstrate ethical responsibility in its widest sense – affecting the treatment of employees, the community, the environment, working conditions and so forth.
- *Employees*: much of the employer/employee relationship now consists of them working together. For employer/employee relationships to be successful there has to be a balance of interests: the employer wants to plan for the future of the business, make profits and keep employees motivated; the employee wants the best possible conditions and living standards. This needs to work to ensure profits.

- *Shareholders*: the business needs to make a profit for its shareholders, but is this the most important aspect of business ethics?
- *Government*: the law of the land needs to be obeyed – taxes paid, health and safety guaranteed and so forth.
- *Local community*: an aspect of corporate social responsibility is to aid the local community and improve the quality of life of the people who live there.
- *Suppliers*: need to be paid fairly and promptly for their goods. This is also an important aspect of corporate social responsibility.
- *Environment*: balancing business growth and environmental quality is always going to be a challenge for business. Businesses are encouraged to have an environmental policy, just as they do for many other issues – again this has often been a reaction to consumer pressure, and also international pressure from organisations, such as the World Wide Fund for Nature.

Globalisation: 'the reduction of the difference between one economy and another, so trade all over the world, both within and between different countries, becomes increasingly similar'. The main reasons for the increase in globalisation are:

- Technological change
- Cheaper and quicker transport
- Deregulation
- Free trade
- Easy movement of money between countries
- Change in consumer tastes
- Emerging markets in developing countries.

However, businesses ethics is not simple, as there is no longer one agreed moral code and multinationals operate in different parts of the world, employing and serving people from different cultures.

Whistle-blowing: relationships between employers and employees do not always work out. The Internet now allows for rapid sharing of information across the world – and multinationals operate across the world. There are a multitude of websites that publicise and discuss the behaviour of businesses. Whistle-blowing is now more acceptable, access to secret information is now better and it is even protected by law in some countries.

Utilitarian approach to business ethics: utilitarianism considers the majority affected by a certain action – general welfare is important, and this is often seen as good business policy: the general good of the organisation is more important than that of individuals. This means that when making business decisions all options need considering – no one can act just on intuition if they wish to maximise utility. Utilitarianism may be good economically but does not consider rights.

Kantian approach to business ethics: Kant believed that morality, in all spheres of human life, including business, should be grounded in reason. Duty, universalisation and not using others as a means to an end need to be considered. Kant's theory implies the necessity of trust, adherence to rules and fulfilment of promises (i.e. contracts). Kantian ethics sees a business as a moral community. If Kantian ethics is applied, there is the possibility of business (commerce) bringing people together and then the chance of peace among nations improves.

 # Examination questions practice

SAMPLE EXAM-STYLE QUESTION

'Kantian ethics is the best approach to the issues surrounding business.' Discuss.

AO1 (15 marks)

- In your answer to this question you will need to explain the main principles of Kantian ethics – for example duty, good will, the categorical and hypothetical imperatives – and how they might be applied to business.
- It would be better to concentrate on one or two business issues, such as relations between business and shareholders, the question of profit and what business methods could be universalised, the relations between employers and employees, and the importance of not treating others as a means to an end, or your essay may tend to be too much about business issues and not enough about ethical theories.

AO2 (15 marks)

- However, you also need to ask if it is the 'best' approach and this means contrasting it with other approaches (e.g. utilitarianism).
- You need to assess the advantages and disadvantages of Kantian ethics in relation to business issues.

Further possible questions

- **Assess the usefulness of utilitarianism as an ethical approach to business.**
- **Critically assess the view that the main aim of a business is to produce a profit.**

FURTHER READING

Bowie, N.E. 1999. *Business Ethics: A Kantian Perspective*. Oxford: Blackwell.

Chryssides, G. and Kaler, J. 1996. *Essentials of Business Ethics*. London: McGraw-Hill.

Crane, A. and Matten, D. 2003. *Business Ethics*. Oxford: OUP.

Frederick, R. 1999. *A Companion to Business Ethics*. Oxford: Blackwell.

Friedmann, M. September 13, 1970. 'The Social Responsibility of Business Is to Increase Its Profits', in *The New York Times Magazine*, New York: New York Times.

FTSE4Good [www.ftse.com/products/downloads/F4G-Index-Inclusion-Rules.pdf]

Singer, P. 2004. *One World: The Ethics of Globalization*. Yale: Yale University Press.

Solomon, R.C. 1993. *Ethics and Excellence*. New York: Oxford University Press.

DEVELOPMENTS IN CHRISTIAN THOUGHT

PART III

16 Introduction

To some people, the idea that there can be developments in a religion would seem to go against the idea that Christianity was 'revealed' in the first century. Surely this means that what needed to be taught was done then and it is up to followers to keep to these laws and teachings. However, this is certainly not the case. One of the most hackneyed clichés must be 'What would Jesus do?' This seems to be used at any time when there is a difficult moral decision to be made. It makes some sense as Christians accept that Jesus was the Son of God and, as part of the Trinity, actually God. Therefore, the question 'What would God do?' might be seen as having some merit. Nevertheless, the only real answer to this question is 'how can we know?'

Christianity has not passed through 2,000 years like a seamless robe. In the past, a popular examination question was 'If Jesus was to enter a church today would he recognise any aspect of the service taking place?' The answer to this is almost certainly that he would not, probably not even the Eucharist.

People might say that they have the Bible and that this is all they need along with their faith. However, if we look at this claim in more detail it makes very little sense.

The Old Testament: Christians number the Old Testament books at 39, while Judaism (for which it forms the Tenakh) numbers the books as 24. This is because Judaism considers Samuel, Kings and Chronicles to form one book each, groups the 12 minor prophets into one book, and regards Ezra and Nehemiah as a single book. The books are also in a different order, concluding with Chronicles and the hope of a return to Jerusalem when the Messiah comes. On the other hand, the Christian Old Testament ends with the prophet Malachi, the end times and the coming of the Messiah. This then leads into the New Testament and Matthew's account of the birth of Jesus.

What makes things confusing is that the Roman Catholic Church uses a Bible which contains 1 & 2 Maccabees, while the Orthodox Church also has 3 & 4 Maccabees. The Roman Catholic Church also has Tobit and Judith and longer versions of the books of Esther and Daniel. The Protestant Church regards these extra books and chapters as apocryphal, meaning that people are not sure whether they are authentic revealed scripture. It was not until 8 April 1546 that the Council of Trent agreed on the canon of Old Testament scripture which exists today.

Unfortunately, when we come to the New Testament, a similar problem arises. The New Testament consist of 27 books: the four Gospels, the Acts of the Apostles, 21 letters or epistles and the Revelation of St John – the Apocalypse. This canon is agreed upon by the Protestant and Roman Catholic Churches but, for example, the churches of the Orthodox Tewahedo tradition also recognise an additional eight books.

The present generally accepted canon was agreed at the 1546 Council of Trent. However, when we look at the Apocryphal New Testament there are at least 28 other gospels, 10 epistles, 15 books of Acts and 7 books of the Apocalypse as well as many other texts. Unless it is attributed to the work of the Holy Spirit, it is difficult to see how the present 27 books were chosen out of over 80 texts.

There were moves to introduce some of the disputed texts into the canon: these include 1 & 2 Clement, the Shepherd of Hermas, the Didache, 3 Corinthians and the Epistle of Barnabas, but the canon still stands as it did following the Council of Trent and the work of Irenaeus, who largely compiled it. So, the Bible might be considered less final and complete than it generally is.

As to biblical accuracy, there are also many questions to be answered. It is generally accepted that the Pauline Epistles were written down by the second century. Mark, the earliest of the four canonical Gospels, seems to date after CE 70 as it appears to relate to the conquest of Jerusalem in that year. Although it seems likely that the three synoptic Gospels date from the first century, many scholars place John in the second century, before CE 150.

There are various theories of the sources of the Gospels too complex to look at here, but it is widely accepted that Luke and Matthew share a common source, known as Q (*quelle*; German: source). Attempts to reconstruct this lost text suggest that it contained passages such as the Devil's three temptations of Jesus, the Beatitudes, the Lord's Prayer and many individual sayings. Many of these sayings are found in the Sermon on the Mount (Matthew 5–7) and the Sermon on the Plain (Luke 6:17–49).

Apocrypha

In relation to the Old Testament: those books included in the Septuagint and Vulgate versions, which were not originally written in Hebrew and not counted as genuine by the Jews, and which, at the Reformation, were excluded from the Sacred Canon by the Protestant party, as having no well-grounded claim to inspired authorship.

The New Testament Apocrypha contains books disputed for various reasons.

The *Council of Trent* was held between 1545 and 1563 in Trento (Trent) and Bologna, northern Italy, and was one of the Roman Catholic Church's most important ecumenical councils, having been prompted by the Protestant Reformation.

Irenaeus the man (*c.* CE 130–200)

Irenaeus originated from Smyrna in Asia Minor. He was a Christian preacher and later became the bishop of Lyon, France. He died in the year 200.

Irenaeus

World History Archive/Alamy

GOSPEL DIFFERENCES

There are also a significant number of differences in the Gospels, which of necessity raise the question of their accuracy, especially taking into account the fact that their earliest form was almost certainly an oral tradition. Some of the most significant are listed ahead.

The Infancy narratives appear in only Luke and Matthew. The genealogies with which they begin were probably bought from professional scribes in the Temple.

The Virgin Birth appears with these narratives. However, it may well be an error or deliberate change in the translation. The writer of Matthew's Gospel was working in Greek and was quoting the Book of Isaiah, which was written in Hebrew:

> Therefore the Lord himself will give you a sign. Look, the young woman is with child and shall bear a son, and shall name him Immanuel.
>
> (Isaiah 7:14)

> Look, the virgin shall conceive and bear a son, and they shall name him Emmanuel.
>
> (Matthew 1:23)

The Hebrew word used in Isaiah was עלמה *'almāh*, which means 'young woman or a girl past puberty'. When, in the second century, the Hebrew was translated into the Greek Septuagint, the closest translation would have been neania (neania), 'young woman', but instead it was translated as παρθένος (parthenos), a 'virgin'.

As the Roman Catholic Church teaches the Perpetual Virginity of Mary this could be seen as an issue.

Erasmus in his Paraphrase of Matthew (*The First Tome or Volume of the Paraphrase of Erasmus Upon the New Testament*) acknowledges that the translation has changed the meaning of the quotation from Isaiah and says that although 'no one would think that we would tolerate anyone' who did not accept the doctrine of the perpetual virginity of Mary, he did point out that the doctrine could not be proved from the Scriptures.

Also, if Mary was indeed a virgin all her life it raises issues about Jesus' brothers and sisters. These appear as the following:

> Is not this the carpenter, the son of Mary and brother of James and Joses and Judas and Simon, and are not his sisters here with us?
>
> (Mark 6:3a)

> Is not this the carpenter's son? Is not his mother called Mary? And are not his brothers James and Joseph and Simon and Judas?
>
> (Matthew 13:55)

> So his brothers said to him, 'Leave here and go to Judea so that your disciples also may see the works you are doing; for no one who wants to

Desiderius Erasmus Roterodamus (1466–1536)

Known as Erasmus or Erasmus of Rotterdam, he was a Dutch/Netherlandish Renaissance humanist, Catholic priest, social critic, teacher and theologian.

He has been called 'the crowning glory of the Christian humanists'. Erasmus rejected Luther's emphasis on faith alone and remained a member of the Roman Catholic Church all his life. He also held to the Catholic doctrine of free will. His middle road ('Via Media') approach disappointed and angered scholars in both the Roman Catholic Church and the Protestant movement. Erasmus died suddenly in Basel in 1536 while preparing to return to Brabant and was buried in Basel Minster, the former cathedral of the city.

be widely known acts in secret. If you do these things, show yourself to the world.' (For not even his brothers believed in him.)

(John 7:3–5)

All these were constantly devoting themselves to prayer, together with certain women, including Mary the mother of Jesus, as well as his brothers.

(Acts 1:14)

Do we not have the right to be accompanied by a believing wife as do the other apostles and the brothers of the Lord and Cephas?

(1 Corinthians 9:5)

The usual explanation given is that 'brothers' means 'cousins' in this context because there are examples of usage in that form in the Old Testament, but these references seem too specific for that.

THE BIRTH OF JESUS

In the Gospel of Luke it says,

In the days of King Herod of Judea . . . In those days a decree went out from Emperor Augustus that all the world should be registered. This was the first registration and was taken while Quirinius was governor of Syria. All went to their own towns to be registered. Joseph also went from the town of Nazareth in Galilee to Judea, to the city of David called Bethlehem, because he was descended from the house and family of David. He went to be registered with Mary, to whom he was engaged and who was expecting a child.

(Luke 1:5, 2:1–5)

The issues here are several: Herod ruled from 37 BCE to 4 BCE. In CE 6 Publius Sulpicius Quirinius was appointed Imperial Legate (governor) of the province of Roman Syria. In the same year Judea was declared a Roman province, and Quirinius was tasked to carry out a census of the new territory for tax purposes. The new territory was one of the three portions into which the kingdom of Herod the Great had been divided on his death in 4 BCE. In this division, Galilee remained autonomous. There was no census of the entire empire under Augustus and no Roman census required people to travel from their own homes to those of distant ancestors. Anyway, the census of Judea would not have affected Joseph and his family as they lived in Galilee.

So it seems that Luke got this part of the infancy narrative very wrong.

A different but similar problem arises if we compare the infancy narratives in Luke and Matthew.

> In the sixth month the angel Gabriel was sent by God to a town in Galilee called Nazareth, to a virgin engaged to a man whose name was Joseph, of the house of David. The virgin's name was Mary.
>
> (Luke 1:26–27)

> After eight days had passed, it was time to circumcise the child; and he was called Jesus, the name given by the angel before he was conceived in the womb. . . . When they had finished everything required by the law of the Lord, they returned to Galilee, to their own town of Nazareth. The child grew and became strong, filled with wisdom; and the favor of God was upon him.
>
> (Luke 2:21, 39–40)

> Now after they had left, an angel of the Lord appeared to Joseph in a dream and said, 'Get up, take the child and his mother, and flee to Egypt, and remain there until I tell you; for Herod is about to search for the child, to destroy him.' Then Joseph got up, took the child and his mother by night, and went to Egypt, and remained there until the death of Herod. This was to fulfill what had been spoken by the Lord through the prophet, 'Out of Egypt I have called my son.' . . . When Herod died, an angel of the Lord suddenly appeared in a dream to Joseph in Egypt and said, 'Get up, take the child and his mother, and go to the land of Israel, for those who were seeking the child's life are dead.' Then Joseph got up, took the child and his mother, and went to the land of Israel. But when he heard that Archelaus was ruling over Judea in place of his father Herod, he was afraid to go there. And after being warned in a dream, he went away to the district of Galilee. There he made his home in a town called Nazareth, so that what had been spoken through the prophets might be fulfilled, 'He will be called a Nazorean.'
>
> (Matthew 2:13–15, 19–23)

It is very difficult to rationalise these accounts in any way. According to Luke, Joseph and Mary lived in Nazareth before Jesus was born. Matthew has them moving there when they came back from Egypt.

Luke has the family returning to Nazareth after Jesus' circumcision. Matthew has an unspecified length of time which they spent in Egypt and again we have the problem of when Herod died.

Herod Archelaus (23 BCE – c. CE 18) was ethnarch (a king who ruled over half of the land of his father) Herod the Great. This included Samaria and Judea. He ruled for nine years (*c.* 4 BCE to CE 6), and was removed by Emperor Augustus when Judaea province was formed under direct Roman rule, at the time of the Census of Quirinius.

MIRACLES

The feeding of the 5,000 is the only miracle (apart from the resurrection) which is recorded in all four canonical Gospels: Matthew 14:13–21, Mark 6:31–44, Luke 9:10–17 and John 6:5–15. This involves two fish and five loaves. The feeding of the 4,000 appears only in Matthew 15:32–16:10 and Mark 8:1–9 and involves a few fish and seven loaves.

The only real difference in the two events is that in Mark 6 the baskets used for collecting the food which remained were 12 κοφινους (hand baskets), but in Mark 6 there were seven σπυριδας. This, of course, loses the symbolism of the 12 baskets representing the Twelve Tribes of Israel.

It would seem, therefore, that this is a variant duplet introduced by mistake and copied from Mark by the writer of Matthew.

THE DATE OF THE LAST SUPPER

The Synoptic Gospels present the Last Supper as a Passover meal (Matthew 26:17, Mark 14:1–2, Luke 22:1–15). However, the Gospel of John (John 13:1) says that the Jewish Passover feast was began in the evening a few hours *after* the death of Jesus. John implies therefore that the Friday of the crucifixion was the day of preparation for the feast (14 Nisan), not the feast itself (15 Nisan).

THE TRIALS OF JESUS

The four Gospels all contain accounts of the trials of Jesus. In all there were six trials, three before the Jews and three before the Romans. However, only Luke recounts the trial before Herod and John omits the trial by the Sanhedrin. It is difficult to see how these can all have been carried out in one night as it was already late when Jesus and the disciples went to the Mount of Olives.

1   The trial before Annas: (John 18:12–14, 19–23). Annas was the father-in-law of Caiaphas, the high priest.
2   The trial before Caiaphas: all four Gospels record this trial (Matthew 26:57–68; Mark 14:53–65; Luke 22:54, 63–65; John 18:24). Caiaphas

The Six Trials of Jesus

	Judge	Texts	Decision	Place
Religious trials by the Jews	Annas	Mt 26:57–58; Mk 14:53–54; Lk 22:54–55; Jn 18:12–23	Guilty	House of the High Priest
	Caiaphas	Mt 26:59–75; Mk 14:55–65; Lk 22:56–65; Jn 18:24	Guilty	House of the High Priest
	Sanhedrin	Mt 27:1, Mk 15:1; Lk 22:66–71	Guilty	Court of the Sanhedrin
Civil trials by the Romans	Pilate	Mt 27:2–14; Mk 15:2–5; Lk 23:1–6; Jn 18:28–38	Innocent	Praetorium
	Herod	Lk 23:7–12	Innocent	Herod visiting Jerusalem
	Pilate	Mt 27:15–26; Mk 15:6–15; Lk 23:13–25; Jn 18:39–19:16	Innocent	Praetorium

was high priest and had predicted one man should die on behalf of the people. In this second trial, the religious leaders gathered together, bringing many false witnesses against Jesus. Jesus spoke of himself as the Son of Man, sitting at the right hand of power, a clear reference to himself as Messiah. The high priest tore his clothes.

3   The trial before the Sanhedrin: the three Synoptic Gospels record this third Jewish trial (Matthew 27:1; Mark 15:1; Luke 22:66–71) that took place 'as soon as it was day' (Luke 22:66). Jesus again referred to himself as the Son of Man and was delivered to the Roman leader Pilate for trial.

4   The trial before Pilate: all four Gospels record this trial (Matthew 27:1–2, 11–14; Mark 15:1–5; Luke 23:1–7; John 18:28–32, 33–38). Pilate found nothing worthy of death to condemn and sent Jesus to King Herod.

5   The trial before Herod: only Luke records this trial (Luke 23:6–12). Herod hoped to see a miracle, although Jesus answered none of the

charges against Him. Herod and his men mocked Jesus and sent him back to Pilate with a kingly robe.

6 The second trial before Pilate: all four Gospels record this trial (Matthew 27:15–23; Mark 15:6–14; Luke 23:13–22; John 18:39–19:6). Pilate claimed to have nothing to do with the punishment of Jesus, leaving his fate to the crowd in the form of allowing them to choose freedom for Jesus or to release a known criminal named Barabbas.

A final note on this is that according to all four canonical Gospels there was a prevailing Passover custom in Jerusalem that allowed or required Pilate, the governor of Judea, to commute one prisoner's death sentence by popular acclaim, and the 'crowd' was offered a choice of whether to have Barabbas or Jesus released from Roman custody. According to the Synoptic Gospels of Matthew, Mark and Luke, and the account in John, the crowd chose Barabbas to be released and Jesus of Nazareth to be crucified.

Barabbas' name appears as *bar-Abbas* in the Greek texts of the Gospels. It comes from the Aramaic בר-אבא, *Bar-abbâ*, meaning 'son of the father'. Some ancient manuscripts of Matthew 27:16–17 give his full name as 'Jesus Barabbas'. The early church father Origen (184/185–253/254) was troubled by the fact that copies of the Gospels gave Barabbas' name as 'Jesus Barabbas' and said that 'Jesus' must have been added to the name by a heretic. It appears that later scholars removed the name 'Jesus' from the text (Warren, 'Who Changed the Text and Why?').

The custom of releasing prisoners in Jerusalem at Passover is referred to as the *Paschal Pardon*, but is not recorded in any historical document other than the Gospels.

THE EMPTY TOMB

After the sabbath, as the first day of the week was dawning, Mary Magdalene and the other Mary went to see the tomb. And suddenly there was a great earthquake; for an angel of the Lord, descending from heaven, came and rolled back the stone and sat on it. His appearance was like lightning, and his clothing white as snow. For fear of him the guards shook and became like dead men. But the angel said to the women, 'Do not be afraid; I know that you are looking for Jesus who was crucified. He is not here; for he has been raised, as he said. Come, see the place where he lay.'

(Matthew 28:1–6)

When the sabbath was over, Mary Magdalene, and Mary the mother of James, and Salome bought spices, so that they might go and anoint him. And very early on the first day of the week, when the sun had risen, they went to the tomb. They had been saying to one another, 'Who will roll away the stone for us from the entrance to the tomb?' When they looked up, they saw that the stone, which was very large, had already been rolled back. As they entered the tomb, they saw a young man, dressed in a white robe, sitting on the right side; and they were alarmed. But he said to them, 'Do not be alarmed; you are looking for Jesus of Nazareth, who was crucified. He has been raised; he is not here. Look, there is the place they laid him.'

(Mark 16:1–6)

(Longer versions of Mark add another 11 verses but suggest that only Mary Magdalene was at the tomb.)

But on the first day of the week, at early dawn, they came to the tomb, taking the spices that they had prepared. They found the stone rolled away from the tomb, but when they went in, they did not find the body. While they were perplexed about this, suddenly two men in dazzling clothes stood beside them. The women were terrified and bowed their faces to the ground, but the men said to them, 'Why do you look for the living among the dead? He is not here, but has risen. Remember how he told you, while he was still in Galilee, that the Son of Man must be handed over to sinners, and be crucified, and on the third day rise again.' Then they remembered his words, and returning from the tomb, they told all this to the eleven and to all the rest. Now it was Mary Magdalene, Joanna, Mary the mother of James, and the other women with them who told this to the apostles.

(Luke 24:1–10)

Early on the first day of the week, while it was still dark, Mary Magdalene came to the tomb and saw that the stone had been removed from the tomb. So she ran and went to Simon Peter and the other disciple, the one whom Jesus loved, and said to them, 'They have taken the Lord out of the tomb, and we do not know where they have laid him.' Then Peter and the other disciple set out and went toward the tomb. The two were running together, but the other disciple outran Peter and reached the tomb first. He bent down to look in and saw the linen wrappings lying there, but he did not go in. Then Simon Peter came, following him, and went into the tomb. He saw the linen wrappings lying there, and the cloth that had been on Jesus' head, not lying with the linen wrappings but rolled up in a place by itself. Then the other disciple, who reached the tomb first, also went in, and he saw and believed; for as yet they did not understand the scripture, that he must rise from the dead. Then the disciples returned to their homes. But Mary stood weeping outside the tomb. As she wept, she bent over to look into the tomb; and she saw two angels in white, sitting where the body of Jesus had been lying, one at the head and the other at the feet. They said to her, 'Woman, why are you weeping?' She said to them, 'They have taken away my Lord, and I do not know where they have laid him.' When she had said this, she turned around and saw Jesus standing there, but she did not know that it was Jesus.

(John 20:1–14)

So it remains quite unclear who visited the tomb and what they saw.

GNOSTIC INFLUENCE?

John 1:1–14 is a very well-known text and is particularly used at Christmas services. However, a number of scholars have suggested that it is, in fact, a Gnostic text added to the beginning of the Gospel:

In the beginning was the Word, and the Word was with God, and the Word was God. He was in the beginning with God. All things came into being through him, and without him not one thing came into being. What has come into being in him was life, and the life was the light of all people. The light shines in the darkness, and the darkness did not overcome it.

(John 1:1–5)

In Book 1 of *Adversus Haereses* (*Against Heresies*) Irenaeus quotes a lengthy Gnostic commentary on this prologue. According to this the Gnostics believed the opening verses revealed the very origin of the Pleroma (the spiritual universe as the abode of God and of the totality of the divine powers and emanations). The commentary also mentions the names of several entities or Aions which came from the Father. In Greek these are: Monogenes (also called Arche), Aletheia, Logos, Zoe, Anthropos and Charis. All of these names appear in the prologue. It just so happens that these very names are also mentioned in the opening verses of John.

Read more: the possible Gnostic influences on the New Testament are explored in *The Jesus Mysteries* by T. Freke and P. Gandy, Harmony Books; 1st American edition (Aug. 2000).

WAS JESUS REALLY A PACIFIST OR JUST INCONSISTENT?

Compare 'Blessed are the peacemakers, for they will be called children of God' (Matthew 5:9) and 'Then Jesus said to him, "Put your sword back into its place; for all who take the sword will perish by the sword"' (Matthew 26:52) with

> Do not think that I have come to bring peace to the earth; I have not come to bring peace, but a sword. For I have come to set a man against his father, and a daughter against her mother, and a daughter-in-law against her mother-in-law; and one's foes will be members of one's own household.
>
> (Matthew 10:34–36)

and

> As for this worthless slave, throw him into the outer darkness, where there will be weeping and gnashing of teeth.
>
> (Matthew 25:30)

So, to what extent can we learn about the person and teachings of Jesus from the New Testament?

This is, as we have seen, a very difficult question to answer. Although if we look at the biblical evidence we see that there are, of course, major agreements on some teaching, there is such diversity that it is hard to attest to what is true and reliable and what is not.

In an attempt to resolve these differences there have been many attempts to produce a gospel which includes everything from the four canonical ones.

Probably the first was the *Diatessaron* (c. 160–175) by Tatian (www.earlychristianwritings.com/text/diatessaron.html). A sample reading of this shows the complexity of trying to weave together the different accounts.

A more recent attempt can be found in Arthur Moss' (1971) *Jesus: A New Translation of the Four Gospels, Arranged as One*, The Citadel Press.

Gnosticism (Greek: γνωστικός gnostikos, 'having knowledge'. A collection of ancient religions whose adherents kept apart from the material world – which they viewed as created by the demiurge – and embraced the spiritual world. Gnostic ideas are that gnosis (knowledge, enlightenment, salvation, emancipation or 'oneness with God') can be reached by practising philanthropy to the point of personal poverty and searching for wisdom by helping others.

THE SYNOPTIC PROBLEM

The 'synoptic problem' looks at the relationship between the three 'synoptic' Gospels: Matthew, Mark and Luke. The question is what source materials the writers had to work with.

There are many similarities between the three books in wording, order, quotations and so forth. Most scholars have seen this as 'documentary dependence'.

Augustine said that the Gospels were written in the order in which they appear in the New Testament – that is Matthew, Mark, Luke, John.

This view was largely accepted until the late eighteenth century, when in 1776, Johann Jakob Griesbach (1745–1812), a German textual critic, published his Greek Gospel synopsis of Matthew. This did not follow the route of works such as the *Diatessaron*, which tried to harmonise the Gospels. Instead it placed them side by side.

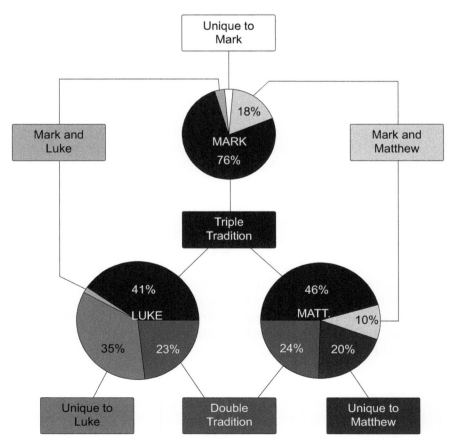

The similarities between the Gospels

The following figures show the main theories which have been proposed for the documentary dependency of the three Gospels.

If the Bible and teaching of the Church are the evidence for the Christian religion, is there anywhere else we can look?

Synoptic theories			
Priority	Theory	Diagram	Notes
Marcan priority	Two-source (Mark-Q)		Perhaps the most common theory. Matthew and Luke independently used Q, which is believed to have been a Greek document largely consisting of the sayings of Jesus.
	Farrer (Mark-Matthew)		This is a double tradition based entirely on the idea of Luke's use of Matthew.

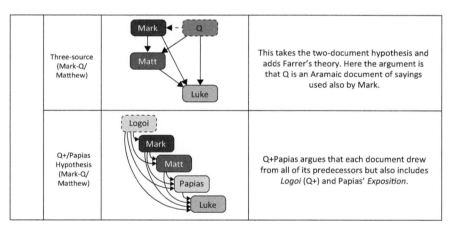

	Three-source (Mark-Q/ Matthew)		This takes the two-document hypothesis and adds Farrer's theory. Here the argument is that Q is an Aramaic document of sayings used also by Mark.
	Q+/Papias Hypothesis (Mark-Q/ Matthew)		Q+Papias argues that each document drew from all of its predecessors but also includes *Logoi* (Q+) and Papias' *Exposition*.

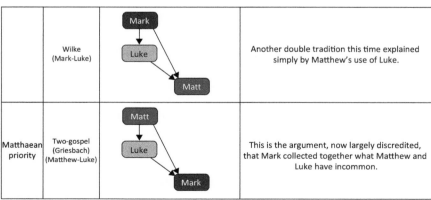

	Wilke (Mark-Luke)		Another double tradition this time explained simply by Matthew's use of Luke.
Matthaean priority	Two-gospel (Griesbach) (Matthew-Luke)		This is the argument, now largely discredited, that Mark collected together what Matthew and Luke have incommon.

The most common hypotheses

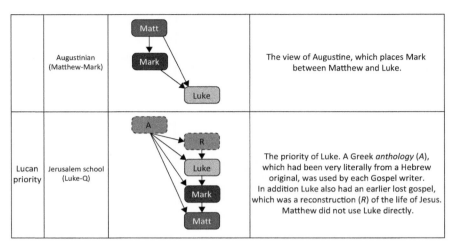

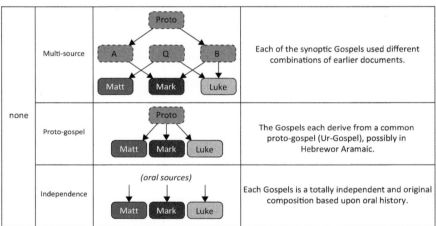

(Continued) The most common hypotheses

Deepak Chopra (1946–)

An American author, public speaker, alternative medicine advocate and a prominent figure in the New Age movement, Chopra has often been accused of preaching pseudoscience but in 2016 he was promoted to full professor at the University of California, San Diego, in its Department of Family Medicine.

THE THIRD JESUS

Deepak Chopra has written that the universe is a 'reality sandwich' with three layers: the 'material' world, a 'quantum' zone of matter and energy, and a 'virtual' zone outside of time and space, which is the domain of God, and from which God can direct the other layers. He says that human beings' brains are 'hardwired to know God' and the functions of the human nervous system mirror divine experience. The great influence on his spiritual thinking was Jiddu Krishnamurti (1895–1986), a famous philosopher, speaker and writer.

In 2008 he published *The Third Jesus*. In this book he suggests that there are three persons of Jesus that the believer needs to understand: Jesus the man,

Deepak Chopra
ZUMA Press Inc./Alamy

whose words and actions form the foundation of Christian theology, Jesus the
Son of God, who represents a specific branch of religion, and the Third Jesus,
who is the spiritual guide whose teachings embrace all of humanity.

Jesus is in trouble. When people worship him today – or even speak his
name – the object of their devotion is unlikely to be who they think he
is. A mythical Jesus has grown up over time. He has served to divide
people and nations. He has led to destructive wars in the name of religious fantasies. The legacy of love found in the New Testament has been
tainted with the worst sort of intolerance and prejudiced that would
have appalled Jesus in life. Most troubling of all, his teachings have been
hijacked by people who hate in the name of love.

Millions of people worship another Jesus, however, who never
existed, who doesn't even lay claim to the fleeting substance of the first
Jesus. This is the Jesus built up over thousands of years by theologians
and other scholars . . . He became the foundation of a religion that has
proliferated into some twenty thousand sects. They argue endlessly over
every thread in the garments of a ghost.

Jesus embodied the highest level of enlightenment. He spent his
brief adult life describing it, teaching it, and passing it on to future
generations.

Jesus intended to save the world by showing others the path to God-consciousness.

We aren't talking about faith. Conventional faith is the same as belief in the impossible (such as Jesus walking on water), but there is another faith that gives us the ability to reach into the unknown and achieve transformation.

(Chopra, 2008)

Chopra argues that this Third Jesus presents a way in which the world can deal with the issues which trouble it, such as abortion, gay rights, women's rights and war. He helps people to do this by his examples of courage, love and forgiveness.

Chopra concludes his book by answering the question with which we began: 'What would Jesus do in my shoes? He would keep walking he path. He would manifest as much courage, truth, sympathy, and love as he actually possessed. He wouldn't pretend to be what he wasn't.'

You might think that in this introduction we have savaged the Bible and wronged the Church but in fact we have considered and explained why there have always been developments in Christian thought and why this will continue.

FURTHER READING

Armstrong, K. 2008. *The Bible: The Biography*. New York: Atlantic Books.

Armstrong, K. 2011. *A History of God*. New York: Vintage Books.

Grant, J. 1989. *White Women's Christ and Black Women's Jesus*. New York: OUP.

Maccoby, H. 1998. *The Mythmaker: Paul and the Invention of Christianity*. London: Barnes & Noble.

Mack, R. 1994. *The Lost Gospel: The Book of Q & Christian Origins*. New York: HarperOne.

Miles, J. 1996. *God: A Biography*. New York: Vintage Books.

Pullman, P. 2011. *The Good Man Jesus and the Scoundrel Christ*. London: Canongate Books.

Wesselow, T. De. 2012. *The Sign: The Shroud of Turin and the Secret of the Resurrection*. London: Viking.

Wilson, A.N. 2003. *Jesus*. London: Pimlico.

Insight

17 Augustine's teaching on human nature

WHAT YOU WILL LEARN ABOUT IN THIS CHAPTER

- Augustine's teaching on human nature
- Augustine's interpretation of Genesis 3 (the Fall)
- Original sin and its effects on the will and human societies
- God's grace

THE OCR CHECKLIST

Augustine's teaching on human nature

- Human relationships pre- and post-Fall
  - Augustine's interpretation of Genesis 3 (the Fall) including:
    - the state of perfection before the Fall and Adam and Eve's relationship as friends
    - lust and selfish desires after the Fall
- Original sin and its effects on the will and human societies
  - Augustine's teaching that original sin is passed on through sexual intercourse and is the cause of:
    - human selfishness and lack of free will
    - lack of stability and corruption in all human societies
- God's grace
  - Augustine's teaching that only God's grace, his generous love, can overcome sin and the rebellious will to achieve the greatest good (*summum bonum*).

Essential terminology

Akrasia
Concupiscence
Continence
Enlightenment
Fall
Grace
Manichaeism
Neo-Platonism
Original Sin
Postlapsarian
Privation and lack
Summum bonum

Key scholars

Epicurus (341 BCE –270 BCE)
Cicero (106 BCE – 43 BCE)
Mani (c. 216–276)
Aurelius Ambrosius (Saint Ambrose of Milan) (c. 340–397)
Augustine of Hippo (354–430)
Pelagius (354–420/440)
Friedrich Schleiermacher (1768–1834)
Sigmund Freud (1856–1939)
Alfred North Whitehead (1861–1947)
Reinhold Niebuhr (1892–1971)
J.L. Mackie (1917–1981)
John Hick (1922–2012)
Anthony Flew (1923–2010)
Herbert McCabe (1926–2001)
Alvin Plantigna (1932–)
Richard Swinburne (1934–)
Richard Dawkins (1941–)
David Griffin (1943–)

continued overleaf

Learners should have the opportunity to discuss issues related to Augustine's ideas on human nature, including:

- whether Augustine's teaching on a historical Fall and original sin is wrong
- whether Augustine is right that sin means that humans can never be morally good
- whether Augustine's view of human nature is pessimistic or optimistic
- whether there is a distinctive human nature.

Contextual references

For reference, the ideas of Augustine listed earlier can be found in:

- *City of God*, Book 14, Chapters 16–26
- *Confessions*, Book 8.

Suggested scholarly views, academic approaches and sources of wisdom and authority

Learners will be given credit for referring to any *appropriate* scholarly views, academic approaches and sources of wisdom and authority; however, the following examples may prove useful.

- Chapman, G. (1994) *Catechism of the Catholic Church*, paras. 385–409
- McGrath, A. (2010, 5th edition) *Christian Theology*, Wiley-Blackwell, pages 348–355, 371–372
- Romans 7:15–20.

(From *OCR AS Level Religious Studies Specification H173*)

Thought point

What does it mean when something or someone is described as 'evil'?

Augustine the man (CE 354–430)

As a young man Augustine turned against the Christian faith of his mother and investigated a number of different schools of philosophical thought.

Aged 16 he went to Carthage in order to study law. However, he soon changed his studies to rhetoric. He did not enjoy life in Carthage, which he later described as a 'hissing cauldron of lust'. Nevertheless he enjoyed life with the rowdy and misbehaving students who were there.

One of the books he read as part of his course in rhetoric is a now lost book on the philosophical pursuit of happiness by Cicero (106 BCE – 43 BCE), *Hortensius*. He was fascinated by this and came to the opinion that the Bible was a very confused book which could not provide answers to the questions raised by Cicero. Around the same time he became influenced by a religious group called the Manicheans, which had been founded by an Iranian prophet, Mani (c. CE 216–276).

Manichaeism was a dualistic religion which taught that existence was a struggle between a good, spiritual world of light and an evil and material world of darkness. This theology was based on Gnostic and other religious movements. Manichaeism addressed the origins of evil by teaching that God was not omnipotent. There are two powers: good, represented by God, and a semi-eternal evil power (Satan). Humans are then a battleground for these powers: the soul defines the person but is under the influence of light and dark. Therefore the existence of evil is explained by a flawed creation which was not made by God but was the result of Satan striking out against God.

At first this theology was very attractive to Augustine. As a result his mother, Monica, sought help from a local bishop, who advised her not to let him come home.

Aged 19, Augustine started an affair with a young woman in Carthage. She was to remain his lover for more than 15 years and together they had a son, Adeodatus. Unlike many other rich young men who often had several mistresses, they lived together as husband and wife. This relationship was very important for Augustine and he subsequently often referred to the very powerful psychological effects associated with sex.

Shocked by the bad behaviour of his pupils, in CE 383 he took employment in Rome to teach rhetoric. Shortly afterwards he was offered the post of orator at the imperial court in Milan. To improve his respectability he sent his mistress back to Carthage and became engaged to a wealthy heiress. 'My mistress being torn from my side as an impediment to my marriage, my heart, which clave to her, was racked, and wounded, and bleeding.' However, Augustine was not seeking marriage but rather was looking for sexual satisfaction. As he had to wait two years before his fiancée came of age, he took another mistress. He eventually broke off his engagement to

Cicero the man (106 BCE – 43 BCE)

Cicero

Chronicle/Alamy

Marcus Tullius Cicero was a Roman philosopher, politician, lawyer, orator, political theorist, consul and constitutionalist. He was a member of a wealthy Roman family and is regarded as one of Rome's greatest orators.

his 11-year-old fiancée, but never renewed his relationship with either of his mistresses. Alypius of Thagaste (fourth century) persuaded Augustine away from marriage, saying that they would not be able live a life together in the love of wisdom if he married.

Soon Augustine began to tire of the Manichean teachings, as he writes in his *Confessions* (397–400):

> O Truth, Truth, how inwardly even then did the marrow of my soul sigh for thee when, frequently and in manifold ways, in numerous and vast books, [the Manicheans] sounded out thy name though it was only a sound! And in these dishes – while I starved for thee – they served up to me, in thy stead, the sun and moon thy beauteous works – but still only thy works and not thyself; indeed, not even thy first work. For thy spiritual works came before these material creations, celestial and shining though they are. But I was hungering and thirsting, not even after those first works of thine, but after thyself the Truth, 'with whom is no variableness, neither shadow of turning.' Yet they still served me glowing fantasies in those dishes. And, truly, it would have been better to have loved this very sun – which at least is true to our sight – than those illusions of theirs which deceive the mind through the eye. And yet because I supposed the illusions to be from thee I fed on them – not with avidity, for thou didst not taste in my mouth as thou art, and thou wast not these empty fictions. Neither was I nourished by them, but was instead exhausted. Food in dreams appears like our food awake; yet the sleepers are not nourished by it, for they are asleep. But the fantasies of the Manicheans were not in any way like thee as thou hast spoken to me now. They were simply fantastic and false. In comparison to them the actual bodies which we see with our fleshly sight, both celestial and terrestrial, are far more certain. These true bodies even the beasts and birds perceive as well as we do and they are more certain than the images we form about them. And again, we do with more certainty form our conceptions about them than, from them, we go on by means of them to imagine of other greater and infinite bodies which have no existence. With such empty husks was I then fed, and yet was not fed.
>
> (*Confessions* 3:6)

He next turned his attention to the teachings of the Platonists (now referred to as neo-Platonists). A major influence on this school of thought was the philosopher Plotinus (*c.* 204/5–270). They adapted Plato's theories and argued that some human minds can ascend from the world of reality to the One (God). Although the soul and body should work together it is their failure to do so which brings about evil and suffering.

Neo-Platonists created a view of Christianity which denied that Christ died for the sins of the world but saw him as logos, a spiritually enlightened being:

> In the beginning was the Word, and the Word was with God, and the Word was God. He was in the beginning with God. All things came into being through him, and without him not one thing came into being. What has come into being in him was life, and the life was the light of all people. The light shines in the darkness, and the darkness did not overcome it.
>
> He was in the world, and the world came into being through him; yet the world did not know him. He came to what was his own, and his own people did not accept him. But to all who received him, who believed in his name, he gave power to become children of God, who were born, not of blood or of the will of the flesh or of the will of man, but of God.
>
> And the Word became flesh and lived among us, and we have seen his glory, the glory as of a father's only son, full of grace and truth.
>
> (John 1:1–5, 10–14)

Augustine's later theology was significantly influenced by neo-Platonism and the view that the soul is able to find wisdom and happiness on its own. It offered a solution to the problem of evil by seeing it not as a separate force but as the absence of good.

Despite the hope of these teachings, Augustine was still struggling with his sense of guilt and feelings of unhappiness.

Augustine then met the bishop of Milan, Aurelius Ambrosius (Saint Ambrose of Milan) (c. 340–397).

> And to Milan I came, to Ambrose the bishop, famed through the whole world as one of the best of men, thy devoted servant. His eloquent discourse in those times abundantly provided thy people with the flour of thy wheat, the gladness of thy oil, and the sober intoxication of thy wine. To him I was led by thee without my knowledge, that by him I might be led to thee in full knowledge. That man of God received me as a father would, and welcomed my coming as a good bishop should. And I began to love him, of course, not at the first as a teacher of the truth, for I had entirely despaired of finding that in thy Church – but as a friendly man. And I studiously listened to him – though not with the right motive – as he preached to the people. I was trying to discover whether his eloquence came up to his reputation, and whether it flowed fuller or thinner than others said it did. And thus I hung on his words

intently, but, as to his subject matter, I was only a careless and contemptuous listener. I was delighted with the charm of his speech, which was more erudite, though less cheerful and soothing, than Faustus' style. As for subject matter, however, there could be no comparison, for the latter was wandering around in Manichean deceptions, while the former was teaching salvation most soundly. But 'salvation is far from the wicked,' such as I was then when I stood before him. Yet I was drawing nearer, gradually and unconsciously.

(*Confessions* 5.13)

Ambrose showed him how the Old Testament could be understood symbolically and thereby resolved many of the problems which Augustine was having.

In the summer of 386 Augustine converted to Christianity. He wrote that he heard a childlike voice telling him to 'take up and read'. He took this as a message from God and opened it at random. The passage he read was the following:

Let us live honourably as in the day, not in revelling and drunkenness, not in debauchery and licentiousness, not in quarrelling and jealousy. Instead, put on the Lord Jesus Christ, and make no provision for the flesh, to gratify its desires.

(Romans 13:13–14)

Ambrose baptised Augustine and Adeodatus at Easter 387 in Milan. Monica died in Italy in 388 just as Augustine and Adeodatus were preparing to return to Africa. Soon after their arrival Adeodatus died and Augustine sold his family estate, keeping only his house at Thagaste, which he turned into a monastic foundation.

In 391 Augustine was ordained and in 395 became bishop of Hippo, a position he held until his death in 430. He wrote a large number of books about Christian doctrine and beliefs, the most famous of which are probably the autobiographical *Confessions in Thirteen Books* (397–398) and *The City of God*, which he wrote to comfort his fellow Christians after the Visigoths had sacked Rome in 410.

Augustine and Donatism

Donatism was named after the fourth-century bishop of Carthage and primate of North Africa, Donatus Magnus. Donatism argued that Christian priests must be faultless for the prayers and sacraments they conduct to be valid. It had its roots in the Roman Africa province (Algeria and Tunisia), during the persecutions of Christians by Diocletian. They flourished in the fourth and fifth centuries.

Augustine campaigned against this belief throughout his time as bishop of Hippo and succeeded in restoring the place of the orthodox Catholic Church. He argued that it was the office of a priest, not their their person, that made the sacraments valid and gave validity to the celebration of the sacraments.

Augustine and Pelagianism

This theory is named after the 'British' monk Pelagius (354–420/440). Pelagians believed that the human will was created by God and therefore was sufficient to live a sinless life. Nevertheless he believed that God's grace assisted all good works.

Pelagius taught that people could obtain moral perfection in this life without needing the assistance of divine grace. Augustine argued that perfection was impossible without grace because people are born sinners with a sinful heart and will. The Pelagians said that Augustine had departed from the teaching of the Apostles: 'Jesus straightened up and said to her, "Woman, where are they? Has no one condemned you?" She said, "No one, sir." And Jesus said, "Neither do I condemn you. Go your way, and from now on do not sin again."' They said that his teaching was Manichaeism claiming the flesh was sinful in itself.

The 415 Council of Diospolis found Pelagius' teachings to be orthodox. However, they were condemned in 418 at the Council of Carthage and this was confirmed at the Council of Ephesus in 431.

The teachings of Pelagius are most often associated with rejecting the concept of original sin and the practice of infant baptism. The writings of Pelagius are lost but corrections to his teachings were made at the Council of Carthage:

- Death did not come to Adam from a physical necessity, but through sin.
- Newborn children must be baptised on account of original sin.
- Justifying grace not only avails for the forgiveness of past sins but also gives assistance for the avoidance of future sins.
- The grace of Christ not only discloses the knowledge of God's commandments but also imparts strength to will and execute them.
- Without God's grace it is not merely more difficult but absolutely impossible to perform good works.

- Not out of humility but in truth must we confess ourselves to be sinners.
- The saints refer the petition of the Our Father, 'Forgive us our trespasses,' not only to others but also to themselves.
- The saints pronounce the same supplication not from mere humility but from truthfulness.
- Children dying without baptism do not go to a 'middle place' because, not having been baptised, they are excluded both from the 'kingdom of heaven' and from 'eternal life'.

In respect of this last point, Augustine said that because of original sin, unbaptised infants receive the mildest punishment of all. However, he continued to say that anyone who denies this punishment is deceiving themselves and others. He quotes from Paul:

> And the free gift is not like the effect of the one man's sin. For the judgment following one trespass brought condemnation, but the free gift following many trespasses brings justification. If, because of the one man's trespass, death exercised dominion through that one, much more surely will those who receive the abundance of grace and the free gift of righteousness exercise dominion in life through the one man, Jesus Christ. Therefore just as one man's trespass led to condemnation for all, so one man's act of righteousness leads to justification and life for all.
>
> (Romans 5:16–18)

AUGUSTINE'S THEOLOGY – THE FALL

Augustine's teaching on the Fall is influenced by the creation stories found in Genesis 1–3. Augustine interpreted the Genesis stories as literal accounts of the origins of the world and also as a mythological story that communicated values and meaning.

Key ideas

God: God is the Creator and as such is omnipotent and omnibenevolent.

Harmonious creation: Creation is good and from the beginning was harmonious.

Hierarchy of beings: Angels, humans, animals.

Privation: Evil is a privation or lack of goodness in something.

The Fall: Angels and human beings can fall through their own free choices by and giving in to temptation. Sin entered the world through Adam and Eve.

Natural evil: Disharmony in the world followed the fall of angels, leading to natural evil.

Free will: Free will is valuable so that God sustains a world within which moral and natural evil occur.

Aesthetic value: The existence of evil demonstrates the goodness of creation because of the contrast between good and evil.

God the Creator: Augustine had a very traditional view of God: God is omnibenevolent, omnipotent and omniscient. This of course creates a problem:

- If God is omnibenevolent and omnipotent, and he created the world, why is there evil in it?
- If God created the universe and continues to sustain it in existence for every moment of every day, it means that if people commit acts of evil, God is sustaining and keeping alive those very people while they do those acts.

Epicurus
© Tarker/Bridgeman Images

The same problem was raised by the Greek philosopher Epicurus (341–270 BCE):

- Is God willing to prevent evil, but not able to? Then he is not omnipotent.
- Is God able to prevent evil, but not willing to? Then he is not omnibenevolent.
- Is God able to prevent evil and willing to? Then why is there evil?

Privation and evil: Augustine attempted to solve the problem by defining evil as a *'privation'*. What this means is that when we use words such as 'evil' and 'bad' we are saying that something does not meet our expectations of what, by nature, it should be like:

> For one of the leaders of this heresy, whose instructions we attended with great familiarity and frequency, used to say with reference to a person who held that evil was not a substance, 'I should like to put a scorpion in the man's hand, and see whether he would not withdraw his hand; and in so doing he would get a proof, not in words but in the thing itself, that evil is a substance, for he would not deny that the animal is a substance.' He said this not in the presence of the person, but to us, when we repeated to him the remark which had troubled us, giving, as I said, a childish answer to children. For who with the least tincture of learning or science does not see that these things hurt by disagreement with the bodily temperament, while at other times they agree with it, so as not only not to hurt, but to produce the best effects? For if this poison were evil in itself,

the scorpion itself would suffer first and most. In fact, if the poison were quite taken from the animal, it would die. So for its body it is evil to lose what it is evil for our body to receive; and it is good for it to have what it is good for us to want. Is the same thing then both good and evil? By no means; but evil is what is against nature, for this is evil both to the animal and to us. This evil is the disagreement, which certainly is not a substance, but hostile to substance. Whence then is it? See what it leads to, and you will learn, if any inner light lives in you. It leads all that it destroys to non-existence. Now God is the author of existence; and there is no existence which, as far as it is existing, leads to non-existence: Thus we learn whence disagreement is not; as to whence it is, nothing can be said.

(Augustine, *Confessions*)

Herbert McCabe (McCabe, 'God, Evil and Divine Responsibility', 1980) gives the example of bad grapes and a bad deckchair:

If you know what it is like for a deckchair to be a bad deckchair you do not for that reason know what it is like for a grape to be a bad grape. A bad deckchair collapses when you sit down on it, but the fact that a grape collapses when you sit on it is not what would show it to be a bad grape. We call something a bad deckchair when it doesn't come up to our expectations for deckchairs, and we call something a bad grape when it doesn't come up to our expectations for grapes. But they are different expectations. And similarly when we say that a thing is a good grape or a good deckchair we mean that they do come up to our respective expectations for grapes and deckchairs. Goodness, like badness, is different from redness in that what it is like for one thing to be good isn't the same as what it is like for another. The fact that wine can be made from good grapes has no tendency at all to suggest that wine can be made from good deckchairs.

Augustine held the same idea about evil. He rejects the idea that evil is a force or power opposing God because this would mean that God had a rival and was not omnipotent. This would, of course, go against traditional Christian belief about God.

The idea of evil being a privation also applies to human beings. According to Augustine, if you say that a human being is evil, or that they are acting in an evil fashion, you are simply saying that the way they behave does not match expectations about how a human being should behave. For example if you racially abuse people, rob or torture them, you are not living up to the standards expected of human beings. It is the failure to be what you should be that is wrong.

Privation: Means something is lacking a particular thing that it should have. Augustine gave the example of 'blindness'. He called this a privation, because if you are blind it means that you are unable to see – in other words you lack the attribute of 'sight'.

Thought point

Evil and privation

Is evil a 'privation' or 'lack' of something? What do you think?

Absence and lack: There is a very important difference between the concepts of absence and lack. Augustine is not saying that it is bad or evil that human beings cannot bark like dogs because that is not what human beings are supposed to be like. Human beings cannot do this naturally as the ability to do so is just *absent*. The idea of privation applies when people *lack* something they should have – for example:

1 If someone cannot use their legs – they lack the health which they should have.
2 If someone is very mean – they lack the qualities of generosity and charity.

These are two examples of what Augustine meant by privation. Of course they are different because the second example is a choice, whereas the first is not.

Thought point

What does the word 'inhuman' mean?

AUGUSTINE'S THINKING ABOUT THE ORIGINS OF EVIL

Augustine believed that both moral and natural evil came from moral choices. If you choose to hurt someone then you lack the quality of respecting other people. It is the lack that makes the action wrong.

God is infinitely good and all his works are good. Yet no one can escape the experience of suffering or the evils in nature which seem to be linked to the limitations proper to creatures: and above all to the question of moral evil. Where does evil come from? 'I sought whence evil comes and there was no solution', said St. Augustine, and his own painful quest would only be resolved by his conversion to the living God. For 'the mystery of lawlessness' is clarified only in the light of the 'mystery of our religion'. The revelation of divine love in Christ manifested at the same time the extent of evil and the superabundance of grace. We must therefore approach the question of the origin of evil by fixing the eyes of our faith on him who alone is its conqueror. I. WHERE SIN ABOUNDED, GRACE ABOUNDED ALL THE MORE.

(*Catechism of the Catholic Church* §385)

Thought point

So is God to blame for evil?

'And it seemed to me better to believe that you had created no evil than to suppose that evil, such as I imagined to be, had its origin in you' (Augustine, *Confessions* 5.10).

'Evil comes from God'

This claim seems impossible in relation to an omnibenevolent God.

However, Augustine believed that God causes everything to exist. God caused human beings to exist and keeps them in existence; and as human beings have free will they can become evil through their free choices.

Augustine did not believe that anyone could be totally evil. He said to be evil you have to lack any goodness, which means you had goodness to start with. Therefore, even the devil has some good.

It was obvious to me that things which are liable to corruption are good. If they were the supreme goods, or if they were not good at all, they could not be corrupted. For if they were supreme goods, they would be incorruptible. If there were no good in them there would be nothing capable of being corrupted.

(Augustine, *Confessions* 3.18)

Thought point

What is meant by 'supreme goods'?

Thought point

The Genesis stories

Read the two creation stories in the book of Genesis, Chapters 1–3.

> **Harmony**
>
> Objects existing in an ordered way together or living creatures existing in a state of peace with each other.

The Garden of Eden

God created the Garden of Eden and created humans from dust. In the first account of creation it states that:

1   Creation is good.
2   Human beings are made in *imago dei* (the image and likeness of God).

Human beings are therefore both physical and spiritual creatures. This is usually understood as meaning that they are capable of rational thought because this is a God-like quality.

The Garden of Eden is in a state of harmony. Everything there is at peace and there is no suffering. Suffering is caused by disharmony.

> **The Fall**
> Refers to the story of Adam and Eve in the Garden of Eden and their disobedience to God (Genesis 2:4 to 3:1).

> **Original sin**
> The first sin of Adam in the Garden of Eden and its effects, according to traditional Christian beliefs.

The Fall

In the story, Adam and Eve choose to eat the fruit of the tree of the knowledge of good and evil. They have a choice about whether to know good and evil. In Hebrew the word translated as 'know' – יָדַע (yada) does not mean just learning a list of facts. It can also mean knowing by experience. Eve was tempted by the serpent and used her free will to choose to do what she was told not to do. Adam is then tempted by Eve. The important feature of this story is that Adam and Eve choose to break their harmony with God – this is the first sin, often called original sin. The original peaceful state of the

Garden cannot be restored. The fact that Adam and Eve realise they are naked is a sign that they are no longer in harmony with the natural world.

From here on the term 'postlapsarian' (after the Fall) is used to describe the world.

THE HIERARCHY OF BEINGS

Augustine discusses the creation of spiritual beings as well as life on Earth. He says that God created all types of life, from physical life to purely spiritual life, like angels. He considered that creation was good and perfect. That meant that it must include all types of beings, otherwise it would lack something and therefore not be good and perfect.

Devils are sometimes said to be fallen angels who chose to turn away from God.

> And one from out the order of angels, having turned away with the order that was under him, conceived an impossible thought, to place his throne higher than the clouds above the earth, that he might become equal in rank to my power. And I threw him out from the height with his angels, and he was flying in the air continuously above the bottomless [*sic*].
>
> (2 Enoch 29:3)

Augustine believed that it was this act that introduced disharmony. He thought that it was the actions of devils that led to natural evil, because of the disharmony they caused. Therefore he taught that both natural and moral evils are the result of free will.

Disharmony causes suffering, and in Genesis 3 God punishes the man with hard work to survive, the woman with pain in childbirth and the serpent with losing its legs. Augustine stresses that it was moral choices which led to evil in the world.

> The LORD God said to the serpent, 'Because you have done this, cursed are you among all animals and among all wild creatures; upon your belly you shall go, and dust you shall eat all the days of your life. I will put enmity between you and the woman, and between your offspring and hers; he will strike your head, and you will strike his heel.'
>
> To the woman he said, 'I will greatly increase your pangs in childbearing; in pain you shall bring forth children, yet your desire shall be for your husband, and he shall rule over you.'

And to the man he said, 'Because you have listened to the voice of your wife, and have eaten of the tree about which I commanded you, 'You shall not eat of it,' cursed is the ground because of you; in toil you shall eat of it all the days of your life; thorns and thistles it shall bring forth for you; and you shall eat the plants of the field. By the sweat of your face you shall eat bread until you return to the ground, for out of it you were taken; you are dust, and to dust you shall return.'

(Genesis 3:14–19)

Therefore, just as sin came into the world through one man, and death came through sin, and so death spread to all because all have sinned.

(Romans 5:12)

Augustine said that therefore all human beings were present in Adam's sin.

Why did God create creatures with free will?

Augustine believed that free will was more valuable than people being automata who always did God's will. He said that allowing evil to happen was a price worth paying for human freedom. The problems with this are that:

1 It means that God allows evil things to happen and has made and sustains a world and people who do evil things, such as murder, rape, torture and discrimination.
2 If there was no free will it would remove the chance of people making good choices. People would not be able to choose actions that bring joy, happiness and hope.

Augustine taught the will was God-given at the creation. The will is love – a force which pulls people in different directions. It is driven by *cupiditas* (self-love) and *caritas* (generous love). Therefore people must love themselves as well as others as this is the only way in which to love God.

Augustine believed that the contrast between what is good and what is evil demonstrates the beauty of goodness. This is often referred to as the *aesthetic principle*: meaning that the contrast between what is good and what lacks goodness is made clearer in the contrast between goodness and lack of goodness (privation).

Augustine had a very powerful sense of sin, possibly because of his own earlier life. He believed that priests, monks and nuns, despite their religious lives, could never be free from the draw of concupiscence.

Perfection

A characteristic or quality of God. God lacks nothing and can be no different or better.

Original sin

Original sin has been defined in many ways. One way is to see it as the inbuilt tendency that humans have to do things wrong despite their good intentions.

Augustine meant that as all human beings are descended from Adam and Eve they all share in the consequences of Adam and Eve's choice. In Christian theology all people are said to share in Adam's sin because they were 'seminally present' in Adam. Since the Fall everyone has been born into a disharmonious world. 'Hence from the misuse of free will there started a chain of disasters: mankind is led from that original perversion, a kind of corruption at the root, right up to the disaster of the second death' (*City of God* 13.14). The First Death occurred when humans disobeyed God in the Garden of Eden, which killed their relationship

continued overleaf

with God, and the Second Death is the mortal state of every human being and God's punishment.

Grace
Unmerited favour from God.

This led him to his teaching on predestination. He believed that only God knew who was worthy of grace and would be rewarded with heaven – the elect. All people can do is to live in love and faith and hope that they are part of this.

Grace

Augustine taught that it was only through God's grace that people could be healed and their relationship with him restored. It was only through the atoning death of Jesus Christ that this could be achieved and the effects of original sin removed. It is necessary for the relationship between humans and God to be restored in order to reach the *summum bonum* (greatest good).

Divided will

Augustine said that after the Fall, the human soul was divided. It still knew right from wrong but despite wanting to do good, it was weakened by desire and could end up doing evil instead.

Paul wrote the following about this state:

> For we know that the law is spiritual; but I am of the flesh, sold into slavery under sin. I do not understand my own actions. For I do not do what I want, but I do the very thing I hate. Now if I do what I do not want, I agree that the law is good. But in fact it is no longer I that do it, but sin that dwells within me. For I know that nothing good dwells within me, that is, in my flesh. I can will what is right, but I cannot do it. For I do not do the good I want, but the evil I do not want is what I do. Now if I do what I do not want, it is no longer I that do it, but sin that dwells within me.
>
> (Romans 7:14–20)

This idea was known to the Greek philosophers as *akrasia* (weakness of will), although Augustine did not agree with Aristotle's teaching interpretation of this weakness.

In Augustine's *Confessions* he describes this teaching from Romans as 'half wounded' and one which even Continence (self-restraint) cannot control.

> I could see the chaste beauty of Continence in all her serene, unsullied joy, as she modestly beckoned me to cross and hesitate no more . . . I was overcome with shame, because I was still listening to the futile mutterings of lower self.
>
> (*Confessions* 8.11)

Concupiscence
Sexual desire or lust.

Concupiscence

Augustine did not accept the Manichaen or neo-Platonist teachings that the body is evil or imperfect because it is flesh. It could not be these things because it created by God to be good. It is therefore the weakened will which leads to lust and desire, particularly for sexual intercourse.

> Human nature then is, without any doubt, ashamed about lust and rightly ashamed.
>
> > (*City of God* 14.20)

> The snare of concupiscence awaits me in the very process of passing from the discomfort to the contentment which comes when it is satisfied.
>
> > (*Confessions* 10.31)

Today many Christians consider that the events of Genesis 2–3 were not historical 'one-offs' but in fact are a reflection of a human being's spiritual journey. This is how Jews have traditionally interpreted the passages.

CRITICISMS OF AUGUSTINE'S VIEWS

Augustine's ideas have dominated Christian thinking for over 1,000 years but modern philosophers have put forward a number of criticisms of them.

Plausibility

Are Augustine's views still believable in today's understanding of science? After all, Augustine interpreted the creation stories fairly literally. Of course, many people believe that there is no convincing evidence that angels exist. John Hick in *Evil and the God of Love* suggests that Augustine's ideas are implausible for modern people.

Responses

Alvin Plantinga has suggested that, for Augustine's ideas to be successful, the existence of angels has to be possible. It is not necessary to demonstrate the existence of angels.

Plantinga and Richard Swinburne have both defended the idea that evil arises from humans misusing their free will.

Many Christians today would say that the importance of the story of creation and the Fall lies in what the story tries to tell people about the world, God the Creator and human beings' relationship with God's creation.

Science

Augustine understood the Fall as taking place in a perfect world which had been created by God and was then harmed by humans and angels misusing free will. However, biologists have now demonstrated that life has developed through the mechanism of evolution by natural selection. So the idea of a perfect world that has been spoilt by evil cannot be accepted as literally true.

Adam's sin

Augustine wrote that all people share in the effects of the Fall because they were seminally present in Adam's sin. Biology has since shown that every person is a unique individual inheriting half of their DNA from each parent. Augustine had an ancient understanding of biology, which taught that the life-giving force for a baby came from the man and the flesh from the woman. So, if human beings were not seminally present in Adam it would be unjust if God punished all human beings for the first human beings' sin.

How could the perfect world go wrong?

Friedrich Schleiermacher (1768–1834) and other philosophers questioned why a perfect world would go wrong. If it is the case that angels were created to live in the presence of God, why would they turn away from God?

Nevertheless, the evidence would suggest that when people carry out actions that ruin the good situation they are in, it is only afterwards, with hindsight, that they can see that they were better off before.

Friedrich Schleiermacher
Georgios Kollidas/Alamy

Thought point

The perfect house

If everyone had the same perfect house, would you change your house in any way to make it different from the others?

How does this question relate to Augustine's ideas?

Thought point

Criminal tendencies

1   Do people assume that children's attitudes and behaviour are simply a reflection of those of their parents? Is it right to assume this and then to act on this basis?
2   Does an assumption such as this affect the way people relate to the children of:

- Cleaners
- Criminals
- Doctors
- Solicitors
- Prostitutes
- Teachers?

Thought point

Free choice?

Think about your time in school. Have you ever misbehaved? If you have, would you have behaved in the same way if your mother had been sitting next to you in class?

In some schools teachers ask the parents to come into class with their child if the child misbehaves. Can you think of any disadvantages of this system of discipline?

Richard Swinburne

Richard Swinburne argued that evil is necessary in order for people to achieve higher-order goods. He accepts that if God is omnipotent he could stop evil, but would do so only if there was no possibility of humans ever choosing to exercise virtues, such as courage and selflessness. He argues that it is better to live in a world where there are evil and suffering than in a 'toy world' where the consequences of human actions do not matter. If there was no possibility of human actions producing evil consequences then humans would not need to make moral decisions. God cannot intervene in the world as this would mean there would be no human freedom and no need for responsibility and development. Death is necessary as it means that humans have to take responsibility for their actions, for if humans were immortal there would always be a second chance and so no risk. Swinburne thought that God created a 'half-finished' universe which gives humans the possibility to choose to make it better. This idea depends on humans having free will.

Richard Dawkins

Unsurprisingly perhaps, Richard Dawkins has no time for Augustine's teachings:

> What kind of ethical philosophy is it that condemns every child even before it is born, to inherit the sin of a remote ancestor . . . But now the sadomasochism. God incarnated himself as a man, Jesus, in order that he should be tortured and executed in *atonement* for the hereditary sin of Adam.
>
> (Dawkins, *The God Delusion*)

Steven Pinker

The psychologist Steven Pinker argues that Christianity was responsible for much of the suffering and violence in the world until the seventeenth- and eighteenth-century Enlightenment. Post-enlightenment thinking dismisses what are regarded as superstitions, such as the Fall and original sin, and replaces them with the humanitarian principle. This states that humans relate better to each other when they respect the interests of other people. There is therefore no requirement for a belief in God's grace. He evidences this by the curtailment of torture, misogynism and capital punishment.

Reinhold Niebuhr

The American theologian Reinhold Niebuhr disagreed with this view of post-enlightenment thinking and argues that it has failed because it does not talk about sin. He believed that both non-religious and religious people were ignorant if they believed that reason and moral goodness were sufficient to create peaceful and just societies. He said that the only way in which life could be improved was by people allowing their ego to form a relationship with God.

Niebuhr produced three paradoxes:

- Original sin is 'inevitable but not necessary';
- Good and evil are present in both good and evil people;
- Good individuals may not continue to act in this way when they are part of a group.

FREE WILL

For Augustine human misuse of free will resulted in the introduction of evil into a perfect world and so evil is the responsibility of humans, not of God. Swinburne argues that free will is vital in order for people to improve both themselves and the world in which they live. Both approaches see evil as the result of the human free will; however, without free will there is no possibility of humans having a free loving relationship with God.

Anthony Flew questions the actual meaning of free will. According to Flew freely chosen actions cannot have external causes; they have to be internal to the person in order to be really freely chosen. Flew goes on to say that God could have created a world in which humans could always freely choose to do the right thing – they would be naturally good, but still make free choices, according to Flew's definition of a free choice.

According to this approach, however, God is manipulating his creation in order to bring about certain results, whereas the free will defence hinges on humans being free to love and worship God and free to reject him.

J.L. Mackie extends the argument further by saying that God could have created a world in which humans were really free but would never have chosen to do evil. Mackie's argument is a logical one: if it is possible for a person who is free to do the right thing on one occasion, then it is possible for a person to do the right thing on every occasion, so God could have created a world in which everyone is genuinely free, and yet chooses always to do the right thing. Mackie concluded that as God failed to do this he cannot be omnipotent and omnibenevolent.

HUMAN NATURE AND SEX

It has been argued that Augustine is responsible for the guilt about sex found in many Western societies.

A major challenge to Augustine's views came from the writings of the psychoanalyst Sigmund Freud. Freud was an atheist but did not reject all of Augustine's ideas. He did not believe that people fell from God's grace but he did say

Sigmund Freud was born
in Freiberg, Moravia,
although he moved to
Vienna in 1860, where he
remained until 1938. He
fled to London in 1938
to escape the Nazis as
his extended family was
Jewish, and although
Freud was an atheist,
culturally he was from a
Jewish background.

Freud worked at the
Salpêtrière mental hospi-
tal in Paris in 1885, and it
was from his work there
that he was led to the
idea of the existence of
the unconscious. In 1895
he and Josef Breuer
published the important
book *Studies in Hysteria*,

that, from observation, most psychological problems could be traced back to childhood events. So he agreed with the idea that people do not choose their personality but that it is the result of their history and environment. He also taught that sexual neurosis can be passed on through society and culture.

Freud's work has had a great influence on Christian theology. Today most Christians do not share Augustine's view that sex is only for procreation, that it passes on guilt or that it is a sign of sin.

SUMMARY

- Influences on Augustine's life

  - Manicheans
  - Pelagians
  - Neo-Platonists
  - Donatism

- Augustine's theology – the Fall

  - God the Creator
  - Privation and evil
  - The origins of evil
  - Sharing in Adam's sin
  - Original sin – double death
  - Grace
  - Concupiscence

- Criticisms of Augustine's views

  - Plausibility
  - Science
  - Adam's sin
  - How could the perfect world go wrong?
  - Richard Swinburne
  - Free will
  - Human nature and sex
  - Sigmund Freud.

REVIEW QUESTIONS

Look back over the chapter and check that you can answer the following questions:

continued opposite

1   What was the teaching of Donatism?
2   What was the teaching of Pelagianism?
3   What did Augustine mean by 'privation'?
4   What do you think are the main strengths and weaknesses of Augustine's teachings?

which suggests the use of hypnotism to recall suppressed traumatic experiences from the unconscious part of the mind in order to treat mental illnesses.

Terminology

Do you know your terminology?

Try to explain the meaning of the following ideas without looking at your books and notes:

- Concupiscence
- Continence
- Enlightenment
- Manichaeism
- Neo-Platonism
- Postlapsarian
- Privation and lack
- Summum bonum.

Examination questions practice

Read the question carefully – remember that although Augustine's life is important in understanding him, it is his teachings which you will be questioned on. Answer the question set, not the one you would like to have been set.

To help you improve your answers look at the levels of response.

SAMPLE EXAM-STYLE QUESTION

Critically assess Augustine's teaching on the Fall.

AO1 (15 marks)

This question requires you to consider exactly what Augustine said about the Fall and to explain it. You need to cite the Fall in Genesis 3 and explain what happened and the consequences of this. This is a very straightforward passage so ensure that you know it and explain it accurately.

AO2 (15 marks)

In critically assessing Augustine's teaching about the Fall you need to show your understanding of his interpretation of the biblical account and how he related this to his beliefs about human nature and sin. You might also look at some of the criticisms made of Augustine's theology, particularly those of Dawkins, and use these in your assessment.

Further possible questions

- 'Augustine's theology cannot withstand the challenges posed by modern science.' Discuss.
- To what extent do you think that Augustine was influenced by his past sex life and feelings of guilt?
- Assess the influence of neo-Platonism on Augustine's theology.
- 'Augustine's teachings have little meaning for Christians in the twenty-first century.' Discuss.

FURTHER READING

There are many books available on Augustine's theology. You should certainly read §385–409 of the *Catechism of the Catholic Church*. As well as the texts in the OCR checklist you could read some of the following:

Chadwick, H. 1986. *Augustine: A Very Short Introduction*. Oxford: Oxford University Press

Hukanovic, R. 1998. *The Tenth Circle of Hell: A Memoir of Life in the Death Camps of Bosnia*. London: Abacus.

Wiesel, E. 2008. *Night*. London: Penguin.

Williams, R. 2016. *On Augustine*. London: Bloomsbury.

Insight

18 Death and the afterlife

WHAT YOU WILL LEARN ABOUT IN THIS CHAPTER

Christian teaching about life after death
Who will be saved.

In this chapter you will consider Christian ideas about life after death. You will consider whether these Christian concepts are coherent. You will also consider what is meant by body and soul and consider the relationship between definitions of body and soul and discussions of life after death. You will consider what Christians mean by heaven, hell and purgatory, and the relation of these concepts to life after death.

THE OCR CHECKLIST

Christian teaching on:

- heaven
- hell
- purgatory
  - different interpretations of heaven, hell and purgatory, including:
    - heaven, hell and purgatory are actual places where a person may go after death and experience physical and emotional happiness, punishment or purification
    - heaven, hell and purgatory are not places but spiritual states that a person experiences as part of his or her spiritual journey after death

---

Essential terminology

Disembodied existence
Dualism
Election
Eschatology
Existentialism
Heaven
Hell
Judgement
Kingdom of God
Life after death
Materialism
Millenarianism
Monism
Parousia
Predestination
Purgatory
Resurrection
Soul

Key scholars

Plato (428/427 or 424/423–348/347 BCE)
Aristotle (384–322 BCE)
Augustine (354–430)
Aquinas (1225–1274)
Dante Alighieri (1265–1231)
John Calvin (1509–1564)
John Milton (1608–1674)
Bertrand Russell (1872–1970)
Albert Schweitzer (1875–1965)
C.H. Dodd (1884–1973)
Karl Barth (1888–1968)

continued overleaf   continued overleaf

Paul Tillich (1886–1965)
Gilbert Ryle (1900–1976)
Oscar Cullman (1902–1999)
Jean-Paul Sartre (1905–1980)
John Hick (1922–2012)
Richard Dawkins (1941–)
Alister McGrath (1953–)

Life after death
The belief that life continues in some fashion post-mortem.

Resurrection
Refers to the belief that life continues after death through the existence of the person, body and soul, in a new but distinct form of life. Resurrection is a feature of Jewish, Christian and Muslim beliefs.

Soul
The word 'soul' is used to refer to the spiritual or non-physical part of a human being, or to the mind. The soul is often seen as the centre or core of identity of a person.

- heaven, hell and purgatory are symbols of a person's spiritual and moral life on Earth and not places or states after death
- election
  - different Christian views of who will be saved, including:
    - limited election (that only a few Christians will be saved)
    - unlimited election (that all people are called to salvation but not all are saved)
    - universalist belief (that all people will be saved)
  - the foregoing to be studied with reference to the key ideas in Jesus' parable on final judgement, 'The Sheep and the Goats' (Matthew 25:31–46).

Learners should have the opportunity to discuss issues related to Christian ideas on death and the afterlife, including:

- whether God's judgement takes place immediately after death or at the end of time
- whether hell and heaven are eternal
- whether heaven is the transformation and perfection of the whole of creation
- whether purgatory is a state through which everyone goes.

Suggested scholarly views, academic approaches and sources of wisdom and authority

- McGrath, A. (2011) *Theology: The Basics,* Blackwell, Chapter 4
- Theissen, G. (2010) *The Shadow of the Galilean,* SCM Press
- Chapman, G. (1994) *Catechism of the Catholic Church,* paras. 422–478.

Thought point

Ask people to explain what the following words and phrases mean to them:

- Soul
- Body
- Resurrection
- Life after death.

Thought point

Why does death matter? Discuss what you think about this passage.

> Accustom yourself to the belief that death is of no concern to us, since all good and evil lie in sensation and sensation ends with death. Therefore the true belief that death is nothing to us makes a mortal life happy, not by adding to it an infinite time, but by taking away the desire for immortality. For there is no reason why the man who is thoroughly assured that there is nothing to fear in death should find anything to fear in life. So, too, he is foolish who says that he fears death, not because it will be painful when it comes, but because the anticipation of it is painful; for that which is no burden when it is present gives pain to no purpose when it is anticipated. Death, the most dreaded of evils, is therefore of no concern to us; for while we exist death is not present, and when death is present we no longer exist. It is therefore nothing either to the living or to the dead since it is not present to the living, and the dead no longer are.
>
> (Epicurus, *Letter to Menoeceus*)

> ### Reincarnation
>
> The belief that the soul of a person is reincarnated after death. Its status in the next life depends on the conduct of the incarnated soul in its previous existence. Belief in reincarnation or rebirth is associated with Hinduism and other Eastern religions.

Birth and death are the only events which are common to every human being's life. It is clear that birth is the beginning of human life. However, does death matter?

Attitudes to death vary enormously from person to person: the death of a loved one tends to distress people a great deal; the death of a child is often seen as a tragedy, and the death of someone in an accident or from malnutrition is sad. People see death on the television, whether in news or drama programmes, but this rarely, if ever, produces the same feeling as the experience of the death of a loved one.

Thought point

Why do you think that people's reactions to the death of other human beings and living creatures vary so much?

If you do not believe in an afterlife, then once you are dead, if there is no afterlife, even a wish for continued life has no meaning. Epicurus makes this very point, but many people do not find Epicurus' thought helpful. Why do you think this is?

For people who believe in life after death, death obviously matters. Death is an unknown and the end of reality as people experience it in their lives. Death is a final parting with people we may have loved and whom we will continue to miss. For religious people death is the beginning of a new stage of life, either with God or, perhaps, separated from God in hell.

CAN I SURVIVE MY DEATH?

For centuries people and philosophers have discussed whether life after death (post-mortem) is possible. Belief in life after death is widespread throughout all cultures of the world. It can be traced back to the cultures of ancient China, India and the Middle East. The pyramids of Egypt are an example of a culture in which the afterlife played a significant part in the belief system.

More recently, theologians, philosophers and scientists have examined the idea of survival post-mortem. This question has generally been broken down into the following aspects:

- What must survive if I am to talk meaningfully of life after death?
- Is belief in life after death coherent?
- Is belief in life after death possible?

The first question points to the debates that have continued through history concerning the nature of personal identity. This is important because if someone talks of personal survival after death, a clear definition of what is meant by 'you' is required. This is a philosophical debate about the mind-body problem and personal identity.

In the history of philosophy two main approaches have been used in relation to this problem. One approach, often labelled dualist, argues that human beings consist of a body and soul. According to this view survival after death is possible if the soul can survive death. The body is less important in dualist thinking, as it functions merely as the carrier of the soul.

An alternative approach is called monist. This suggests that human beings' minds or centres of identity cannot be separated from their bodies. Human beings are a unity of what may be called body and soul. Therefore the concept of life after death is possible only if humans survive death in some way as a body-soul unity.

The views of dualism and monism then lead to the second and third questions.

Dualism

The view that a human person consists of two distinct elements: the mind/soul and the body. The mind/soul is immaterial, whereas the body is physical.

Monism

The belief that human beings are a single unity of body and mind. The mind's existence is dependent on the body.

HOW DO PEOPLE KNOW WHO THEY ARE?

Thought point

- Who are you?
- How do you know who you are?
- How do other people recognise you as you?
- Are you the same person today as yesterday?
- Will you be the same person tomorrow morning as today?
- Are you:

  - Your mind?
  - Your body?
  - Something else?

Materialism

This is the view that humans are physical beings rather than consisting of a physical body and an immaterial soul.

Many philosophers are monists. By monism, philosophers mean that the mind and body are not separate and distinct. Instead, the mind is one with the body and inseparable from it. According to this view the mind is the product of the functioning of the brain, and the brain in turn is a physical organ of the body. Most monists are materialists and argue that the only form of existence is physical, so it is not possible to talk about the existence of a soul separate from the body. Materialists can support life after death only if that life is physical, such as in religious teaching about resurrection. The appeal of this view is that it accords with our knowledge of the world. Since the writings of Kant human beings have been aware that our knowledge is limited to the physical world even if there is a numinous world beyond the possibility of our sense experiences.

> The body is the source of endless trouble to us by reason of the mere requirement of food; and is liable also to diseases which overtake and impede us in the search after true being: it fills us full of loves, and lusts, and fears, and fancies of all kinds, and endless foolery, and in fact, as men say, takes away all power of thinking.
>
> (Plato, *Phaedo*)

Soul and psyche

The word 'soul' originates from the Greek word *psyche*. It is translated as 'soul', not 'psyche', because in ancient Greek *psyche* means life or the principle that keeps a person alive. Plato means more than this when he talks about the 'soul'.

Thought point

Death and philosophy

In *Phaedo*, Plato suggests that philosophy is a preparation for death. Why do you think he says this?

Does the soul survive after death?

Aristotle's unity of the Form and matter of the body suggests that the soul does not survive after death, as the Form of the body is inseparable from the body. Furthermore, Aristotle's book *De Anima* does not focus on the question of the immortality of a soul. It is concerned with plant and animal life. However, confusion has been brought about by the fact that Aristotle also suggested that intellectual thought could possibly be separated from the soul and be eternal. Even if thought can survive after death, this is clearly not the same as saying that one's personal identity survives death. Aristotle's writings about the intellectual faculty of the soul are described as 'inconstant' by Anthony Kenny (*A Brief History of Western Philosophy*), by which he means that what Aristotle thought about the soul surviving death is unclear and some of these ideas conflict with other ideas of his.

Aristotle and Christianity

Aristotle's ideas are of great importance to understanding Christian theology. His ideas were preserved through the Dark Ages of Europe in Islamic and Jewish cultures. During the Middle Ages the works of Aristotle reappeared in Western European culture from the Arabic and Jewish centres of learning in Spain. Thomas Aquinas came across Aristotle's rediscovered works as a student and he spent much of his life incorporating many of Aristotle's ideas into Christian teaching.

- Aquinas produced ideas now known as cosmological arguments that are greatly influenced by Aristotle's ideas.
- The philosophy of Aristotle was used to explain Roman Catholic beliefs about the presence of Jesus in the bread and wine used in the Eucharistic service, the Mass.
- The transcendent Prime Mover, who is pure activity, was a strong influence on medieval ideas about the nature of God, as may be seen in Aquinas' *Summa Theologiae*.

However, with regard to the soul, Christianity was influenced by Plato more than by Aristotle. Can you think of why this was the case?

MATERIALISM AND MONISM

Materialists generally argue against any concept of the afterlife, but a materialist could believe in bodily resurrection. Materialists are often called monists. 'Monist' refers to anyone who believes that there is only one sub-stance – matter – and therefore dualism is incorrect, since it postulates the existence of matter and a non-physical substance (body and soul).

Thought point

Materialism and bodily resurrection

If you are a materialist you cannot be a dualist or believe in rebirth, but you could believe in bodily resurrection. Why?

For materialists, the identity of a person is linked inextricably to the phys-ical body. When the physical body's life ends then that person ends. Emotions, feelings and thoughts derive from our brains and are mental processes in the brain. According to materialism, all of these characteristics of our experience are explainable by reference to the mental activity of the brain.

Identity theory claims that all mental activities are centred in the brain. This approach is supported by scientific research which can point to the modification of mood, behaviour and character by drugs. If drugs such as alcohol or antidepressants affect our character, which they clearly do, this suggests that mental activity is not to be linked to an immaterial soul or identity but to our brain. When our physical life ends, then mental activity ceases. The argument is that it is not that a soul has gone to another place but that the life has just ended.

However, many criticisms of identity theory have been made. Stephen T. Davis ('Philosophy and Life after Death: The Questions and the Options') points to the fact that identity theory has been criticised concerning how intentionality can be explained. By this, philosophers mean that brain activ-ity consists of nerves functioning in the brain. When you as an individual make a decision, such as whether to listen to music or to open the window, you form an intention. The challenge, however, is that neural activity in the brain has no intentionality. Other philosophical criticisms include the fact that mental events are private, and so do not have a physical location.

Recent scientific discoveries have suggested that mental activity is fully explainable in terms of neurone activity in the brain. For example NASA (Newscientist.com., 22 March 2004) has developed sensors which, when placed on the throat, can detect and recognise words that you say silently to yourself without voicing aloud. Scientists at University College London and the University of California, Los Angeles, carried out research in which peo-ple viewed different images ('Thoughts Read via Brain Scans', http://news.bbc.co.uk/1/hi/health/4715327.stm, 7 August 2005). The researchers used a functional magnetic imaging scanner to detect, successfully, when people's attention was focused on different images. In other words, they could read the thoughts of the people in the study.

While this research is not 'mind-reading', it strongly suggests that mental activities, such as thoughts, can be readable as they are caused by physical events in the brain. If this is true it would support philosophers who argue against the dualistic ideas that separate the body and the soul/mind/identity or physical activity in the brain from mental activity and thoughts.

RICHARD DAWKINS

Dawkins presents a case in favour of a materialist view of personal identity with no survival post-mortem. He argues that individual human beings cannot survive death. The only sense in which human beings survive death is through the memories of them in other people's minds or through their genes, some of which are passed on to the next generation of offspring. This may be seen in Richard Dawkins' discussion of God's covenant with Abraham:

> He didn't promise Abraham eternal life as an individual (though Abraham was only 99 at the time, a spring chicken by Genesis standards). But he did promise something else.
>
> 'And I will make my covenant between me and thee, and will multiply thee exceedingly . . . and thou shalt be a father of many nations . . . And I will make thee exceeding fruitful, and I will make nations of thee, and kings shall come out of thee.' (Genesis 17)
>
> Abraham was left in no doubt that the future lay with his seed, not his individuality. God knew his Darwinism.
>
> (Dawkins, *Unweaving the Rainbow*)

Genes do not have a sense of goal or direction. Instead, genes are what DNA is made of. DNA is a protein that makes copies of itself. Dawkins argues that genes are '*potentially immortal*' as they are the '*basic unit of natural selection*' (Dawkins, *The Selfish Gene*). Genes have been passed on from the previous generations of living organisms.

The role of the body is as '*a survival machine*' for genes. Genes that survive into another generation survive because they make bodies that enable them to be passed on to the next generation:

> A gene can live for a million years, but many new genes do not even make it past their first generation. The few new ones that succeed

do so partly because they are lucky, but mainly because they have what it takes, and that means that they are good at making survival machines.

(Dawkins, *The Selfish Gene*)

The human brain has evolved over three million years and the genes for growth in our brain size were passed on because genes in bodies with bigger brains had a survival advantage. The exact reason why the larger brains of human beings evolved is not fully understood; however, possibilities include the evolution of language, which actually stimulated further evolution, because language offers a distinct survival advantage.

Human beings' consciousness has evolved due to the survival advantage it gives. Genes cause each person to develop a brain as it grows and the sense of consciousness arises from the brain. This does not mean that genes control or direct our thoughts. Dawkins made the point that you can program a computer to play chess, but when it is actually playing it is not being directed by the programmer – it is playing on its own.

Human consciousness means that the body has a greater chance of survival and provides a greater chance for the body's genes to be passed on to the next generation. The survival advantage of being conscious is high. Therefore, genes which specify the development of a brain and consciousness have an advantage over those that do not. Another way to think about this is the fact that conscious human beings have managed to wipe out some illnesses, such as smallpox. The consciousness coded by the genes of human doctors gave them a survival advantage over the genes of consciousless smallpox.

Whatever the philosophical problems raised by consciousness, for the purpose of this story it can be thought of as the culmination of an evolutionary trend towards the emancipation of survival machines as executive decision-takers from their ultimate masters, the genes. Not only are brains in charge of the day-to-day running of survival-machine affairs, they have acquired the ability to predict the future and act accordingly. They even have the power to rebel against the dictates of the genes, for instance in refusing to have as many children as they are able to.

(Dawkins, *The Selfish Gene*)

However, this is not the only value of consciousness to us, as thinking human beings. This is just one way in which the origins of consciousness can be explained. Consciousness is of value to us in different ways because we have the capacity to understand, enjoy and live life. As Dawkins stated,

Gene

A gene is the term which scientists use for the smallest unit of DNA which can have an effect on the growth of the organism containing the DNA. DNA guides the development of every cell in a living organism. Different genes in isolation or combination have different effects they cause different tissues or cells to develop). Similarly, the reason that human beings are different from monkeys, earthworms or yeast is precisely because the DNA in every cell of each of these living organisms is different.

Biologists refer to the effect that a gene has on its environment (i.e. how the organism develops) as its phenotypic effect.

What is the use of bringing a baby into the world if the only thing it does with its life is just work to go on living? . . . There must be some added value. At least a part of life should be devoted to living that life, not just working to stop it ending.

(Dawkins, *Unweaving the Rainbow*)

Gilbert Ryle's 'ghost in the machine'

Gilbert Ryle's book *The Concept of Mind*, first published in 1949, challenged philosophical dualism, such as that of Descartes. He argued that philosophers often make a category error by assuming that mind and the body can be spoken of as though they are the same kind of thing:

'the dogma of the ghost in the machine'. I hope to prove that it is entirely false, and false not in detail but in principle. It is not merely an assemblage of mistakes. It is one big mistake and a mistake of a special kind. It is namely, a category mistake. It represents the facts of mental life as if they belonged to one logical type or category . . ., when they actually belong to another.

(*The Concept of Mind* 2000 [1949, 1984])

Ryle noted that a person can talk about mental and physical events, but it does not mean that the mental and physical events are the same type of thing, or that they can be compared. In his book Ryle attacked Descartes' dualism and suggested a new approach to understanding the mind-body problem.

JOHN HICK

John Hick's replica theory (Hick, 'Resurrection of the Person') presents one way in which the concept of resurrection may be understood. The significance of Hick's theory is that he rejects dualism, while at the same time presenting a defence of belief in bodily resurrection. This contrasts with many philosophers in history who have held monist views and not accepted life after death, or dualist views and accepted life after death.

Hick regards human beings as a 'psycho-somatic unity'. By this, he means that human beings are a unity of physical body and the mind or soul. The two cannot be separated. He does not think that a soul is like Gilbert Ryle's ghost in a machine (see ahead). 'The concept of mind or soul is thus not that of a "ghost" in the "machine" but of the more flexible and sophisticated ways in which human beings behave and have it in them to behave' (Hick, 'Resurrection of the Person'). Hick argues that the soul is not a separate part of human beings, such as in the work of Plato or other dualists. Hence, his views are not suitably described as dualistic.

Thought point

Dualism and Hick

Students writing examination answers often make the mistake of calling Hick a dualist. Why is this incorrect?

Instead of a dualistic view of the soul surviving death, Hick uses a 'replica theory' to explain what is meant by resurrection. Paul spoke of the resurrection involving spiritual bodies, and Hick's replica theory is one way to understand Paul.

Hick argues that resurrection is a divine action in which an exact replica of ourselves is created in a different place. 'I wish to suggest that we can think of it as the divine creation in another space of an exact psycho-physical "replica" of the deceased person' (Hick, 'Resurrection of the Person'). The replica is in all respects the same as us, but the location of the replica is not on earth.

Hick argues that resurrection could take place instantaneously at death or after a time lapse determined by God. The replica exists in a 'different space' from us that is observable by God and not by us.

However, the replica of the person is not the same as a copy. Hundreds of copies can be made of an article or picture using a photocopier. Instead, Hick uses the word 'replica' because each person can exist in only one place and time. Hick does not accept the idea of there being hundreds or thousands of possible copies of a person, because part of being a human person is that we are individuals. What matters is that the replica is the real you; there cannot be another replica floating around in some other place.

In 'Resurrection of the Person', Hick suggested an example to explain replica theory. He starts by considering the case of a person disappearing in London and reappearing in New York. He suggested that, for the person who appears in New York to be identifiable, the particular appearance of the person, his or her character, the arrangement of the matter that makes the person have to enable someone observing the person in New York, who knew the person first in London, to recognise who he or she is. What matters for Hick is the arrangement of matter in the person in New York being such that it is the same as the person who disappeared in London.

Hick continues by suggesting that you imagine a person who dies in London and is recreated in New York. Hick argues that if a replica of that person exists in New York and a dead body exists in London, it is easier to identify the replica in New York as the person rather than the dead body. He suggests that resurrected persons do not doubt that they are the same person as before. Thus, resurrection is understood by Hick as the creation of a replica by God in a different space.

Understandably, philosophers have raised many issues concerning Hick's replica theory.

Identification of the replica with the original person

Hick argued that the replica and the original person cannot exist at the same time, as persons are individuals. For the replica to be you, it has to be individual. Hick argued that if the replica has the same *'consciousness, memory, emotion and volition'* as the original person, it is logical to identify the replica as the same individual as the original person.

However, for some philosophers, what matters is the physical continuity of the person through life – that is an individual person consists not just of *'consciousness, memory, emotion and volition'* but also of the fact that these are linked to the same physical body throughout life. If the body's life comes to an end then the unity which was that person ends.

Hick insisted that there is continuity because the replica has the *'consciousness, memory, emotion and volition'* of the person and there can only ever be one replica of an individual. However, if physical continuity of the body is important when explaining identity, then replica theory is problematic.

Multiple replicas

Some philosophers have suggested that there could be multiple replicas. If this were the case then the individuality of a replica would be lost and so none of the copies would be a replica. Hick rejected this suggestion as not fitting with people's understanding of what a person is:

'Our concept of "the same person" has not developed to cope with such a situation' (Hick, 'Resurrection of the Person'). Any discussion of life after death is inevitably limited by human beings' inability to talk about what lies beyond their sense experience. Hick acknowledged that discussion of the nature of life as a replica is impossible. Typical questions concern what stage in life the replica is a copy of. If it is a copy at death, are terminal illnesses replicated? Hick suggested that one possibility might be that the healing of illness and disease takes place in the new existence as a replica.

HEAVEN AND HELL

Christianity and Islam, along with many other religious traditions, believe in a state of existence with God after death, called heaven, and a state of punishment, called hell.

Heaven

In Christianity the idea of afterlife with God is described as a state of existence with God in which people see God face to face – that is people see or experience God in a new way. In Catholic tradition the idea of seeing God face to face is called the *beatific vision*. The same belief is found in Orthodox Christianity.

This belief comes from the first followers of Jesus who witnessed the events surrounding Jesus' death and resurrection, and it is found in the Bible in the writings of Paul and in the Book of Revelation. Paul stated that, in heaven, God is experienced in a different way:

> Love never ends. But as for prophecies, they will come to an end; as for tongues, they will cease; as for knowledge, it will come to an end. For we know only in part, and we prophesy only in part; but when the complete comes, the partial will come to an end. When I was a child, I spoke like a child, I thought like a child, I reasoned like a child; when I became an adult, I put an end to childish ways. For now we see in a mirror, dimly, but then we will see face to face. Now I know only in part; then I will know fully, even as I have been fully known. And now faith, hope, and love abide, these three; and the greatest of these is love.
>
> (1 Corinthians 13:8–13)

Secondly, heaven is described in Christian tradition as a state of fulfilment; it is a place where all human longings and wishes are to be in a right relationship with God:

> This perfect life with the Most Holy Trinity – this communion of life and love with the Trinity, with the Virgin Mary, the angels and all the blessed – is called 'heaven.' Heaven is the ultimate end and fulfilment of the deepest human longings, the state of supreme, definitive happiness.

To live in heaven is 'to be with Christ.' The elect live 'in Christ,' but they retain, or rather find, their true identity, their own name.

For life is to be with Christ; where Christ is, there is life, there is the kingdom.

By his death and Resurrection, Jesus Christ has 'opened' heaven to us. The life of the blessed consists in the full and perfect possession of the fruits of the redemption accomplished by Christ. He makes partners in his heavenly glorification those who have believed in him and remained faithful to his will. Heaven is the blessed community of all who are perfectly incorporated into Christ.

This mystery of blessed communion with God and all who are in Christ is beyond all understanding and description. Scripture speaks of it in images: life, light, peace, wedding feast, wine of the kingdom, the Father's house, the heavenly Jerusalem, paradise: 'no eye has seen, nor ear heard, nor the heart of man conceived, what God has prepared for those who love him.'

Because of his transcendence, God cannot be seen as he is, unless he himself opens up his mystery to man's immediate contemplation and gives him the capacity for it. The Church calls this contemplation of God in his heavenly glory 'the beatific vision'.

(*Catechism of the Catholic Church* §1024–1028)

Heaven is believed to be the ultimate goal of human existence to which all human beings are called. For Roman Catholic and Orthodox Christians life after death with God in heaven is something they have to achieve through their actions in life. People have to want to do what is good (i.e. God's will) and actually do it.

But the throne of God and of the Lamb will be in it, and his servants will worship him; they will see his face, and his name will be on their foreheads. And there will be no more night; they need no light of lamp or sun, for the Lord God will be their light, and they will reign forever and ever.

(Revelation 22:3b–5)

However, within Christian tradition there is also much emphasis placed upon hell as the fate of people who do wrong in life.

Hell

Hell is traditionally described by two features: it is a state of separation from God and it is a place of punishment by God. Imagery of fire, pain, suffering and torture is frequently used to describe hell. Many of these images originate from Dante Alighieri's (1265–1231) poetry. His major work was *La divina commedia* (Divine Comedy) (*c.* 1308). This contains three books: *Inferno* (Hell), *Purgatorio* (Purgatory) and *Paradiso* (Heaven). In these books Dante is guided by the Roman poet Virgil, representing the best of human knowledge. They pass through a dark wood and then the descending circles of the pit of hell. Lucifer's (Satan) pit is at the centre of the world. They then emerge on a beach of the island mountain of purgatory. At the top of the mountain, where the sinners are purged of their sins, Virgil leaves as this is as far as human knowledge can go. On the threshold of Paradise Dante is met by Beatrice, who holds the knowledge of the divine mysteries, which are bestowed by Grace. She leads him through the ascending levels of heaven to the Empyrean, the highest level, where for a moment he sees the glory of God.

According to Dante's poem, hell was created by an earthquake at the moment of Jesus' death on the cross.

> At that moment the curtain of the temple was torn in two, from top to bottom. The earth shook, and the rocks were split. The tombs also were opened, and many bodies of the saints who had fallen asleep were raised. After his resurrection they came out of the tombs and entered the holy city and appeared to many.
>
> (Matthew 27:51–53)

This is the inscription over the gate to hell according to Dante:

> Through me the way into the woeful city,
> Through me the way to eternal pain,
> Through me the way among the lost people.
> Justice moved my maker on high,
> Divine power made me and supreme wisdom and primal love;
> Before me nothing was created but eternal things and I endure eternally.
> Abandon every hope, ye that enter.
>
> (Dante, *Divine Comedy*, 'Inferno', canto 3:1–9)

John Milton described hell as:

> A dungeon horrible on all sides round,
> As one great furnace flamed; yet from those flames,
> No light, but rather darkness visible
> Served only to discover sights of woe
> Regions of sorrow, doleful shades
>
> (Milton, *Paradise Lost*)

These words convey the idea that hell is a state of suffering after death. In traditional Christian teaching hell is seen as a place of suffering and punishment. It is a state of suffering because the wicked people who are in hell lose the chance of a beatific vision with God and they know they have lost it. It is a state of punishment because God's justice demands that wrongdoers are punished.

This is found in the Book of Revelation:

Then I saw an angel coming down from heaven, holding in his hand the key to the bottomless pit and a great chain. He seized the dragon, that ancient serpent, who is the Devil and Satan, and bound him for a thousand years, and threw him into the pit, and locked and sealed it over him, so that he would deceive the nations no more, until the thousand years were ended. After that he must be let out for a little while.

Then I saw thrones, and those seated on them were given authority to judge. I also saw the souls of those who had been beheaded for their testimony to Jesus and for the word of God. They had not worshiped the beast or its image and had not received its mark on their foreheads or their hands. They came to life and reigned with Christ a thousand years. (The rest of the dead did not come to life until the thousand years were ended.) This is the first resurrection. Blessed and holy are those who share in the first resurrection. Over these the second death has no power, but they will be priests of God and of Christ, and they will reign with him a thousand years.

When the thousand years are ended, Satan will be released from his prison and will come out to deceive the nations at the four corners of the earth, Gog and Magog, in order to gather them for battle; they are as numerous as the sands of the sea. They marched up over the breadth of the earth and surrounded the camp of the saints and the beloved city. And fire came down from heaven and consumed them. And the devil who had deceived them was thrown into the lake of fire and sulphur, where the beast and the false prophet were, and they will be tormented day and night forever and ever.

Then I saw a great white throne and the one who sat on it; the earth and the heaven fled from his presence, and no place was found for them. And I saw the dead, great and small, standing before the throne, and books were opened. Also another book was opened, the book of life. And the dead were judged according to their works, as recorded in the books. And the sea gave up the dead that were in it, Death and Hades gave up the dead that were in them, and all were judged according to what they had done. Then Death and Hades were thrown into the lake of fire. This is the second death, the lake of fire; and anyone whose name was not found written in the book of life was thrown into the lake of fire.

(Revelation 20:1–15)

In much of Christian teaching hell is seen as an aspect of God's justice. People who do wrong deserve to be punished and it is through their own wrong actions that people bring punishment on themselves. This is a retributive theory of justice. Many Christians might argue that a failure by God to punish people would contradict the idea of God being just.

Today, some people find these images unhelpful as they do not believe that they communicate the idea of a loving and forgiving God. For others, the idea of eternal punishment appears unjust – the punishment is punishment alone – it is does not educate or rehabilitate the person.

Therefore these images act as a type of negative reinforcement education that might encourage people not to commit an act, but it does not necessarily persuade them to choose what is right for its own sake.

If hell is a place of physical suffering, where is it? In the history of Christian belief and teachings there have been many suggestions as to the location of hell, such as under the Earth or on the other side of the moon, but we now know that these places, though they may be inhospitable, are not hell in this traditional sense.

Some theologians have focused on the idea that hell is a state of separation from both God and other people that is caused by a person becoming aware of others' 'judgement' on them. In this way, hell may be understood as a state of utter loneliness and separation. Sometimes, through choices in life, people may bring this situation on themselves. For example if you steal from your family and friends and get caught, the effect is that you lose their good will and your relationship with them.

In medieval Christian thought hell is both a state of separation from God and a state of punishment. 'For mortal sin which is contrary to charity a person is expelled for ever from the fellowship of the saints and condemned to everlasting punishment' (Aquinas, *Summa Theologiae*, Supp. 3a, q. 91, a. 1). In the Catholic tradition mortal sin is the most serious type of sin and it causes the sinner to be separated from God – for example murder is a mortal sin. The origins of this teaching are found in Jesus' parable of the sheep and the goats (see p. 363).

To die in mortal sin without repenting and accepting God's merciful love means remaining separated from him for ever by our own free choice. This state of definitive self- exclusion from communion with God and the blessed is called 'hell.'

The teaching of the Church affirms the existence of hell and its eternity. Immediately after death the souls of those who die in a state of mortal sin descend into hell, where they suffer the punishments of hell, 'eternal fire.' The chief punishment of hell is eternal separation from God, in whom alone man can possess the life and happiness for which he was created and for which he longs.

(*Catechism of the Catholic Church* §1033, 1035)

In the thinking of medieval theologians like Aquinas hell is a state of punishment and separation from God which mirrors the separation from the community of people who do wrong on earth. Aquinas argued that hell serves two purposes:

> First, because thereby the Divine justice is safeguarded which is acceptable to God for its own sake . . . Secondly, they are useful, because the elect rejoice therein, when they see God's justice in them, and realize that they have escaped them.
>
> (*Summa Theologiae*, Supp. 3a, q. 91, a. 1)

Jean-Paul Sartre, an atheist philosopher, suggested that hell is an experience of separation from other people. Having poor relationships with other people is an experience of hell.

> So that's what hell is; I'd never have believed it. . .
> Do you remember brimstone, the stake, the gridiron? . . .
> What a joke! No need for the gridiron – Hell is other people.
>
> (Sartre, 'Huis Clos')

The Fall

Paradise Lost is an epic poem by John Milton (1608–1674) which tells the story of the Fall according to Christian tradition. If you have time to read only a short extract, read Book 1.

Gehenna

The image of flames and burning in hell almost certainly originates from a rubbish dump outside Jerusalem. In the times of the Jewish scriptures rubbish was burned in Gehenna and pagan gods were worshipped there. Jews did not live there as it was unclean and associated with pagan worship. Eventually a link was made between the place where unclean people were and cleansing and punishment by fire.

> But I say to you that if you are angry with a brother or sister, you will be liable to judgment; and if you insult a brother or sister, you will be liable to the council; and if you say, 'You fool,' you will be liable to the hell of fire.
>
> (Matthew 5:22)

Retributive justice

A retributive theory of justice is one in which people who commit wrong acts are punished by law in a manner that is proportionate to their wrongdoing. The strength of such a theory is that it emphasises that justice involves punishing the wrongdoer and leaving the good person in peace.

The word translated here as 'hell' is in the Ge'enna (γέεννα) – Gehenna.

According to existentialist theologians, such as Paul Tillich (1886–1965), these images are metaphors which can now be interpreted as spiritual and psychological descriptions of the human condition in a state of alienation. 'Heaven and hell must be taken seriously as metaphors for the polar ultimates in the experience of the divine' (Tillich, *Systematic Theology*

III). In this teaching Tillich was following the ideas of the theologian Origen (*c.* 185–*c.* 254). Origen taught that as God is omnibenevolent and reconciles all things, then eventually everyone will be forgiven and go to heaven. In this he also included Satan.

Purgatory

Purgatory is a traditional Christian belief in a place where all people who die in relationship with God, but who are not yet perfect, are purified after death. The imagery again is of a place of suffering; in purgatory the suffering is for the purpose of purifying a person of his or her wrongdoings in life. Sometimes people think that purgatory is a place of judgement from where people will go to either heaven or hell; however, the judgement has already taken place and those in purgatory will all eventually go to heaven.

Belief in purgatory is said to derive from a passage in the Bible which talks about praying for the dead.

> But if he [Judas Maccabee] was looking to the splendid reward that is laid up for those who fall asleep in godliness, it was a holy and pious thought. Therefore he made atonement for the dead, so that they might be delivered from their sin.
>
> (2 Maccabees 12:45)

There would not appear to be any reason to pray for the dead if they were already in Hell.

Purgatory became an important part of Christian teaching in the Middle Ages.

Ambrose of Milan believed purgatory to be a place where people were given a foretaste of the future but he also considered that some people would fail to be purified there.

Origen said that purgatory was a place where people could perfect themselves over thousands of years.

Gregory of Nyssa (*c.* 335–*c.* 394) shared Origen's belief and said that everyone there would eventually get to heaven.

> All who die in God's grace and friendship, but still imperfectly purified, are indeed assured of their eternal salvation; but after death they undergo purification, so as to achieve the holiness necessary to enter the joy of heaven. The Church gives the name Purgatory to this final purification of the elect, which is entirely different from the punishment of the damned. The Church formulated her doctrine of faith on

Existentialism
This is a doctrine that concentrates on the existence of the individual who, because he or she is free and responsible, can be held to be what he or she makes themselves by the self-development of his or her essence through acts of the will (in Christian existentialism this leads to God).

> Purgatory especially at the Councils of Florence and Trent. The tradition of the Church, by reference to certain texts of Scripture, speaks of a cleansing fire.
>
> (*Catechism of the Catholic Church* §1030–1031)

Some Christians today find the idea of purgatory hard to believe as it is very difficult to understand how an individual who has died can spend time in a physical place being purified if his or her life in the physical, time-bound existence of the earth has come to an end.

The Protestant churches have generally rejected the idea of purgatory. However, in recent times a number of Protestant theologians have come to see it as part of the continuing journey of the soul. John Hick shared this view. He rejected the ideas of judgement, heaven and hell in favour of the idea of a person-making process. This starts on earth and continues through many stages on the journey to be with God.

CHRISTIANITY AND RESURRECTION

Christians believe that death is not the end of human existence but simply an end to physical life and the beginning of a new stage in life. The New Testament refers to the afterlife as a paradise, a state of continued existence with God after death.

The resurrection of Jesus is interpreted by Christians as a sign that death is not the end of human existence and that God does not abandon people, even when they are dying.

> But we do not want you to be uninformed, brothers and sisters, about those who have died, so that you may not grieve as others do who have no hope. For since we believe that Jesus died and rose again, even so, through Jesus, God will bring with him those who have died.
>
> (1 Thessalonians 4:13–14)

The story of Jesus in the Gospels concludes with his resurrection and ascension. In Christian belief this is the most important event. Jesus not only dies for people but also rises from the dead. There are a number of important events in the accounts of the resurrection: Jesus is somehow changed and different. His followers do not at first recognise him and his body is different. Secondly, Jesus is not described as being a ghost or vision; he is physically risen from the dead, but his body is transformed and different.

There are many people, both Christians and non-Christians, who believe that some sort of non-physical life after death is possible. What is different about Christianity is that it traditionally believes in the resurrection of the body in some way, not just a person's soul or centre of identity. Many philosophers challenge the concept of bodily resurrection, but Peter Geach suggests that resurrection is the only meaningful way in which one can speak of life after death. He states this view on the grounds that a person could not be meaningfully identified with a spiritual existence after death. Instead, he suggests that because people are a unity of body and soul, the only meaningful way to talk about survival after death is to say that souls can be reunited 'to such a body as would reconstitute a man identifiable with the man who died' (Geach, 'What Must Be True of Me if I Survive My Death').

From the time that Paul wrote 1 Corinthians 15, Christian belief has been in resurrection and life after death, though it has not always been clearly stated what is meant by resurrection of the body. Christian belief centres on Jesus' resurrection, as illustrated by the following example:

> We firmly believe, and hence we hope that, just as Christ is truly risen from the dead and lives for ever, so after death the righteous will live for ever with the risen Christ and he will raise them up on the last day. Our resurrection, like his own, will be the work of the Most Holy Trinity:
>
> If the Spirit of him who raised Jesus from the dead dwells in you, he who raised Christ Jesus from the dead will give life to your mortal bodies also through his Spirit who dwells in you.
>
> The term 'flesh' refers to man in his state of weakness and mortality. The 'resurrection of the flesh' (the literal formulation of the Apostles' Creed) means not only that the immortal soul will live on after death, but that even our 'mortal body' will come to life again.
>
> (*Catechism of the Catholic Church* §989–990)

While Christianity has argued in favour of the unity of body and soul in an individual person, it has also at times sounded dualistic. From biblical stories Christians believe that at death the soul of a person is separated from her or his body, awaiting the final resurrection and transformation of the person's body to be resurrected like Jesus. At death each person is judged by God in what is called 'The Particular Judgment'. This sounds dualistic, but Christianity also emphasises resurrection of the physical body after death; whether this takes place at the point of death is not always clear.

Jesus' resurrection and the Kingdom of God

The Gospel writers portray Jesus' resurrection in a very simple way and show it to mean that:

Eschatology

The part of theological science which is concerned with 'the four last things: death, judgement, heaven, and hell'.

- The end of the world had not arrived but it was the beginning of Christianity.
- The resurrection replaced despair over the human condition with hope for the afterlife.
- It was an occasion when God acted in a very mysterious way.

Jesus' teaching about life after death was based on Jewish eschatology and in particular in the writings of the Pharisees, who had been in part influenced by Greek philosophical teaching about the soul.

Jesus taught that his death was a sacrifice for the sins of the world and would restore the relationship between God and humanity, which had been broken at the Fall. He also said that God would bring in a new kingdom and that he and his followers would have a place in this kingdom, together with the saints and martyrs who had died before.

Jesus' teaching on this found in the Gospels leaves quite a muddled idea of the nature of this kingdom:

> Now after John was arrested, Jesus came to Galilee, proclaiming the good news of God, and saying, 'The time is fulfilled, and the kingdom of God has come near; repent, and believe in the good news.'
>
> (Mark 1:14–15)

> And he said to them, 'Truly I tell you, there are some standing here who will not taste death until they see that the kingdom of God has come with power.'
>
> (Mark 9:1)

> But if it is by the finger of God that I cast out the demons, then the kingdom of God has come to you.
>
> (Luke 11:20)

There are three distinctive forms of eschatology, all deriving much of their teachings from the Book of Revelation.

The following approaches arose from the study of Christianity's most central eschatological document, the Book of Revelation, but the principles embodied in them can be applied to all prophecy in the Bible. They are by no means mutually exclusive and are often combined to form a more complete and coherent interpretation of prophetic passages. Most interpretations fit into one, or a combination, of these approaches.

Preterism

This is an approach which sees prophecy as chiefly being fulfilled in the past, especially during the first century. Prophecies in general, therefore, have already been fulfilled. Some preterists see the Book of Revelation as a text using symbols in communicating prophecies to the early Church about the destruction of the Temple in CE 70. Other preterists see Revelation as a symbolic prophetic presentation of the struggle of Christianity to survive the persecutions of the Roman Empire. This view is found in the writings of Eusebius and John Chrysostom.

Historicism

Historicism views prophecy as being fulfilled in the past, present and future, including during the previous two millennia, according to Revelation. Historists see Revelation as a symbolic prophetic view of the struggle of Protestantism to survive the persecutions of the papacy.

Futurism

In futurism, parallels can be drawn with historical events, but most eschatological prophecies are seen as referring to events which have not yet been fulfilled, but will take place at the end of this age and the end of the world.

Realised eschatology was made famous by C.H. Dodd (1884–1973). It says that the eschatological passages in the New Testament are not referring to the future but refer to the ministry of Jesus and his legacy. In this view eschatology is not the end of the world but its rebirth instituted by Jesus and continued by his disciples.

Inaugurated eschatology was pioneered by the Lutheran theologian Oscar Cullman (1902–1999). It says that the end times began in the life, death and resurrection of Jesus and that therefore there are aspects to the Kingdom of God which are both 'already' and 'not yet'. The following text is used to explain this: 'Very truly, I tell you, anyone who hears my word and believes him who sent me has eternal life, and does not come under judgment, but has passed from death to life' (John 5:24). Cullmann sought to combine the 'thorough-going eschatology' of Albert Schweitzer (1875–1965) with the 'realised eschatology' of C.H. Dodd. Schweitzer believed that the life of Jesus must be interpreted in the light of Jesus' own beliefs, which reflected those of Jewish eschatology. Schweitzer writes,

> Paul's imminent eschatology (from his background in Jewish Eschatology) causes him to believe that the kingdom of God has not yet come and that Christians are now living in the time of Christ. Christ-mysticism holds the field until God-mysticism becomes possible, which is in the near future.
>
> (Schweitzer, *The Mysticism of Paul the Apostle*, 1931)

Cullmann suggested (Pate, 1995) the analogy of D-Day and V-Day to illustrate the relationship between Jesus' death and resurrection on the one hand and his *parousia* on the other.

Parousia

It appears from the New Testament that many Christians at that time were expecting an imminent parousia – the return of Jesus to usher in the new Kingdom of God.

This is reflected in the Book of Revelation, with passages such as the following:

> Then I saw a new heaven and a new earth; for the first heaven and the first earth had passed away, and the sea was no more. And I saw the holy city, the new Jerusalem, coming down out of heaven from God, prepared as a bride adorned for her husband. And I heard a loud voice from the throne saying,
>
> 'See, the home of God is among mortals.
> He will dwell with them as their God;
> they will be his peoples,
> and God himself will be with them;
> he will wipe every tear from their eyes.
> Death will be no more;
> mourning and crying and pain will be no more,
> for the first things have passed away.'
>
> And the one who was seated on the throne said, 'See, I am making all things new.' Also he said, 'Write this, for these words are trustworthy and true.' Then he said to me, 'It is done! I am the Alpha and the Omega, the beginning and the end. To the thirsty I will give water as a gift from the spring of the water of life. Those who conquer will inherit these things, and I will be their God and they will be my children. But as for the cowardly, the faithless, the polluted, the murderers, the fornicators, the sorcerers, the idolaters, and all liars, their place will be in the lake that burns with fire and sulphur, which is the second death.'
>
> (Revelation 21:1–8)

Problems with eschatological teaching and the Kingdom of God

Theologians have suggested that the Kingdom could be an actual place, a spiritual place or state, or a symbol of Christian moral life.

As previous texts here have shown, Jesus' teaching about the Kingdom was not clear. His healing miracles seem to be signs of the future Kingdom which reflect the promises found in the Old Testament.

On the other hand he appears to have a traditional Pharisaic view of eschatology that in the Kingdom that is to come the righteous will live in perfect harmony with God.

Paul appears to suggest that the resurrection shows that the world has been restored.

Love never ends. But as for prophecies, they will come to an end; as for tongues, they will cease; as for knowledge, it will come to an end. For we know only in part, and we prophesy only in part; but when the complete comes, the partial will come to an end. When I was a child, I spoke like a child, I thought like a child, I reasoned like a child; when I became an adult, I put an end to childish ways. For now we see in a mirror, dimly, but then we will see face to face. Now I know only in part; then I will know fully, even as I have been fully known. And now faith, hope, and love abide, these three; and the greatest of these is love.

(1 Corinthians 13:8–13)

The Gospel of Luke stresses that when the Kingdom comes that good people will be rewarded and the wicked punished. This is made clear in the parable of the rich man and Lazarus:

There was a rich man who was dressed in purple and fine linen and who feasted sumptuously every day. And at his gate lay a poor man named Lazarus, covered with sores, who longed to satisfy his hunger with what fell from the rich man's table; even the dogs would come and lick his sores. The poor man died and was carried away by the angels to be with Abraham. The rich man also died and was buried. In Hades, where he was being tormented, he looked up and saw Abraham far away with Lazarus by his side. He called out, 'Father Abraham, have mercy on me, and send Lazarus to dip the tip of his finger in water and cool my tongue; for I am in agony in these flames.' But Abraham said, 'Child, remember that during your lifetime you received your good things, and Lazarus in like manner evil things; but now he is comforted here, and you are in agony. Besides all this, between you and us a great chasm has been fixed, so that those who might want to pass from here to you cannot do so, and no one can cross from there to us.' He said, 'Then, father, I beg you to send him to my father's house – for I have five brothers – that he may warn them, so that they will not also come into this place of torment.' Abraham replied, 'They have Moses and the prophets; they should listen to them.' He said, 'No, father Abraham; but if someone goes to them from the dead, they will repent.' He said to him, 'If they do not listen to Moses and the prophets, neither will they be convinced even if someone rises from the dead.'

(Luke 16:19–31)

In fact, Jesus had warned his followers not to try to calculate the date of the parousia. 'But about that day and hour no one knows, neither the angels of heaven, nor the Son, but only the Father' (Matthew 24:36). This is further stressed by Paul:

Now concerning the times and the seasons, brothers and sisters, you do not need to have anything written to you. For you yourselves know very well that the day of the Lord will come like a thief in the night. When they say, 'There is peace and security,' then sudden destruction will come upon them, as labour pains come upon a pregnant woman, and there will be no escape! But you, beloved, are not in darkness, for that day to surprise you like a thief; for you are all children of light and children of the day; we are not of the night or of darkness.

(1 Thessalonians 5:1–5)

On the matter of judgement, the author of John's Gospel is harsh:

For God so loved the world that he gave his only Son, so that everyone who believes in him may not perish but may have eternal life.

Indeed, God did not send the Son into the world to condemn the world, but in order that the world might be saved through him. Those who believe in him are not condemned; but those who do not believe are condemned already, because they have not believed in the name of the only Son of God. And this is the judgment, that the light has come into the world, and people loved darkness rather than light because their deeds were evil. For all who do evil hate the light and do not come to the light, so that their deeds may not be exposed. But those who do what is true come to the light, so that it may be clearly seen that their deeds have been done in God.

(John 3:6–21)

Do not be astonished at this; for the hour is coming when all who are in their graves will hear his voice and will come out – those who have done good, to the resurrection of life, and those who have done evil, to the resurrection of condemnation.

(John 5:28–29)

Judgement: general and particular

The Church has always taught that there are two judgements.

When a person dies he or she will receive 'particular judgement'. Based on how the person has lived his or her life the person will then go to heaven, hell or purgatory. General Judgement will come at the Last Judgement.

> In the presence of Christ, who is Truth itself, the truth of each man's relationship with God will be laid bare. The Last Judgement will reveal even to its furthest consequences the good each person has done or failed to do during his earthly life.
>
> (*Catechism of the Catholic Church* §1039)

Christian teaching on judgement is found in the parable of the sheep and the goats.

> When the Son of Man comes in his glory, and all the angels with him, then he will sit on the throne of his glory. All the nations will be gathered before him, and he will separate people one from another as a shepherd separates the sheep from the goats, and he will put the sheep at his right hand and the goats at the left. Then the king will say to those at his right hand, 'Come, you that are blessed by my Father, inherit the kingdom prepared for you from the foundation of the world; for I was hungry and you gave me food, I was thirsty and you gave me something to drink, I was a stranger and you welcomed me, I was naked and you gave me clothing, I was sick and you took care of me, I was in prison and you visited me.' Then the righteous will answer him, 'Lord, when was it that we saw you hungry and gave you food, or thirsty and gave you something to drink? And when was it that we saw you a stranger and welcomed you, or naked and gave you clothing? And when was it that we saw you sick or in prison and visited you?' And the king will answer them, 'Truly I tell you, just as you did it to one of the least of these who are members of my family, you did it to me.' Then he will say to those at his left hand, 'You that are accursed, depart from me into the eternal fire prepared for the devil and his angels; for I was hungry and you gave me no food, I was thirsty and you gave me nothing to drink, I was a stranger and you did not welcome me, naked and you did not give me clothing, sick and in prison and you did not visit me.' Then they also will answer, 'Lord, when was it that we saw you hungry or thirsty or a stranger or naked or sick or in prison, and did not take care of you?' Then he will answer them, 'Truly I tell you, just as you did not do it to one of the least

of these, you did not do it to me.' And these will go away into eternal punishment, but the righteous into eternal life.

(Matthew 25:31–46)

Some people claim that God will forgive them whatever they do. However, this is not supported by the Christian as justice demands that people make up for wrongdoing if they are to be forgiven. God accepts people as they are; forgiveness is therefore on offer if people really repent, but it also requires people to acknowledge their wrongdoing (contrition), admit their wrongdoing (confession) and make up for their wrongdoing (an act of satisfaction).

Millenarianism – chiliastic doctrine

He seized the dragon, that ancient serpent, who is the Devil and Satan, and bound him for a thousand years, and threw him into the pit, and locked and sealed it over him, so that he would deceive the nations no more, until the thousand years were ended. After that he must be let out for a little while.

Then I saw thrones, and those seated on them were given authority to judge. I also saw the souls of those who had been beheaded for their testimony to Jesus and for the word of God. They had not worshiped the beast or its image and had not received its mark on their foreheads or their hands. They came to life and reigned with Christ a thousand years. (The rest of the dead did not come to life until the thousand years were ended.) This is the first resurrection.

(Revelation 20:2–6)

Revelation 20 is generally seen as being about the rule of the Church preparing for Christ's return.

However, followers of millenarianism believe that the present state of the world is reflecting the teachings in Revelation and that environmental and nuclear disasters will hasten the coming of the 1,000-year rule of Jesus on earth.

Predestination and election

The word 'elect' comes from the Greek ἐκλογή, meaning 'choice'.

The teachings of both election and predestination are attempts to explain why some people will have eternal life after their death while others will not.

There are two different versions of election but they are incompatible with each other.

Limited election

This states that the afterlife is only for people whom God chooses in his perfect, just nature. This has led to a belief in 'limited atonement' – that is Jesus died for the sins of the elect, not for everyone.

Unlimited election

Classic Image/Alamy

Everyone has the opportunity to reach the afterlife. Christ's atonement was therefore 'unlimited'.

Within Christian tradition much emphasis has been placed on the importance of free will, moral responsibility and a rejection of any idea of predestination. However, it is important to note that some Christians believe in divine election. While this is not the same as predestination, it has led some people to believe in predestination.

The sixteenth-century Protestant reformer John Calvin is generally associated with what he called the doctrine of divine election. By the doctrine of divine election, Calvin meant that some people are destined for relationship with God while some are not. This may be seen by the way that some people believe in Jesus and some do not. What is noticeable is that whether one is saved or goes to hell is not a matter of human choice. Calvin ultimately argues that whether a person is among God's elect is a matter for God, who is omnipotent and omniscient, and is therefore believed to be something beyond human comprehension.

Augustine is largely responsible for belief in predestination. He taught that even having faith in the redeeming act of the Crucifixion was insufficient to overcome sin and concupiscence. Salvation can come only from God's grace. This grace is not prompted by the human condition or merit. It is freely given and unprompted by the recipient. So from the very beginning God knew that only the elect would go to heaven. 'This is right and is acceptable in the sight of God our Saviour, who desires everyone to be saved and to come to the knowledge of the truth' (1 Timothy 2:3–4). Following Augustine's teachings, some theologians have argued that there are different types of predestination:

* Single predestination – God lets only those he has chosen enter heaven.
* Double predestination – God lets only those who he chosen enter heaven and also says that sinners must be punished in hell.

There are also different beliefs about when God chose these people:

- Antilapsarian Decree – God chose who would be saved and who would be punished at Creation.
- Postlapsarian Decree – God chose who would be saved and who would be punished after the Fall.

Among some Protestant groups which are offshoots from Calvinism (e.g. followers of Théodore de Bèze) the doctrine of predestination became an important article of belief separating Catholics and Lutherans from some other Protestants. Some support for belief in predestination may be found in the Bible in the Book of Revelation, which refers to the 144,000 servants of God (Revelation 7:9–14) who are to be saved.

> After this I looked, and there was a great multitude that no one could count, from every nation, from all tribes and peoples and languages, standing before the throne and before the Lamb, robed in white, with palm branches in their hands. They cried out in a loud voice, saying, 'Salvation belongs to our God who is seated on the throne, and to the Lamb!'
>
> And all the angels stood around the throne and around the elders and the four living creatures, and they fell on their faces before the throne and worshiped God, singing, 'Amen! Blessing and glory and wisdom and thanksgiving and honour and power and might be to our God forever and ever! Amen.'
>
> Then one of the elders addressed me, saying, 'Who are these, robed in white, and where have they come from?' I said to him, 'Sir, you are the one that knows.' Then he said to me, 'These are they who have come out of the great ordeal; they have washed their robes and made them white in the blood of the Lamb.'

Calvinism is generally seen as a holding a belief in double predestination; this is found in the Westminster Confession of Faith, which was produced by the 1646 Westminster Assembly as part of the Westminster Standards to be a confession of the Church of England. Chapter 3 is about predestination. It says that God preordained who would be among the elect (and therefore saved), while others would be punished for their sins. It continues to state that from eternity God did 'freely, and unchangeably ordain whatsoever comes to pass . . . By God's decree, some men and angels are predestinated unto everlasting life; and others foreordained to everlasting death.'

Calvin himself did not agree totally with Augustine's interpretation of the text from 1 Timothy. He argued that God's will is hidden and people cannot presume to know what the future will be. God lets humans know only as much as they can understand. When Paul talks about 'all people' he means 'all types of people'. Christians must preach the gospel and treat the future as unlimited election even if this is not the case. If the non-elect reject gospel teachings then they have no excuse when they are punished.

Calvin himself called double predestination 'this dreadful decree' but said that if some people take issue with the decree 'let them answer why they are men rather than oxen or asses'.

Calvin's is a Protestant view. The teachings of the Roman Catholic Church are based on the work of Aquinas. He did not believe that the Fall had removed human freedom and supported single predestination, which means that sinners choose their fate themselves.

> God predestines no one to go to hell; for this, a wilful turning away from God (a mortal sin) is necessary, and persistence in it until the end. In the Eucharistic liturgy and in the daily prayers of her faithful, the Church implores the mercy of God, who does not want 'any to perish, but all to come to repentance': Father, accept this offering from your whole family. Grant us your peace in this life, save us from final damnation, and count us among those you have chosen.
>
> (*Catechism of the Catholic Church* §1037)

Belief in divine election is ultimately a belief that God's justice triumphs; the good are saved while the wicked go to hell.

Universalism (Greek ἀποκατάστασις, 'return' or 'restoration')

Is it true that you will go to hell if you do not believe in God?

This question has long been debated across the passage of Christian history. Many Christians over the centuries have argued that Jesus died to save people who believe in him. Since atheism is a denial of God's existence, such people would be judged and condemned by God. In the past, for example in medieval Europe or ancient Greece, atheism was punishable by death. This attitude was supported in Christian culture by passages in the Bible which clearly say that if someone knowingly rejects the Holy Spirit he or she will go to hell. This is the 'unforgiveable sin' – blasphemy against the Holy Spirit.

However, while this attitude has been a part of mainstream popular Christian culture over the centuries, it is not necessarily reflective of Christian teaching. For example the Roman Catholic Church states that all people must follow their consciences, as well as seek guidance to inform their consciences. Compulsion or threats cannot be used to make people believe.

More specifically, to say 'extra ecclesia nulla salus' ('outside the Church there is no salvation') is rejected by most Christian denominations, such as Roman Catholics.

This rejection of the belief that you must believe in God to be saved developed among Catholic missionaries who were scandalised by the way the conquerors of the New World (the Americas) treated the native populations. In particular, theologians from Spain suggested that if the person preaching Christianity was scandalous in his behaviour, it was unreasonable to say that people should believe the preaching. Ultimately, God is seen by Christians as the judge of people who decides whether they go to heaven or hell; Christians cannot decide this themselves.

Christian teaching today, such as that of the Roman Catholic Church, clearly states that judgement is a matter for God and also that people can be expected to believe in Christianity only if the witness they have seen is credible. In Roman Catholic theology it is possible to be a good person and go to heaven by following your conscience and natural law if you are not a Christian and have had no credible opportunity to become a Christian:

> To the extent that they [Christians] are careless about their [non-Christians] instruction in the faith, or present its teachings falsely, or even fail in their religious, moral, or social life, they must be said to conceal rather than reveal the true nature of God and of religion.
>
> (Vatican II, *Gaudium et Spes*, 1965)

The main tenet of universalism is the idea that hell will not exist for eternity and that eventually the world with all creation will be restored to its pre-Fall state of perfection. It also states that God's omnibenevolence and grace mean that eventually all humans will reach salvation because they have free will and so will eventually achieve perfection themselves. Universalism means that salvation embraces people of any faith or none. Despite cultural, sociological or geographical influences no one will be excluded from reconciliation with God.

John Hick

Hick did not accept that the God who Jesus taught about would judge people and send them to hell. He believed that the main message of the New Testament was reconciliation. He argued that if the purpose of life was to follow a spiritual journey an eternity in hell would not help people to be educated into a more moral way of life.

Karl Barth (1888–1968)

Barth was a Calvinist but, although not a direct follower of universalism, he created a distinct theory of election. He wrote that the idea of some people going to heaven and others to hell was too simplistic. In the incarnation Jesus was both the elector and the elected. Therefore he was both the subject and the object of election.

In Christ, God elects to save all of humanity by overcoming death. In Christ God reveals his love of humanity by entering into the fallen state and dying for others.

Barth says that humans cannot fully understand the mystery of salvation.

It has been argued that although Barth rejected universalism as a principle for salvation, in fact he had created his own form of it, which included everyone who is 'in Christ'. 'I don't believe in universalism, but I do believe in Christ, the reconciler of all' (Barth).

ARGUMENTS AGAINST BELIEF IN LIFE AFTER DEATH

Many philosophers have rejected belief in life after death of any sort. Their arguments focus on three key ideas:

- Belief in an afterlife is the product of human wishful thinking.
- There is no evidence to suggest that people do survive death.
- It makes no sense to talk of a person surviving death, since a person is a physical entity.

Many people fear death because it is something unknown. Some philosophers argue that fear of death being the end leads people to believe in continued existence after death.

In the essay 'Can a Man Witness His Own Funeral?' Anthony Flew argues against belief in an afterlife. He points out that people are mortal and their minds are united to a physical body, which is mortal. As far as is known mental processes do not survive physical death. Furthermore, Flew suggests that *people are what you meet,*' meaning that when we talk about Theresa May or Martin Luther King Jr we mean a particular physical person. We do not mean a disembodied soul that is called Martin Luther King Jr's soul. For Flew, talk of life after death was 'self-contradictory' – it made no sense.

Bertrand Russell also argued that there was no such thing as life after death. His arguments focus on the claim that humans' wishful thinking was the cause of belief in life after death. For Russell, *'All that constitutes a person is a series of experiences connected by memory and by certain similarities of the sort we call habit'* (Russell, 'Belief in Life After Death Comes From Emotion Not Reason').

Russell argues that a person is in fact the experiences that are connected together in his or her memory. He suggested that memories are linked to the brain just as a river is associated with its bed. If the river bed is destroyed, so is any sense of the use of the word 'river' for what was there before. In the same way, at death a person's brain ceases to function and his or her body starts to decay.

For Russell, 'fear of death' is 'instinctive' and the result of this fear is that people believe in life after death. However, Russell argues that the universe is indifferent to people and there is no evidence of life after death.

Russell also puts forward an argument for rejecting belief in life after death:

> Of men in the concrete, most of us think the vast majority very bad. Civilised states spend more than half their revenue on killing each other's citizens. Consider the long history of activities inspired by moral fervour: persecution of heretics, witch-hunts, pogroms leading up to wholesale extermination by poison gas.
>
> (Russell, 'Belief in Life After Death Comes From Emotion Not Reason')

So Russell continues by questioning two things: first, whether the ethical beliefs that led to these types of activities are really from an intelligent creator God, and second, whether people really want those who do conduct events such as witch-hunts or pogroms to live forever. Russell suggests that the world is better understood without God and an afterlife, because if there is evidence in the world for *'deliberate purpose, the purpose must have been that of a fiend'* ('Belief in Life After Death Comes From Emotion Not Reason').

Thought point

Good or bad?

Choose some of the following people. Decide whether what you know of the person's actions supports Russell's arguments. If you do not know who any of these people are, research them online:

* Christopher Columbus
* Adolf Hitler

continued opposite

- Mira Hindley
- Ian Brady
- Alexander Fleming
- Albert Einstein
- Pol Pot
- Chairman Mao
- Arthur 'Bomber' Harris.

SUMMARY

Does death matter?

No

If you do not believe in an afterlife, death is not something that you personally experience, because your life ends at death.

Yes

Death is an unknown.
A final parting with people whom we love.
For religious people it is the dawn of a new stage of life with God, or separated from God in hell.

The origin of belief in the afterlife

Belief in life after death can be traced back to the cultures of ancient China, India and the Middle East.

How do you know who you are?

Personal identity is linked to one's body, mind or both.

Dualism

For example: Plato and Descartes
The mind/soul and the body are separate.
The mind (or soul) forms the centre of identity; it is somehow joined with the body.

Support for dualism

We clearly do experience ourselves as thinking beings distinct from our bodies.
Reports concerning people having out-of-body or near-death experiences.

Plato

> People consist of a body and a soul.
>
> The soul is imprisoned in the body.
>
> After death, the souls of wrongdoers would be re-imprisoned in a body.
>
> Two related arguments to support his belief in an immortal soul:
>
> Argument from opposites
>
> Argument that education is about remembering.

Monism and materialism

The belief that the mind is one with the body and inseparable from it. 'Monist' refers to anyone who believes that there is only one substance. Typically, monists are materialists.

For materialists the identity of a person is linked to the physical body. Identity theory claims that all mental activities are centred in the brain. Materialists can support life after death only if that life is physical, such as in religious teaching about resurrection.

Richard Dawkins

> The only sense in which human beings survive death is through the memories of them in other people's minds or through their genes, some of which are passed on to the next generation of offspring.
>
> Human beings' consciousness has evolved because of the survival advantage it gives.
>
> Support for materialism and monism
>
> It accords with our knowledge of the physical world.
>
> Some support for claims that mental activity is fully explainable in terms of neurone activity in the brain from recent scientific discoveries.

Challenges to this view

Stephen T. Davis pointed to the fact that identity theory has difficulty explaining intentionality.

John Hick's replica theory

> Rejects dualism, while at the same time presenting a defence of belief in bodily resurrection.
>
> Human beings are a 'psycho-somatic unity' (Hick, 'Resurrection of the Person').
>
> Hick's replica theory is one way to understand Paul.
>
> Resurrection is a divine action in which an exact replica of ourselves is created in a different place.
>
> Resurrection could take place instantaneously at death or after a time lapse determined by God.

The replica exists in a 'different space' from us that is observable by God and not by us.

The replica of the person is not the same as a copy.

John Hick suggested the example of a person disappearing in London and reappearing in New York.

Challenges to replica theory:

Identification of the replica with the original person

Multiple replicas

The nature and state of the resurrected body.

Religious views on the afterlife

Christianity – resurrection

Resurrection and the New Testament

The New Testament refers to the afterlife as a paradise, a state of continued existence with God after death (1 Thessalonians 4: 13–14).

Seeing God face to face is called the *beatific vision* (1 Corinthians 13: 12). Christianity since the writing of 1 Corinthians 15 traditionally believes in the resurrection of the body, not just a person's soul or centre of identity.

Peter Geach suggests that resurrection is the only meaningful way in which one can speak of life after death.

At death the soul of a person is separated from her or his body, awaiting the final resurrection, and each person is judged by God (the particular judgment).

God offers forgiveness if people really repent, but forgiveness also requires contrition, confession and an act of satisfaction.

Heaven and hell

Christianity and Islam traditionally believe in a state of existence with God after death (heaven) and a state of separation from God (hell).

Heaven is described in Christian tradition:

As a state of fulfilment of all human longings

As the ultimate goal or end of human existence.

Hell is traditionally characterised as:

A state of separation from God

A place of punishment by God

As an aspect of God's justice.

Problems with belief in hell:

Images do not communicate the idea of a loving and forgiving God.

For some people, the eternal nature of the punishment appears unjust; it is not educative.

If hell is a place of physical suffering, where is it?

Purgatory

A traditional Christian belief in a place where all people who die in relationship with God, but who are not yet perfect, are purified after death.

Heaven, hell and the problem of evil

For some Christians the justification of the existence of God comes from the belief that ultimately God holds everyone to account and judges them according to their actions.

Within Roman Catholic and Orthodox Christian traditions no one is predestined to go to hell.

Richard Swinburne: universal salvation is not traditional belief (*Providence and the Problem of Evil*).

Many theories rely on the concept of God judging people as the basis of moral responsibility.

Predestination and divine election

Some Christians believe in divine election.

By the doctrine of divine election Calvin meant that some people are destined for relationship with God and some are not; this is an aspect of God's sovereignty.

Among some Protestant groups which are offshoots from Calvinism (e.g. followers of Théodore de Bèze) the doctrine of predestination became important.

Some support for belief in predestination in the Bible in Revelation (Revelation 7: 12).

Universalism

John Hick
Karl Barth

Arguments against belief in life after death

There is no evidence to suggest that people do survive death. It makes no sense to talk of a person surviving death, since a person is a physical entity

Flew suggested that 'people are what you meet,' meaning that when we talk about a person we mean a particular physical person.

Bertrand Russell

> Belief in an afterlife is the product of human wishful thinking.
> At death the person's memories that make the person who he or she is also are lost because the brain, like the rest of the body, dies and rots.
> Russell argues that the universe is indifferent to people.
> Russell questions whether people really want those who do conduct events such as witch-hunts or pogroms to live forever.
> Russell suggests that the world is better understood without God and an afterlife.

REVIEW QUESTIONS

Look back over the chapter and check that you can answer the following questions:

1   What is the appeal of materialism?
2   Is replica theory more persuasive than belief in a soul?
3   Which argument against life after death is the strongest in your opinion? Justify your answer.
4   Outline Russell's reasons for rejecting belief in life after death. Is his argument persuasive?

Terminology

Do you know your terminology?

Try to explain the following ideas without looking at your books and notes:

- Replica theory
- Universalism
- Resurrection
- Materialism
- Divine election.

Examination questions practice

EXAM MISTAKES TO AVOID

It is very important that you are able to explain clearly the different views of writers on life after death and the existence of the soul. If you confuse different ideas you will not achieve high marks. In particular, you need to be able to apply the terms 'monism' and 'dualism' accurately to different philosophers. In addition, make sure that you can clearly explain replica theory.

The word 'possible' indicates that you need to discuss whether embodied existence after death happens or can happen. The emphasis of the second question is different from that of the first because the focus of the question is whether embodied life after death happens.

Examination questions practice

Read the question carefully – remember that although Augustine's life is important in understanding him, it is his teachings which you will be questioned on. Answer the question set, not the one you would like to have been set.

To help you improve your answers look at the LEVELS OF RESPONSE.

SAMPLE EXAM-STYLE QUESTION

'Heaven is an idea not a place.' Discuss.

AO1 (15 marks)

This question requires you to consider exactly what the Church teaches about heaven and how this has changed through history. You need to explain that although many people may still have a very literal belief about the sort of heaven described in the Book of Revelation, increasingly people look upon hell as union with God and perhaps the beatific vision.

AO2 (15 marks)

In evaluating the statement you need to show your understanding of the biblical accounts, such as 1 Corinthians 13 and Revelation 22, as well as Church teaching, such as is found in the

Catechism of the Catholic Church. You then need to weigh up the 'evidence' and consider which arguments seem strongest.

Further possible questions

- **'Biblical teaching about the Kingdom of God is very unclear.' Discuss.**
- **To what extent are Richard Dawkins' views on death and the afterlife convincing?**
- **Critically assess different Christian views about election.**
- **Assess the strengths and weaknesses of John Calvin's teachings about predestination.**

FURTHER READING

Chapman, G. 1994. *Catechism of the Catholic Church*, paras. 356–368, 1020–1050.

Hick, J. 1985. *Death and Eternal Life*, Palgrave Macmillan, Part 3.

Hick, J. 1985. *Death and Eternal Life*, Part 3. London: Palgrave Macmillan.

McGrath, A. 2011. *Theology: The Basics*, Ch. 8. Oxford: Blackwell.

McGrath, A. (2011) *Theology: the Basics*, Blackwell, Chapter 8

Craig, W.L. 2001. *The Son Rises: The Historical Evidence for the Resurrection of Jesus*. Oregon: Wipf & Stock.

Davies, B. 1993. *The Thought of Thomas Aquinas* (new ed.). New York: OUP.

Russell, B. 2004. *Why I Am Not a Christian and Other Essays on Religion* (2nd ed.). Oxford: Routledge.

Revelation 20: 2–6, 7–15 and 21:1–8.

Swinburne, R. 1997. *Evolution of a Soul* (rev. ed.). New York: OUP.

Edwards, P. (ed.). 1992. *Immortality*. New York: Prometheus Books.

19 Knowledge of God's existence

Essential terminology

Divine inspiration
Fideism
Inerrant
Infallible
Innate
Magisterium
Non-propositional revelation
Numinous experience
Process theology
Propositional revelation
Revelation
Revelation
Sola gratia
Teleological
Verbal inspiration

Key scholars

Aristotle (384–322 BCE)
Cicero (106 BCE – 43 BCE)
Thomas Aquinas (1225–1274)
John Calvin (1509–1564)
John Locke (1602–1734)
A.N. Whitehead (1861–1947)
Rudolph Otto (1869–1937)
Karl Barth (1886–1968)
Emil Brunner (1889–1966)
Alvin Plantigna (1923–)
Richard Dawkins (1941–)

WHAT YOU WILL LEARN ABOUT IN THIS CHAPTER

- How humans can have knowledge of God's existence
- How knowledge of God's existence can be revealed
- How people can have knowledge of God's existence through Jesus Christ.

THE OCR CHECKLIST

- Natural knowledge of God's existence:
  - as an innate human sense of the divine
    - as all humans are made in God's image they have an inbuilt capacity and desire to know God, including:
    - human openness to beauty and goodness as aspects of God
    - human intellectual ability to reflect on and recognise God's existence
  - as seen in the order of creation
    - what can be known of God can be seen in the apparent design and purpose of nature
- Revealed knowledge of God's existence:
  - through faith and God's grace
    - as humans are sinful and have finite minds, natural knowledge is not sufficient to gain full knowledge of God; knowledge of God is possible through:

continued opposite

- faith
- grace as God's gift of knowledge of himself through the Holy Spirit
○ revealed knowledge of God in Jesus Christ
  - full and perfect knowledge of God is revealed in the person of Jesus Christ and through:
  - the life of the Church
  - the Bible.

Learners should have the opportunity to discuss issues related to Christian ideas on knowledge of God, including:

- whether God can be known through reason alone
- whether faith is sufficient reason for belief in God's existence
- whether the Fall has completely removed all natural human knowledge of God
- whether natural knowledge of God is the same as revealed knowledge of God
- whether belief in God's existence is sufficient to put one's trust in him.

Suggested scholarly views, academic approaches and sources of wisdom and authority

- Romans 1:18–21
- Calvin, J., Institutes of the Christian Religion, I.I and I.II
- Acts 17:16–34.

The earlier chapters on Plato and Aristotle presented ideas which suggest that God is a distant, separate, transcendent being. They both suggest that God is neither part of the universe nor clearly understandable or observable from within our physical universe. This is quite different from the religious understanding of God in faiths, such as Christianity.

'Knowing' is a word used in many different ways. It could mean that we 'know' that something is true because it has proven facts in support of it. It could mean that we 'know' something is true because we believe there is good evidence to support it. On the other hand it can mean that we 'know' somebody, such as a friend, or even just that we 'know' about someone.

Discussion

Give examples of these four ways of knowing. Discuss which of these might apply to God.

	Faith	Philosophy
God	1 This is the view of many believers. 2 It derives from tradition and from holy books, such as the Bible.	1 The understanding of God developed in philosophical argument 2 Emphasises the logical and rational explanation of belief in God
God's existence	1 It is known through faith, revelation and religious experience. 2 The existence of God is beyond doubt.	1 This is demonstrated through rational argument (natural theology). 2 The cosmological, teleological arguments
Creator	1 Genesis (creation narratives), Psalms, Job and Isaiah 2 God is immanent.	1 God is the final cause (Aristotle), or the Prime Mover (Aquinas). 2 God's relationship to the world is non-interventionalist.
Goodness of God	1 This is revealed through God's actions, such as miracles, God's gifts to the world, such as the Ten Commandments, and people's experiences of God. 2 God's actions are described as those of a person acting morally.	1 God is the ultimate source of Good. 2 God is perfect and immutable. 3 God is incapable of lacking goodness. 4 There are links between Plato's Form of the Good and Christian ideas about God's goodness.
Language applied to God	1 God is described using anthropomorphic and anthropopathic language. 2 God is love, a warrior, the lord, a king. 3 God is immanent and personal.	1 God is impersonal and transcendent. 2 The language used to describe God is not anthropomorphic or anthropopathic.

Natural knowledge of God's existence

Natural theology

Natural theology refers to the process of learning about God from the natural world by using reason. Aquinas emphasised the role of propositional revelation and natural theology. In Aquinas' thought, revelations can be accepted as genuine if they accord with Church teaching because the existence of God, who makes the revelations, may be demonstrated using arguments for God's existence.

A difficulty here is that God is completely different from any other thing which we might try to explain, define or understand. God is not an object and, therefore, by definition lies beyond reason.

Natural theology attempts to provide a justification but nevertheless has to acknowledge that God is beyond reason.

Revealed theology talks about knowledge derived from revelations for God to humans and is therefore even more difficult to justify.

Greek philosophers spoke about 'true knowledge', which was said to be incontrovertible fact. However, true knowledge could also be described as 'wisdom', which came from people 'knowing' themselves. The word 'philosophy' itself comes from the Greek words *philos* (φιλία; love) and *sophos* (σοφός; wisdom).

However, true knowledge might indeed be knowledge that comes from God.

> The desire for God is written in the human heart, because man is created by God and for God; and God never ceases to draw man to himself. Only in God will he find the truth and happiness he never stops searching for:
>
> The dignity of man rests above all on the fact that he is called to communion with God. This invitation to converse with God is addressed to man as soon as he comes into being. For if man exists it is because God has created him through love, and through love continues to hold him in existence. He cannot live fully according to truth unless he freely acknowledges that love and entrusts himself to his creator.
>
> (*Catechism of the Catholic Church* §27)

If humans are indeed made 'in imago Dei' (in the image of God) (Genesis 1:27) then it might be natural to assume that they have an inclination to know and understand God to some degree. God is the creator of the cosmos and everything in it so therefore it is through creation that humans can come to know God.

> Our wisdom, in so far as it ought to be deemed true and solid Wisdom, consists almost entirely of two parts: the knowledge of God and of ourselves. But as these are connected together by many ties, it is not easy to determine which of the two precedes and gives birth to the other. For, in the first place, no man can survey himself without forthwith turning his thoughts towards the God in whom he lives and moves; because it is perfectly obvious, that the endowments which we possess cannot possibly be from ourselves; nay, that our very being is nothing else than

Revealed theology

This is theology based on the idea that all religious truth is derived exclusively from the revelations of God to humans.

Revelation

Refers to any act in which God is revealed to human beings. The characteristic of revelation is that it reveals knowledge of God/God's nature.

subsistence in God alone. In the second place, those blessings which unceasingly distil to us from heaven, are like streams conducting us to the fountain. Here, again, the infinitude of good which resides in God becomes more apparent from our poverty. In particular, the miserable ruin into which the revolt of the first man has plunged us, compels us to turn our eyes upwards; not only that while hungry and famishing we may thence ask what we want, but being aroused by fear may learn humility. For as there exists in man something like a world of misery, and ever since we were stripped of the divine attire our naked shame discloses an immense series of disgraceful properties every man, being stung by the consciousness of his own unhappiness, in this way necessarily obtains at least some knowledge of God.

(Calvin, *Institutes of Religion* 1:1)

So the same view was held by the sixteenth-century Protestant reformer as by the Catholic Church today.

Calvin wrote that this knowledge of the divine was innate and so was a 'sense of the divine' (sensus divintatis).

However, it is very difficult to support this argument. Various theories have been put forward. Cicero (first century BCE) developed a theory called the universal consent argument. This says that so many people believe in gods that they or it must exist and even if this does not prove their existence, at least it suggests that it is probable.

There is in fact no subject upon which so much difference of opinion exists, not only among the unlearned but also among educated men; and the views entertained are so various and so discrepant, that, while it is no doubt a possible alternative that none of them is true, it is certainly impossible that more than one should be so.

(*De Natura Deorum* [On the Nature of the Gods] I, 5)

John Locke (1632–1704) dismisses this idea of universal consent being innate. He says the following:

- All ideas must be imprinted on the mind. (definition of idea)
- Innate ideas are ideas; therefore, they are imprinted on the mind. (from 1)
- It is claimed that we have understanding or knowledge, some of which anyway is in the form of innate ideas. (by hypothesis)
- If I know or understand something, p, then I must be aware of or conscious of p. (definition of knowledge)
- Take any innate idea, I; I is imprinted on the mind. (from 2)
- I is or produces knowledge or understanding. (from 3)
- Therefore, whosoever has I must be aware of I. (from 4)

Paul and the unknown god

> While Paul was waiting for them in Athens, he was deeply distressed to see that the city was full of idols. So he argued in the synagogue with the Jews and the devout persons, and also in the marketplace every day with those who happened to be there. Also some Epicurean and Stoic philosophers debated with him. Some said, 'What does this babbler want to say?' Others said, 'He seems to be a proclaimer of foreign divinities.' (This was because he was telling the good news about Jesus and the resurrection.) . . . Then Paul stood in front of the Areopagus and said, 'Athenians, I see how extremely religious you are in every way. For as I went through the city and looked carefully at the objects of your worship, I found among them an altar with the inscription, 'To an unknown god.' What therefore you worship as unknown, this I proclaim to you. The God who made the world and everything in it, he who is Lord of heaven and earth, does not live in shrines made by human hands, nor is he served by human hands, as though he needed anything, since he himself gives to all mortals life and breath and all things.
>
> (Acts 16:17–18, 22–25)

Paul then tries to explain to the Athenians that they are worshipping God at this particular altar. Therefore they have an innate sense of belief.

Finally, the Catholic Church acknowledges a sort of universal consent because prayer, meditation and rituals are so widespread in the world, although they are different:

> In many ways, throughout history down to the present day, men have given expression to their quest for God in their religious beliefs and behaviour: in their prayers, sacrifices, rituals, meditations, and so forth. These forms of religious expression, despite the ambiguities they often bring with them, are so universal that one may well call man a religious being: From one ancestor [God] made all nations to inhabit the whole earth, and he allotted the times of their existence and the boundaries of the places where they would live, so that they would search for God and perhaps grope for him and find him – though indeed he is not far from each one of us. For 'in him we live and move and have our being.' . . . 'Let the hearts of those who seek the LORD rejoice.' Although man can forget God or reject him, He never ceases to call every man to seek him, so as to find life and happiness. But this search for God demands of man every effort of intellect, a sound will, 'an upright heart', as well as the witness of others who teach him to seek God.
>
> (*Catechism of the Catholic Church* §28, 30)

The passage echoes exactly the continuation of Paul's teaching in Acts 17.

Numinous experience

Rudolph Otto (1869–1937) pointed out that a central element of direct experiences of God was an 'apprehension of the wholly other', which Otto called the 'numinous'. By 'numinous' Otto meant the world that is beyond the physical observable universe in which we live. Hence, Otto refers to direct experiences of God as experiences of the 'wholly other' (Otto, *The Idea of the Holy*).

Beauty and goodness as aspects of God

The human person: with his openness to truth and beauty, his sense of moral goodness, his freedom and the voice of his conscience, with his longings for the infinite and for happiness, man questions himself about God's existence. In all this he discerns signs of his spiritual soul. The soul, the 'seed of eternity we bear in ourselves, irreducible to the merely material', can have its origin only in God.

(*Catechism of the Catholic Church* §33)

Human beings can appreciate the beauty of the world around them and the cosmos as a whole. Rudolf Otto described this is a 'numinous experience' – seeing, hearing or feeling something 'wholly other'.

As can be seen through the teachings of the *Catechism*, the Catholic Church believes that this awareness can come only directly from God.

A very similar view is found in Calvin's writings:

It must be acknowledged, therefore, that in each of the works of God, and more especially in the whole of them taken together, the divine perfections are delineated as in a picture, and the whole human race thereby invited and allured to acquire the knowledge of God, and, in consequence of this knowledge, true and complete felicity. Moreover, while his perfections are thus most vividly displayed, the only means of ascertaining their practical operation and tendency is to descend into ourselves, and consider how it is that the Lord there manifests his wisdom, power, and energy, – how he there displays his justice, goodness, and mercy. For although David (Psalm 92:6) justly complains of the extreme infatuation of the ungodly in not pondering the deep counsels of God, as exhibited in the government of the human race, what he elsewhere says (Psalm 40) is most true, that the wonders of the divine wisdom in this respect are more in number than the hairs of our head.

(Calvin, *Institutes* 5.10)

Teachings about moral goodness are similarly found in Catholic and Calvinist teachings.

The Catholic Church sees natural moral law (see Chapter 10) as demonstrating that the human sense of goodness is innate. Similarly, Calvin regarded conscience as being God-given.

Therefore, lest this prove a stumbling-block to any, let us observe that in man government is twofold: the one spiritual, by which the conscience is trained to piety and divine worship; the other civil, by which the individual is instructed in those duties which, as men and citizens, we are bold to perform (see Book 4, chap. 10, sec. 3–6). To these two forms are commonly given the not inappropriate names of spiritual and temporal jurisdiction, intimating that the former species has reference to the life of the soul, while the latter relates to matters of the present life, not only to food and clothing, but to the enacting of laws which require a man to live among his fellows purely honourably, and modestly. The former has its seat within the soul, the latter only regulates the external conduct. We may call the one the spiritual, the other the civil kingdom . . . Simple knowledge may exist in man, as it were shut up; therefore this sense, which sits man before the bar of God, is set over him as a kind of sentinel to observe and spy out all his secrets, that nothing may remain buried in darkness. Hence the ancient proverb, Conscience is a thousand witnesses. For the same reason Peter also employs the expression, 'the answer of a good conscience' (1 Pet. 3:21), for tranquillity of mind; when persuaded of the grace of Christ, we boldly present ourselves before God. And the author of the Epistle to the Hebrews says, that we have 'no more conscience of sins' (Heb. 10:2), that we are held as freed or acquitted, so that sin no longer accuses us.

(Calvin, *Institutes* 3.19.15)

The order of creation

Arguments for the existence of God have developed particularly in the last millennium. Some centre on the belief that the cosmos could have been brought into existence only by an 'uncaused causer' and this causer must inevitably be God.

Created in God's image and called to know and love him, the person who seeks God discovers certain ways of coming to know him. These are also called proofs for the existence of God, not in the sense of proofs in the natural sciences, but rather in the sense of 'converging and convincing arguments', which allow us to attain certainty about the truth. These 'ways' of approaching God from creation have a twofold point of departure: the physical world, and the human person.

The world: starting from movement, becoming, contingency, and the world's order and beauty, one can come to a knowledge of God as the origin and the end of the universe.

As St. Paul says of the Gentiles: For what can be known about God is plain to them, because God has shown it to them. Ever since the creation of the world his invisible nature, namely, his eternal power and deity, has been clearly perceived in the things that have been made.

And St. Augustine issues this challenge: Question the beauty of the earth, question the beauty of the sea, question the beauty of the air distending and diffusing itself, question the beauty of the sky . . . question all these realities. All respond: 'See, we are beautiful.' Their beauty is a profession [confessio]. These beauties are subject to change. Who made them if not the Beautiful One [Pulcher] who is not subject to change?

(*Catechism of the Catholic Church* §31–32)

Calvin and God as creator

John Calvin
Classic Image/Alamy

Calvin taught that God demonstrated his existence to human beings by 'accommodating' to their limited minds. The finite cannot understand the infinite and the problem of reason was shown at the beginning of this chapter. Humans cannot experience God directly but can see his 'appearance' in the world around them.

Since the perfection of blessedness consists in the knowledge of God, he has been pleased, in order that none might be excluded from the means of obtaining felicity, not only to deposit in our minds that seed of religion of which we have already spoken, but so to manifest his perfections in the whole structure of the universe, and daily place himself in our view, that we cannot open our eyes without being compelled to behold him. His essence, indeed, is incomprehensible, utterly transcending all human thought; but on each of his works his glory is engraven in characters so bright, so distinct, and so illustrious, that none, however dull and illiterate, can plead ignorance as their excuse. Hence, with perfect truth, the Psalmist exclaims, 'He covereth himself with light as with a garment' (Psalm 104:2); as if he had said, that God for the first time was arrayed in visible attire when, in the creation of the world, he displayed those glorious banners, on which, to whatever side we turn, we behold his perfections visibly portrayed. In the same place, the Psalmist aptly compares the expanded heavens to his royal tent, and says, 'He layeth the beams of his chambers in the waters, maketh the clouds his chariot, and walketh upon the wings of the wind,' sending forth the winds and lightnings as his swift messengers. And because the glory of his power and wisdom is more refulgent in the firmament, it is frequently designated as his palace. And, first, wherever you turn your eyes, there is no portion of the world, however minute, that does not exhibit at least some sparks of beauty; while it is impossible to contemplate the vast and beautiful fabric as it extends around, without being overwhelmed by the immense weight of glory. Hence, the author of the Epistle to the Hebrews elegantly describes the visible worlds as images of the invisible

(Heb. 11:3), the elegant structure of the world serving us as a kind of mirror, in which we may behold God, though otherwise invisible. For the same reason, the Psalmist attributes language to celestial objects, a language which all nations understand (Psalm 19:1), the manifestation of the Godhead being too clear to escape the notice of any people, however obtuse. The apostle Paul, stating this still more clearly, says, 'That which may be known of God is manifest in them, for God has showed it unto them. For the invisible things of him from the creation of the world are clearly seen, being understood by the things that are made, even his eternal power and Godhead' (Rom. 1:20).

(Calvin, Institutes 1.5.1)

Teleological arguments

The teleological arguments for the existence of God look at the universe and everything in it and attempt to show that it has all been designed for a purpose. Teleological arguments examine if there is a designer of things that appear to have been designed, and whether the designer is God. It looks at the features of the universe and asks whether they can account for their own existence.

Usually teleological arguments infer the existence of God from a particular aspect or character of the world – namely the presence of order, regularity and purpose. Order, regularity and purpose are seen as marks of design, and the arguments conclude that God must be the source of that design. The kind of thing that is usually appealed to as evidence of order in the universe is the solar system, with the planets revolving in their predictable orbits, or the human eye.

Paley's argument from design (see Chapter 4) starts with the analogy of a watch and says that if someone found a watch by chance they would inevitably infer that someone had designed and made it. This could not have happened by chance and therefore it is logical to say the same thing about the world.

The twentieth century saw the development of process theology.

Process theology was developed by A.N. Whitehead (1861–1947), Charles Hartshorne (1897–2000) and J.B. Cobb (1925–).

Whitehead and Hartshorne argued that God affects and is affected by temporal processes. This is therefore different from the view that God is non-temporal (eternal), unchanging (immutable) and unaffected by the world (impassible).

Whitehead's original principles were as follows:

* It is as true to say that God is permanent and the World fluent, as that the World is permanent and God is fluent.

- It is as true to say that God is one and the World many, as that the World is one and God many.
- It is as true to say that, in comparison with the World, God is actual eminently, as that, in comparison with God, the World is actual eminently.
- It is as true to say that the World is immanent in God, as that God is immanent in the World.
- It is as true to say that God transcends the World, as that the World transcends God.
- It is as true to say that God creates the World, as that the World creates God.

(Whitehead, *Process and Reality*, 1978)

This theory argues that God and the world work together and that God therefore reveals himself through every moment in the cosmos.

Revealed knowledge of God's existence

In Christianity there are two types of revelations:

- Propositional revelation
- Non-propositional revelation.

Propositional revelation

The phrase '*propositional revelation*' refers to God revealing truths about himself to human beings. It is called 'propositional' to show that the revelations are statements of facts. Since these revelations demonstrate facts from God or about God, Christians argue that they are true.

Christians believe that the Ten Commandments revealed to Moses on Mount Sinai were a revelation from God. For most Christians the Ten Commandments are not up for discussion or question; they are simply facts laid down by God. The distinctive feature of propositional revelation is that it reveals knowledge from God, which is without error or need of reinterpretation.

There are many possible types of propositional revelations, such as through holy books like the Bible, visions or other religious experiences of God. In relation to propositional revelation, faith is to accept the revelation from God.

Thomas Aquinas (*Summa Theologiae*) argued that 'faith' is about knowledge of God who is transcendent. Therefore, although this is more certain than opinion, it is not certain in the way scientific knowledge is. Aquinas said that even if faith cannot be demonstrated in the same way as science, it is still better than opinions. He believed that faith is based on something which is factual, and opinion is not. Nevertheless, faith cannot be proved true by reason. Propositional revelations cannot be demonstrated using human reason.

People who believe in propositional revelation do not reject the use of reason. They accept that God's revelations cannot be proved by human reason, but that God can be revealed through using reason in the world. An example of this is the attempts to prove that God exists using the cosmological and teleological arguments.

Aquinas is a good example of a person who emphasised the role of propositional revelation and natural theology. Aquinas said that revelations could be accepted as genuine if they were in accordance with Church teaching because this teaching was also revealed from Jesus and the apostles.

The Magisterium
Within the Roman Catholic Church the teaching authority of the Church is called 'the Magisterium'.

The genuineness of a revelation could be assessed by referring to previous teaching of the Magisterium.

Criticisms of propositional revelation

- Propositional revelation assumes that the person receiving the revelation is passive. Many philosophers have suggested that, from the perspective of psychology, the human mind actively receives knowledge. So, when you learn something your mind remembers it accurately. If you hear a piece of gossip you have to remember it actively to be able to repeat it. Secondly, we make mistakes even when trying to learn things accurately. This could mean that propositional revelations of God may not be recorded accurately.
- How can anyone tell which propositions are true? The criteria of agreeing with accepted Church teaching do not guarantee that a revelation is genuine. The after-effects of a revelation could be given, such as Paul becoming a Christian after the revelation on the road to Damascus (Acts 9: 1–31). This does not provide absolute proof of whether the revelation is genuine.
- Although many religions claim to have received propositional revelations, often their truth claims conflict. How can this be resolved? How can it be shown which truth claim is correct? Does this show that all revelations from God are limited by the fact that when they are revealed to human beings the person experiencing the revelation may misunderstand it?
- There is no way directly to verify or prove that propositional revelations happen.

Sherlock Holmes

Baker Street Scans/Alamy

Non-propositional revelation

Non-propositional revelation is the idea that God does not reveal facts or truths to people. Rather, the believer recognises where God is acting in human history and human experience. A religious believer may see God in a beautiful natural scene which reveals God to the person observing it. William Paley was famously impressed by the structure of the human eye, while Arthur Conan Doyle's character Sherlock Holmes was impressed by the beauty of nature.

> How sweet the morning air is! See how that one little cloud floats like a pink feather from some gigantic flamingo. Now the red rim of the sun pushes itself over the London cloud-bank. It shines on a good many folk, but on none, I dare bet, who are on a stranger errand than you and I. How small we feel with our petty ambitions and strivings in the presence of the great elemental forces of Nature!
>
> (Doyle, *Sign of Four*)

> He [Sherlock Holmes] walked past the couch to the open window, and held up the drooping stalk of a moss rose, looking down at the dainty blend of crimson and green. It was a new phase of his character to me, for I had never before seen him show any keen interest in natural objects.
>
> 'There is nothing in which deduction is so necessary as in religion', said he, leaning with his back against the shutters. 'It can be built upon an exact science by the reasoner. Our highest assurance of the goodness of providence seems to rest in the flowers. All other things, our powers, our desires, our food, are really necessary for our existence in the first instance. But this rose is an extra. Its smell, its colour are an embellishment of life, not a condition of it. It is only goodness which gives extras so I say again we have much hope from the flowers.'
>
> (Doyle, *The Adventures of Sherlock Holmes*)

For many people their thoughts are raised to the possibility of God through the beauty that is found in the world around them. For them, nature reveals God to them. However, this revelation is indirect and can be a matter of interpretation. Therefore, this type of revelation is called non-propositional as it is a human being's recognition of God's acts in and through the world.

In this view of revelation, religious books, such as the Bible, witness to and record how God's revelation has been understood in history by believers. God acted in history, and the views of people who witness these acts are what are recorded in the Bible. It could be said that people learn about God through the miracles (signs) that Jesus worked and people who witnessed these acts interpreted what they saw. These non-propositional revelations are indirect experiences of God, which can lead a person to understand something about God. In this sense faith can be seen as how a person experiences God through events in daily life – faith is a way of seeing the world. A Christian may look at a beautiful landscape and come to understand something about God as the Creator, while an atheist may look at the same landscape and gain no understanding of God.

If the Bible is regarded as a non-propositional revelation, then the role of the reader and his or her interpretation is of crucial importance, as the revelation takes place in the reader's life. The authority given to non-propositional revelation comes from the fact that people are free to respond to God's revelation or not, as it is not received passively.

> For the wrath of God is revealed from heaven against all ungodliness and wickedness of those who by their wickedness suppress the truth. For what can be known about God is plain to them, because God has shown it to them. Ever since the creation of the world his eternal power and divine nature, invisible though they are, have been understood and seen through the things he has made. So they are without excuse; for though they knew God, they did not honor him as God or give thanks to him, but they became futile in their thinking, and their senseless minds were darkened.
>
> (Romans 1:18–21)

Criticisms of non-propositional revelation

- Non-propositional revelations are the result of human understanding and interpretation of events and do not reveal direct knowledge of God. They cannot be considered as free from error (infallible). In this case there is no way of resolving theological debates apart from appealing to one's own experience. On the other hand the propositional view is that one can appeal to facts revealed by God as a basis for debate.
- In the non-propositional view of revelation, the content of the revelation is inevitably a matter of interpretation. Although Arthur Conan Doyle wrote about the beauty of nature revealing God, as did William Paley and many other writers, it is equally possible to wonder at the beauty of nature and not experience a non-propositional revelation. Richard Dawkins, the evolutionary biologist and critic of religious belief, is equally moved by the beauty he finds in the world around him. However, for Dawkins the fact that we evolved through our genes and developed a sense of consciousness which enables us to understand a little of our place in the universe and in the process of evolution is wonderful.

Non-propositional revelation

This refers to the idea that God does not reveal facts or truths to people; instead the religious believer recognises God acting in human history and human experience. For example a religious believer may come to see God in a beautiful natural scene; the scene reveals God to the person observing it.

Consciousness is a great thing but it does not lead Richard Dawkins to a belief in God.

The spotlight passes but, exhilaratingly, before doing so it gives us time to comprehend something of this place in which we fleetingly find ourselves and the reason that we do so. We are alone among the animals in being able to say before we die: Yes, that is why it was worth coming to life in the first place.

(Dawkins, *Unweaving the Rainbow*)

Faith and God's grace

Humans are sinful and have finite minds. Therefore natural knowledge is not sufficient to gain full knowledge of God; knowledge of God is possible through faith and grace, which is God's gift of knowledge of himself through the Holy Spirit.

It is possible to argue that knowledge of God which is discovered by the creation of the cosmos and the work of the conscience should be sufficient to enable human beings to enter into a relationship with God. However, this does not take into account the consequences of the Fall.

By the knowledge of God, I understand that by which we not only conceive that there is some God, but also apprehend what it is for our interest, and conducive to his glory, what, in short, it is befitting to know concerning him. For, properly speaking, we cannot say that God is known where there is no religion or piety. I am not now referring to that species of knowledge by which men, in themselves lost and under curse, apprehend God as a Redeemer in Christ the Mediator. I speak only of that simple and primitive knowledge, to which the mere course of nature would have conducted us, had Adam stood upright. For although no man will now, in the present ruin of the human race, perceive God to be either a father, or the author of salvation, or propitious in any respect, until Christ interpose to make our peace; still it is one thing to perceive that God our Maker supports us by his power, rules us by his providence, fosters us by his goodness, and visits us with all kinds of blessings, and another thing to embrace the grace of reconciliation offered to us in Christ. Since, then, the Lord first appears, as well in the creation of the world as in the general doctrine of Scripture, simply as a Creator, and afterwards as a Redeemer in Christ, – a twofold knowledge of him hence arises.

(Calvin, *Institutes* 1.2.1)

Calvin is saying that without Jesus Christ as Redeemer and the salvation he offered it would not be possible for humans to achieve the knowledge of God which restores the relationship with him.

The consequences of original sin are seen in ignorance, desire and bad behaviour.

> But this 'intimate and vital bond of man to God' can be forgotten, overlooked, or even explicitly rejected by man. Such attitudes can have different causes: revolt against evil in the world; religious ignorance or indifference; the cares and riches of this world; the scandal of bad example on the part of believers; currents of thought hostile to religion; finally, that attitude of sinful man which makes him hide from God out of fear and flee his call.
>
> (*Catechism of the Catholic Church* §29)

> By natural reason man can know God with certainty, on the basis of his works. But there is another order of knowledge, which man cannot possibly arrive at by his own powers: the order of divine Revelation. Through an utterly free decision, God has revealed himself and given himself to man. This he does by revealing the mystery, his plan of loving goodness, formed from all eternity in Christ, for the benefit of all men. God has fully revealed this plan by sending us his beloved Son, our Lord Jesus Christ, and the Holy Spirit.
>
> (*Catechism of the Catholic Church* §50)

However strong someone's faith is it still needs some form of reason behind it. 'Faith is the great cop-out, the great excuse to evade the need to think and evaluate evidence. Faith is belief in spite of, even perhaps because of, the lack of evidence' (Richard Dawkins, Lecture from 'The Nullifidian'). Aquinas maintained a distinction between two types of faith:

- Unformed faith – an example might be of someone who may believe that Jesus was God but cannot bring him- or herself to believe that this is true.
- Formed faith – this is faith which is prepared to accept what the person can believe through his or her intellect. This type of faith takes discipline and prayer to develop.

Calvin's teaching about faith is found in the *Institutes*:

> We have also seen, that since the knowledge of the divine goodness cannot be of much importance unless it leads us to confide in it, we must

Special revelation is the belief that knowledge of God and of spiritual matters can be discovered through means such as miracles or the scriptures. It is a way of knowing God's truth through means other than human reason.

General revelation (natural revelation) is knowledge about God and spiritual matters which are discovered through natural means, such as looking at the physical universe, philosophy and reasoning. Christians use the term to describe knowledge of God which is plainly available to all humans.

exclude a knowledge mingled with doubt, – a knowledge which, so far from being firm, is continually wavering. But the human mind, when blinded and darkened, is very far from being able to rise to a proper knowledge of the divine will; nor can the heart, fluctuating with perpetual doubt, rest secure in such knowledge. Hence, in order that the word of God may gain full credit, the mind must be enlightened, and the heart confirmed, from some other quarter. We shall now have a full definition of faith if we say that it is a firm and sure knowledge of the divine favour toward us, founded on the truth of a free promise in Christ, and revealed to our minds, and sealed on our hearts, by the Holy Spirit.

(Calvin, *Institutes* 3.2.7)

Both the Catholic Church and Calvin state that it is the Holy Spirit which bestows grace on people. Grace is required to mend the relationship with God. This can happen only if it is his will.

The New Testament is said to provide a complete and final revelation of Christ. However, does the knowledge from the Bible explain the essence of God? The answer is made clear by Paul:

Therefore, since it is by God's mercy that we are engaged in this ministry, we do not lose heart. We have renounced the shameful things that one hides; we refuse to practice cunning or to falsify God's word; but by the open statement of the truth we commend ourselves to the conscience of everyone in the sight of God. And even if our gospel is veiled, it is veiled to those who are perishing. In their case the god of this world has blinded the minds of the unbelievers, to keep them from seeing the light of the gospel of the glory of Christ, who is the image of God. For we do not proclaim ourselves; we proclaim Jesus Christ as Lord and ourselves as your slaves for Jesus' sake. For it is the God who said, 'Let light shine out of darkness,' who has shone in our hearts to give the light of the knowledge of the glory of God in the face of Jesus Christ.

(2 Corinthians 4:1–4)

The Catholic Church continues by saying,

'The Christian economy, therefore, since it is the new and definitive Covenant, will never pass away; and no new public revelation is to be expected before the glorious manifestation of our Lord Jesus Christ.' Yet even if Revelation is already complete, it has not been made completely explicit; it remains for Christian faith gradually to grasp its full significance over the course of the centuries.

(*Catechism of the Catholic Church* §66)

Revelation through the Bible

What is the Bible?

- The Bible is the divinely inspired and revealed Word of God.
- The Bible is a collection of separate books that were first written down in the period from 1200 BCE to CE 97.

INTRODUCTION – HOLY SCRIPTURE

People speak of 'holy scripture' revealing God or containing revelations from God, but what does this mean?

In religious tradition, some books, such as the Bible, are given the title 'holy'. 'Holy' originally meant 'separate' or 'set apart' and therefore came to be associated with God. Calling books such as the Bible holy is suggesting a special status linked to God. For religious believers, books such as the Bible are set apart by the fact that they are revelation – they reveal God to the world.

THE REVELATION OF GOD THROUGH SCRIPTURE

What sort of revelation of God is found in the Bible? For some people the Bible is a propositional revelation from God that reveals his divine word; for other people the Bible is a non-propositional revelation in which God is revealed through the writings in the Bible that record the individual authors' experiences of God.

THE BIBLE IS THE DIVINELY INSPIRED WORD OF GOD

A propositional revelation view

People who believe that the Bible is a propositional revelation of God would say that it is the Word of God. The role of the writers of the books of the Bible is limited or non-existent as it is God's revelation. The Bible is divinely inspired and this is what caused the author to write each book.

Some fundamentalist Christians use the term *'verbal inspiration'* to indicate the divine origins or authorship of every word in the Bible. In this view

Verbal inspiration
Refers to the divine origins or authorship of every word in the Bible. According to this view God effectively dictates the books of the Bible by divine inspiration.

God effectively dictated the books of the Bible. Therefore, someone who believed in divine dictation would believe that the Bible is inerrant (without error).

While people may disagree about divine versus verbal inspiration, all Christians who believe that the Bible is, or contains, propositional revelations from God would point out that the Bible reveals propositions about God and God's wishes for human beings that are true. For example the Ten Commandments were given to Moses by God, and these reveal basic commands for human beings about how they should live.

Biblical fundamentalism

The term 'fundamentalism' comes from nineteenth-century theologians and biblical scholars who were opposed to liberal approaches to biblical interpretation, which cast doubt on things such as the miracles in the Bible and the Genesis creation stories.

Biblical fundamentalists today believe that the Bible is the inspired Word of God and that it is without errors. The Bible is the authoritative Christian book that reveals God's will to people. Many of them accept stories such as the Genesis creation accounts as historically true documents.

Limitations of this approach

- Fundamentalism does not help in interpreting the Bible. The Bible's authoritative status may be accepted, but unless the reader also has inspiration to read the Bible in the way God wants, how is the Bible's message any clearer?
- A fundamentalist accepts only one way of interpreting the Bible, but there is no proof that this is the correct one. To claim that their view is correct is a purely subjective view.

Thought point

If the Bible and its contents are revealed by God, do you have to obey them?

Read the following passages in the Bible and then answer the questions that follow:

continued opposite

- Leviticus 19:27–28
- Leviticus 20:9
- Deuteronomy 21:18–21
- Matthew 5:27–30
- Mark 10:21–22
- What is each passage about?
- Do you agree with the teaching in every passage? Give reasons to support your answer.
- If the Bible is a propositional revelation, what do you think the revelation is which is contained in these passages?
- Could a person be a Christian who believes that the Bible is inspired and a propositional revelation from God and yet not follow the teaching contained in these passages?

A fundamentalist maintains that the role of the author role is just that of a passive recorder of God's revelation. Other Christians believe that the Bible reveals true propositions about God but that they have been recorded by human beings in their manner. Therefore a reader has to interpret and understand it in order to know the revelation it contains from God. These approaches are different but both would still claim that the Bible is without errors.

An example of the propositional revelation approach to the Bible

The Catholic Church is one tradition which believes that the Bible is a propositional revelation from God and is therefore the Word of God: God is the author of sacred scripture. 'The divinely revealed realities, which are contained and presented in the text of sacred scripture, have been written down under the inspiration of the Holy Spirit' (*Catechism of the Catholic Church* §105). The Church also stresses the role of the human authors. God communicates to Christians through the Bible in a human way. Therefore the reader has to try to understand the intentions of the authors.

> In order to discover the sacred authors' intention, the reader must take into account the conditions of their time and culture. The literary genres in use at that time, and the modes of feeling, speaking and narrating then current. For the fact is that truth is differently presented and expressed in the various types of historical writing, prophetical and poetical texts, and in other forms of literary expression.
>
> (*Catechism of the Catholic Church* §110)

The Catholic Church indicates that while the Bible is a propositional revelation of the Word of God, it still needs to be interpreted if its message is to speak to Christians today. It is important to remember that Roman Catholics do not interpret the Bible literally.

A non-propositional revelation view: the Bible is a record of human experiences of God

Many Christians believe that the Bible is divinely inspired but do not accept the idea that it is a propositional revelation from God. They would consider the Bible to be a record of human beings' experiences of God. Therefore, the Bible is a non-propositional revelation of God since it reveals God to people indirectly.

This non-propositional view of the Bible sees the scriptures as presenting pictures and images of God's revelation. However, Jesus' significance can be understood only through faith, not through statements in the text. Therefore, people read the Bible and then work out what the revelation means to them today.

This non-propositional understanding of revelation in the Bible is often associated with what has been called liberal biblical interpretation. An important person in this movement was Friedrich Schleiermacher (1768–1834), who said that religious faith is a matter of experience and feeling in the life of the believer. Schleiermacher concluded that the Bible reveals that Jesus' mission was not about saving people but about raising their awareness of God.

Thought point

Is the non-propositional revelation of Jesus clear?

c Image of Jesus

Dorling Kindersley Ltd/
Alamy

a Image of Jesus

CBW/Alamy

b Image of Jesus

FineArt/Alamy

continued opposite

- Which picture best represents Jesus as revealed in the Gospels?
- Which picture appeals most to you?
- Discuss your answers.
- Can you identify a problem related to the non-propositional view of the Bible? Think about how you could use these pictures as examples in your answer.

THE AUTHORITY OF SCRIPTURE

The Church of England

> Holy Scripture containeth all things necessary to salvation: so that whatsoever is not read therein, nor may be proved thereby, is not to be required of any man, that it should be believed as an article of the Faith, or be thought requisite or necessary to salvation. In the name of the Holy Scripture we do understand those canonical Books of the Old and New Testament, of whose authority was never any doubt in the Church
> (*The 39 Articles*, Article 6)

Apostolic authority

The link between the books of the Bible and Jesus is very important to Christians. Jesus gave his authority to the apostles (Mark 16:12–20) and the apostles were witnesses of Jesus' life and work. Peter was commissioned by Jesus as the leader of the apostles (Matthew 16) and given authority by Jesus on earth in his name. Bishops of the Church are successors to the apostles because the authority of the apostles has been handed on to the bishops.

THE AUTHORITY OF THE BIBLE

For an atheist or agnostic the Bible may be a historically important text. It may help to inform people about the society and beliefs of peoples living 2,000 to 3,500 years ago. However, does this mean that the Bible is an authoritative document? For Christians the Bible is a document that is authoritative. Calling the Bible 'scripture' implies this point.

Maurice Wiles ('The Authority of Scripture in a Contemporary Theology') says that authority may have more than one sense. In a 'hard' sense, authority suggests something having the status of a law. Authority in a 'soft sense' might be saying someone is an 'authority' on politics, for example.

This is a statement about the way a person speaks on a subject; it does not necessarily imply that the speaker is always correct.

The Bible has traditionally been seen as an authority similar to the 'law' rather than to an authoritative and learned speaker on a subject. Also, if someone believes that the Bible is divinely inspired and reveals the Word of God, then clearly it is authoritative and should be followed.

Sometimes, however, 'laws' can need clarification and interpretation to meet new issues. Christians disagree about whether the Bible is a law in this sense. If the Bible is divinely inspired and inerrant, it should not need to be reinterpreted and, unlike human laws, the Bible would be seen as timeless.

So, saying the Bible is authoritative may imply that the Bible requires interpretation, and that what it reveals about God is not always straightforward and clear.

What if the Bible is divinely inspired?

Verbal inspiration

If the Bible is verbally inspired, every word comes from God, and therefore every word should be respected and followed. However, what this might mean is disputed:

- The Bible says that the death penalty can be used as a punishment for many offences, and many of the punishments in the Jewish scriptures appear harsh to modern readers (Exodus 21).
- The meaning of the Genesis creation stories is disputed among Christians.
- Can the Bible be disobeyed? If the Bible is a verbally inspired revelation from God, then disobeying any instruction in the Bible would be a rejection of God's commands.

Divine inspiration

- The majority of Christians believe that the Bible is divinely inspired, but this still leaves questions.
- The idea of disobeying specific instructions from God is problematic, but an issue arises about what the specific instructions from God are. If the book is divinely inspired but not verbally inspired, then the revelation of God is within the text. Identifying it could be problematic.
- Many Christians have difficulty accepting some of the laws about moral behaviour from both the New and Old Testaments. For example Jesus

clearly states that divorce is wrong, but many Christian Churches permit divorce and in some circumstances remarriage.

- Some of the passages found within the Bible conflict with many Christians' views today. Paul's statements about women, for example, do not fit well with modern ideas about male and female equality.

If Christians believe that the Bible is divinely inspired but is expressed in the language and culture of the times in which the Bible books were written, then the problem for any reader of the Bible is to identify the knowledge revealed about God in the biblical books.

Natural versus revealed theology

Calvin's theology raises questions about natural and revealed theology: are we looking at the transcendent creator or the immanent redeemer?

The Catholic Church would appear to accept God as known through natural theology.

'Our holy mother, the Church, holds and teaches that God, the first principle and last end of all things, can be known with certainty from the created world by the natural light of human reason.' Without this capacity, man would not be able to welcome God's revelation. Man has this capacity because he is created 'in the image of God'.

In the historical conditions in which he finds himself, however, man experiences many difficulties in coming to know God by the light of reason alone:

Though human reason is, strictly speaking, truly capable by its own natural power and light of attaining to a true and certain knowledge of the one personal God, who watches over and controls the world by his providence, and of the natural law written in our hearts by the Creator; yet there are many obstacles which prevent reason from the effective and fruitful use of this inborn faculty. For the truths that concern the relations between God and man wholly transcend the visible order of things, and, if they are translated into human action and influence it, they call for self-surrender and abnegation. The human mind, in its turn, is hampered in the attaining of such truths, not only by the impact of the senses and the imagination, but also by disordered appetites which are the consequences of original sin. So it happens that men in such matters easily persuade themselves that what they would not like to be true is false or at least doubtful.

(*Catechism of the Catholic Church* §36–37)

This question was the topic of a famous debate of 1934 between Emil Brunner and Karl Barth.

The heart of the debate is whether one can attain knowledge of God 'naturally' or whether, on the other hand, the grace of God is strictly required for that.

Barth is very clear in stating that there is no way to knowledge of God by way of human reason – in other words, there is absolutely no source of authority aside from the Word of God. For Brunner instead, natural theology is the result of the theoretical possibility for humanity to be addressed by God. The actual realisation of this depends on Grace. Therefore, Brunner maintains, the traditional doctrine of *sola gratia* is not endangered by this conception of natural theology.

Brunner followed Calvin's idea that the general revelation of God in nature is a means for people to become aware of what God wants and also of their state as a consequence of the Fall.

Sola gratia
By grace alone.

Brunner

Brunner makes a distinction between two questions: the question of the revelation in creation, and the question of man's natural knowledge of God. He says that a theology which remains true to the Bible cannot deny the reality of revelation in creation. He believes that this distinction between natural theology and revelation is essential: one should be rejected, but one is biblically affirmed.

He points to the sinfulness of humans as proof of a revelation in nature. Since people are sinners and cannot propose a genuine natural theology but nevertheless try, there must be a revelation in creation behind their attempts. He says that God cannot be known through nature but that trying to know shows people's sin and points to a revelation in creation beyond their understanding.

Human beings, even those who know nothing of the historical revelation, are such that they cannot help forming an idea of God and making pictures of God in their minds. Brunner says that the history of religions is proof of this.

Brunner says that there is a revelation in creation and cited Romans 1:19–20a:

> For what can be known about God is plain to them, because God has shown it to them. Ever since the creation of the world his eternal power and divine nature, invisible though they are, have been understood and seen through the things he has made.

He points to the existence of some kind of original revelation in nature, which, because of sin, people cannot understand and will always distort.

Brunner argues that the Apostles had no interest in explaining theoretically how sinful human beings could understand natural theology, but wanted to answer the question, 'How should we address the man to whom the message of Jesus Christ is to be proclaimed?' He says that the Fall does not mean that humans are no longer responsible, but that they cease to understand their responsibility properly. He said, 'It is sin which makes idols out of the revelation in Creation.'

He concludes that philosophy cannot form any true knowledge of God. The gods of philosophy are ultimately 'intellectual idols'. This is a straightforward rejection of philosophical, natural theology.

He continues that true knowledge of God can be achieved only through the revelation of Christ.

Barth

Barth's response to Brunner was 'Nein!' (No!). Barth believed that human nature was so damaged by the Fall that only God could take the initiative in revealing himself to humanity. He said that Brunner did not take into account the amount of corruption caused by the Fall and that humans are now so corrupted that they cannot know God's existence unaided. He did not think that nature, the prodding of the conscience or a sense of guilt provided any way of being in contact with God. He continues that these are felt only after someone has received God's grace.

He said that although people can see order in nature it is not a source of moral guidance or salvation for the fallen state. Again he says that the order of creation can be understood only after the receipt of grace.

Scholars remain divided over which of these two correctly interpreted Calvin's teachings.

A modern response to the debate

Alvin Platingna (1932–) – working again from Calvin's argument – argued that natural theology will never give sufficient reason to believe in God. On the other hand he believes that revealed theology is reasonable and can lead to understanding of God.

He argues that Christian revealed truths constitute 'basic knowledge'.

He continues to argue that if God did not exist then people would not claim to know God. Therefore, the knowledge of God can be regarded as basic knowledge. This basic knowledge is available only to Christians

Atheological

Opposed to theology.

Basic knowledge

A belief which is maintained to be the truth because it makes sense of experiences.

because Christ is needed to remove sin and allow the Holy Spirit access to the believer.

He says that there can be no indisputable proof of belief but there can be good reasons to hold to it.

In response to people who reject all theological claims he said,

> Upon grasping this argument, perhaps I have a substantial reason for accepting a defeater of theistic belief, namely that X is improbable. But in order to defeat this potential defeater, I need not know or have very good reason to think that it is false that is improbable on Y; it would suffice to show that the atheologian's argument (for the claim that X is improbable on Y is unsuccessful. To defeat this potential defeater, all I need to do is refute this argument; I am not obliged to go further and produce an argument for the denial of its conclusion.
>
> (Plantinga, 'Intellectual Sophistication and Basic Belief in God')

(X= God exists and is omniscient, omnipotent, and wholly good; Y= evil)

Objections to Plantinga

Plantinga's ideas are called 'reformed epistemology'. Criticism of his theories include the following:

- He claims that people have claimed to have a sense of God for millennia. However, they could all have been wrong.
- He regards Christian beliefs as true but does not give a reason for believing this.
- His argument could be used to support any belief system, however ridiculous.

Reformed epistemology is often regarded as fideism.

Fideism

Any doctrine according to which all (or some) knowledge depends upon faith or revelation, and reason or the intellect is to be disregarded.

Fideism was condemned in the *Dogmatic Constitution on the Catholic Faith*, First Vatican Council (1869–1870), which lists among other errors atheism, pantheism, rationalism, fideism, biblicism and traditionalism. These were either utterly wrong – for example atheism – or wrong in emphasising merely one element of the whole truth – for example rationalism.

It is disputed whether natural theology can really be seen as Christian theology as it tends to reduce teachings such as the resurrection as no more than an attempt to conquer despair with hope.

SUMMARY

Natural knowledge of God's existence
   Natural theology
      Natural theology refers to the process of learning about God from the natural world by using reason.
      Paul and the unknown God
      The order of creation
      Calvin and God as Creator
      Teleological arguments
   Process theology
   Revealed knowledge of God's existence
   Propositional revelation
   Criticisms of propositional revelation
   Non-propositional revelation
   Criticisms of non-propositional revelation
   Faith and God's grace
      Revelation through the Bible
      The revelation of God through scripture
      The Bible is the divinely inspired Word of God
      Biblical fundamentalism
      The authority of scripture
   A non-propositional revelation view: the Bible is a record of human experiences of God
      The authority of the Bible
      What if the Bible is divinely inspired?
   Natural versus revealed theology
      Barth/Brunner debate 1934
      A modern response to the debate – Alvin Plantinga
      Objections to Plantinga

REVIEW QUESTIONS

Look back over the chapter and check that you can answer the following questions:

1   What is the main argument of natural theology?
2   What is the main argument of revealed theology?
3   Which of these types of theologies do you think is stronger? Justify your answer.
4   Outline how people can have knowledge of God's existence through Jesus Christ.

Terminology

Do you know your terminology?

Try to explain the following ideas without looking at your books and notes:

- Innate
- Revelation
- Numinous experience
- Teleological
- Process theology
- Magisterium

Examination questions practice

Exam mistakes to avoid: it is very important that you are able to explain clearly the different views of theologians and philosophers on the knowledge of God's existence. In particular, you need to be able to use the terms and theories accurately and not confuse them. In particular you must be able to explain natural and revealed theology.

To help you improve your answers look at the levels of response.

SAMPLE EXAM-STYLE QUESTION

'God cannot be known through the natural world.' Discuss.

AO1 (15 marks)

This question requires you to consider exactly what teachings there are about God as Creator of the world. Consider whether humans have the ability have a natural capacity to experience God. Consider the arguments for God's existence and whether they help understanding. *Imago dei* suggests humans have a special relationship with God as part of creation.

AO2 (15 marks)

In evaluation you need to weigh up the 'evidence' and consider the strengths and weaknesses of the statement. You might consider teleological arguments and the beauty of nature. On the other hand you could consider whether the human soul is so corrupted by the Fall that nothing can happen without God's grace.

Further possible questions

- 'Biblical teaching about the Kingdom of God is very unclear.' Discuss.
- To what extent are Richard Dawkins' views on death and the afterlife convincing?
- Critically assess different Christian views about election.
- Assess the strengths and weaknesses of John Calvin's teachings about predestination.

FURTHER READING

Manning, R.E.M. 2015. *The Oxford Handbook of Natural Theology*, reprint. Oxford: OUP.

McGrath, A. 2011. *Christian Theology* (5th ed.). Oxford: Wiley-Blackwell

Schneider, S.M. 1999. *The Revelatory Text: Interpreting the New Testament as Sacred Scripture* (2nd ed.). Wilmington: Michael Glazier.

Foundations

20 The person of Jesus Christ

WHAT YOU WILL LEARN ABOUT IN THIS CHAPTER

- The person of Jesus Christ
- Jesus' authority as the Son of God
- Jesus' authority as a teacher of wisdom
- Was Jesus a liberator?

THE OCR CHECKLIST

The person of Jesus Christ

- Jesus Christ's authority as:
  - the Son of God
    - Jesus' divinity as expressed in his:
      - knowledge of God
      - miracles
      - resurrection
    - With reference to Mark 6:47–52 and John 9:1–41
  - a teacher of wisdom
    - Jesus' moral teaching on:
      - repentance and forgiveness
      - inner purity and moral motivation
    - With reference to Matthew 5:17–48 and Luke 15:11–32
  - a liberator
    - Jesus' role as liberator of the marginalised and the poor, as expressed in his:

continued opposite

- challenge to political authority
- challenge to religious authority
  - With reference to Mark 5:24–34 and Luke 10:25–37.

Learners should have the opportunity to discuss issues related to Christian ideas regarding

- Jesus Christ as a source of authority, including:
- whether Jesus was only a teacher of wisdom
- whether Jesus was more than a political liberator
- whether Jesus' relationship with God was very special or truly unique
- whether Jesus thought he was divine.

Suggested scholarly views, academic approaches and sources of wisdom and authority

- McGrath, A. (2011) *Theology: The Basics,* Blackwell, Chapter 4
- Theissen, G. (2010) *The Shadow of the Galilean,* SCM Press
- Chapman, G. (1994) *Catechism of the Catholic Church,* paras. 422–478.

Anselm (1033/1034–1109)

Bernard of Clairvaux (1090–1153)

Thomas Aquinas (1225–1274)

David Hume (1711–1776)

David Strauss (1808–1874)

Rudolf Karl Bultmann (1884–1976)

John Hick (1922–2012)

David Jenkins (1925–2016)

Wolfhart Pannenburg (1928–2014)

Gustavo Gutiérrez Merino (1928–)

Camilo Torres Restrepo (1929–1966)

Leonardo Boff (1938–)

Jesus of Nazareth
God, saint or sinner?

For two millennia theologians and other scholars have tried to work out what can actually be known about Jesus of Nazareth. The 'quest for the historical Jesus' was particularly important in the nineteenth and twentieth centuries. Two important texts are *Das Leben Jesu, kritisch bearbeitet* (1835–1836) (The Life of Jesus, Critically Examined), by David Strauss (1808–1874), and *The Quest of the Historical Jesus* (1906), by Albert Schweitzer (1875–1965).

Extra-biblical texts were initially seen as the most important proof of the historical Jesus. However, in the twentieth century, the works usually cited, by Philo (*c.* 20 BCE–*c.* CE 50), Pliny (23–79), Josephus (37–*c.* 100) and Tacitus (56 – *c.* 120), were all discredited as forgeries or forged insertions into the text.

There is no archaeological evidence available as again, items such as the sarcophagus inscription, which says, 'James, son of Joseph, brother of

Jesus', cannot be shown to have any further connection to Jesus and, of course, although many Christians accept this family link, it is not clear in the New Testament. Therefore, people have to accept that apart from the biblical text and perhaps the pseudepigraphal and apocryphal books, there is no 'proof' that Jesus ever existed. Many might regard the Bible as proof because in the New Testament it says, 'All scripture is inspired by God and is useful for teaching, for reproof, for correction, and for training in righteousness' (2 Timothy 3:16). However, it requires very little skill in verbal logic to see that this text is a circular argument which proves nothing.

The best-known official statement of the Christian Church about Jesus is found in the Nicene Creed:

> I believe in one God the Father Almighty,
> Maker of heaven and earth,
> And of all things visible and invisible:
> And in one Lord Jesus Christ, the only-begotten Son of God,
> Begotten of his Father before all worlds,
> God of God, Light of Light,
> Very God of very God,
> Begotten, not made,
> Being of one substance with the Father,
> By whom all things were made;
> Who for us men, and for our salvation came down from heaven,
> And was incarnate by the Holy Ghost of the Virgin Mary,
> And was made man,
> And was crucified also for us under Pontius Pilate.
> He suffered and was buried,
> And the third day he rose again according to the Scriptures,
> And ascended into heaven,
> And sitteth on the right hand of the Father.
> And he shall come again with glory to judge both the quick and the dead:
> Whose kingdom shall have no end.
> And I believe in the Holy Ghost,
> The Lord and giver of life,
> Who proceedeth from the Father and the Son,
> Who with the Father and the Son together is worshipped and glorified,
> Who spake by the Prophets.
> And I believe one Catholick and Apostolick Church.
> I acknowledge one Baptism for the remission of sins.
> And I look for the Resurrection of the dead,
> And the life of the world to come.
> Amen.

(*Book of Common Prayer*, 1662)

This creed was formulated at the Council of Nicaea in CE 325 and expanded at the Council of Constantinople in CE 381.

The creed was necessary to counter the many Christological heresies of the time.

The most significant of these are as follows.

Adoptionism

This was a belief which said that Jesus was born as man and because he was so virtuous he was adopted as the 'Son of God' when the Holy Spirit descended to him on the banks of the river Jordan.

> And when Jesus had been baptized, just as he came up from the water, suddenly the heavens were opened to him and he saw the Spirit of God descending like a dove and alighting on him. And a voice from heaven said, 'This is my Son, the Beloved, with whom I am well pleased.'
> (Matthew 3:16–17)

The Gospel of Mark is believed by most modern scholars to be the first of the four canonical gospels to have been written but in the earliest manuscripts of Mark the phrase 'Son of God' does not appear Mark 1:1. Therefore the first use of the title for Jesus comes at his baptism.

Also, the letters of Paul do not mention a virgin birth. Paul describes Jesus as 'born of a woman, born under the law' (Galatians 4:4b) and 'the gospel concerning his Son, who was descended from David according to the flesh and was declared to be Son of God with power according to the spirit of holiness' Romans 1:3-4a).

This was promoted in Rome by Theodotus of Byzantium but condemned by the Synod of Antioch in 268.

Apollinarism

This belief stated that Jesus had a human body and lower soul but a divine mind. Apollinaris of Laodicea also said that human souls contained other souls, as well as their bodies. This heresy was condemned by the first Council of Constantinople in 381.

Arianism

In the third and fourth centuries Arius (250/256–336) did not accept the true divinity of Jesus Christ but agreed that Jesus Christ was created by the Father and that he had a beginning in time. The title 'Son of God' was purely a courtesy.

In order to make clear the relationship of Jesus Christ to God, the Nicene Creed used *homoousion* (ὁμοούσιος) – 'one in being'. In the fourth century, the Arian heresy argued against the use of *homoousion*. Homoeanism declared that the Son was 'similar' to God, while heteroousianism said that God the Father and God the Son were different in both their substance and attributes.

This was condemned at the Council of Nicaea in 325 and again at the Council of Constantinople in 359.

Docetism

This was a belief dating from the first century that Jesus' physical body was an illusion, as was his crucifixion. He only appeared to be physical but, in fact, was incorporeal and therefore pure spirit.

Macedonians or pneumatomachians

This fourth-century heresy accepts the divinity of Jesus Christ as stated at the Council of Nicaea but denies that of the Holy Spirit. It sees the Spirit as a creation of the Son, and a servant of the Father and the Son. It was opposed by the Cappadocian Fathers and condemned at the Council of Constantinople.

This is what prompted the addition of the following to the Nicene Creed:

And I believe in the Holy Ghost,
The Lord and giver of life,
Who proceedeth from the Father and the Son,
Who with the Father and the Son together is worshipped and glorified,
Who spake by the Prophets.

Monophysitism or Eutychianism

This is a fifth-century heresy promulgated by Eutches of Constantinople. It stated that Christ's divinity dominates and overwhelms his humanity. It was rejected by the Council of Chalcedon in 451.

Monothelitism

A seventh-century heresy from Armenia and Syria which stated that although Christ had two natures he had only one will.

Monothelitism was a development of Monophysitism. Patriarch Sergius I of Constantinople was the force behind this heresy with the blessing of the Emperor Heraclius. In 622, Heraclius wrote to Bishop Paul of Armenia and asserted that the active force of Jesus was single (*Monoenergism*).

Nestorianism

This heresy was put forward by Nestorius of Constantinople in the fifth century. It teaches that Jesus Christ was a natural union between the flesh and the Word and therefore is not identical to the divine Son of God. It was condemned at the First Council of Ephesus in 431 and the Council of Chalcedon in 451. It rejected the title Theotokos (Θεοτόκος) – 'God carrier' – for the Virgin Mary and used Christotokos (Χριστοτόκος) – 'Christ carrier'.

Patripassianism

This stressed that the Father and Son were not two distinct persons, and therefore it was God the Father who was crucified as Jesus.

Similarly, it stressed that God the Father, Jesus Christ, and the Holy Spirit were three different aspects of one God, as seen by the believer, not three distinct persons. There were no real or differences between the three, so there was no true identity for the Spirit or the Son.

Psilanthropism

This is an approach to Christology which teaches that Jesus was human, the literal son of human parents. It denied the virgin birth of Jesus, and his divinity. The 19th century poet Samuel Taylor Coleridge was an example of a psilanthropist. However, later he rejected it totally. The heresy was rejected by the first Council of Nicaea.

Sabellianism

This second-century heresy taught by Noetus of Smyran and Sabellius that the Father, Son and Holy Spirit were three characterisations of one God, not three distinct 'persons' in one God.

So, what did Jesus think?

- Was he confused?
- Did he know he was the Messiah or divine?
- Did he know much about the afterlife?

The authority of Jesus Christ

What is authority? According to the *Oxford English Dictionary* it is 'Power or right to enforce obedience; moral or legal supremacy; the right to command, or give an ultimate decision.' Jesus apparently had the power to command

and carry out his Father's work; however, he was under control of his Father as he was to be the ultimate sacrifice. Although he could do anything he wanted, he showed obedience, respect and submission to authority over him. His main purpose was to fulfil the plans of his Father. In stating this, was Jesus in control of every single moment or did he have free will? Did he have complete authority over his disciples or did his Father actually have that control?

If this is the case, then how do Christians live and walk in this power and authority? Many Christians believe that the world they live in has two realms – the natural and the spiritual. People need to know how to live in this spiritual realm in a way that affects the natural realm. Instead of the spiritual realm affecting only an individual, he or she needs to be living in a way that affects the spiritual realm, which in turn affects the natural realm.

Son of God

Christology is the study within Christian theology primarily of the relationship of Jesus with God the Father.

- Christology from above begins with the divinity of Christ and his pre-existence as Logos – the Word.

    In the beginning was the Word, and the Word was with God, and the Word was God. He was in the beginning with God. All things came into being through him, and without him not one thing came into being. What has come into being in him was life, and the life was the light of all people. The light shines in the darkness, and the darkness did not overcome it.

(John 1:1–5)

- Christology from below is an approach that begins with human aspects of Jesus and his ministry and then moves on to his divinity and the mystery of incarnation.
- Cosmic Christology begins with St Paul and how the arrival of the Son of God fundamentally changed the nature of the entire cosmos.
- Monastic Christology is used to describe spiritual approaches developed by people such as Anselm (1033/1034–1109) and Bernard of Clairvaux (1090–1153).
- Popular Christology derives from Franciscan teachings on piety.
- Scholastic Christology refers to the systematic approach by people such as Aquinas.

Jesus is given many titles in the New Testament. The primary one is Son of God. Jesus never used this of himself, however.

The title is in frequent use in the Old Testament, where it is seen as referring to a ruler or king who it was believed had been chosen by God to exercise his will. The Hebrew word מָשִׁיחַ – Moshiach – is translated as 'messiah', which means 'anointed one'. It is a direct parallel with the Greek Christos (Χρίστος) – Christ.

A hope that a specially anointed person would arrive and free Israel politically, morally and spiritually. The Hebrew for 'anointed one' is messiah or Christos (in Greek). In other words, Son of God and Christ are equivalent terms.

One of the most famous references to this is found in the words of the Roman centurion at the crucifixion: 'Truly this man was God's Son!' (Mark 15:39b). However, if a centurion said this it is not at all clear what he meant.

Knowledge of God

Was Jesus Christ only an ordinary man? Novatian (*c.* 200–258), a theologian and writer, answered this question at a time when there was much debate about how to deal with Christians who had lapsed and wished to return, and the issue of penance.

> If Christ was only man, why did he lay down for us such a rule of believing as that in which he said, 'And this is life eternal, that they should know you, the only and true God, and Jesus Christ, whom thou hast sent?' (John 17:3). Had he not wished that he also should be understood to be God, why did he add, 'And Jesus Christ, whom thou hast sent,' except because he wished to be received as God also? Because if he had not wished to be understood to be God, he would have added, 'And the man Jesus Christ, whom thou hast sent;' but, in fact, he neither added this, nor did Christ deliver himself to us as man only, but associated himself with God, as he wished to be understood by this conjunction to be God also, as he is. We must therefore believe, according to the rule prescribed, on the Lord, the one true God, and consequently on him whom he has sent, Jesus Christ, who by no means, as we have said, would have linked himself to the Father had he not wished to be understood to be God also. For he would have separated himself from him had he not wished to be understood to be God.
>
> (Novation, 235, *Treatise on the Trinity*, 16)

There are many passages in the Bible which say that knowledge of and about God the Father and Jesus Christ is of crucial importance.

> May grace and peace be yours in abundance in the knowledge of God and of Jesus our Lord. His divine power has given us everything needed for life and godliness, through the knowledge of him who called us by his own glory and goodness.
>
> (2 Peter 1:2–3)

The Bible also states that God is the source of all knowledge. By seeking God, humanity can discover God's truth. Jesus brought this knowledge to earth.

> For it is the God who said, 'Let light shine out of darkness,' who has shone in our hearts to give the light of the knowledge of the glory of God in the face of Jesus Christ.
>
> (2 Corinthians 4:6)

> He will be the stability of your times, abundance of salvation, wisdom, and knowledge; the fear of the LORD is Zion's treasure.
>
> (Isaiah 33:6)

Miracles

Thomas Aquinas (1225–1274) defined the word 'miracle' as 'that which has a divine cause, not that whose cause a human person fails to understand' (Thomas Aquinas, *Summa Contra Gentiles*). Aquinas' definition is important, as it highlights a fundamental point for religious believers: miracles are events caused by God. This is reflected in the meaning of the word 'miracle', which comes from the Latin 'miraculum' – an object of wonder.

> As he walked along, he saw a man blind from birth. His disciples asked him, 'Rabbi, who sinned, this man or his parents, that he was born blind?' Jesus answered, 'Neither this man nor his parents sinned; he was born blind so that God's works might be revealed in him. We must work the works of him who sent me while it is day; night is coming when no one can work. As long as I am in the world, I am the light of the world.' When he had said this, he spat on the ground and made mud with the saliva and spread the mud on the man's eyes, saying to him, 'Go, wash in the pool of Siloam' (which means Sent). Then he went and washed and came back able to see. The neighbours and those who had seen him before as a beggar began to ask, 'Is this not the man who used to sit and beg?' Some were saying, 'It is he.' Others were saying, 'No, but it is someone like him.' He kept saying, 'I am the man.' But they kept asking him, 'Then how were your eyes opened?' He answered, 'The man called Jesus made mud, spread it on my eyes, and said to me, 'Go to Siloam and wash.' Then I went and washed and received my sight.' They said to him, 'Where is he?' He said, 'I do not know.'
>
> (John 9:1–12)

If we take a story such as this passage from John's Gospel, it is of no interest to a religious believer whether we understand how Jesus performed this miracle. The point of the story is that God caused the man to be cured and this is an event to be wondered at. In the story, people cannot stop talking about what Jesus did and how God worked through him.

The second point to note is that Aquinas' idea of miracle comes from Aristotle. Aquinas and Aristotle both believed that everything which exists has a nature. Basically, this nature is a statement about what a thing is able to do. For example you could say that part of the nature of human beings that makes them different from animals is that they can think about the future and the meaning of life and death. When Aquinas talks about a miracle having a 'divine cause' he means that the event in question is not a normal part of the nature of things.

However, many Christians today would add a further point to what Aquinas says. They would add that miracles not only are caused by God but also reveal something about God to people.

DAVID HUME'S DEFINITION OF A MIRACLE

The most famous definition of a miracle in the modern world is probably that of David Hume (1711–1776). Hume defined a miracle as a *'violation of the laws of nature'* (David Hume, *An Enquiry Concerning Human Understanding*).

For Hume, a miracle, such as Jesus curing the paralytic, is an example of an event which suggests that something happened which broke the laws of nature. It is important to understand what Hume means by the laws of nature, as his ideas are rather different from those of scientists today. Hume uses the laws of nature to show how the universe works. For example if you throw a book off your desk you know that it will fall to the floor. Why?

For Hume, a law of nature is something which can be tested scientifically and you say something is a law of nature only if every time you test the law you find the same result. If you want to put this philosophically, Hume would say that laws of nature are proved inductively. What this means is that evidence is collected and a conclusion reached, like a judge listening to the evidence in a court case. The conclusion is beyond reasonable doubt. Hume is not saying that the laws of nature necessarily have to be this way, but he is saying that the laws of nature are the best description of the way in which the universe works, beyond any reasonable doubt. Secondly, Hume believed that the laws of nature are rigid and fixed – meaning that they are statements which describe how the world works. Once discovered, laws of nature are unchanging.

In terms of events recorded in the New Testament a miracle is an unusual and significant event (τέρας) which requires the working of a supernatural power (δύναμις) and is performed for the purpose of authenticating the message or the messenger (σημεῖον).

Parousia

This means presence, arrival or official visit. In the New Testament it is also used for the Second Coming of Jesus.

Jesus himself uses the term ἔργον (erga) – 'work' – when referring to the miracles. This comes from Jewish tradition, where miracles are seen as a sign of God's mighty and saving power.

Jesus performed many miracles which demonstrated his power over nature and spirits to indicate that the Kingdom of God was immanent (παρουσία, or parousia).

According to the accounts in the synoptic Gospels, Jesus refused to perform miraculous signs simply in order to prove his authority. However, in John's Gospel he performs seven miraculous signs:

- Turning water into wine (John 5:1–30).
- Jesus heals the son of an official (John 4:46–54).
- Pool of Bethesda (John 4:46–54).
- Feeding of the 5,000 (John 5:42).
- Jesus walking on the water (John 6:16–24).
- A man born blind receives sight (John 9:1–41).
- The raising of Lazarus (John 11:1–44).

Many Christians believe Jesus' miracles were historical events and that his miraculous works were an important part of his life which showed his divinity and the hypostatic union – that is the dual natures of Jesus as God and Man. His experiences of hunger, weariness and death are seen as evidence of his humanity, and the miracles as evidence of his divinity.

So, what could be understood from the following miracle?

> When evening came, the boat was out on the sea, and he was alone on the land. When he saw that they were straining at the oars against an adverse wind, he came towards them early in the morning, walking on the sea. He intended to pass them by. But when they saw him walking on the sea, they thought it was a ghost and cried out; for they all saw him and were terrified. But immediately he spoke to them and said, 'Take heart, it is I; do not be afraid.' Then he got into the boat with them and the wind ceased. And they were utterly astounded, for they did not understand about the loaves, but their hearts were hardened.
>
> (Mark 6:47–52; see also John 6:15–21)

- Absence of faith in the person of Jesus Christ brings failure.
- He has the power over the natural elements.
- Was the storm sent to test and strengthen the faith of the disciples?
- It was the hardened hearts of the disciples which kept them from seeing Christ for who he was.

- The disciples had failed to understand the feeding of the 5,000 because they did not have sufficient faith and now they are failing again.
- The miracle indicates that there is safety in the person and power of Christ.

Jesus accompanies his words with many 'mighty works and wonders and signs', which manifest that the kingdom is present in him and attest that he was the promised Messiah.

    The signs worked by Jesus attest that the Father has sent him. They invite belief in him. To those who turn to him in faith, he grants what they ask. So, miracles strengthen faith in the One who does his Father's works; they bear witness that he is the Son of God. But his miracles can also be occasions for 'offence'; they are not intended to satisfy people's curiosity or desire for magic. Despite his evident miracles some people reject Jesus; he is even accused of acting by the power of demons.

    (Catechism of the Catholic Church §547–548)

Resurrection

Salvific
Causing salvation.

The resurrection of Jesus – and the salvific nature of his sacrifice, atoning for the sins of the world, restoring the relationship between God and humanity and conquering death – is generally seen as probably the most important event in his life.

    The Pharisees of the first century held a belief in resurrection that in a future age the dead would rise from their graves to live again. This is closely associated with their teaching about the Messiah and the immortality of the soul. However, there are only two references to the idea in the Jewish scriptures:

> Your dead shall live, their corpses shall rise.
> O dwellers in the dust, awake and sing for joy!
> For your dew is a radiant dew,
> and the earth will give birth to those long dead.
>
> (Isaiah 26:19)

> Many of those who sleep in the dust of the earth shall awake, some to everlasting life, and some to shame and everlasting contempt. Those who are wise shall shine like the brightness of the sky, and those who lead many to righteousness, like the stars forever and ever.
>
> (Daniel 12:2–3)

What might be considered different about Jesus' resurrection was that it happened so soon after his death and that the people who experienced the resurrected Christ were left with a belief that something fundamental had changed in their relationship with God.

Paul saw Jesus as the first fruits of a new order and wrote,

> But in fact, Christ has been raised from the dead, the first fruits of those who have died. For since death came through a human being, the resurrection of the dead has also come through a human being; for as all die in Adam, so all will be made alive in Christ. But each in his own order: Christ the first fruits, then at his coming those who belong to Christ. Then comes the end, when he hands over the kingdom to God the Father, after he has destroyed every ruler and every authority and power. For he must reign until he has put all his enemies under his feet. The last enemy to be destroyed is death.
>
> (1 Corinthians 15:20)

Some theologians who do not believe that Jesus was more than a human being during his lifetime nevertheless believe that it was at the resurrection that Jesus is shown as the actual Son of God. Key among these is Wolfhart Pannenburg (1928–2014).

On the other hand, the late bishop of Durham, David Jenkins (1925–2016) was perhaps more challenging. His selection as bishop of Durham was controversial due to allegations that he held heterodox (not orthodox) beliefs in relation to the virgin birth and bodily resurrection. Just before his consecration in 1984 he said in an interview, 'I wouldn't put it past God to arrange a virgin birth if he wanted. But I don't think he did.'

He was very widely quoted as describing the resurrection of Christ as being 'just a conjuring trick with bones'. What he actually said was '[the Resurrection] is real. That's the point. All I said was "literally physical". I was very careful in the use of language. After all, a conjuring trick with bones proves only that somebody's very clever at a conjuring trick with bones.'

He believed that the resurrection was not a single event but a series of experiences that gradually convinced people that Jesus' life, power, purpose and personality were actually continuing.

What do people believe?

According to a 2017 survey carried out for the BBC there is a wide diversity of belief about Jesus' resurrection.

ComRes surveyed 2,010 British adults by telephone, between 2 and 12 February 2017. The research was commissioned by BBC local radio for Palm Sunday.

The survey suggested the following:

- 17% of all people believe the Bible version word-for-word.
- 31% of Christians believe word-for-word the Bible version, rising to 57% among 'active' Christians (those who go to a religious service at least once a month).
- Exactly half of all people surveyed did not believe in the resurrection at all.
- 46% of people say they believe in some form of life after death and 46% do not.
- 20% of non-religious people say they believe in some form of life after death.
- 9% of non-religious people believe in the Resurrection, 1% of whom say they believe it literally.

Jesus Christ's authority as a teacher of wisdom

Many scholars have accepted that Jesus' wisdom teaching and the resurrection are signs of his relationship with God.

However, others have rejected events such as the miracles on the basis that these were invented by the early Church to prove his divinity.

Rudolf Karl Bultmann (1884–1976) was a German Lutheran theologian who is probably most remembered for his controversial ideas. In 1941 he gave a lecture called *New Testament and Mythology: The Problem of Demythologizing the New Testament Message,* calling on interpreters to replace traditional supernaturalism (demythologise) with the temporal and existential categories. He rejected teachings such as the pre-existence of Christ. He believed that the 'mythical picture' presented by the early Church alienated many people from Christianity in the twentieth century. He believed that faith should not be made to rest on provable facts; rather it is the decision to choose a new life in Christ.

For many scholars this was welcome because it largely removed arguments about the divinity of Christ and therefore did not put Christianity in opposition to other faiths.

John Hick (1922–2012) saw wisdom teachers, such as Moses, Jesus, Buddha and Muhammad (pbuh), as 'gifts to the world'. This means that the authority of Jesus' moral teaching lies in an actual engagement with and affirmation of life. It is no longer reliant on abstract concepts.

> ### Form criticism
>
> This is a method of biblical criticism that classifies scriptural units by literary pattern and attempts to trace each type to its period of oral transmission. It attempts to establish the original form of each unit from its historical context.

Jesus' moral teaching

Many scholars have suggested that Jesus was, in fact, a travelling rabbi. There is very little in his teachings in the Gospels which is different from that of the Judaism of the first century. This is therefore different from the teachings found in many of the epistles.

The bulk of Jesus' moral teaching is found in the Sermon on the Mount (Matthew 5–7), opening with the Beatitudes. (Much of this teaching is also found in the Sermon on the Plain; Luke 6:17–49.)

While it is almost certain that Luke was written before Matthew, many of these teachings are now attributed by some scholars to Q (see p. 297).

One of the difficulties with deciding about Jesus' moral teaching is a passage which comes three verses after the Beatitudes:

> Do not think that I have come to abolish the law or the prophets; I have come not to abolish but to fulfil. For truly I tell you, until heaven and earth pass away, not one letter, not one stroke of a letter, will pass from the law until all is accomplished. Therefore, whoever breaks one of the least of these commandments, and teaches others to do the same, will be called least in the kingdom of heaven; but whoever does them and teaches them will be called great in the kingdom of heaven. For I tell you, unless your righteousness exceeds that of the scribes and Pharisees, you will never enter the kingdom of heaven.
>
> (Matthew 5:17–20)

It is difficult to decide what the text actually means. At face value it would appear that Jesus was saying that the Law (Torah) was not being followed and he had come to make sure that this was corrected. He seems to be saying that this had to be observed until the coming of the kingdom.

Certainly, in the Acts of the Apostles it appears that after Pentecost and the coming of the Holy Spirit (Acts 2:1–4) many of the laws began to be seen as outdated.

> Awe came upon everyone, because many wonders and signs were being done by the apostles. All who believed were together and had all things in common; they would sell their possessions and goods and distribute the proceeds to all, as any had need. Day by day, as they spent much time together in the temple, they broke bread at home and ate their food with glad and generous hearts, praising God and having the goodwill of all the people. And day by day the Lord added to their number those who were being saved.
>
> (Acts 2:43–47)

Peter's vision

About noon the next day, as they were on their journey and approaching the city, Peter went up on the roof to pray. He became hungry and wanted something to eat; and while it was being prepared, he fell into a trance. He saw the heaven opened and something like a large sheet coming down, being lowered to the ground by its four corners. In it were all kinds of four-footed creatures and reptiles and birds of the air. Then he heard a voice saying, 'Get up, Peter; kill and eat.' But Peter said, 'By no means, Lord; for I have never eaten anything that is profane or unclean.' The voice said to him again, a second time, 'What God has made clean, you must not call profane.' This happened three times, and the thing was suddenly taken up to heaven.

(Acts 10:9–16)

THE COUNCIL OF JERUSALEM

Then certain individuals came down from Judea and were teaching the brothers, 'Unless you are circumcised according to the custom of Moses, you cannot be saved.' And after Paul and Barnabas had no small dissension and debate with them, Paul and Barnabas and some of the others were appointed to go up to Jerusalem to discuss this question with the apostles and the elders . . . The apostles and the elders met together to consider this matter. After there had been much debate, Peter stood up and said to them, 'My brothers, you know that in the early days God made a choice among you, that I should be the one through whom the Gentiles would hear the message of the good news and become believers. And God, who knows the human heart, testified to them by giving them the Holy Spirit, just as he did to us; and in cleansing their hearts by faith he has made no distinction between them and us. Now therefore why are you putting God to the test by placing on the neck of the disciples a yoke that neither our ancestors nor we have been able to bear? On the contrary, we believe that we will be saved through the grace of the Lord Jesus, just as they will.'

(Acts 15:1–3, 6–11)

Council of Jerusalem
The First Council of Jerusalem found in Acts 15 is generally said to have taken place in CE 50. However, as it is never mentioned in the letters of St Paul, many scholars have doubted its authenticity.

Apart from the Sermon of the Mount, which may be a compilation of teachings, Jesus seemed to prefer the use of parables.

Metanoia (Greek μετάνοια) is 'a transforming change of heart' and suggests 'repentance'.

Repentance and forgiveness

The announcement of the Kingdom of God was also a call from Jesus to repentance.

There are many examples of repentance in the New Testament but perhaps the most famous and significant is in the parable of the lost (prodigal) son.

> Then Jesus said, 'There was a man who had two sons. The younger of them said to his father, "Father, give me the share of the property that will belong to me." So he divided his property between them. A few days later the younger son gathered all he had and travelled to a distant country, and there he squandered his property in dissolute living. When he had spent everything, a severe famine took place throughout that country, and he began to be in need. So he went and hired himself out to one of the citizens of that country, who sent him to his fields to feed the pigs. He would gladly have filled himself with the pods that the pigs were eating; and no one gave him anything. But when he came to himself he said, "How many of my father's hired hands have bread enough and to spare, but here I am dying of hunger! I will get up and go to my father, and I will say to him, 'Father, I have sinned against heaven and before you; I am no longer worthy to be called your son; treat me like one of your hired hands.'" . . . Now his elder son was in the field; and when he came and approached the house, he heard music and dancing. He called one of the slaves and asked what was going on. He replied, "Your brother has come, and your father has killed the fatted calf, because he has got him back safe and sound." Then he became angry and refused to go in. His father came out and began to plead with him. But he answered his father, "Listen! For all these years I have been working like a slave for you, and I have never disobeyed your command; yet you have never given me even a young goat so that I might celebrate with my friends. But when this son of yours came back, who has devoured your property with prostitutes, you killed the fatted calf for him!" Then the father said to him, "Son, you are always with me, and all that is mine is yours. But we had to celebrate and rejoice, because this brother of yours was dead and has come to life; he was lost and has been found."'
>
> (Luke 15:11–19, 25–32)

The key issues in the parable are both repentance for sin and its forgiveness.

The requirement for both is found in the Lord's Prayer (Matthew 6:9–13, Luke 11:2–4). The need to show forgiveness is taught by Jesus to Peter:

> Then Peter came and said to him, 'Lord, if another member of the church sins against me, how often should I forgive? As many as seven

times?' Jesus said to him, 'Not seven times, but, I tell you, seventy-seven times.'

(Matthew 18:21–22)

Note: the Greek for 77 times can also be translated as '70 times 7'.

Jesus' teaching on inner purity and moral motivation

In the Sermon on the Mount, Jesus gives clear teaching on six topics.

Anger

Jesus expands on the commandment 'You shall not murder' and explains that God cannot be worshipped unless a person is at peace with their family and neighbours.

> You have heard that it was said to those of ancient times, 'You shall not murder'; and 'whoever murders shall be liable to judgment.' But I say to you that if you are angry with a brother or sister, you will be liable to judgment; and if you insult a brother or sister, you will be liable to the council; and if you say, 'You fool,' you will be liable to the hell of fire. So when you are offering your gift at the altar, if you remember that your brother or sister has something against you, leave your gift there before the altar and go; first be reconciled to your brother or sister, and then come and offer your gift.
>
> (Matthew 5:21–24)

Adultery

Again Jesus extends the teaching of the commandment 'You shall not commit adultery': 'You have heard that it was said, "You shall not commit adultery." But I say to you that everyone who looks at a woman with lust has already committed adultery with her in his heart' (Matthew 5:27–28).

Divorce

> It was also said, 'Whoever divorces his wife, let him give her a certificate of divorce.' But I say to you that anyone who divorces his wife, except on the ground of unchastity, causes her to commit adultery; and whoever marries a divorced woman commits adultery.

The Greek term *porneia* (πορνεία), meaning adultery in this translation, is often translated as 'prostitution'. It is unclear therefore which Jesus meant.

Oaths

Here Jesus is expanding on the commandment 'You shall not make wrongful use of the name of the LORD your God, for the LORD will not acquit anyone who misuses his name':

> Again, you have heard that it was said to those of ancient times, 'You shall not swear falsely, but carry out the vows you have made to the Lord.' But I say to you, Do not swear at all, either by heaven, for it is the throne of God, or by the earth, for it is his footstool, or by Jerusalem, for it is the city of the great King. And do not swear by your head, for you cannot make one hair white or black. Let your word be 'Yes, Yes' or 'No, No'; anything more than this comes from the evil one.
>
> (Matthew 5:33–37)

Retaliation

> You have heard that it was said, 'An eye for an eye and a tooth for a tooth.' But I say to you, Do not resist an evildoer. But if anyone strikes you on the right cheek, turn the other also; and if anyone wants to sue you and take your coat, give your cloak as well; and if anyone forces you to go one mile, go also the second mile. Give to everyone who begs from you, and do not refuse anyone who wants to borrow from you.
>
> (Matthew 5:38–42)

The passage being referred to here is 'Anyone who maims another shall suffer the same injury in return: fracture for fracture, eye for eye, tooth for tooth; the injury inflicted is the injury to be suffered' (Leviticus 24:19–20). It is often referred to as lex talionis and means a retaliation authorised by law, in which the punishment corresponds in kind and degree to the injury. However, it is very important to remember that this was an instruction to limit revenge, not to insist on it. Also, some New Testament scholars have suggested that, in fact, to turn the other cheek was an insult.

Love for enemies

> You have heard that it was said, 'You shall love your neighbour and hate your enemy.' But I say to you, Love your enemies and pray for those who

persecute you, so that you may be children of your Father in heaven; for he makes his sun rise on the evil and on the good, and sends rain on the righteous and on the unrighteous. For if you love those who love you, what reward do you have? Do not even the tax collectors do the same? And if you greet only your brothers and sisters, what more are you doing than others? Do not even the Gentiles do the same? Be perfect, there-fore, as your heavenly Father is perfect.

(Matthew 5:43–48)

The phrase 'You shall love your neighbour and hate your enemy' is often thought to have its origins in the Old Testament, but, in fact, it does not appear anywhere and is the total opposite to what the scriptures teach (see Leviticus 19 *et al.*).

It can be seen that Jesus strengthens the Jewish law rather than try-ing to change it. However, he sometimes interpreted it differently from the scribes and the Pharisees.

The prime example of this is the fourth commandment:

Remember the sabbath day, and keep it holy. Six days you shall labour and do all your work. But the seventh day is a sabbath to the LORD your God; you shall not do any work – you, your son or your daughter, your male or female slave, your livestock, or the alien resident in your towns. For in six days the LORD made heaven and earth, the sea, and all that is in them, but rested the seventh day; therefore the LORD blessed the sab-bath day and consecrated it.

(Exodus 20:8–11)

Jesus of course taught that people should follow the commandment and worship on the Sabbath but also said that the 39 categories of work which were banned were preventing people from carrying out their duties to oth-ers who needed help.

Now he was teaching in one of the synagogues on the sabbath. And just then there appeared a woman with a spirit that had crippled her for eighteen years. She was bent over and was quite unable to stand up straight. When Jesus saw her, he called her over and said, 'Woman, you are set free from your ailment.' When he laid his hands on her, imme-diately she stood up straight and began praising God. But the leader of the synagogue, indignant because Jesus had cured on the sabbath, kept saying to the crowd, 'There are six days on which work ought to be done; come on those days and be cured, and not on the sabbath day.' But the Lord answered him and said, 'You hypocrites! Does not each of you on the sabbath untie his ox or his donkey from the manger, and lead it away to give it water? And ought not this woman, a daughter of Abraham whom Satan bound for eighteen long years, be set free from this bondage on the sabbath day?' When he said this, all his opponents were put to shame; and the entire crowd was rejoicing at all the wonderful things that he was doing.

(Luke 13:10–17)

One sabbath he was going through the grainfields; and as they made their way his disciples began to pluck heads of grain. The Pharisees said to him, 'Look, why are they doing what is not lawful on the sabbath?' And he said to them, 'Have you never read what David did when he and his companions were hungry and in need of food? He entered the house of God, when Abiathar was high priest, and ate the bread of the Presence, which it is not lawful for any but the priests to eat, and he gave some to his companions.' Then he said to them, 'The sabbath was made for humankind, and not humankind for the sabbath; so the Son of Man is lord even of the sabbath.'

(Mark 2:23–28)

As a reminder:

Do not think that I have come to abolish the law or the prophets; I have come not to abolish but to fulfil. For truly I tell you, until heaven and earth pass away, not one letter, not one stroke of a letter, will pass from the law until all is accomplished.

(Matthew 5:17–18)

Jesus' role as liberator of the marginalised and the poor, as expressed in his challenge to political and religious authority

From the New Testament it appears that much of Jesus' ministry was spent in conflict with both the Roman and Jewish authorities.

For centuries Jesus has largely been portrayed as a pacifist, and some have taken this to mean that the Church should play no part in politics or conflict. However, there are many scholars who maintain that his teaching on the Kingdom of God requires a change to society and the oppression of the poor and marginalised.

Liberation

The period from the 1970s to the 1990s was a time of civil wars in South America and the continuing oppression of the poor.

Jesus a Zealot

The Zealots were a first-century group who used violence and rebellions in order to free Palestine from the Roman occupation. The argument that Jesus himself was a Zealot was put forward in a controversial book *Jesus and the Zealots* (1967), by S.G.F. Brandon (1907–1971), a British priest and professor of comparative religion. This book argues that Jesus was a freedom fighter and that the Gospels deliberately changed this image.

This saw the development of liberation theology, particularly by Roman Catholic priests. The idea of Jesus as a Zealot was understandably attractive.

This theology argued that the almost totally neutral Jesus portrayed and built upon by the Church was wrong. They saw Jesus' actions and teachings as having a bias towards the poor and marginalised. These were the people who were now viewed as the 'underside of history' – the majority of people in the world who are ignored or forgotten about. This could be changed, they argued, only by portraying Jesus as a liberator. This should then ensure that Christianity is at the forefront of the struggle to free people from poverty and oppression as Jesus demonstrated in his own life.

The liberation which Jesus offers is universal and integral and transcends national boundaries, attacks the foundation of injustice and exploitation, and eliminates politico-religious confusions, without therefore being limited to a purely 'spiritual' plane.

It is not enough, however, to say that Jesus was not a Zealot. There are those who seek, in good faith but uncritically, to cleanse Jesus from anything which can give even an inkling of a political attitude on his part. But Jesus' posture precludes all oversimplification. To close one's eyes to this complexity amounts to letting the richness of his testimony on this score escape (Gustavo Gutiérrez: *A Theology of Liberation*, 2001).

Preferential option for the poor

Liberation theology sees a bias in Jesus' life and teachings towards the oppressed and describes this as a preferential option for the poor. The option should be seen as central to the lives of all Christians at all times.

A Christology that proclaims Jesus Christ as the Liberator seeks to be committed to the economic, social and political liberation of those groups that are oppressed and dominated. It purports to see the theological relevance of the historic liberation of the vast majority of people in our continent. Such a Christology believes that its thinking and practice should be centred on such liberation. It seeks to create a style and to develop the content of Christology in such a way that it can bring out the liberative dimensions present in Jesus' historical course (Boff, *Jesus Christ Liberator: A Critical Christology for Our Time*, 1972).

Some priests saw Jesus as a type of Zealot. Camilo Torres Restrepo, for example, was a Roman Catholic priest who joined the communist people's army as a soldier in the guerrilla war against the government troops. As he said, 'If Jesus were alive today, He would be a guerrillero.'

Camilo Torres Restrepo (1929–1966) was a Colombian socialist, a Roman Catholic priest, a predecessor of the liberation theology movement and a member of the National Liberation Army (ELN) guerrilla organisation. He tried to reconcile revolutionary Marxism and Catholicism.

Gustavo Gutiérrez Merino, O.P. (1928–)

A Peruvian philosopher, theologian and Dominican priest, Merino is regarded as one of the founders of liberation theology.

Leonardo Boff (1938–)

Keystone Pictures USA/ Alamy

He was born *Genézio Darci Boff* in 1938 in Concórdia, Santa Catarina. He entered the Franciscan Order in 1959 and was ordained as a Catholic priest in 1964. He studied at the University of Munich and his 1970 doctoral thesis *Die Kirche*

continued overleaf

als Sakrament im Horizont der Welterfahrung considered how the Church could be a sign of the sacred and the divine in the secular world and in the work of the liberation of the oppressed.

Boff is one of the best-known supporters of the early liberation theologians. He is a controversial figure in the Catholic Church for his criticism of the church's hierarchy and his past critical support of communist regimes. Boff left the Church and the Franciscan Order in 1992 as he considered them to be fossilised.

Samaritans

The Samaritans still exist in Israel. They are a group of Jews from Samaria (now largely the West Bank). The first-century Judean Jews regarded them as being ritually impure and the fact that they had built their own temple as heresy.

Denarii

The denarius was the usual day's wage for a labourer.

He was on the academic staff of the National University of Colombia; however, his involvement in student and political movements brought him many detractors, especially from the Colombian government and the church itself. Due to the growing pressure to end his involvement with radical politics, Torres saw himself as persecuted and went into hiding, joining the guerrillas in Colombia. He was killed in his first combat experience, and after his death, he was made an official martyr of the Ejército de Liberación Nacional (ELN; National Liberation Army).

In 1970 in the Dominican Republic a revolutionary group that included Catholic clergy and university students was founded under the name CORECATO, which stands for Comando Revolucionario Camilo Torres or Revolutionary Command Camilo Torres.

There are many events in Jesus' life and parables which show his concern for the poor, oppressed and marginalised.

Luke's Gospel in particular shows his association with people whom the Pharisees and scribes considered to be sinners. These include tax collectors, dung collectors and prostitutes. He chose his disciples from those whom the Pharisees largely considered to be ignorant, such as fishermen. Also, he ate with people whom the Pharisees would have refused to sit at a table with because they did not observe all the food laws and rituals.

Parable of the good Samaritan

This parable demonstrates that Jesus taught love for all people regardless of their race, religion or social status.

Just then a lawyer stood up to test Jesus. 'Teacher,' he said, 'what must I do to inherit eternal life?' He said to him, 'What is written in the law? What do you read there?' He answered, 'You shall love the Lord your God with all your heart, and with all your soul, and with all your strength, and with all your mind; and your neighbour as yourself.' And he said to him, 'You have given the right answer; do this, and you will live.'

But wanting to justify himself, he asked Jesus, 'And who is my neighbour?' Jesus replied, 'A man was going down from Jerusalem to Jericho, and fell into the hands of robbers, who stripped him, beat him, and went away, leaving him half dead. Now by chance a priest was going down that road; and when he saw him, he passed by on the other side. So likewise a Levite, when he came to the place and saw him, passed by on the other side. But a Samaritan while traveling came near him; and when he saw him, he was moved with pity. He went to him and bandaged his wounds, having poured oil and wine on them. Then he put him on his own animal, brought him to an inn, and took care of him. The next day he took out two denarii, gave them to the innkeeper, and said, 'Take care of him; and when I come back, I will repay you whatever more you spend.' Which of these three, do you think, was a neighbour to the man who fell into the hands of the robbers?' He said, 'The one who showed him mercy.' Jesus said to him, 'Go and do likewise.'

(Luke 10:25–37)

The healing of a woman with bleeding

Jewish law had very strict rules about contact between a menstruating woman and other people.

> When a woman has a discharge of blood that is her regular discharge from her body, she shall be in her impurity for seven days, and whoever touches her shall be unclean until the evening. Everything upon which she lies during her impurity shall be unclean; everything also upon which she sits shall be unclean. Whoever touches her bed shall wash his clothes, and bathe in water, and be unclean until the evening. Whoever touches anything upon which she sits shall wash his clothes, and bathe in water, and be unclean until the evening; whether it is the bed or anything upon which she sits, when he touches it he shall be unclean until the evening. If any man lies with her, and her impurity falls on him, he shall be unclean seven days; and every bed on which he lies shall be unclean.
>
> If a woman has a discharge of blood for many days, not at the time of her impurity, or if she has a discharge beyond the time of her impurity, all the days of the discharge she shall continue in uncleanness; as in the days of her impurity, she shall be unclean. Every bed on which she lies during all the days of her discharge shall be treated as the bed of her impurity; and everything on which she sits shall be unclean, as in the uncleanness of her impurity. Whoever touches these things shall be unclean, and shall wash his clothes, and bathe in water, and be unclean until the evening.

(Leviticus 15:19–28)

In this account, the woman had been bleeding for 12 years and therefore was an outcast for all that time.

> And a large crowd followed him and pressed in on him. Now there was a woman who had been suffering from haemorrhages for twelve years. She had endured much under many physicians, and had spent all that

she had; and she was no better, but rather grew worse. She had heard about Jesus, and came up behind him in the crowd and touched his cloak, for she said, 'If I but touch his clothes, I will be made well.' Immediately her haemorrhage stopped; and she felt in her body that she was healed of her disease. Immediately aware that power had gone forth from him, Jesus turned about in the crowd and said, 'Who touched my clothes?' And his disciples said to him, 'You see the crowd pressing in on you; how can you say, "Who touched me?"' He looked all around to see who had done it. But the woman, knowing what had happened to her, came in fear and trembling, fell down before him, and told him the whole truth. He said to her, 'Daughter, your faith has made you well; go in peace, and be healed of your disease.'

(Mark 5:24b–34)

So here Jesus raises the status of women as well as healing here even though this was against Jewish law.

Of course, not all scholars or Christians accept the idea of Jesus as a liberator. Many consider that his authority was simply spiritual. They may cite texts in support of this, such as the following:

Then Pilate entered the headquarters again, summoned Jesus, and asked him, 'Are you the King of the Jews?' Jesus answered, 'Do you ask this on your own, or did others tell you about me?' Pilate replied, 'I am not a Jew, am I? Your own nation and the chief priests have handed you over to me. What have you done?' Jesus answered, 'My kingdom is not from this world. If my kingdom were from this world, my followers would be fighting to keep me from being handed over to the Jews. But as it is, my kingdom is not from here.' Pilate asked him, 'So you are a king?' Jesus answered, 'You say that I am a king. For this I was born, and for this I came into the world, to testify to the truth. Everyone who belongs to the truth listens to my voice.' Pilate asked him, 'What is truth?'

(John 18:33–38)

Others would refer to Matthew 19:30: 'But many who are first will be last, and the last will be first' – showing Jesus as liberator of the poor and oppressed.

SUMMARY

The historical Jesus

- Heresies
- Nicene Creed

Jesus' authority as the Son of God

- Christology

Jesus' divinity as expressed in his:

- knowledge of God
- miracles
  - Aquinas
  - David Hume

- Resurrection
  - What do people believe?
    Jesus as a teacher of wisdom
    Jesus' moral teaching on repentance and forgiveness
    The disciples after Pentecost
- Council of Jerusalem

  Jesus' moral teaching on inner purity and moral motivation
  Jesus' role as liberator of the marginalised and the poor, as expressed in
     his challenge to political and religious authority

  - Jesus as a Zealot
  - Liberation theology
  - Preferential option for the poor.

REVIEW QUESTIONS

Look back over the chapter and check that you can answer the following questions:

1   What were the purposes of the Councils of Nicaea and Constantinople?
2   How did the life of the disciples begin to change after Pentecost?
3   What did Bultmann mean by demythologising the New Testament?
4   What different types of Christology can you name and explain?

Terminology

Do you know your terminology?

Try to explain the following ideas without looking at your books and notes:

continued overleaf

- Arianism
- Homoousion
- Hypostatic union
- Parousia
- Zealot.

Examination questions practice

Exam mistakes to avoid: it is very important that you do not confuse autonomous, heteronomous and theonomous. May sure you can give clear examples of each.

To help you improve your answers look at the levels of response.

SAMPLE EXAM-STYLE QUESTION

'There is no justification for claiming that Jesus was a Zealot.' Discuss.

AO1 (15 marks)
- You might refer to the book *Jesus and the Zealots* by S.G.F. Brandon. This book argues that Jesus was a freedom fighter and that the Gospels deliberately changed this image.
- You might also refer to the work and writings of liberation theologians and activists, such as Gustavo Gutiérrez Merino, Camilo Torres Restrepo, Leonardo Boff and Óscar Romero.
- You could use the preferential option for the poor as an example of putting Jesus' teachings into practice.

AO2 (15 marks)
In evaluation the point could be made that there are many different ways of interpreting and understanding the New Testament. There are arguments to support the traditional view of the Church that Jesus was a pacifist and would have nothing to do with politics. Similarly, it is possible to argue in favour of liberation theology. You should also consider what Jesus meant by his teaching about the Kingdom of God.

Further possible questions

- **To what extent do you think that Christology is important in understanding who Jesus was?**
- **'Jesus said that he came "not to change the Law" but he did change it in his teachings in the Sermon on the Mount.' To what extent do you agree with this statement?**
- **Critically analyse the strengths and weaknesses of liberation theology.**
- **'Jesus was no more than another travelling rabbi.' Discuss.**

FURTHER READING

Chapman, G. (1994) *Catechism of the Catholic Church*, paras. 422–478.

Maccoby, H. 1987. *The Mythmaker: Paul and the Invention of Christianity*. New York: HarperCollins.

Maccoby, H. 2000. *Jesus the Pharisee*. London: SCM Press.

McGrath, A. 2011. *Theology: The Basics*. Oxford: Blackwell.

McGrath, A. (2011) *Theology: The Basics*, Blackwell, Chapter 4

Theissen, G. 2010. *The Shadow of the Galilean*. London: SCM Press.

Theissen, G. (2010) *The Shadow of the Galilean*, SCM Press

Essential terminology

Autonomous
Divine command theory
Heteronomous
Magisterium
Natural law
Theonomous

Key scholars

Plato (428–347 BCE)
Thomas Aquinas (1225–1274)
Immanuel Kant (1724–1804)
Jeremy Bentham (1748–1832)
John Stuart Mill (1806–1873)
Joseph Fletcher (1905–1991)
Pope John Paul II (1920–2005)
Cardinal Joseph Ratzinger (later Pope Benedict XVI) (1927–)
Hans Küng (1928–)
Stanley Hauerwas (1940–)

Living

21 Christian moral principles

WHAT YOU WILL LEARN ABOUT IN THIS CHAPTER

- Christian ethics from the New Testament.
- The role of authority, tradition and conscience in Christian ethics.
- The link between religion and morality.
- Absolutism and relativism in Christian ethics.
- Christian ethical theories: divine command theory and natural moral law.
- The relationship between Christian ethics and contemporary moral thought.

THE OCR CHECKLIST

The diversity of Christian moral reasoning and practices and sources of ethics, including:

- the Bible as the only authority for Christian ethical practices
  - as the Bible reveals God's will, then only biblical ethical commands must be followed
- Bible, Church and reason as the sources of Christian ethical practices
  - Christian ethics must be a combination of biblical teaching, Church teaching and human reason
- love (agape) as the only Christian ethical principle which governs Christian practices

  - Jesus' only command was to love and that human reason must decide how best to apply this

continued opposite

Learners should have the opportunity to discuss issues related to diversity of Christian moral principles, including:

* whether Christian ethics are distinctive
* whether Christian ethics are personal or communal
* whether the principle of love is sufficient to live a good life
* whether the Bible is a comprehensive moral guide.

Suggested scholarly views, academic approaches and sources of wisdom and authority

* Exodus 20:1–17
* 1 Corinthians 13:1–7
* Messer, N. (2006) *SCM Study Guide to Christian Ethics*. SCM Press.

WHAT IS CHRISTIAN ETHICS?

There is no easy answer to this question, as there is so much diversity within Christianity. Some Christians will base their ethics solely on the Bible and its teachings, others will base their ethics on the biblical teachings but also on Church tradition and natural law, others will follow a situation ethics approach and others will look to their conscience as a guide. As a result of this diversity, Christians have different responses to ethical issues, whether it is euthanasia, abortion, genetic engineering, foetal research, sex and relationships, war, peace or justice. It is important to understand not only what Christians think on different ethical issues but also why they think as they do and the basis of their ideas.

In many ways Christian ethics does not look at right and wrong actions, but at the sort of person we are called to become. The Bible teaches that humans are created by God in his image and called to live free and responsible lives, but sin and ignorance have led us to misuse this freedom. In many ways, therefore, Christian ethics has more in common with virtue ethics than any other ethical theory.

Natural law
The theory that an eternal, absolute, moral law can be discovered by reason.

The Jewish roots of Christian ethics

The early Church brought into Christianity much that belonged to Judaism, and many today would still claim that we can obtain absolute moral rules

Moses and the Ten Commandments
North Wind Picture Archives/Alamy

from the Bible: the Ten Commandments are rules that must be followed without exception, and in the Bible we can find many acts such as homosexuality and divorce that are utterly condemned. However, it is clear that Christianity left behind the Jewish ethic of law as a divine command made known in a comprehensive legal code and interpreted by lawyers into many ritual requirements and practices. Christians attempted to drop the legalism and keep the law, especially the Ten Commandments, which were seen as an important part of God's revelation and good guidelines for human existence and human flourishing, in accordance with the human nature which God gave us. Jewish ethical teaching, at its core, is based on relationships: our relationship with God and all our many and varied relationships with other people.

The basis of Christian ethics in the Bible

Many Christians rely on the Bible as their source of ethics as they believe that it is a revelation from God. 'All scripture is inspired by God and is useful for teaching, for reproof, for correction, and for training in righteousness, so that everyone who belongs to God may be proficient, equipped for every good work' (2 Timothy 3:16–17). This approach is called theonomous Christian ethics.

However, the use of the Bible, both the Old and New Testaments, in Christian ethics is not as straightforward as some would believe; some passages need careful exegesis which is beyond the scope of this book. The Bible is a collection of writings put together over a long period of time and reflecting many different cultural contexts. It is important that this fact is borne in mind and that its diversity is recognised. There is no biblical morality or even New Testament teaching that can be followed in every detail, as it all needs to be understood in its cultural context. Christian denominations have always chosen the Bible teachings that back up their particular take on Christianity, such as the Catholic use of Mark's teaching on divorce and total disregard for Matthew's exception clause, or the Lutheran misuse of Romans (7:1–20):

> For we know that the law is spiritual; but I am of the flesh, sold into slavery under sin. I do not understand my own actions. For I do not do what I want, but I do the very thing I hate. Now if I do what I do not want, I agree that the law is good. But in fact it is no longer I that do it, but sin that dwells within me. For I know that nothing good dwells within me, that is, in my want, but the evil I do not want is what I do. Now if I do what I do not want, flesh. I can will what is right, but I cannot do it. For I do not do the good if it is no longer I that do it, but sin that dwells within me.

The following section will necessarily take a broad-brush approach and follow general themes.

> ### Theonomous Christian ethics
>
> The word 'theonomous', which comes from ϙϵos (theos) god and nómos (nomos) law, is the belief that God's laws, including those in the Old Testament, should be observed by modern societies.

The ethics of Jesus

Although Christian ethics carries with it the Ten Commandments, it is of a totally different mindset from a law-based ethic. It was, from the beginning, attempting to reply to the philosophical questions of happiness and salvation. Therefore the most concentrated body of ethical teaching in the Gospels, the Sermon on the Mount, begins with the Beatitudes: 'Blessed are the poor . . .'

The Sermon on the Mount may seem to be a set of impossible commands, but although its teaching is challenging, underlying it all is the commandment of love. However, it is not always easy to see what is meant by 'love': for Jesus in the Synoptics it is love of God and love of neighbour; for Paul it is mostly love of neighbour, especially Christians; John's Gospel seems to speak of love in an even narrower sense. It may be summed up as follows:

> 'You shall love the Lord your God with all your heart, and with all your soul, and with all your mind.' This is the greatest and first commandment. And a second is like it: 'You shall love your neighbour as yourself.'
>
> (Matthew 22:37b–39)

> **Agape** (ἀγάπη)
>
> Agape love: 'the highest form of love, charity' . . . 'the love of God for man and of man for God' (Liddell and Scott 2010).

Or 'In everything do to others as you would have them do to you' (Matthew 7:12a). The ultimate Christian ethical teaching seems to centre on love: 'Love is the fulfilling of the law' (Romans 13:10b). This New Testament ethical teaching is part of the relationship with God – what makes Christian ethics different is the 'faith' element; Christian ethics comes from a need to interpret, understand and respond to ethical issues from the point of their particular relationship with God.

There are a number of specific teachings about agape in the New Testament:

> Jesus answered, 'The first is, "Hear, O Israel: the Lord our God, the Lord is one; you shall love the Lord your God with all your heart, and with all your soul, and with all your mind, and with all your strength." The second is this, "You shall love your neighbor as yourself." There is no other commandment greater than these.'
>
> (Mark 12:29–31)

> Jesus answered him, 'Those who love me will keep my word, and my Father will love them, and we will come to them and make our home with them. Whoever does not love me does not keep my words; and the word that you hear is not mine, but is from the Father who sent me.'
>
> (John 14:23–24)

Beloved, let us love one another, because love is from God; everyone who loves is born of God and knows God. Whoever does not love does not know God, for God is love. God's love was revealed among us in this way: God sent his only Son into the world so that we might live through him. In this is love, not that we loved God but that he loved us and sent his Son to be the atoning sacrifice for our sins. Beloved, since God loved us so much, we also ought to love one another. No one has ever seen God; if we love one another, God lives in us, and his love is perfected in us.

(1 John 4:7–12)

> Read Chapters 14–16 of John's Gospel. Make notes on what it says about love.

Thought point

This idea of the special relationship with God is carried on in the idea of the Kingdom of God. What the Kingdom of God actually means has been debated endlessly, but it seems to be a state which has arrived, but not yet – a little like a visitor who has arrived at a friend's house and rung the doorbell, but the door has not yet been opened. The problem is how this paradox is to be maintained as far as ethics is concerned. Jesus' ethics can be connected with the idea of the Kingdom of God only by seeing entry into the Kingdom as a result of responding to the appeal to the desire to be children of God; a joyful acceptance of forgiveness and a desire to do God's will. This is no blind obedience, nor is it a morality of law, command, duty and obligation; nor is it motivated by the promise of reward in heaven or punishment in hell, but by a desire to follow God's will – the love commandment.

The ethics of Paul

The other source of biblical Christian ethics is found in the Epistles of Paul. He wrote at a time when the early Christians were attempting to interpret the teachings of Jesus and apply them to a variety of new situations. Paul stresses the importance of Christian freedom, but to be free from the law means to be united with Christ and with one another in love and service. It is life lived in the Spirit: 'Live by the Spirit, I say, and do not gratify the desires of the flesh. . . . But if you are led by the Spirit, you are not subject to the law. . . . If we live by the Spirit, let us also be guided by the Spirit' (Galatians 5:16, 18, 25).

If then there is any encouragement in Christ, any consolation from love, any sharing in the Spirit, any compassion and sympathy, make my joy complete: be of the same mind, having the same love, being in full accord and of one mind. Do nothing from selfish ambition or conceit, but in humility regard others as better than yourselves. Let each of you look not to your own interests, but to the interests of others.

(Philippians 2:1–5)

Look up some of the following texts to see how Jesus' ethics is based on, yet seems to reinterpret, the Jewish law:

Matthew 5–7
Mark 2:23 to 3:6
Mark 7:1–23

For Paul, the whole law may be summed up in love of neighbour and this love is limitless, as is shown in the great hymn to love in the Letter to the Corinthians. Paul also calls the Christians to imitate the virtues of Jesus in their daily lives: meekness, gentleness, humility, generosity, mercy and self-giving love. However, the words and life of Jesus could not be made into a blueprint for Christian ethics in the early Church without becoming legalistic, and so it was recognised that following Christ depended on the gift and guidance of the Holy Spirit, which was given to the community of believers. Paul's list of virtues is called 'the fruit of the Spirit' (Galatians 5:22–23) and love is the greatest sign of the presence and activity of the Holy Spirit (I Corinthians 13).

If I speak in the tongues of mortals and of angels, but do not have love, I am a noisy gong or a clanging cymbal. And if I have prophetic powers, and understand all mysteries and all knowledge, and if I have all faith, so as to remove mountains, but do not have love, I am nothing. If I give away all my possessions, and if I hand over my body so that I may boast, but do not have love, I gain nothing. Love is patient; love is kind; love is not envious or boastful or arrogant or rude. It does not insist on its own way; it is not irritable or resentful; it does not rejoice in wrongdoing, but rejoices in the truth. It bears all things, believes all things, hopes all things, endures all things.

(1 Corinthians 13:1–7)

Christian ethics in this developing Church could be called a community ethic: the ethic of a community guided by the Holy Spirit, rather than by law or tradition.

If then there is any encouragement in Christ, any consolation from love, any sharing in the Spirit, any compassion and sympathy, make my joy complete: be of the same mind, having the same love, being in full accord and of one mind. Do nothing from selfish ambition or conceit, but in humility regard others as better than yourselves. Let each of you look not to your own interests, but to the interests of others.

(Philippians 2:1–4)

However, there is no explicit concern with changing society as a whole. The main attitude towards rulers was that of obedience, as their authority was given by God, but if the commands of the state and those of God conflict, then the Christian should obey God. According to Paul the barriers between slaves and free men and women have been broken, both marriage and celibacy are seen as gifts, and wealth is to be shared with those in need. However, there is no evidence of struggling for justice, as it was believed that God would soon intervene in history and establish his kingdom, apart from which Christians were few in number with no political clout. The teaching of love for one's neighbour, however, did eventually lead Christians to exercise greater social responsibility.

Love

This distinctive moral teaching based on love continued to dominate the work of Christian thinkers:

Love, and do what you will. If you keep silence, keep silence in love; if you speak, speak in love; if you correct, correct in love; if you forbear, forbear in love. Let love's root be within you, for from that root nothing but good can spring.

(Augustine, *Epistola Joannis* 7.8)

Love, according to Thomas Aquinas, is the reason why we were made; it unites us with God, and to love is to share his life. Without love no virtue is possible, and love alone leads to happiness and fulfilment.

AUTHORITY AND TRADITION IN CHRISTIAN ETHICS

Although Aquinas followed the early Christian idea of morality as love and grace, not law, it is true that legalism has justifiably been associated with Christian ethics, both in theory and in practice. Peter Singer criticises this legalism and accuses Christianity of obscuring the true nature of morality: human fulfilment – happiness. He thinks that the end of the Christian

Heteronomous Christian ethics

This is a system of normative ethics based not on the individual's own moral principles but also on beliefs and teachings taken from other sources.

influence on our moral standpoints will open up a 'better way of life for us' and the Judaeo-Christian ethic is 'an empty shell, founded on a set of beliefs that most people have laid aside'. Christian ethics have been seen as deontological and authoritarian, with an emphasis on certain acts as being either right or wrong.

Many Christians believe that ethics should be a combination of Biblical teaching, human reason and teaching from the authority of the Church. This is called heteronomous Christian ethics.

There are problems with Christian heteronomous ethics. Apart from the Bible, what other sources should be consulted while others should be ignored? Also, do these sources have a hierarchy of importance or are they all equal?

The issue of authority and tradition is treated differently by the different Christian churches. Some Protestants see the Bible as the sole authority in every matter and view this as more important than the role given to tradition in Catholicism.

While, particularly in the past, there have been Protestant theologians who taught natural law, today most Protestants would accept the Bible as the primary source. Others would argue that the Bible evolved over time and the development of Christian ethics should also be based on reason, conscience and particular Church traditions.

An exception to this perhaps is the American theologian Stanley Hauerwas (1940–). Hauerwas is strongly influenced by Karl Barth and maintains that Christian ethics evolve within the worshipping community of the Church. He says that that Christian Church is ongoing and developing.

In collaboration with William Willimon, Hauerwas wrote *Resident Aliens: Life in the Christian Colony* (1989). The book considers the nature of the church and how it relates to the culture around it. It argues that churches should focus on developing Christian life and community rather than trying to reform secular culture. The authors do not accept that any country is a Christian nation. They say that Christians should regard themselves as 'resident aliens' in a foreign land. Instead of trying to make the world confirm to the gospel or the gospel to the world, they say that Christians should focus on conforming to the gospel themselves. The role of Christians is therefore to live lives which model the love of Christ. So instead of trying to convince other people to change or redefine their ethics they should present a new set of ethics which are derived from the life, death and resurrection of Christ.

The Catholic Church

Catholics would argue that scripture does not give guidance on many important matters and so Church tradition is important, as interpreted by the Magisterium (the pope and the bishops). This teaching does not claim to be absolutely accurate or infallible, but is teaching on behalf of the community of the people of God. It can become authoritarian, especially when the issues are new or there is no consensus of views among the episcopacy or the Catholic community – for example the teaching of *Humanae Vitae* (1968), which banned artificial contraception and has been totally ignored by many Catholics.

> The Church, the 'pillar and bulwark of the truth,' 'has received this solemn command of Christ from the apostles to announce the saving truth.' 'To the Church belongs the right always and everywhere to announce moral principles, including those pertaining to the social order, and to make judgments on any human affairs to the extent that they are required by the fundamental rights of the human person or the salvation of souls.'
>
> The Magisterium of the Pastors of the Church in moral matters is ordinarily exercised in catechesis and preaching, with the help of the works of theologians and spiritual authors. Thus from generation to generation, under the aegis and vigilance of the pastors, the 'deposit' of Christian moral teaching has been handed on, a deposit composed of a characteristic body of rules, commandments, and virtues proceeding from faith in Christ and animated by charity. Alongside the Creed and the Our Father, the basis for this catechesis has traditionally been the Decalogue which sets out the principles of moral life valid for all men.
>
> The Roman Pontiff and the bishops are 'authentic teachers, that is, teachers endowed with the authority of Christ, who preach the faith to the people entrusted to them, the faith to be believed and put into practice.' The ordinary and universal Magisterium of the Pope and the bishops in communion with him teach the faithful the truth to believe, the charity to practice, the beatitude to hope for.
>
> (*Catechism of the Catholic Church* §2032–2034)

In addition, the Church stresses the role of the conscience and the importance of natural law.

> The authority of the Magisterium extends also to the specific precepts of the natural law, because their observance, demanded by the Creator, is necessary for salvation. In recalling the prescriptions of the natural law, the Magisterium of the Church exercises an essential part of its prophetic office of proclaiming to men what they truly are and reminding them of what they should be before God.
>
> (*Catechism of the Catholic Church* §2036)

Magisterium

The *Magisterium* of the Catholic Church is the church's authority to establish its own teachings. That authority is rests in the pope and the bishops because it is believed that they are in communion with the correct teachings of the faith. Sacred scripture and sacred tradition 'make up a single sacred deposit of the Word of God, which is entrusted to the Church' (Dei Verbum 2:10).

Liberation theology

Another development of Catholic ethical heteronomy is liberation theology, which developed in South America in the 1950s and 1960s. In 1955 the Latin American Episcopal Conference (CELAM) was founded in Brazil.

Liberation theology is based firmly on the Bible as the central source of ethics. Liberation theology aims to fight poverty by addressing its source, which is believed to be sin. It looks at the relationship between Christian theology (particularly Catholic) and political activism in relation to social justice, poverty and human rights. It focuses on seeing theology from the perspective of the poor and the oppressed.

CELAM attempted to push the Second Vatican Council (1962–65) towards a socially oriented stance. Liberation theology was opposed by the Vatican, and Pope Paul VI tried to slow the movement after the Council. The Church saw liberation theology as being related to Marxism.

In 1979 at a conference in Puebla, Pope John Paul II criticised radical liberation theology, saying, 'this idea of Christ as a political figure, a revolutionary, as the subversive of Nazareth, does not tally with the Church's catechesis.' He did, however, continue by speaking about 'the ever increasing wealth of the rich at the expense of the ever increasing poverty of the poor'.

In 1983, Cardinal Joseph Ratzinger (later Pope Benedict XVI), said that he objected that the spiritual concept of the Church as 'People of God' is transformed into a 'Marxist myth'.

The idea of the 'agreement of the faithful' has been further developed by many free churches, which have built their forms of church government on congregational lines – this is going back to Paul's idea of attempting to discern the will of God by the Holy Spirit working in the Christian community. However, many Christian legalists would argue that Christians should keep rules because God has revealed them – is this why Christian ethics has become so irrelevant to many people?

Ethical autonomy

The Catholic Church views ethical autonomy as a development of liberal Catholicism. It teaches that people should have much greater autonomy in making their own ethical decisions. The Swiss Catholic theologian Hans Küng (1928–) argued that the essence of Christian ethics could be discovered by any 'person of good will'. He created the idea of a 'global ethic' to save the environment and to prevent humanity from destroying itself.

Küng's teachings angered the Magisterium and he had his official license to teach withdrawn in 1979.

My permission to teach was withdrawn by the church, but nevertheless I retained my chair and my institute. For two further decades I remained unswervingly faithful to my church in critical loyalty, and to the present day I have remained professor of ecumenical theology and a Catholic priest in good standing. I affirm the papacy for the Catholic Church, but at the same time indefatigably call for a radical reform of it in accordance with the criterion of the gospel.

(Küng, 2002, *The Catholic Church: A Short History*)

This type of ethical autonomy was condemned by Pope John Paul II (1920–2005) and Pope Benedict XVI (1927–).

The Protestant Church

Radical Protestant theologians, such as Joseph Fletcher (1905–1991) (see Chapter 9), argued that goodness is just a condition of being human and does not have to be revealed or derived from natural law. While agreeing that Christianity stressed the idea of agape, he argued that ethics are autonomous and teleological – striving to create the most loving situation. Opponents of this idea have said that 'love' is not sufficient in itself but that ethics must be developed internally to develop a relationship with God. 'Do not think that I have come to abolish the law or the prophets; I have come not to abolish but to fulfil' (Matthew 5:17).

DIVINE COMMAND THEORY

Divine command theory
Actions are right or wrong depending on whether they follow God's commands.

If God's will is taken as arbitrary, then this does not give any satisfactory explanation for why anyone is morally bound to follow it. If God commands something for good reasons, then it is these reasons that are the source of moral obligations, regardless of God or any religious law.

Does religion give people a reason to be moral? Is there any meaning to life that would make it even possible to talk about morality? In Dostoyevsky's *The Brothers Karamazov*, Ivan says that 'without God everything is permitted' – so does God give a reason to be moral? In Albert Camus' *The Stranger*, the issue of meaning is a central theme – Mersault does not condemn any action as wrong, and when he ends up shooting a complete stranger, he is sorry only that he got caught – killing someone has no more meaning than any other action. However, we do make judgements about what is right and wrong, and many people do so without seeing any involvement from God.

Euthyphro dilemma

The dilemma first identified by Plato – is something good because God commands it or does God command it because it is good?

The whole problem of doing something because God commands it was examined by Plato in what has become known as the Euthyphro dilemma. Plato asks, 'Is X good because God wills it or does God will it because it is good?'

The first option says that certain actions are good because God commands them – it is the command of God that makes something good or bad. This means that if God commanded, 'Make a fat profit,' then it would be right – this makes God's commands arbitrary. Leibniz in his *Discourse on Metaphysics* sums this up:

> So in saying that things are not good by any rule of goodness, but sheerly by the will of God, it seems to me that one destroys, without realising it, all the love of God and all his glory. For why praise him for what he has done if he would be equally praiseworthy in doing the contrary?

Deontological ethics

Ethical systems which consider that the moral act itself has moral value (e.g. telling the truth is always right, even when it is difficult or causes problems.).

The idea that moral rules are true because God commands them is called the divine command theory. In many ways the laws of the Old Testament may be seen as a good example of this theory (e.g. 'Thou shalt not commit murder'). This view of Christian ethics goes completely against the morality of love and grace, but it was held by many Christian thinkers, such as Duns Scotus, William of Ockham and Descartes, as well as many conservative Protestants today. If we do good acts simply out of obedience to God, are we being good for the right reasons?

The second option says that God commands things because they are right or wrong in themselves. Murder is wrong in itself and that is why God forbids it. God can see that it destroys life and makes people unhappy, and so it is unlikely that he would ever command it. However, this option seems to be arguing that there is a standard of right and wrong which is independent of God and which influences his commands. James Rachels argued that it is unacceptable for religious belief to involve unqualified obedience to God's commands as it means abandoning personal autonomy – the rightness of an action must come from the fact that the action is right in itself.

Absolutism

An objective moral rule or value that is always true in all situations and for everyone without exception.

Divine command theory

Actions are right or wrong depending on whether they follow God's commands.

Thought point

1. Do we need God to give meaning to life?
2. Do you agree that 'without God everything is permitted'?
3. Explain the difference between 'X is good because God wills it' and 'God wills X because it is good'.

continued opposite

4 Read the Euthyphro dilemma and work out the key criticisms of the argument.
5 Can morality ever be founded on authority?
6 How do you decide what is good or bad? Justify your view.

> **Conscience**
>
> Our sense of right and wrong.

NATURAL LAW

A full treatment of natural law may be found in Chapter 10.

Natural law is often seen as centred on law, and so on obligation, and Aquinas himself speaks of natural law. However, by this he meant that our nature is objectively knowable and our reason will help us to understand what is meant by it. Ethics is a matter of our common humanity, not a set of principles from which we make moral decisions, and its purpose is to enable us to become complete and whole humans, and to achieve our desires. Morality is rooted in the desire for happiness, but for Aquinas natural law is not enough if we are to attain final happiness – for this God's grace is needed.

Natural law has come to be seen as deontological and authoritarian with its application of the primary precepts, but Aquinas said that the primary precepts were always true, as they point us in the right direction; however, different situations require secondary precepts and if our reasoning is faulty these may be wrong – we need to discern what is good and what will help us to become complete and whole human beings. Intention is important, but in natural law it is not possible to say that the end justifies the means, although there is certainly flexibility in the natural law approach. Aquinas wrote, 'The more you descend into the details the more it appears how the general rule admits of exceptions, so that you have to hedge it with cautions and qualifications.'

However, Aquinas is certain that there is an absolute natural law and this has led the Catholic Church, following Aquinas, to emphasise reason as a tool for showing that certain acts are intrinsically right or wrong, as they go against our true purpose; certain absolutes, such as the sanctity of life, cannot be changed by the circumstances.

CONSCIENCE

Catholics consider that conscience plays an important part in Christian ethical decision making. Here conscience is not seen as some inner voice or oracle that will point us in the right direction – conscience is not about feelings but about reason and judgement. Aquinas saw conscience as reason making moral decisions. But conscience as the 'voice of God' can easily become what we mean by 'right' and 'wrong' – so men persecute 'heretics', slaughter enemies and become suicide bombers in the name of God.

However, conscience does not make the law; it recognises law and uses it to assess conduct. So, for religious ethics, conscience is not so much the voice of God as a response to God's voice. Conscience can be mistaken; doing a bad action when following the guidance of conscience does not make that action good. Conscience is just a way of using reason to come to a decision, but it needs to be informed, and in following conscience we need to be prepared to accept the costs, not just do what we want.

SUMMARY

- The Jewish roots of Christian ethics
- The basis of Christian ethics in the Bible
- Theonomous Christian ethics

  - The ethics of Jesus

    - Agape

  - The ethics of Paul

- Authority and tradition in Christian ethics
- Heteronomous Christian ethics

  - The Catholic Church
  - Liberation theology.

- Ethical autonomy

  - The Catholic Church
  - The Protestant Church.

- Divine command theory
- Natural law
- Euthyphro dilemma

REVIEW QUESTIONS

Look back over the chapter and check that you can answer the following questions:

1   What is the principle of heteronomous Christian ethics?

continued opposite

2   What is the principle of theonomous Christian ethics?

3   Which of these principles do you think most convincing? Justify your answer.

4   What is the connection between conscience and Christian religious ethics?

Terminology

Do you know your terminology?

Try to explain the following ideas without looking at your books and notes:

- Magisterium
- Divine command theory
- Natural law
- Agape.

Examination questions practice

Exam mistakes to avoid: it is very important that you do not confuse autonomous, heteronomous and theonomous. May sure you can give clear examples of each.

To help you improve your answers look at the levels of response.

SAMPLE EXAM-STYLE QUESTION

'The Bible and the teaching authority of the Church are both necessary for Christian ethics.' Discuss.

AO1 (15 marks)
- You might say that if the Bible is the revealed word of God then it must have moral authority. However, some Christians might question how much authority it has in twenty-first century.
- You could also say that although Christians ethics are largely based on the Bible and, in particular on the Ten Commandments and Jesus' teaching, some people believe that

the teaching of the Church, human reason and the overarching concept of agape have a very strong influence.

AO2 (15 marks)

In evaluation the point could be made that without the Bible people would make the wrong choices and decisions. Can human reason be trusted as it often appears to reach different conclusions? The writers of the Bible of necessity were influenced by the social and geographical influences of where they lived and the time of writing. Therefore, it could be concluded that the teachings of the Church and reason are vital in understanding Christian ethics.

Further possible questions

- To what extent do you agree that the most important principle of Christian ethics is agape?
- 'Theonomous Christian ethics are based on the word of God and so are more reliable than heteronomous ethics.' Discuss.
- To what extent are Christian ethics personal rather than communal?
- 'The principle of love is all that is needed to live a good life.' Discuss.

FURTHER READING

Cook, D. 1983. *The Moral Maze*. London: SPCK.

Hoose, B. (ed.). 1998. *Christian Ethics: An Introduction*. London: Cassell (contains an excellent chapter on the Bible and Christian ethics by Tom Deidum).

Macquarrie, J. and Childress, J. 1986. *A New Dictionary of Christian Ethics*. London: SCM.

Messer, N. 2006. *SCM Study Guide to Christian Ethics*. London: SCM Press.

Plato. 1969. 'Euthyphro', in *The Last Days of Socrates*, Tredennick, H. (trans.). London: Penguin.

Rachels, J. and Rachels, S. 2007. *The Elements of Moral Philosophy*. New York: McGraw-Hill.

Living

22 Christian moral action

WHAT YOU WILL LEARN ABOUT IN THIS CHAPTER

The life and teachings of Dietrich Bonhoeffer

The relevance of Bonhoeffer's teachings in the twentieth century and today.

Essential terminology

Aryan paragraph
Christology
Civil disobedience
Confessing Church
Discipleship
Duty
Grace
Religionless Christianity
Secular pacifism
Systematic theology
Tyrannicide

Key scholars

Karl Barth (1886–1968)
Dietrich Bonhoeffer (1906–1945)

THE OCR CHECKLIST

Christian moral action
- The teaching and example of Dietrich Bonhoeffer on:
  - duty to God and duty to the state
    - Bonhoeffer's teaching on the relationship of Church and state, including:
      - obedience, leadership and doing God's will
      - justification of civil disobedience.
  - Church as community and source of spiritual discipline
    - Bonhoeffer's role in the Confessing Church and his own religious community at Finkenwalde
  - the cost of discipleship
    - Bonhoeffer's teaching on ethics as action, including:
      - 'costly grace'
      - sacrifice and suffering
      - solidarity.

continued overleaf

Learners should have the opportunity to discuss issues related to Christian moral action in the life and teaching of Bonhoeffer, including:

- whether Christians should practise civil disobedience
- whether it is possible always to know God's will
- whether Bonhoeffer puts too much emphasis on suffering
- whether Bonhoeffer's theology has relevance today.

Contextual references:

For reference, the ideas of Bonhoeffer listed earlier can be found in: *Letters and Papers from Prison and The Cost of Discipleship,* Chapter 1. Suggested scholarly views, academic approaches and sources of wisdom and authority:

- Romans 13:1–7
- *Barmen Declaration* (www.sacred-texts.com/chr/barmen.htm)
- Luke 10:38–42.

The life of Dietrich Bonhoeffer (1906–1945)

Dietrich Bonhoeffer

Mary Evans Picture Library/Alamy

Early life

Dietrich Bonhoeffer was born to Karl and Paula Bonhoeffer, on 4 February 1906 in Breslau (now Wrocław, Poland). His father was a psychiatrist and neurologist and his mother was a teacher. In addition to his other siblings, Dietrich had a twin sister, Sabine Bonhoeffer Leibholz: he and Sabine were the sixth and seventh children out of eight.

continued overleaf

INTRODUCTION

'The church as we know it has got to change.' Is this the reality that Bonhoeffer was trying to achieve for his times and the twenty-first century? In this chapter, you will be studying the key concepts and ideologies of Bonhoeffer, including his views of sacrifices, duty and responsibility to Christ and humanity: 'Not hero worship, but intimacy with Christ' (Bonhoeffer, *The Cost of Discipleship*).

The key questions are:

- Did Bonhoeffer base his lifestyle on the life and teachings of Jesus?
- Did he want the changes that Jesus made to become relevant today?

Systematic theology

Systematic theology attempts to create an ordered, rational and coherent account of Christian teachings based on the Bible. It includes dogmatics, ethics and philosophy.

The early 1930s were a period of great upheaval in Germany, with the instability of Weimar Republic and the mass unemployment of the Great Depression leading to the election of Adolf Hitler (1889–1945) as chancellor in 1933.

Bonhoeffer was a firm opponent of Hitler's philosophy; however, it was widely welcomed by the German population, including significant parts of the Church.

Two days after Hitler's election Bonhoeffer made a radio broadcast criticising him, and the dangers that awaited due to the Führer. As Bonhoeffer spoke his radio broadcast was cut off mid-air. (The cause of this is not known.)

In the same year, Bonhoeffer spoke out about the persecution of Jews and argued that the Church had a responsibility to act against this kind of policy. This idea stemmed from his deep conviction in the idea of ecumenism. He said the church must not just 'bandage the victims under the wheel, but jam the spoke in the wheel itself' (Bonhoeffer, *No Rusty Swords*).

Adolf Hitler
Everett Historical/Shutterstock

The Confessing Church

Bonhoeffer sought to organise the Protestant Church to reject Nazi ideology from infiltrating the church. This started a new revolution and eventually led to the formation of the Confessing Church, with help from Martin Niemöller. The Confessing Church sought to stand in stark contrast with the Nazi-supported, German Christian movement.

In 1933 Bonhoeffer was offered a parish post in eastern Berlin. However, he refused it in protest of the nationalist policy and instead accepted a two-year appointment as a pastor of two German-speaking Protestant churches in London. He explained to the theologian Karl Barth that he had found little support for his views and that 'it was about time to go for a while into the desert.' Barth saw this as running away from the problems in German and said, 'I can only reply to all the reasons and excuses which you put forward: "And what of the German Church?"'

After two years in London, Bonhoeffer returned to Berlin. He felt a call to go back to his native country and share in its struggles, despite the bleak outlook. Shortly after his return, Bonhoeffer had his authorisation to teach revoked after being denounced as a pacifist and enemy of the state.

In 1937, as Nazi control of the country intensified, the Confessing Church seminary was closed down by Heinrich Himmler Reichsführer of the Schutzstaffel (commander of the Protection Squad). During this period, Bonhoeffer wrote extensively on subjects of theological interest which were deep-rooted in his stance on ecumenism and social injustice in the world.

Education

His family were not religious, although his mother's grandfather was the Protestant theologian Karl von Hasse. However, at the age of 14 he announced that he wanted to train to become a priest and study theology. This was clearly a shock to his family due to their backgrounds having strong musical and artistic heritages. This was an opportunity for Bonhoeffer to express his ideas and worldviews. He began his studies at the University of Tübingen in 1923. He went on to gain a doctorate in theology for his influential thesis, *Sanctorum Communio: eine Dogmatische Untersuchung zur Soziologie der Kirche*

continued overleaf

(Communion of Saints) and graduated in 1927 from the University of Berlin. His second thesis, *Akt und sein* (Act and Being), was published in 1931.

After his request to be ordained was not granted, because at the age of 24 he was too young, Bonhoeffer went to America to pursue postgraduate studies at New York City's Union Theological Seminary. He also spent time in Spain, and this gave him more confidence in his opinions of the Church's practical understanding and interpretation of the Gospels and, in particular, the stance which it took in supporting the social and injustices that these societies were facing. This was to contribute to his radical thinking in challenging both Church and state. Through his experiences in the USA, Spain and so forth, Bonhoeffer came to realise the importance and necessity of the churches working together across all their divisions.

Return to Germany

In 1931, aged 25, Bonhoeffer returned to Berlin and was ordained as a priest. He also joined the staff of the University of Berlin as a lecturer in systematic theology.

The Cost of Discipleship is a study on the Sermon on the Mount and argues for greater spiritual discipline and practice to achieve 'the costly grace'.

> Cheap grace is the grace we bestow on ourselves. Cheap grace is the preaching of forgiveness without requiring repentance, baptism without church discipline, Communion without confession . . . Cheap grace is grace without discipleship, grace without the cross, grace without Jesus Christ, living and incarnate.
>
> (Bonhoeffer, *The Cost of Discipleship*)

Worried by a fear of being asked to take an oath to Hitler or be arrested, Bonhoeffer left Germany for the USA in June 1939. After less than two years, he returned to Germany because he felt guilty for seeking sanctuary and not having the courage to practise what he preached.

It was at this time that he developed the idea of secular pacifism. He had always considered that he was a pacifist but came to realise that this form of pacifism was based on a secular belief that did not take account of a Christian's preparation for the Kingdom of God and that there were occasions when evil must be challenged.

On 8 April 1945, Bonhoeffer was given a cursory court martial and sentenced to death by hanging. Like many of the conspirators, he was hung by wire, to prolong the death. He was executed with fellow conspirators, such as Admiral Wilhelm Canaris and Hans Oster.

Just before his execution, he asked a fellow inmate to relate a message to Bishop George Bell of Chichester: *'This is the end – for me the beginning of life.'*

The camp doctor at Flossenbürg who witnessed the execution of Bonhoeffer later wrote,

> I saw Pastor Bonhoeffer . . . kneeling on the floor praying fervently to God. I was most deeply moved by the way this lovable man prayed, so devout and so certain that God heard his prayer. At the place of execution, he again said a short prayer and then climbed the few steps to the gallows, brave and composed. His death ensued after a few seconds. In the almost fifty years that I worked as a doctor, I have hardly ever seen a man die so entirely submissive to the will of God.

Duty to God and duty to the state

The definition of the word according to the *Oxford English Dictionary*: 'Moral obligation; the binding force of what is morally right.' e.g. *'It's my duty to uphold the law.'*

Does Bonhoeffer try to distinguish between Christian duties and secular ones?

Bonhoeffer's work *Ethics* was written from 1940 to 1943. Christian ethics, he says, must be concerned with the regenerated person, whose chief desire should be to please God, not with the one who is looking for an airtight philosophical system.

Bonhoeffer wrote that 'instead of knowing only the God who is good to him and instead of knowing all things in Him, [man] knows only himself as the origin of good and evil.' With this statement, he entered into one of the most difficult philosophical and theological problems in the history of the Church: the problem of evil. Bonhoeffer believed that the problem of evil could be understood only considering the Fall of man (Genesis 3:1–24). Due to modern humanity having a vagueness about what is right or wrong, Bonhoeffer urged Christians to be concerned with the living will of God rather than the set of rules people may follow.

Bonhoeffer knew that the opposition to Hitler and the decision to overthrow him were going to be a very difficult time. He got to the point that acknowledging the Hitler's assassination was the only hope for the freedom of the Church; however, this caused a great dilemma: 'Is murder ever right?' Bonhoeffer came to believe that evil must be opposed even if this involved murder. He relied on the principle that God would forgive the person who became a sinner by opposing evil in this way.

World War II was at its severest point, and the greatest problem facing Christians and the Church was that of ethics. They found themselves opposing sides of war. For the difficulties they faced, Bonhoeffer advised them to turn to Christ, in whom they could receive answers.

The key controversy was that Bonhoeffer suggested that the state cannot represent the Church and therefore cannot have any power or authority over it. The questions we should consider are: 'Should the state and Church be separate?' 'Should the Church get exclusivity from the state?' 'If we live in the land, should we not abide by the laws of the land?'

Obedience to the will of God

We in live a world where the views of the public are mixed and varied due to political leadership, which is probably at an all-time low. There are many uncertainties surrounding the choices people in power make for others. The times in which we live and the people who rule have divided the people in either accepting their rules or rebelling against them. The focus in obeying God's will is made clear in the New Testament and is set out in the teachings of Paul in the Epistle to the Romans.

Let every person be subject to the governing authorities; for there is no authority except from God, and those authorities that exist have been

---

Karl Barth the man (1886–1968)

Karl Barth

Granger Historical Picture Archive/Alamy

Karl Barth was a Swiss Reformed theologian who is often considered to be the greatest Protestant theologian of the twentieth century.

His father, Johann Friedrich Barth, was a professor of theology and a pastor. From 1911 to 1921 Karl Barth was a Reformed pastor in the village of Safenwil in Aargau. Later he became a professor of theology at Göttingen (1921–1925), Münster (1925–1930) and Bonn (1930–1935).

He left Germany in 1935 after refusing to swear allegiance to Adolf Hitler. He returned to Switzerland and became a professor in Basel (1935–1962).

His most famous work is the 13-volume *Church Dogmatics*, published between 1932 and 1967.

instituted by God. Therefore whoever resists authority resists what God has appointed, and those who resist will incur judgment. For rulers are not a terror to good conduct, but to bad. Do you wish to have no fear of the authority? Then do what is good, and you will receive its approval; for it is God's servant for your good. But if you do what is wrong, you should be afraid, for the authority does not bear the sword in vain! It is the servant of God to execute wrath on the wrongdoer. Therefore one must be subject, not only because of wrath but also because of conscience. For the same reason you also pay taxes, for the authorities are God's servants, busy with this very thing. Pay to all what is due them – taxes to whom taxes are due, revenue to whom revenue is due, respect to whom respect is due, honour to whom honour is due.

(Romans 13:1–7)

The purpose of this quotation is so that Christians might better understand how it is that God would have people relate to those whom he, in his sovereignty, has placed in authority.

However, Bonhoeffer was asking the question, 'Is it God's will to obey the state?'

Christianity stands or falls with its revolutionary protest against violence, arbitrariness and pride of power and with its plea for the weak. Christians are doing too little to make these points clear rather than too much. Christendom adjusts itself far too easily to the worship of power. Christians should give more offense, shock the world far more, than they are doing now. Christian should take a stronger stand in favor of the weak rather than considering first the possible right of the strong.

(Bonhoeffer, *Sermon*)

For discussion

What does he mean by this quote? Does he suggest that people bow down too much to the state and the rules of others rather than spreading the truth about the Church's beliefs?

Remembering what he had faced under the reign of Hitler, Bonhoeffer fought fervently for social justice. Bonhoeffer's conviction is clear in the quote, stating that people must submit, abandon their selfish ways and become selfless. He is saying that taking a strong stance can help people stand together so that justice can prevail. There must be balance, but people should not forget others in doing so. It comes down to the basics of the importance of Christian love. Bonhoeffer is very focused on Christian autonomy; however, Christians can achieve this by living moral lives. His argument extends to the concepts of people submitting to prayer and focusing on Christ as their role model.

Leadership

Bonhoeffer spent much of his life opposing what he considered to be bad leadership. When Hitler was elected chancellor in 1933, his was one of the first voices in Germany to urge for caution. He wrote extensively on topics concerning Christian theology and effective spiritual practices. Considering his personal perspective witnessing Hitler's rise, he also addressed the nature of leadership and power.

The primary focus on leaders, whoever they may be, is linked with the degree of power; however, this can be challenged by this statement attributed to Abraham Lincoln: *'Nearly all men can stand adversity, but if you want to test a man's character, give him power.'* Bonhoeffer claimed that Germany allowed a leader with his own motives and agendas to lead the country. In doing so the people had submitted to giving up who they were. Leadership should be an area where someone takes everyone's views into perspective. They should realise that leadership goes beyond the leader.

Bonhoeffer's words about true leadership, therefore, are appropriate for anybody. He certainly had Hitler in mind and political leaders in general while writing this passage:

> If [the true Leader] understands his function in any other way than as it is rooted in fact, if he does not continually tell his followers quite clearly of the limited nature of his task and of their own responsibility, if he allows himself to surrender to the wishes of his followers, who would always make him their idol – then the image of the Leader will pass over into the image of the mis-leader, and he will be acting in a criminal way not only towards those he leads, but also towards himself. The true Leader must always be able to disillusion. It is not just that this is his responsibility and real object. He must lead his following away from the authority of his person to the recognition of the real authority of orders and offices . . . He must radically refuse to become the appeal, the idol, i.e. the ultimate authority of those whom he leads . . . He serves the order of the state, of the community, and his service can be of incomparable value. But only so long as he keeps strictly in his place . . . He has to lead the individual into his own maturity . . . Now a feature of man's maturity is responsibility towards other people, towards existing orders. . .

> ... Only when a man sees that office is a penultimate authority in the face of an ultimate, indescribable authority, in the face of the authority of God, has the real situation been reached. And before this Authority the individual knows himself to be completely alone. The individual is responsible before God. And this solitude of man's position before God, this subjection to an ultimate authority, is destroyed when the authority of the Leader or of the office is seen as ultimate authority ... Alone before God, man becomes what he is, free and committed to responsibility at the same time.
>
> (Bonhoeffer, 'Leadership Principle', 1933)

Bonhoeffer acknowledged that leadership is a normal and necessary part of life. Authentic leadership, in Bonhoeffer's view, is the administration of an objective office.

> The first service that one owes to others in the fellowship consists of listening to them. Just as love of God begins with listening to his word, so the beginning of love for our brothers and sisters is learning to listen to them.
>
> (*Life Together*)

Justification of civil disobedience

Civil disobedience is the active, professed refusal to obey certain laws, demands and commands of a government, or of an occupying international power. Civil disobedience is sometimes, though not always, defined as non-violent resistance.

Bonhoeffer believed in non-violent resistance but considered that it was his Christian duty to use force against an evil regime. He was arrested on 5 April 1943 on the grounds that he helped Jews escape to Switzerland. He then spent 18 months in a military prison in Berlin. He was accused of involvement in the July 1944 attempt to assassinate Hitler and was placed in the Buchenwald concentration camp. From there he was taken to Flossenbürg, where he was hung for treason in 1945. This stance might seem to oppose or contradict his views on modelling life on Jesus and Christianity being about love. The key to understanding Bonhoeffer's view on civil disobedience is that Christians have a responsibility towards the state; however, this does not mean that they require the state to become Christian, but must do things in accordance with the will of God.

Bonhoeffer was truly against the state in the rule of Hitler; he felt that the Church was being sidetracked into Nazism.

In the Old Testament, revenge or retribution is seen as a legitimate aim of punishment.

'Anyone who maims another shall suffer the same injury in return: fracture for fracture, eye for eye, tooth for tooth; the injury inflicted is the injury to be suffered' (Leviticus 24:19–20). The commandment's original intention was to limit revenge.

So, was Bonhoeffer justified in plotting to assassinate Hitler?

In the Sermon on the Mount Jesus tells his disciples that they must offer no resistance or retaliation towards their enemies.

> Blessed are the peacemakers, for they will be called children of God.
>
> (Matthew 5:9)

> But I say to you, Do not resist an evildoer. But if anyone strikes you on the right cheek, turn the other also.
>
> (Matthew 5:39)

When Jesus was arrested one of the disciples cut off the ear of one of the guards. 'Then Jesus said to him, "Put your sword back into its place; for all who take the sword will perish by the sword"' (Matthew 26:52).

Tyrannicide – the killing or assassination of a tyrant.

For discussion

This appears to contradict Jesus' attitude or behaviour on two separate occasions, or does it? Can one do anything to stand up for what they believe in?

Jesus cleanses the Temple (Matthew 21:12–17):

> Then Jesus entered the temple and drove out all who were selling and buying in the temple, and he overturned the tables of the money changers and the seats of those who sold doves. He said to them, 'It is written, "My house shall be called a house of prayer"; but you are making it a den of robbers.'
>
> The blind and the lame came to him in the temple, and he cured them. But when the chief priests and the scribes saw the amazing things that he did, and heard the children crying out in the temple, 'Hosanna to the Son of David,' they became angry and said to him, 'Do you hear what these are saying?' Jesus said to them, 'Yes; have you never read, "Out of the mouths of infants and nursing babies you have prepared praise for yourself"?'

He left them, went out of the city to Bethany, and spent the night there.

Jesus curses the fig tree (Matthew 21:18–22):

In the morning, when he returned to the city, he was hungry. And seeing a fig tree by the side of the road, he went to it and found nothing at all on it but leaves. Then he said to it, 'May no fruit ever come from you again!' And the fig tree withered at once. When the disciples saw it, they were amazed, saying, 'How did the fig tree wither at once?' Jesus answered them, 'Truly I tell you, if you have faith and do not doubt, not only will you do what has been done to the fig tree, but even if you say to this mountain, "Be lifted up and thrown into the sea," it will be done. Whatever you ask for in prayer with faith, you will receive.'

Historical examples of civil disobedience

Martin Luther – freedom of religion
American Revolution – tax protest
Martin Luther King Jr. – racial equality
Rosa Parks – racial equality
Mohandas Gandhi – inspires civil rights and protested for social justice to prevail.

So, to conclude, the key aspect of Bonhoeffer's views was that people should not allow themselves to become consumed with the euphoria of the moment and time, but have the will of God in mind on all occasions. If God's will is fulfilled, then whatever the consequences of your action God will forgive.

The Church as community and source of spiritual discipline

Bonhoeffer said that the Church must act as a source of morality and hope for all. The focus must be God's will; however, this needs to encompass everyone even if they are not Christian. The Church needs to be a beacon of hope and willing to be able to give the communities the strength and focus to live moral lives, through either teachings or actions. It needs to stop hiding behind its four walls and embrace everyone, even a society without religion. Bonhoeffer said that *'Your life as a Christian should make non-believers question their disbelief in God.'*

The key focus of Bonhoeffer was that people should not judge anyone, but embrace everyone: '*Judging others makes us blind, whereas love is illuminating. By judging others, we blind ourselves to our own evil and to the grace which others are just as entitled to as we are.*'

If a community is to unite then it starts with the Church. The Church needs to come out of a place complacency and contentment and make a more practical impact in society. The Church needs to assert itself in a confident powerful manner that can influence people by example; the key to this is showing love and empathy to all.

> We do God's work for our brothers and sisters when we learn to listen to them. So often Christians, especially preachers, think that their only service is always to have to 'offer' something when they are together with other people. They forget that listening can be a greater service than speaking. Many people seek a sympathetic ear and do not find it among Christians, because these Christians are talking even when they should be listening.

The Church has an unconditional obligation to the victims of any ordering society, even if they do not belong to the Christian community.

We have approached a 'religionless' age. Some call it a post-Christian world. Ethics and politics are no longer directly influenced by religious beliefs. For many self-describing Christians, their lives show no visible difference from unbelievers. So how can the Church change this? Bonhoeffer would argue that if the Church becomes complacent and does not allow God's will to be complete then it is not following God's commandments. Eventually there can be no distinction between state, God's will and emulating a moral source for people to follow.

Bonhoeffer asked, 'How can Christ become Lord of the religionless as well?' and 'Is there such a thing as a religionless Christian?' He answered these questions with 'the nonreligious interpretation of biblical concepts'.

What is religionless Christianity?

Bonhoeffer wrote, '*If religion is only the garb in which Christianity is clothed – and this garb has looked very different in different ages – what then is religionless Christianity?*' In order to make Christianity current and relevant in today's world, he invites the Church to rid itself of all non-essential ideas or concepts. He invites people to rethink the way Christians represent Christ and his Word and work in their lives.

What matters is not the beyond but this world, how it is created and preserved, is given laws, reconciled, and renewed. What is beyond this world is meant, in the gospel, to be there for this world – not in the anthropocentric sense of liberal, mystical, pietistic, ethical theology, but in the biblical sense of the creation and the incarnation, crucifixion, and resurrection of Jesus Christ.

(Letters and Papers from Prison)

Bonhoeffer's idea of religionless Christianity not only opens a door for people to reach a post-Christian world but also can help them understand the relationships and links between God and science.

The Confessing Church

The Confessing Church (*Bekennende Kirche*) was a movement within German Protestantism during the period of Nazi Germany that arose in opposition to the government.

In November 1933 Niemöller founded the Pastors' Emergency League, which resisted the programmes of the German Christians. The Synod of Barmen was held in May 1934, and its theological declaration transformed the defensive movement against Nazi control of the churches into an organised revival, especially where German territorial churches were subject to Nazi administration.

The Confessing Church was formed by Martin Niemöller in 1934 with 6,000 ministers, leaving only 2,000 behind in the National Reich Church. This was a challenge to the Nazis. Around 800 ministers were arrested and sent to concentration camps.

- Niemöller was arrested in 1937 and sent to Dachau and then Sachsenhausen, until 1945.
- Bonhoeffer was imprisoned in 1943 and was later executed.

Christians were not the only ones being persecuted by the Nazis. About one-third of Jehovah's Witnesses were killed in concentration camps as they weren't willing to fight for any cause and therefore refused to serve in the army.

The following religious groups disappeared from Germany:

- The Salvation Army
- Christian Saints
- The Seventh Day Adventist Church.

The following groups were banned:

- Astrologers
- Faith healers
- Fortune tellers.

When the German Christians first proposed the Aryan paragraph, Bonhoeffer became active in a counter-group called the Young Reformation Movement. (His sister's marriage to a converted Jew undoubtedly provided personal motivation.) The Young Reformers advocated an outright rejection of excluding non-Aryans from pulpits or pews.

The Barmen Declaration (The Theological Declaration of Barmen) of 1934 was a document adopted by Christians in Nazi Germany who opposed the German Christian movement. In the view of the delegates to the Synod that met in the city of Barmen in May 1934, the German Christians were said to have corrupted the Church government by making it bow down to the state and had introduced Nazi ideology into the German Protestant churches which went against the Christian gospel.

The Barmen Declaration rejects the following:

(i) the subordination of the Church to the state (8.22–3) and

(ii) the subordination of the Word and Spirit to the Church. '8.27 We reject the false doctrine, as though the Church in human arrogance could place the Word and work of the Lord in the service of any arbitrarily chosen desires, purposes, and plans.' On the contrary, The Declaration proclaims that the Church 'is solely Christ's property, and that it lives and wants to live solely from his comfort and from his direction in the expectation of his appearance.' (8.17) Rejecting domestication of the Word in the Church, The Declaration points to the inalienable lordship of Jesus Christ by the Spirit and to the external character of church unity which 'can come only from the Word of God in faith through the Holy Spirit. Thus, alone is the Church renewed' (8.01): it submits itself explicitly and radically to Holy Scripture as God's gracious Word.

The declaration was mostly written by the Reformed theologian Karl Barth. The declaration states that Christ is in the centre and that the church accepts only things which are in line with Jesus Christ.

In 1936, the unity of the Confessing Church started to disappear because political differences led the Lutheran churches to form the Council of the Evangelical Lutheran Church in Germany. The Reformed and United sections of the Confessing Church remained active in protesting euthanasia and the persecution of the Jews. Due to the pressure from the Nazis the

> **Pagans**
>
> The German faith movement was pro-Nazi. They were racist. They worshipped the sun and the seasons.

> **The Church**
>
> The Nazis did not manage to abolish the Church. The majority chose to keep quiet and appeared to be conforming. There was an intense fear of the Gestapo.

Confessing Church was eventually forced underground. In 1937 Niemöller and many other clergy were arrested. After World War II, the Confessing Church continued, but was seriously damaged by the conscription of both clergy and laity. In 1948, it ceased to exist when the churches formed the reorganised Evangelical Church in Germany.

The religious community of Finkenwalde

In 1935 Bonhoeffer was presented with a much sought-after opportunity. He was asked to return to Germany to take over and lead an illegal preacher's seminary, founded by theologians, who were preparing for the profession of priesthood after studying at the university.

The seminary existed for two years before the Gestapo ordered it closed in August 1937.

The two years of Finkenwalde's existence produced some of Bonhoeffer's most significant theological work as he prepared these young seminarians for the turbulence and risk of parish ministry in the Confessing Church.

Bonhoeffer and his seminarians were under Gestapo surveillance; some of them were arrested and imprisoned. Throughout, he remained dedicated to training them for the ministry and its challenges in a challenging time. In this period Bonhoeffer wrote his classics, *Discipleship* and *Life Together*.

The focus of the community of Finkenwalde was to promote a positive moral living standard for all. The time in Finkenwalde should have characterised young theologians for their whole lives. Bonhoeffer led with them a consistent Christian life, from which these young theologians had the power to withstand the burdens and afflictions to which they were to be subjected in their work within the Confessing Church.

Some of the key practices included:

• Meditation: The concept of meditation was his focus and Bonhoeffer believed that this way of life was a demanding one. By fulfilling this principle of meditation, it therefore will create a strong community of brotherhood, which is of vital importance to understanding and fulfilling God's will.

The restoration of the church will surely come from a sort of new monasticism which has in common with the old only the uncompromising attitude of a life lived according to the Sermon on the Mount in the following of Christ. I believe it is now time to call people to this.

(Bonhoeffer, *Letter to His Brother*, 1935)

- Reflection: To reflect on the will of God was to put God first in every situation. Reflection would also show whether a person is in accordance with the will of God. The Bible was a very vital part of the theologians' training for growth. By reading, reflecting and sharing the word of God, they would eventually gain more understanding and knowledge of who God is and what he wanted for them. 'Christianity without discipleship is always Christianity without Christ' (*Cost of Discipleship*).
- Community for all: ecumenism was Bonhoeffer's key focus – getting people involved with each other, ensuring that God's will was being obeyed even to the point of fighting for social justice, which was his passion, and ensuring that they lived lives that would be beacons of hope for Christians and others outside of Christianity.

We do God's work for our brothers and sisters when we learn to listen to them. So often Christians, especially preachers, think that their only service is always to have to 'offer' something when they are together with other people. They forget that listening can be a greater service than speaking. Many people seek a sympathetic ear and do not find it among Christians, because these Christians are talking even when they should be listening.

(Bonhoeffer, *Life* Together)

The cost of discipleship

'What is Christian discipleship?' By definition, a disciple is a follower, one who accepts and assists in spreading the doctrines of another. A Christian disciple is a person who accepts and assists in the spreading of the good news of Jesus Christ.

This quote states that when someone becomes a disciple of God there are many sacrifices, and the key sacrifice is that the person surrenders everything to God and his will: 'When Christ calls a man, he bids him come and die' (Bonhoeffer, *The Cost of Discipleship*). Bonhoeffer goes on to state that 'Christianity without discipleship is always Christianity without Christ' (*The Cost of Discipleship*). However, what can the call to discipleship, the belief in the word of Jesus, mean to the community? What was the purpose of Jesus? What is God's will for people today?

Bonhoeffer feared that many do not follow because, for example, a human rather than the divine word is preached. Discipleship is much easier than man-made rules and dogmas, but more important. What Jesus wills is to be done and he gives the grace to do this. Discipleship may be hard, but it is not limited – it is a great sacrifice. Discipleship is the road to the fulfilment of Christianity.

Ethics as an action

For Bonhoeffer, the foundation of ethical behaviour is based on how the reality of the world and the reality of God were reconciled by the reality of Christ. Both in his teachings and in his life, ethics was centred on the demand for action by responsible men and women in facing evil. Evil, he claimed, was concrete and specific, and it could be overridden only by the specific actions of responsible people. Bonhoeffer took an uncompromising position in his seminal work *Ethics*, which was directly reflected in his stance against Nazism. In 1940 his early opposition turned into active conspiracy in trying to overthrow the regime. It was during this time, until his arrest in 1943, that he worked on *Ethics*.

> Do and dare what is right, not swayed by the whim of the moment. Bravely take hold of the real, not dallying now with what might be. Not in the flight of ideas but only in action is freedom. Make up your mind and come out into the tempest of living. God's command is enough and your faith in him to sustain you. Then at last freedom will welcome your spirit amid great rejoicing.
>
> (Bonhoeffer, *Ethics*)

Under the guide of Barth, Bonhoeffer was steered towards the belief that God chooses to reveal himself to the people.

Grace
(Greek: Χάρις [charis]) unmerited favour.

Costly grace

> Cheap grace is the grace we bestow on ourselves. Cheap grace is the preaching of forgiveness without requiring repentance, baptism without church discipline, Communion without confession . . . Cheap grace is grace without discipleship, grace without the cross, grace without Jesus Christ, living and incarnate.
>
> (Bonhoeffer, *The Cost of Discipleship*)

Cheap grace means grace as a doctrine, a principle, a system. It means forgiveness of sins proclaimed as a general truth, the love of God taught as the Christian 'conception' of God. In such a community the world finds a cheap covering for its sins, still less has any real desire to be delivered from these sins. Cheap grace therefore amounts to a denial of the living Word of God – in fact, a denial of the incarnation of the Word of God. Cheap grace is the grace people allow themselves. Cheap grace is grace without discipleship.

However, Bonhoeffer mainly focuses on costly grace, which entails making sacrifices. At what cost? Bonhoeffer wanted politics and personal ends to be separate from Church and state. Grace allows people to make choices and assumes they will make the best choice. Grace cannot be bought; it is an ultimate sacrifice. Grace is costly, because there are major implications. Why did Jesus die on the cross? What was the purpose? What does Jesus' sacrifice mean for all Christians?

> Costly grace is the gospel which must be sought again and again and again, the gift which must be asked for, the door at which a man must knock. Such grace is costly because it calls us to follow, and it is grace because it calls us to follow Jesus Christ. It is costly because it costs a man his life, and it is grace because it gives a man the only true life. It is costly because it condemns sin, and grace because it justifies the sinner. Above all, it is costly because it cost God the life of his Son: 'Ye were bought at a price', and what has cost God much cannot be cheap for us. Above all, it is grace because God did not reckon his Son too dear a price to pay for our life, but delivered him up for us. Costly grace is the Incarnation of God.
>
> (Bonhoeffer, *The Cost of Discipleship*)

People should seek life and freedom only in Jesus Christ. He is said to contain the fullness of both grace and truth.

Sacrifice and suffering

Jesus said in Luke 9:23–25, 'If any want to become my followers, let them deny themselves and take up their cross daily and follow me. For those who want to save their life will lose it, and those who lose their life for my sake will save it. What does it profit them if they gain the whole world, but lose or forfeit themselves?'

Robert H. Stein notes that three conditions for following Jesus are laid out in this passage:

- The first involves a need to deny oneself. This is much more radical than simply a denial of certain things. This mandates a rejection of a life based on self-interest and self fulfillment. Instead a disciple is to be one who seeks to fulfill the will and the teachings of Christ.

- The second condition involves the need to take up one's cross . . . Jesus' own crucifixion reveals more fully to Luke's readers that this call is a commitment unto death. There needs to be a willingness to suffer martyrdom if need be.
- The final condition is the need to follow Jesus. In contrast to the other two conditions, indicating that following Jesus must be continual.
(*Luke: An Exegetical and Theological Exposition of Holy Scripture*
[The New American Commentary])

Bonhoeffer's conviction was based on 'costly grace' because it cost Jesus his life. Grace is also costly because it costs people their very lives if they follow Jesus. The ultimate sacrifice that Jesus made had no boundaries, so people in their quest to complete God's will must go through sacrifice and suffering. They will have to embrace the life of sacrificing various aspects of things that could possibly lead them astray.

To Bonhoeffer, true and biblical discipleship had to be costly and self-sacrificing. There really was no other way to follow Jesus. As a Christian, he followed Jesus regardless of the cost to his own safety and position. Even if he had to suffer to follow Jesus then that was the level of sacrifice he was willing to complete. In the *Cost of Discipleship*, he wrote, 'Suffering, then, is the badge of true discipleship. The disciple is not above his Master . . . If we refuse to take up our cross and submit to suffering and rejection at the hands of men, we forfeit our fellowship with Christ and have ceased to follow him.'

My brothers and sisters, whenever you face trials of any kind, consider it nothing but joy, because you know that the testing of your faith produces endurance; and let endurance have its full effect, so that you may be mature and complete, lacking in nothing.

(James 1:2–4)

Suffering to James can result in true joy when trials test a person's faith. The cost of following Jesus comes at a price. The key question is whether people are willing to make that sacrifice.

Solidarity

Right up until the day he was put to death Bonhoeffer was an acting representative of Christ suffering with the victims of Hitler's rule. At the centre of Bonhoeffer's theology of the cross was his ethics of suffering solidarity. Due to Jesus Christ's suffering and pain to set humanity free from sin and bondage, God revealed that he is aware of the suffering. This shows that God is willing to go through suffering with humanity and ensure that he is in solidarity with his people.

The Nazis were ordering all men of his age to register with the military. Bonhoeffer was convinced that this was not God's will for him, so he decided with support from his family and friends to travel to America to avoid the coming war. Once in New York, Bonhoeffer began to question his decision to flee Germany. It appeared that God was calling him back to Germany to face the Nazis with his fellow Germans.

In a letter to Reinhold Niebuhr in July 1939, Bonhoeffer wrote these words (from *A Testament to Freedom: The Essential Writings of Dietrich Bonhoeffer*):

> I have had the time to think and to pray about my situation and that of my nation and to have God's will for me clarified. I have come to the conclusion that I have made a mistake in coming to America. I must live through this difficult period of our national history with the Christian people of Germany. I shall have no right to participate in the reconstruction of Christian life in Germany after the war if I do not share the trials of this time with my people.

In the article, 'Religionless Christianity and Vulnerable Discipleship: The Interfaith Promise of Bonhoeffer's Theology,' David H. Jensen writes,

> Bonhoeffer's participation in Operation 7 . . . offers . . . evidence of his solidarity with those most vulnerable under Nazi terror. By the fall of 1941 and continuing until his arrest, Bonhoeffer's cumulative actions displayed a concern with those victimized most brutally by Nazism and a willingness to put himself at risk on their behalf.

Bonhoeffer was an example of a deeply committed follower of Jesus who submitted to the will of God. He was a man who offered his life where Christ could become present in the world through suffering solidarity and passionate love.

This showed that Bonhoeffer was committed to ensuring that social justice took its place and that justice prevailed. No matter where he was he still made his voice heard, showing the Nazis that he was in solidarity with injustices and the Jews. However, it is important to remember that he believed that eventually all Jews should convert to Christianity.

In his letter to his friend and biographer, Eberhard Bethge, he wrote this testament:

If we are to learn what God promises and what he fulfils, we must persevere in quiet meditation on the life, sayings, deeds, sufferings, and death of Jesus. It is certain that we may always live close to God and in the light of his presence, and that such living is an entirely new life for us; that nothing is then impossible for us, because all things are possible with God; that no earthly power can touch us without his will, and that danger and distress can only drive us closer to him. It is certain that we can claim nothing for ourselves, and may yet pray for everything; it is certain that our joy is hidden in suffering, and our life in death; it is certain that in all this we are in a fellowship that sustains us. In Jesus God has said Yes and Amen to it all, and that Yes and Amen is the firm ground on which we stand.

(391)

Bonhoeffer's relevance today

When looking back at Bonhoeffer's life and work there are many facets to consider: he completed his doctorate in theology at the age of 21 from the University of Berlin, and he was a caring minister whose life and ministry were shortened by the Nazis at a young age. Further to this Bonhoeffer left the Christian world powerful messages in works including: *Grace (Cheap and Costly)*, *Religionless Christianity* and *Cost of Discipleship*. Christology forms the framework of all Bonhoeffer's theology, and there is much which can be learned from this focus.

Christology

(Greek: Χριστός, *Khristós*, messiah, and λογία, *logia*, word) – study which is about the ontology of the person of Jesus as found in the New Testament.

Bonhoeffer's life was extraordinary. He lived in extraordinary times and under very difficult conditions. Still today his life and work continue to engage the minds of Christians and others alike. Bonhoeffer's legacy of a life of faith as personally intense and substantive as it was has proved very influential. It was his stance and conviction that made his faith stronger and more fervent, with the struggles following Hitler becoming chancellor, the churches bowing down to the state and the persecution of the Jews among many others. People rightly continue to be humbled by the courage, faith and self-sacrifice that Bonhoeffer showed until the very end of his life.

Even after his death, Bonhoeffer's life and thought continue to play a vital role for individuals throughout the world. Although his influence has been largely on those within Christian communities, his focus on social injustice and the correct treatment of people is still an inspiration today for people to try to make a difference. However, not everyone would agree with the stance and teachings that he held. One of the main contentions is whether Christians can cope in modern societies. Would they eventually become overwhelmed by allowing distractions to rule them or would they be guided by God's will? Also, would his theology work in today's multifaith societies?

As Christology is the interpretative key to Bonhoeffer's reading of the Bible and practice, so should it be for the Church. What then is the function of Christology?

- To lead Christians towards lives and actions that are different from others
- To cause people to speak out against injustices and the oppression of those people who have become marginalised
- To govern a Christian's life, belief and mission.

SUMMARY

- Bonhoeffer's teaching of putting Christian moral life into action

  - Duty to God and the state

    - Civil disobedience
    - Obedience to the will of God
    - The state should always act in accordance with God's will.
    - Secular pacifism

  - Discipleship

    - The example of Christ
    - Life in a religious community – for example Finkenwalde
    - Costly grace versus cheap grace
    - Sacrifice
    - Suffering
    - Solidarity

  - The Church community

    - The need for religionless Christianity
    - Confessing Church
    - Church communities necessary to provide spiritual and moral skills in society.

REVIEW QUESTIONS

Look back over the chapter and check that you can answer the following questions:

1   Who founded the Confessing Church?
2   What did Bonhoeffer mean by 'religionless Christianity'?

continued overleaf

3   Who was Karl Barth?

4   What do you think are the main strengths and weaknesses of Bonhoeffer's teachings?

Terminology

Do you know your terminology?

Try to explain the meaning of the following ideas without looking at your books and notes:

- Aryan paragraph
- Christology
- Civil disobedience
- Grace
- Secular pacifism
- Systematic theology
- Tyrannicide.

Examination questions practice

Read the question carefully – remember that although Bonhoeffer's life is important in understanding him, it is his teachings which you will be questioned on. Answer the question set, not the one you would like to have been set. To help you improve your answers look at the levels of response.

SAMPLE EXAM-STYLE QUESTION

To what extent do you think that Bonhoeffer's views on civil disobedience are compatible with Christianity?

AO1 (15 marks)

- This question requires you to consider Bonhoeffer's views on civil disobedience and to what extent he sees it as justified in certain circumstances. You also need to give consideration to his ideas about non-violent resistance.

- Then look at the consistency of biblical teaching from the Old and New Testaments about the use of violence.

- Use examples to illustrate your answer.

AO2 (15 marks)

- In evaluating the statement you need to consider whether there are inconsistences in the biblical teachings on the use of violence, particularly in relation to Jesus.
- Compare Bonhoeffer's views and consider whether they are really based on Christian teaching. Civil disobedience as he understood it might seem to oppose or contradict his views on modelling life on Jesus and Christianity being about love.
- However, he believed that Christians have a responsibility to the state but must do things in accordance with the will of God.
- Regardless of the way you argue, it is important to have a clear conclusion which gives reasons as to whether the different views are compatible.

Further possible questions

- 'It is unrealistic of Bonhoeffer to expect the state to take notice of Church teachings when he stresses that they must be separate.' Discuss.
- 'Bonhoeffer's involvement in a plot to assassinate Hitler cannot be justified.' Discuss.
- Assess Bonhoeffer's view that the teachings about authority in Romans 13 are compatible with his statement that 'Christians should give more offense, shock the world far more, than they are doing now.'
- To what extent are Bonhoeffer's views on 'cheap grace' and 'costly grace' aligned with Christian teaching that 'grace' is unmerited favour?
- 'Bonhoeffer's teachings have little relevance for today's societies.' Discuss.

FURTHER READING

Bethge, E. 1999. *Dietrich Bonhoeffer: Biography – Theologian, Christian Man for His Times* (rev. ed.). Minneapolis: Augsburg Fortress

Bonhoeffer, D. 2013. *Letters and Papers From Prison* (An Abridged ed.). London: SCM Press.

Bonhoeffer, D. 2015. *The Cost of Discipleship* (new ed.)., ch. 1. London: SCM Press.

Lawrence, J. 2010. *Bonhoeffer: A Guide for the Perplexed*. London: T & T Clark.

Glossary

A posteriori
A Latin phrase meaning 'from what comes after'. Philosophers use it to apply to knowledge which is known through experience.

A priori
A Latin phrase meaning 'from what comes before'. Philosophers use it to apply to knowledge that is gained irrespective of experience, simply by reasoning.

Absolute
A principle that is universally binding.

Act utilitarianism
A teleological theory that uses the outcome of an action to determine whether it is good or bad.

Active euthanasia
The intentional premature termination of another person's life.

Adoptionism
A belief which said that Jesus was born as man and because he was so virtuous he was adopted as the 'Son of God' when the Holy Spirit descended to him on the banks of the river Jordan.

Agape
'Love: the highest form of love, charity' . . . 'the love of God for man and of man for God' (Liddell and Scott 2010).

Analogy
The act of comparing one thing with another that shares similar characteristics, to help a person learn about the first thing. Thomas Aquinas divided analogy into two types: (1) proportion, telling us the extent to which a thing corresponds to what it should be; (2) attribution, telling us about the qualities of a particular thing.

Analytic
The concept of the subject is contained in the predicate, where the predicate is the part of the sentence which follows after the subject – for example triangles have three sides.

Antilapsarian Decree
God chose who would be saved and who would be punished at creation.

Apocrypha
In relation to the Old Testament: those books included in the Septuagint and Vulgate versions, which were not originally written in Hebrew and not counted genuine by the Jews.

Apollinarism
This belief stated that Jesus had a human body and lower soul but a divine mind.

Apparent good
Something which seems to be good or the right thing to do but which does not fit the perfect human ideal.

Arianism
This heresy did not accept the true divinity of Jesus Christ but agreed that Jesus Christ was created by the Father and that he had a beginning in time.

Aryan paragraph
A clause by which an organisation reserves membership solely for members of the 'Aryan race' and excludes any non-Aryans, particularly Jews or those of Jewish descent.

Assisted dying/suicide
When a person takes his or her own life with the assistance of another person. When the other person is a doctor, it is called physician-assisted suicide.

Atheological
Opposed to theology.

Atman
A Sanskrit word that means 'inner-self' or 'soul'. Atman is the true self of an individual beyond identification with phenomena, the essence of an individual.

Authority
When applied to religious experience, the word 'authority' indicates that the person who has the religious experience has some new insight or knowledge about the world and God's relationship with the world.

Autonomous moral agent
Someone who can make a moral decision freely; someone who is totally responsible for his or her actions.

Body
In Aristotle's thinking 'the body' refers to the matter that a living creature is made of.

Categorical imperative
A command to perform actions that are absolute moral obligations without reference to other ends.

Cause
That which produces an effect; that which gives rise to any action, phenomenon or condition. In philosophy this concept is often linked to the so-called four causes of Aristotle.

Celibacy
Not having sexual relations with another person.

Christian realism
The belief that Christianity may use violence to bring about the Kingdom of God and secure peace on Earth.

Christology
The study within Christian theology primarily of the relationship of Jesus with God the Father.

Concupiscence
Sexual desire or lust.

Consequentialism
The rightness or wrongness of an act is determined by its consequences.

Contingent
Philosophers use the word contingent to mean that something is not immortal but depends on something else for its existence.

Copernican Revolution
Belief that the solar system revolves around the sun.

Council of Jerusalem
The First Council of Jerusalem found in Acts 15 is generally said to have taken place in 50. However, as it is never mentioned in the letters of St Paul, many scholars have doubted its authenticity.

Creatio ex nihilo
This phrase is Latin for 'creation out of nothing'. It is often used by Christians to communicate the idea that God created the universe out of nothing.

Cultural relativism
What is right or wrong depends on the culture.

Decalogue
Another term for the Ten Commandments revealed to Moses on Mount Sinai.

Deism
Belief in a God who starts the world off or creates it and then leaves it to run by itself.

Deontological
Philosophical theories which hold that the morality of an act is not totally dependent on its consequences.

Deontological ethics
Ethical systems which consider that the moral act itself has moral value (e.g. telling the truth is always right, even when it may cause pain or harm).

Descriptive relativism
Different cultures and societies have differing ethical systems and so morality is relative.

Determinism
The view that every event has a cause and so, when applied to moral decisions, we do not have free will.

Direct religious experiences
Refer to events where God reveals her-/himself directly to the person having the experience.

Disembodied existence
The idea that a soul can exist separately from its body. Disembodied existence relies on a dualistic view of personhood.

Divine command theory
Actions are right or wrong depending on whether they follow God's commands.

Divine inspiration
Refers to the belief among Christians that God inspired the writers of the books of the Bible.

Divine law
The Bible – this reflects the eternal law.

Docetism
This was a belief that Jesus' physical body was an illusion, as was his crucifixion. He only appeared to be physical but, in fact, was incorporeal and therefore pure spirit.

Donatism
Donatism argued that Christian priests must be faultless for the prayers and sacraments they conduct to be valid.

Double predestination
God lets only those whom he has chosen to enter heaven and also says that sinners must be punished in hell.

Dualism
The view that a human person consists of two distinct elements: the mind/soul and the body. The mind/soul is immaterial, whereas the body is physical.

Duty
A motive for acting in a certain way which shows moral quality.

Equivocal language
The use of the same word to mean completely different things when applied to different objects.

Eschatology
The part of theological science which is concerned with 'the four last things: death, judgement, heaven, and hell'.

Eternal law
The principles by which God made and controls the universe which are fully known only by God.

Ethical autonomy
The Catholic Church views ethical autonomy as a development of liberal Catholicism. It teaches that people should have much greater autonomy in making their own ethical decisions.

Ethical naturalism/ethical cognitivism
A theory that moral values can be derived from sense experience.

Eudamonia
The final goal of all human activity – happiness, well-being, human flourishing.

Euthyphro dilemma
The dilemma first identified by Plato – is something good because God commands it or does God command it because it is good?

Existentialism
This is a doctrine that concentrates on the existence of individuals who, because they are free and responsible, can be held to be what they make themselves by the self-development of their essence through acts of the will (in Christian existentialism this leads to God).

Fideism
Any doctrine according to which all (or some) knowledge depends upon faith or revelation, and reason or the intellect is to be disregarded.

Form
By 'Form' Plato meant the idea of something. For example if you say 'Look! There's a cat,' you have some idea of what a cat is and you can recognise lots of different types of cats.

Form of the Good
The highest of all the Forms. Plato said it was also the source of the other Forms.

Futurism
In futurism, parallels can be drawn with historical events, but most eschatological prophecies are seen as referring to events which have not yet been fulfilled, but will take place at the end of this age and the end of the world.

General revelation (natural revelation)
Knowledge about God and spiritual matters which is discovered through natural means, such as looking at the physical universe, philosophy and reasoning. Christians use the term to describe knowledge of God which is plainly available to all humans.

Genesis 1–3
The Book of Genesis is the first book of the Christian Bible and Jewish Torah. Chapters 1–3 contain two different accounts of the creation of the world by God.

Gnosticism
A collection of ancient religions whose adherents kept apart from the material world – which they viewed as created by the demiurge – and embraced the spiritual world.

Grace
Unmerited favour from God.

Hedonic calculus
Bentham's method for measuring the good and bad effects of an action.

Hedonism
The view that pleasure is the chief 'good'.

Heteronomous Christian ethics
This is a system of normative ethics based not on the individual's own moral principles but also on beliefs and teachings taken from other sources.

Historicism
Historicism views prophecy as being fulfilled in the past, present and future, including during the previous two millennia, according to Revelation.

Hypothetical imperative
An action that achieves some goal or end.

Immanent
Used to express the idea that God is involved and active in the world.

Inaugurated eschatology
The idea that the end times began in the life, death and resurrection of Jesus and that therefore there are aspects to the Kingdom of God which are both 'already' and 'not yet'.

Indirect religious experiences
Experiences, thoughts or feelings about God that are prompted by events in daily life – for example observing the stars in the sky and having thoughts about the greatness of God the Creator.

Infallible
Used by religious believers to indicate that a teaching does not contain any error or possibility of error.

Instrumental value
Something's value lies in its usefulness for others.

Intelligent design
A theory suggesting that the universe shows evidence that it is created by God.

Intrinsically good
Something which is good in itself, without reference to the consequences.

Involuntary euthanasia
This term is used when someone's life is ended to prevent his or her suffering, without the person's consent, even though the person is capable of consenting.

Karma
In Hinduism, the law of cause and effect.

Kingdom of ends
A world in which people do not treat others as means but only as ends.

Liberation theology
Liberation theology is based firmly on the Bible as the central source of ethics. Liberation theology aims to fight poverty by addressing its source, which is believed to be sin.

Life after death
The belief that life continues in some fashion post-mortem.

Limited election
This states that the afterlife is only for people whom God chooses in his perfect, just nature.

Macedonianism or Pneumatomachians
This fourth-century heresy accepts the divinity of Jesus Christ as stated at the Council of Nicaea but denies that of the Holy Spirit.

Magisterium
The Magisterium of the Catholic Church is the church's authority to establish its own teachings. That authority is rests in the pope and the bishops because it is believed that they are in communion with the correct teachings of the faith.

Materialism
The view that human beings are physical beings rather than consisting of a physical body and an immaterial soul.

Maxim
A general rule in accordance with which we intend to act.

Metanoia
Repentance.

Miracle
This word has a great variety of possible meanings. Some uses of the word 'miracle' are given here:

- A lucky event
- A coincidence
- A sign pointing to God
- An event that breaks the law of nature
- An event that reveals God
- A natural event that is given a special meaning by someone
- God's direct intervention in history.

Monism
The belief that human beings are a single unity of body and mind. The mind's existence is dependent on the body.

Monophysitism or Eutychianism
This is a fifth-century heresy which stated that Christ's divinity dominates and overwhelms his humanity.

Monothelitism
A seventh-century heresy which stated that although Christ had two natures he had only one will.

Moral absolutism
There is only one correct answer to every moral problem.

Moral objectivism
Truth is objectively real regardless of culture.

Moral relativism
There are no universally valid moral principles and so there is no one true morality.

Moral virtues
Qualities of character, such as courage, friendliness and truthfulness.

Mystical experience
Used in many ways by writers on religious experience. In general, it is used to refer to religious experiences where God is revealed directly and the person having the experience is passive.

Myth
A story which communicates the values and/or ultimate beliefs of a culture or society.

Natural laws
When discussing the teleological argument, this phrase refers to physical laws of science, such as gravity. It must not be confused with the ethical theory called natural (moral) law.

Natural moral law
The theory that an eternal, absolute moral law can be discovered by reason.

Natural theology
Natural theology refers to the process of learning about God from the natural world by using reason.

Naturalistic fallacy
The claim that good cannot be defined.

Necessary being
A phrase used in philosophy of religion to refer to something which always exists and cannot fail to exist.

Negative utilitarianism
The principle of minimising pain.

Nestorianism
This heresy taught that Jesus Christ was a natural union between the flesh and the Word and therefore is not identical to the divine Son of God.

Noetic
Refers to something which gives knowledge, such as a revelation from God in which God reveals something.

Non-propositional revelation
Refers to the idea that God does not reveal facts or truths to people; instead the religious believer recognises God acting in human history and human experience.

Normative ethics
A term used to describe different moral codes of behaviour – rules by which we make moral decisions (e.g. utilitarianism, natural moral law, Kantian ethics).

Numinous experience
An 'apprehension of the wholly other'.

Omnibenevolence
Used as a title for God to say that God is 'good'. Means that God always wills goodness or good things towards people, or all-loving.

Omnipotent
Means infinite or unlimited power. It is a philosophical word often used to describe God.

Omnipresent
All-present. It is used in philosophy as a quality for God to refer to God being present throughout every part of creation.

Omniscient
Means infinite knowledge. Most philosophers today use the word as a quality for God to indicate that God knows everything it is logically possible to know.

Ordinary and extraordinary means
According to natural law moral duties apply in ordinary situations. A patient may refuse certain treatments on the grounds that they are 'extraordinary' (i.e. over and above the essential).

Original sin
A reference to the first sin of Adam in the Garden of Eden and its effects, according to traditional Christian beliefs.

'Ought implies can'
The idea that someone cannot be blamed for what he could not do, but only for what he was capable of doing but did not do.

Pacifism
The belief that violence is wrong.

Parousia
This means presence, arrival or official visit. In the New Testament it is also used for the Second Coming of Jesus.

Passive
Passivity describes the common state of a person who has a religious experience. Often people do not seek out or will religious experiences; instead the experience happens to them – they are passive.

Passive euthanasia
Treatment is either withdrawn or not given to the patient in order to hasten death. This could include turning off a life-support machine.

Patripassianism
This stressed that the Father and Son were not two distinct persons and therefore it was God the Father who was crucified as Jesus.

Pelagianism
Pelagians believed that the human will was created by God and therefore was sufficient to live a sinless life.

Perfection
A philosophical term used to indicate the goodness of God. To be perfect means that you lack nothing and could not be better in any way. God is said to be perfect, as God is totally good and could not be more 'good'.

Personhood
Definition of a human being as a person – having consciousness, self-awareness, ability to reason and self-sufficiency.

Pharisees
The Pharisee ('separatist') party came from the groups of scribes and sages in the second century BCE. They were active until the destruction of the Temple in CE 70. They were considered to be the most expert and accurate teachers of Jewish law in the face of assimilation by the Greeks.

Phronesis (practical wisdom)
According to Aristotle the virtue most needed for any other virtue to be developed. Balancing self-interest with that of others. Needs to be directed by the moral virtues.

Postlapsarian Decree
God chose who would be saved and who would be punished after the Fall.

Postulate
Kant uses the word 'postulate' to mean 'assuming as true for the purposes of argument or set forward as a plausible hypothesis'.

Predestination
The belief that God has decided who will be saved and who will not.

Predicate
A quality or property of a subject expressed in a sentence.

Preference utilitarianism
Moral actions are right or wrong according to how they fit the preferences of those involved.

Preferential option for the poor
Liberation theology sees a bias in Jesus' life and teachings towards the oppressed and describes this as a preferential option for the poor.

Prescriptivism
A theory that ethical statements have an intrinsic sense so other people should agree with the statement and follow it.

Preterism
This is an approach which sees prophecy as chiefly being fulfilled in the past, especially during the first century. Prophecies in general, therefore, have already been fulfilled.

Primary precepts
The fundamental principles of natural moral law.

Prime Mover
The unchanging cause of all that exists. Sometimes this is extended to suggest that the Prime Mover is God.

Principle of utility
The theory of usefulness – the greatest happiness for the greatest number.

Privation
Privation means that something is lacking a particular thing that it should have.

Propositional revelation
Refers to God directly revealing truths to people.

Providence
A word used in Christian theology to refer to God's goodness and continuing activity in the world for the benefit of creation.

Psilanthropism
This belief claimed that Jesus was 'merely human'. He either was never divine or did not exist until his incarnation as a man.

Purpose
The idea that the rightness or wrongness of an action can be discovered by looking at whether the action agrees with human purpose.

PVS (persistent vegetative state)
When a patient is in this condition, doctors may seek to end his or her life. The relatives have to agree and usually the patient must be brainstem-dead.

Qualitative
Looking at the quality of the pleasure.

Quality of life
The belief that human life is not valuable in itself; it depends on what kind of life it is.

Quantitative
Looking at the quantity of the happiness.

Real good
The right thing to do – it fits the human ideal.

Realised eschatology
This says that the eschatological passages in the New Testament are not referring to the future but refer to the ministry of Jesus and his legacy.

Realism
Normal moral rules cannot be applied to how states act in time of war.

Reincarnation or rebirth
The belief that the soul of a person is reincarnated after death.

Relativism
Nothing may be said to be objectively right or wrong; it depends on the situation, the culture and so on.

Resurrection
Refers to the belief that life continues after death through the existence of the person, body and soul, in a new but distinct form of life.

Retributive justice
A retributive theory of justice is one in which people who commit wrong acts are punished by law in a way that is proportionate to their wrongdoing.

Revealed theology
This is theology based on the idea that all religious truth is derived exclusively from the revelations of God to humans.

Revelation
Refers to any act in which God is revealed to human beings. The characteristic of revelation is that it reveals knowledge of God/God's nature. In Christianity there are two types of revelations: (1) propositional revelation and (2) non-propositional revelation.

Rule utilitarianism
Establishing a general rule that follows utilitarian principles.

Sabellianism
A heresy teaching that the Father, Son and Holy Spirit were three characterisations of one God, not three distinct 'persons' in one God.

Samsara
The cycle of birth, death and rebirth in Hindu belief. The atman (jiva) is reincarnated as a human or other life form, depending on the conduct of its last incarnation.

Sanctity of life
The belief that human life is valuable in itself.

Secondary precepts
These are worked out from the primary precepts.

Sentience
The ability to feel pleasure and pain.

Single predestination
God lets only those he has chosen enter heaven.

Situation ethics
The morally right thing to do is the most loving in the situation.

Soul
The word 'soul' is used to refer to the spiritual or non-physical part of a human being, or to the mind. The soul is often seen as the centre or core of identity of a person.

Special revelation
The belief that knowledge of God and of spiritual matters can be discovered through means such as miracles or the scriptures. It is a way of knowing God's truth through means other than human reason.

Subjectivism
Each person's values are relative to that person and so cannot be judged objectively.

Summum bonum
The supreme good that we pursue through moral acts.

Symbol
Used in religious thought to indicate something which points people to God and also presents something about God to people.

Synderesis
Aquinas' idea of what he termed 'right' reason, by which a person acquires knowledge of basic moral principles and understands that it is important to do good and avoid evil.

Syneidesis
This means 'to know with'. St Paul uses it to explain the human ability to know and choose what is good.

Systematic theology
Systematic theology attempts to create an ordered, rational and coherent account of Christian teachings based on the Bible. It includes dogmatics, ethics and philosophy.

Teleological
An argument relating to the study of ultimate causes in nature or a study of actions relating them to the ends.

Teleological ethics
The morally right or wrong thing to do is determined by the consequences.

Telos
The Greek word for 'end' or 'result' of a process or course of action.

The Cave
A famous analogy written by Plato which he uses to explain some parts of his theory of Forms.

The Fall
Refers to the story of Adam and Eve in the Garden of Eden and their disobeying of God. It may be read in Genesis 2:4 to 3:1 of the Bible.

The Four Causes
The material cause – what a thing is made of. The efficient cause – the agent or cause of the thing coming to exist as it is. The existence of a painting or work of art is brought about by the artist who makes it. The artist is the efficient cause. The formal cause – what makes the thing recognisable: its structure, shape and activity. The final cause – the ultimate reason why the thing exists.

Theism
Refers to belief in a God who creates the world and continues to sustain it and be involved with it. This is the traditional view of God held by the Jewish, Christian and Islamic traditions.

Theodicy
A philosophical attempt to solve the problem of evil.

Theonomous Christian ethics
The belief that God's laws, including those in the Old Testament, should be observed by modern societies.

Transcendent
The word used to express the idea that God is separate from and completely distinct and different from the physical world.

Transience
Refers to the fact that religious experiences are experiences which are temporary.

Universalisability
If an act is right or wrong for one person in a situation, then it is right or wrong for anyone in that situation.

Univocal language
Words have the same meaning when applied to different objects or things (e.g. Liz is fat, Mark is fat, the pig is fat).

Unlimited election
Everyone has the opportunity to reach the afterlife. Christ's atonement was therefore 'unlimited'.

Utilitarianism
Only pleasure and the absence of pain have utility or intrinsic value.

Verbal inspiration
Refers to the divine origins or authorship of every word in the Bible. According to this view, God effectively dictates the books of the Bible by divine inspiration.

Vision
An event in which God, or something about God, is seen or observed.

Voluntary euthanasia
The intentional premature termination of another person's life at his or her request.

Bibliography

Alston, W.P. 1999. 'Perceiving God', in *Philosophy of Religion: The Big Questions*, Stump, E. et al. (ed.). Oxford: Blackwell.

Alston, W.P. 2000. 'Why Should There Not Be Experience of God?' in *Philosophy of Religion: A Guide and Anthology*, Davies, B. (ed.). Oxford: Oxford University Press.

Annas, J. 1998. *An Introduction to Plato's Republic*. Oxford: Oxford University Press.

Anscombe, G.E.M. 1974. *Whatever Has a Beginning of Existence Must Have a Cause: Hume's Argument Exposed in Philosophy of Religion a Guide and Anthology* (ed. Davies, B). Oxford: Oxford University Press.

Aquinas, T. 1997. 'Summa Theologiae', in *Basic Writings of Thomas Aquinas*, Pegis, A.C. (ed.). Indianapolis: Hackett, Random House.

Aristotle *Physics* II 3

Aristotle. 1986. *De Anima* (translation, introduction and notes, Lawson-Tancred, H). London: Penguin.

Bentham, J. 1948. *An Introduction to the Principles of Morals and Legislation* (ed. Harrison, W). Cambridge: Cambridge University Press.

Bethge, E. 1999. *Dietrich Bonhoeffer: Biography – Theologian, Christian Man for His Times*. Minneapolis: Augsburg Fortress.

Boff, L. 1972. *Jesus Christ Liberator: A Critical Christology for Our Time*. New York: Orbis Books.

Bonhoeffer, D. 2013. *Letters and Papers From Prison (An Abridged Edition)*. London: SCM Press.

Bonhoeffer, D. 2015. *The Cost of Discipleship*. London: SCM Press.

Bowie, N.E. 1999. *Business Ethics: A Kantian Perspective*. Oxford: Blackwell.

Calvin, J. 1970. *The Institutes of the Christian Religion*, Henry Beveridge translation. Grand Rapids, MI: Eerdmans.

Chadwick, H. 1986. *Augustine a Very Short Introduction*. Oxford: Oxford University Press.

Chapman, G. 1994. *Catechism of the Catholic Church*. London: Continuum International.

Chryssides, G. and Kaler, J. 1996. *Essentials of Business Ethics*. London: McGraw-Hill.

Cook, D. 1983. *The Moral Maze*. London: SPCK.

Craig, W.L. 2001. *The Son Rises: The Historical Evidence for the Resurrection of Jesus*. Oregon: Wipf & Stock.

Crane, A. and Matten, D. 2003. *Business Ethics*. Oxford: Oxford University Press.

Davies, B. 1993. *The Thought of Thomas Aquinas* (new ed.). New York: Oxford University Press.

Davies, B. 1997. *God, Reason and Theism*. Edinburgh: Edinburgh University Press.

Davies, B. (ed.) 2003. *Philosophy of Religion*. London: Continuum.

Dawkins, R. 1995. *River Out of Eden*. New York: Basic Books.

Dawkins, R. 2006. *The Blind Watchmaker* (new ed.). London: Penguin.

Dawkins, R. 2016. *The Selfish Gene*. Oxford: Oxford University Press.

Descartes, R. 2010. *Meditations*. London: Penguin.

Descartes, R. 2015. *The Passions of the Soul*. Oxford: Oxford University Press.

Edwards, P. (ed.) 1997. *Immortality*. New York: Prometheus Books.

Fletcher, J. 1997. *Situation Ethics*. Westminster: John Knox Press.

Frederick, R. 1999. *A Companion to Business Ethics*. Oxford: Blackwell.

Friedmann, M. 1970. 'The Social Responsibility of Business Is to Increase Its Profits', *The New York Times Magazine*, 13 September.

Geach, P. 1969. *God and the Soul*. London: Routledge & Kegan Paul.

Gensler, H., Earl, W. and Swindal, J. 2004. *Ethics: Contemporary Readings*. London: Routledge.

Gill, R. 2001. *The Cambridge Companion to Christian Ethics*. Cambridge: Cambridge University Press.

Glover, J. 1990. *Causing Death and Saving Lives*. London: Penguin.

Green, M. 1977. *The Truth of God Incarnate*. London: Hodder.

Hay, D. 1990. *Religious Experience Today*. London: Mowbray, Continuum International.

Hick, J. 1964. *The Existence of God*. New York: Palgrave Macmillan.

Hick, J. 1985a. *Death and Eternal Life*. Basingstoke: Palgrave Macmillan.

Hick, J. 1985b. *Evil and the God of Love*. Basingstoke: Palgrave Macmillan.

Hick, J. 2012. *The Myth of God Incarnate*. London: SCM Press.

Hinman, L. 2012. *Ethics Updates*. Available at http://ethics.sandiego.edu/ (accessed 16 June 2017).

Hoose, B. (ed.) 1998. *Christian Ethics: An Introduction*. London: Cassell.

Hughes, G. 1998. 'Natural Law', in *Christian Ethics: An Introduction*, Hoose, B. (ed.). London: Cassell.

Hukanovic, R. 1998. *The Tenth Circle Of Hell: A Memoir of Life in the Death Camps of Bosnia*. London: Abacus.

James, W. 2007. *The Varieties of Religious Experience: A Study in Human Nature*. New York: Cosimo Classics.

Kant, I. 2005. 'Groundwork of a Metaphysics of Morals', in *The Moral Law*, Paton, H.J. (trans). London: Routledge.

Kenny, A. 1998. *A Brief History of Western Philosophy*. Oxford: Blackwell.

Kuhse, H. and Singer, P. (eds) 1999. *Bioethics – An Anthology* (contains articles by Jonathan Glover, Germain Grisez, Joseph Boyle, James Rachels and Helga Kuhse). Oxford: Blackwell.

Küng, H. 2002. *The Catholic Church: A Short History*. New York: Modern Library.

Lafollette, H. (ed.) 2002. *Ethics in Practice – An Anthology*. Oxford: Blackwell.

Lawrence, J. 2010. *Bonhoeffer: A Guide for the Perplexed*. London: T & T Clark.

Liddell, H.G. and Scott, R. 2010. *An Intermediate Greek-English Lexicon* (7th ed.). Oxford: Benediction Classics.

Maccoby, H. 1987. *The Mythmaker: Paul and the Invention of Christianity*. New York: HarperCollins.

Maccoby, H. 2000. *Jesus the Pharisee*. London: SCM Press.

MacIntyre, A. 1968. *A Short History of Ethics*. London: Routledge.

Mackie, J.L. 1982. *The Miracle of Theism: Arguments for and Against the Existence of God*. Oxford: Oxford University Press.

Macquarrie, J. and Childress, J. 1986. *A New Dictionary of Christian Ethics*. London: SCM Press.

Magee, B. 2016. *The Story of Philosophy*. Oxford: Dorling Kindersley.

Manning, R.E.M. 2015. *The Oxford Handbook of Natural Theology*, reprint. Oxford: Oxford University Press.

McGrath, A. 2011a. *Theology: The Basics*. Oxford: Blackwell.

McGrath, A. 2011b. *Christian Theology* (5th ed.). Oxford: Wiley-Blackwell.

Messer, N. 2006. *SCM Study Guide to Christian Ethics*. London: SCM Press.

Mill, J.S. 2002. *Utilitarianism*. Indianapolis: Hackett.

Moltmann, J. 2015. *The Crucified God*. London: SCM Press.

Norman, R. 1998. *The Moral Philosophers*. Oxford: Oxford University Press.

O'Neill, O. 2013. 'Kantian Approaches to Some Famine Problems' in *Ethical Theory: An Anthology*, Shafer-Landau, R. (ed.). Chichester: Wiley-Blackwell.

Palmer, M. 2001. *The Existence of God*. London: Routledge.

Pate, M.C. *The End of the Age Has Come: The Theology of Paul*. 1995. Grand Rapids: Zondervan Press.

Philips, D.Z. 2004. *The Problem of Evil and the Problem of God*. London: SCM Press.

Plantinga, A. 1986. 'Intellectual Sophistication and Basic Belief in God', *Faith and Philosophy* 3: 306–12.

Plato. 1969. 'Euthyphro', in *The Last Days of Socrates*, Tredennick, H. (trans). London: Penguin.

Plato. 2000. 'Life After Death: An Ancient Greek View', in *Philosophy of Religion: A Guide and Anthology*, Davies, B. (ed.). Oxford: Oxford University Press.

Pojman, L.P. 1989. *Ethical Theory*. Toronto: Wadsworth.

Pojman, L.P. 2002. *Ethics: Discovering Right and Wrong*. Toronto: Wadsworth.

Pojman, L.P. 2006. *Ethics: Inventing Right and Wrong* (5th ed.). Belmont, CA: Thomson and Wadsworth.

Rachels, J. and Rachels, S. 2007. *The Elements of Moral Philosophy*. New York: McGraw-Hill.

Raeper, W. and Smith, L. 1991. *A Beginner's Guide to Ideas*. Oxford: Lion Books.

Rawls, J. 2005a. *Political Liberalism*. Columbia: Columbia University Press.

Rawls, J. 2005b. *A Theory of Justice*. Cambridge, MA: Harvard University Press.

Robinson, J.A.T. 1967. *But That I Can't Believe*. London: HarperCollins.

Robinson, J.A.T. 2000. *Redating the New Testament*. Oregon: Wipf & Stock.

Ross, W.D. 2002. *The Right and the Good*: Oxford: Oxford University Press.

Russell, B. 2004. *Why I Am Not a Christian and Other Essays on Religion* (2nd ed.). Oxford: Routledge.

Ryle, G. 1949 [2002]. *The Concept of Mind*. Chicago: University of Chicago Press.

Sacred Congregation for the Doctrine of the Faith. 1980. *Declaration on Euthanasia*. Rome: s.n.

Schneider, S.M. 1999. *The Revelatory Text: Interpreting the New Testament as Sacred Scripture* (2nd ed.). Wilmington: Michael Glazier.

Singer, P. 1972. 'Famine, Affluence, and Morality', *Philosophy and Public Affairs* 1 (1): 229–243.

Singer, P. 1993. *Practical Ethics*. Cambridge: Cambridge University Press.

Singer, P. 1994. *Rethinking Life and Death: The Collapse of our Traditional Ethics*. Oxford: Oxford University Press.

Singer, P. 2004. *One World: The Ethics of Globalization*. Yale: Yale University Press.

Smart, J.J.C. and Williams, B. 1973. *Utilitarianism: For and Against*. Cambridge: Cambridge University Press.

Smith, A. 1981. *The Wealth of Nations* (eds. Campbell, R.H. and Skinner, A.S.). Indianapolis: Liberty Press.

Solomon, R.C. 1993. *Ethics and Excellence*. New York: Oxford University Press.

Stanford Encyclopedia of Philosophy (2005; rev. 2011) *Aquinas' Moral, Political and Legal Philosophy*. Available at http://plato.stanford.edu/entries/aquinas-moral-political/ (accessed 16 June 2017).

Swinburne, R. 1991. *The Existence of God*. Oxford: Oxford University Press.

Swinburne, R. 1996. *Is There a God*. Oxford: Oxford University Press.

Swinburne, R. 1997a. *Evolution of the Soul*. Oxford: Clarendon Press.

Swinburne, R. 1997b. *Evolution of a Soul* (rev. ed.). New York: Oxford University Press.

Swinburne, R. 1998. *Providence and the Problem of Evil*. Oxford: Oxford University Press.

Swinburne, R. 2004. *The Existence of God*. Oxford: Oxford University Press.

Theissen, G. 2010. *The Shadow of the Galilean*. London: SCM Press.

Vardy, P. 1990. *The Puzzle of God*. London: Fount Paperbacks.

Vardy, P. and Arliss, J. 2003. *The Thinker's Guide to Evil*. Arelsford: John Hunt.

Ward, K. 1972. *The Development of Kant's View of Ethics*. Oxford: Blackwell.

Warnock, M. 1999. *An Intelligent Person's Guide to Ethics*. London: Duckworth.

Warren, W. 2011. 'Who Changed the Text and Why? Probable, Possible, and Unlikely Explanations', in *The Reliability of the New Testament: Bart Ehrman and Daniel Wallace in Dialogue*, Stewart, R. (ed.). New York: Fortress Press.

Whitehead, A. 1978. *Process and Reality*. Corrected ed. New York: The Free Press.

Wiesel, E. 2008. *Night*. London: Penguin.

Wilcockson, M. 1999. *Issues of Life and Death*. London: Hodder & Stoughton.

Williams, B. 1978. *Descartes: The Project of Pure Enquiry*. London: Humanities Press.

Williams, R. 2016. *On Augustine*. London: Bloomsbury.

Index

Page numbers in italic indicate a figure or feature.